#23668

336.1   Clotfelter, Charles
CLO   T.

          Selling hope

$16.95

DATE			

Selling Hope

A National Bureau of Economics Research Book

Selling Hope
State Lotteries in America

Charles T. Clotfelter
and Philip J. Cook

Harvard University Press
Cambridge, Massachusetts
London, England

For Lucile
C.T.C.

For my parents
P.J.C.

Copyright © 1989 by the President and Fellows of Harvard College
All rights reserved
Printed in the United States of America
10   9   8   7   6   5   4   3   2

First Harvard University Press paperback edition, 1991

Library of Congress Cataloging-in-Publication Data
Clotfelter, Charles T.
  Selling hope : state lotteries in America / Charles T. Clotfelter and
Philip J. Cook.
    p.   cm.
  Bibliography: p.
  Includes index.
  ISBN 0–674–80097–4 (alk. paper) (cloth)
  ISBN 0–674–80098–2 (paper)
    1. Lotteries—United States—States.   2. Lotteries—Government
policy—United States—States.   I. Cook, Philip J., 1946–
II. Title.
HG6126.C55   1989   89–32398
336.1'7'0973—dc20   CIP

Contents

Preface to the 1991 edition

The lottery industry in the United States grew tenfold during the 1980s. As a result of this extraordinary growth, the lottery has emerged as the largest form of commercial gambling, generating greater revenues (over $10 billion per year) than all casino operations combined, and much greater revenues than parimutuel betting or bingo. Twenty years ago lotteries were an interesting but rather minor curiosity in public finance and household expenditure patterns. Today they have become a ubiquitous and prominent activity of state governments, and figure importantly in the budgets of an increasing number of households.

Lotteries are important in public finance because they are the fastest-growing source of state revenue and because they engender controversy about the proper role of government. It was the perceived need for a new source of revenue that pushed the New Hampshire legislature to create the first legal lottery of the twentieth century in 1964. Thereafter the quest for new revenues helped sell the lottery to one state after another during the 1970s and 1980s, to the point that now two-thirds of the states are in this business. And business it is, much more so than any other major endeavor of state governments. Lottery directors understand their mission to be that of making as much money as possible for the state treasury. As a consequence, they have been open to a variety of innovations that may increase profits, including new games, improvements in the statewide networks for taking bets, and more appealing and sophisticated advertising campaigns. Such marketing efforts have enhanced sales, but in other respects they may be problematic. Critics assert that it is inappropriate for the government to encourage people to gamble, and that lottery expenditures impose a disproportionate burden on less affluent and less educated families. Still, a strong majority of the public supports the lottery, in part because it does satisfy some of the revenue needs of the state. Lotteries are not just a source of revenue, but also a source of entertainment to the millions who play. They are important, then, when viewed as a new commodity occupying an increasingly prominent place in household budgets. Some 60 percent of the adult public living in lottery states play, though most of these players are only spending a few dollars now and again. However, most lottery sales go to regular participants who spend over $20 per week. Part of the appeal may stem from marketing devices intended to create an exaggerated impression of the chance of winning. But with or without this encouragement, most people are tempted by a chance to win a lot of money, even when the odds are very long. Further, the lottery has become part of popular culture, with its folklore of betting systems and tales of multimillion dollar winners. The lottery thus offers a pleasant diversion akin to professional sports and soap operas, although for some it represents a more serious activity.

The purpose of this book is to document the lottery phenomenon and analyze it as a consumer commodity, a business, and a source of government revenue. In accordance with the National Bureau of Economic Research guidelines for its studies, the book does not offer policy recommendations, although it does present a good deal of evidence for evaluating policy issues. And certainly there are a number of issues to be considered during the 1990s. Most important, perhaps, is the introduction of new games that represent a turn to a "harder" form of gambling. There are various possibilities under consideration, including sports betting (pioneered by the Oregon lottery) and player-operated video slot machines (first introduced in South Dakota). Another possibility is a telephone betting system that would allow people to place bets from their homes while watching a lottery game show. Also important for public consideration is the perennial question of what limits should be placed on advertising and promotion of lottery games. Legislatures in a few states have imposed restrictions on their ads without any obvious harm to their sales trajectories, but most states' advertising is restrained only by the prevailing standards of commercial advertising. Finally, there are difficult questions to be answered about the future of multistate lotteries and interstate competition among lotteries. The limits on interstate commerce in lottery tickets will ultimately be decided by Congress, which also will no doubt revisit the possibility of launching a national lottery. These are among the issues challenging those who are concerned with the growth and evolution of lotteries, and they are relevant both in existing lottery states and in states still debating the question of adoption. We intend our book to serve as a guide in considering these issues.

In contrast to many studies sponsored by the National Bureau of Economic Research, this presentation has been tailored for a readership broader than those conversant with the statistical and mathematical models common in economic scholarship. Econometric analysis, for example, is relegated to notes and appendixes. In this effort to broaden readership we have benefited from the advice and encouragement of the NBER.

The project was begun in 1986 as an equal collaboration. Before long it became clear that Philip Cook's administrative responsibilities as director of Duke University's Institute of Policy Sciences and Public Affairs would make it necessary to revise the basis of our collaboration. As a result, Charles Clotfelter took responsibility for Chapters 1–4 and 9–10, while the two of us wrote the rest together. The framing of the book is decidedly a joint effort, as are its major arguments.

Financial support provided by Duke University, the Ford Foundation, and the National Bureau of Economic Research made our project possible. One of the indispensable items this aid generated was the research assistance of a number of graduate and undergraduate students at Duke. We are grateful for the diligent help of all these students: Graham Barr, Allan Brunner, Susan Coppedge, Jon Danielsson, Sheri Gravett, Eva Herbst, Will Mc-Kinnon, Harriet Morgan, Ying Qian, Ross Ullmer, Meg Wimmer, and Angela Woo. We also thank Sonja Turner, Martha Wall, and Bernice Wheeler for assistance with manuscript preparation, Amanda Heller for many helpful editorial suggestions, Dek Terrell for his commendable work with computer programming and figures, and Marshall Adesman for his invaluable contributions as librarian, research assistant, and manuscript preparer. The Duke University Library helped us with dozens of inquiries and searches; we are especially indebted to Stuart Basefsky and the staff in the public documents, reference, and interlibrary loan departments.

We were also aided by numerous state lottery officials and others in state governments. While a few lottery agencies refused our requests for specific data, for the most part lottery personnel cheerfully cooperated with our many inquiries. They provided annual reports, examples of advertisements, unpublished tabulations, and answers to our survey questions. We also obtained data from the Arizona State University Survey Research Laboratory, Broadcast Advertisers Reports, the Gallup Organization, the *Los Angeles Times*, and the University of California Survey Research Center.

From the beginning we received useful suggestions from dozens of colleagues, too numerous to name. In particular, comments from seminar participants at the NBER, McMaster University, Yale, Rochester, Harvard, and Duke were very helpful, as were detailed remarks from Michael Aronson, Robert Bates, Douglas Bernheim, Richard Bostic, Larry Braidfoot, Roger Brinner, Eugene Christiansen, James Clotfelter, Larry DeBoer, Robert Entman, Edward Gramlich, Joel Huber, Robert Inman, H. Roy Kaplan, Mark Kleiman, Helen Ladd, Terri LaFleur, Theodore Marmor, John McCann, Daniel Nagin, Dick Netzer, Jonathan Skinner, Frederick Stocker, Kip Viscusi, Burton Weisbrod, and Franklin Zimring.

C.T.C.

P.J.C.

January 1991

National Bureau of Economic Research

PART I

The Setting

1.

A New Role for the States

Hope springs eternal in the human breast.

—Alexander Pope, *An Essay on Man*

In the waning days of summer 1984, lines of people stretched outside delicatessens and liquor stores in Chicago, Springfield, and East St. Louis. These people were all waiting to buy a product, one that had become page-one reading and the subject of countless everyday conversations. Sales of this product throughout the state of Illinois reached $8 million a day, representing a rate of roughly thirteen thousand units purchased every minute. The product? A lottery game called lotto, featuring a top prize that had grown to $40 million. This product was remarkable for two reasons. First, it had created a fever pitch of excitement with few parallels in consumer behavior. And second, its manufacturer was not a commercial firm but rather the state of Illinois.

For the first six decades of the twentieth century lotteries were banned in every American state. Yet today three-fourths of the U.S. population lives in states where lotteries are not only legal but provided by state government itself. One after the other states have embraced this form of public finance, adhering for the most part to a single model for the lottery's operation and financing. In each state the government has ended its former prohibition of lotteries, made itself the sole provider, and used the profits from the operation as a new source of revenue. In doing so the states have entered unfamiliar terrain. They have gone into business selling a popular consumer product, and they have carried on with Madison Avenue gusto and an unfettered dedication to the bottom line. The complete about-face from prohibition to promotion in one state after another is remarkable, to say the least.

The purpose of this book is to examine state lotteries and the states' role in them. Lotteries are a historical curiosity, a cultural phenomenon, a rapidly evolving new industry, and a consumer craze, and in this book we pay attention to all of these issues. But there are also more serious points to be considered, including the propriety of this new source of public revenue and the long-term social and economic consequences of the state's giving official encouragement to gambling.

To illustrate the rapid evolution and growth of the lottery as well as the policy issues that have arisen along the way, we begin with an account of one state's experience. For this purpose we have chosen Illinois, one of the first states to climb onto the bandwagon. The state's experience with the lottery provides an interesting case study that touches on all the matters that concern us. It provides a representative story as well, for Illinois is as close to Middle America in demographics and temperament as it is in geography.

One State's Story

As in every other American state, lotteries in Illinois had been illegal since the nineteenth century.[1] To be sure, gambling in the state had remained popular, at least among a large portion of the population. Horse racing had been legal since 1927, and by 1963 attendance at racetracks in the state was almost 6 million a year.[2] Despite the official prohibition of lotteries, people found several ready alternatives. The Irish Sweepstakes was popular in the Midwest, as it was throughout the United States; a Michigan factory worker won half a million dollars in 1972. In Illinois illegal lotteries in the form of "policy" games flourished, especially in the black neighborhoods of Chicago. In the early 1970s an estimated twenty-three policy "wheels" were operating in Chicago, grossing some $20 million a year. A survey of the South Side and West Side of Chicago showed that over 40 percent of the residents of those neighborhoods played policy.[3] And, as in much of the country, bingo had long been played under the auspices of churches and other charities, although it was not until 1971 that the state of Illinois legalized, regulated, and taxed it.

The idea of having a state-run public lottery in Illinois began to receive serious attention in the early 1970s. Lotteries had already appeared in the Northeast, and by 1972 seven states were operating them. In particular, the success of the New Jersey lottery seems to have captured the attention of the Illinois legislature, as it did in other states. A proposal for a lottery patterned after New Jersey's—one operated by a commission appointed by the governor—was passed in one house of the Illinois legislature in 1972 on the strength of a provision that would earmark a portion of the $100 million estimated revenues for financially strapped school systems. The bill died, however, after the governor threatened to veto it.

But debate on the lottery question continued into 1973. Supporters of the idea, including Chicago's Mayor Richard Daley, stressed the potential for revenue to the state. Some proponents argued that a state lottery would cut into the business of the illegal gambling syndicate. But there was vigorous opposition to the lottery idea. Some opponents maintained that it would place an unfair burden on the poor and on compulsive gamblers. Others based their arguments on morality, one calling the lottery "another step toward the destruction of our ethical values."[4] The *Chicago Tribune* editorialized against lotteries on several occasions, criticizing the low proportion of revenues returned as prizes and charging that state sponsorship of a lottery teaches an ethic of easy money over the value of hard work.[5] Despite such opposition, the lottery won approval. What appeared to win the day was a proposed tangible use for the lottery's revenue as well as the support of the new governor, Dan Walker. In a special legislative session the lottery became linked to an emergency funding package for the Chicago area transit system. A poll showed that by a wide margin state residents preferred a lottery over an increase in the sales tax as a source of funding. In December 1973 the state legislature passed a lottery bill, and the governor signed it into law with assurances that the lottery would be run honestly.

The new state lottery agency began selling tickets in July 1974, and honesty was indeed a byword from the beginning—along with publicity. Balls imprinted with winning numbers were selected mechanically rather than by hand, and the device was transported throughout the state for drawings. A congressional ban on televised drawings ended in 1976, and thereafter television became a vital part of the lottery's marketing. Tickets were sold in some 7,500 retail establishments, including grocery stores, convenience stores, liquor stores, and drugstores. According to its director, the lottery agency itself was designed to be operated as a business. It was broken into three conventional business divisions—operations, finance, and marketing—each with its own deputy, who took on the role of a corporate vice president.[6] Following the example of New Jersey rather than the higher-priced lotteries run by New Hampshire and New York, the Illinois lottery set the price of its tickets at fifty cents. Prizes ranged from $20 to $1 million (the latter paid out over twenty years). Subsequently the lottery introduced other games, first a similar one with tickets selling for a dollar, then an "instant game" featuring scratch-off spaces revealing winning combinations. The public responded to the new lottery with enthusiasm. Sales were brisk, winners became celebrities, and predictions of high revenues were fulfilled. In the first fiscal year sales were $129 million, increasing to $163 million in 1976. In 1988 dollars the second year's sales were just under $30 per capita.

But then the bloom began to fade. Sales dropped in 1977 and again in each of the following two years. By 1979 the real value of sales had fallen more than 60 percent, and the number of participating retail agents had dropped to less than half the peak figure. The disappointing sales became a source of concern and criticism, and officials were reduced to blaming heavy snow. Governor James Thompson publicly suggested that the lottery might be phased out if sales could not be increased. With its back to the wall, the lottery agency sought and obtained two changes in its offerings in hopes of producing a turnaround. The first was an increase in the percentage of sales that could be returned in the form of prizes. The 45 percent average in Illinois was slightly lower than that offered by other states and, more important, was seen as significantly lower than the rates available in the state's illegal lotteries.

If this first change was aimed indirectly at illegal gamblers, the second was aimed squarely in that direction. The lottery decided to follow the lead of New Jersey and Massachusetts in offering a daily numbers game in which players could choose their own numbers. A network of computer terminals placed in retail outlets was used to record bets, and winning numbers were announced nightly on television. Fully aware that a ready-made market for a game of this sort already existed among the devotees of illegal numbers games, the lottery agency bet that it could capture a share of that market. The bet paid off handsomely. Sales immediately climbed. In the three years after the introduction of the numbers game lottery business more than tripled; in 1982 for the first time sales in real terms exceeded the previous peak, reached in 1976.

Its continued existence firmly established, the lottery decided to adopt a second major new game, lotto, and the result was still more dramatic increases in sales. A game used widely in Europe but not unlike the old policy game played on the streets of Chicago, lotto had proved exceedingly popular in the states that had adopted it. Introduced in 1983, lotto in Illinois quickly became a consumer craze. Prize jackpots, which were allowed to grow when there was no winner, sometimes reached enormous sums. The game's popularity, along with a change in format, were factors in the $40 million jackpot that accumulated in September 1984. A twenty-eight-year-old printer from Chicago picked the winning numbers, 2, 3, 10, 26, 30, and 43, to become the biggest winner in any lottery game up to that time. Not since the beginning of the lottery had there been so much public attention, and the result was even higher sales, topping $1 billion in 1985. In real terms sales in the state increased at an *annual* rate of over 40 percent from 1979 to 1986, doubling approximately every two years. While few expected that rate to continue, it was extraordinary and certainly unprecedented in comparison to sales of other consumer products. What is doubly remarkable about this boom in sales corresponding with the introduction of lotto is that the two other mainstays of the product line, instant games and daily games (weekly games had by this point been dropped as "obsolete"),[7] did not decline but in fact increased at the same time lotto was beginning its surge. So popular was lotto judged to be that a new game was added in 1987, and Illinois briefly considered joining with other states to run a multistate lotto game that would offer even bigger prizes.

Day in and day out, probably the most visible sign of the lottery agency is its advertising, about half of which appears on television. A typical day's television advertising in Chicago might consist of from a few to two dozen thirty-second spots, distributed among the city's five major television stations, shown largely in the late afternoon and evening and timed to coincide with news programs, sporting events, and other popular programs.[8] On the El or in retail outlets lottery posters proclaimed: "There's another way to get rich quick. Play lotto," and "Now money grows on trees. Play Money Tree Instant Lottery. You could win a million dollars in cash." In addition to its advertising, the lottery seemed constantly on the lookout for ways "to broaden the base of players," in the words of the lottery's director. For example, the state increased the number of lotto drawings per week, offered players the chance to buy subscription books of lotto tickets, and began selling tickets at various locations in O'Hare Airport.[9] A new lottery director appointed in 1987 promised to "keep up the hype" in order to keep sales growing.[10]

By 1986 total lottery sales were $1.3 billion and per capita sales had reached $111 a year. Even adjusting for sales to nonresidents, this per capita figure probably understates average sales to adults. As a revenue source the lottery has grown in importance, though it is not in the same class with state income and sales taxes. From 1 percent of the state's general fund revenues in the first years, it fell to less than half a percentage point but by 1986 had climbed above 5 percent, one of the highest ratios in the country. Average commissions to retail agents were $7,500 in 1986.[11]

Still, the lottery has had its detractors. Some have complained that prizes advertised as "instant" were not in fact paid immediately. Others believe that the lottery encourages immorality and undercuts belief in the virtue of hard work. Members of Gamblers Anonymous have blamed the state's lottery for contributing to the problems of compulsive gamblers. But probably the most common theme of the opposition has been the charge that the lottery preys on the poor and the ignorant. Raised in the initial legislative debate over adoption, this concern surfaced again when the instant game was introduced in 1976. Fearing that the appeal of immediate winnings might tempt some low-income players to bet more than they could afford, the Illinois House of Representatives actually passed a nonbinding resolution against the instant game shortly after its introduction, although the lottery ignored it. It was the daily game, however, that seemed to appeal most directly to minorities and low-income players. Four of the five most active retail outlets for the daily game were in predominantly black neighborhoods in Chicago. Total per capita lottery sales were over twice as high in Chicago's Cook County as in suburban Du Page County. Perhaps the most vivid display of concern over the lottery's purported appeal to the poor was a short-lived boycott of the lottery that was organized in one of Chicago's largely black West Side neighborhoods. In 1986 a billboard appearing on a major street in this neighborhood became a cause célèbre: "How to go from Washington Blvd. to Easy Street—Play the Illinois State Lottery." Boycott leaders charged that the lottery targeted low-income neighborhoods. While this charge was denied at the time, a subsequent state report confirmed that this had in fact been a marketing strategy for a short time.[12]

For the most part, though, the Illinois lottery has faced relatively little opposition since its adoption. Except for an occasional unfriendly statement, the existence of the lottery quickly became a nonissue. Even the *Chicago Tribune,* which had opposed the lottery's adoption and continued to criticize it editorially, lost no time in jumping on the bandwagon, dutifully reporting the details of new games and promising to publish winning numbers as soon as they were known. Most important, the mass media discovered in the lottery winners an appealing source of human interest articles. Who could resist, for example, the story of the state's first big winner in 1975? A welder from Kankakee with a chronically sick child, he got word of his $300,000 prize at work because he could not take time off to attend the drawing. The governor himself called to give him the happy news, offering to fly him to Springfield for a ceremony. The lucky winner promised to give some of his winnings to Easter Seals and some to the hospital that had cared for his child, and some he would spend on a party for his friends.[13] In Illinois and elsewhere stories of winners and how winning changed their lives seem to be an inevitable by-product of state lotteries. According to one observer, the lottery "has given newspapers a sure-fire, once-a-week happy news story."[14]

The Two Faces of the Lottery

As illustrated by the experience of Illinois, the lottery is a phenomenon that has rapidly, if not effortlessly, gained a foothold in contemporary American culture. Where a lottery is legalized, a majority of adults soon begin playing, at least occasionally, and stories of winners and large jackpots become the stuff of everyday conversation. An activity that was outlawed only decades before is officially sanctioned and readily available. The state government, as operator of the lottery, takes on a role unlike virtually any other function performed by the state. In all this the issue of lotteries remains a divisive one. In states considering adopting a lottery, opponents are sure to be vigorous and outspoken. Nor does the opposition to lotteries ever quite die out once a lottery is adopted. Detractors become, for the most part, quietly resigned to the lottery's existence and widespread popularity, but the deep reservations that remain surface occasionally in the critical op-ed piece or letter to the editor. Yet to compare the happy feature stories about lottery winners with the dark picture drawn by lottery critics makes it appear as if two entirely different phenomena were being described.

Supporters view the lottery as the ideal form of public finance—a "painless tax" that raises public funds without coercion. People have always gambled and are going to gamble whether or not it is legal, the argument goes, so why not tap this activity to raise much-needed public revenue? And if in the bargain the lottery takes business away from illegal gambling rackets, the state can reduce crime and the enforcement efforts that are devoted to preventing it. But strongest of all among the arguments for lotteries is their overwhelming popularity. Certainly the verdict of the voters is clear: in state after state the people have endorsed state-run lotteries in public referenda. Once in place the lottery quickly becomes a commonly shared experience; like sports and the weather, the lottery is something that almost everybody knows something about. Especially in the midst of the frenzy created by the occasional giant lotto jackpot, players reportedly indulge in fantasies about what could be done with the prize money. Like a snowstorm or a World Series, a multimillion-dollar jackpot creates excitement that spills over to become a social event. A 1985 *New York Times* editorial described the festival atmosphere and "new camaraderie" created by a $40 million drawing: "They stood in long lines chatting to one another while blocking in the numbers. Birthdays, ages, addresses, fractions of Social Security and telephone numbers. When asked their systems, they answered with old chestnuts like 'Does Macy's tell Gimbels?' When blessed with a 'good luck,' they promptly good-lucked back. Once they'd put the ticket someplace safe, the fantasies took over."[15] Seen in this light, the lottery embodies communal good feeling, the wholesome instinct to take a chance, and innocent fantasies of wealth. But more than this, the lottery becomes almost allegorical when it anoints the honest working person with the realization of the storybook dream of riches, as it did when twenty-one factory workers, most of them immigrants, won a share of that $40 million jackpot.

Detractors see a darker side to the lottery. Some of them view lotteries as a reflection of the boredom and materialism of modern life. Many critics argue that legalized lotteries exacerbate financial and behavioral problems. Others view lotteries as a tax that falls disproportionately on the poor and uninformed. Not only do lotteries harm the players, say the critics, but they are an active instrument in the moral degradation of society. The columnist Russell Baker humorously captures the sense of disenchantment with the lottery's influence:

> Once you could send your innocent babes, hope of the future, off to the candy store to buy some chewing wax, a Baby Ruth, the new Batman comic book and a kazoo, and be secure in the knowledge that good Mrs. Chesley behind the counter would bust their little knuckles if they tried to buy a copy of The Racing Form.
>
>   Not anymore. Now good Mrs. Chesley has turned her shop into a gambling hell where she greets the traffic with a leer that says, "Hello, sucker," and has to keep kicking the kids out of her way so the lottery players can get their bets down.[16]

Still other critics assert that legalized gambling leads to illegal gambling, crime, and corruption. According to former governor Bruce Babbitt of Arizona, the lottery "attracts all kinds of flakey characters who hang around the fringes."[17] To these critics must be added those who oppose lotteries simply because they believe all gambling to be immoral.

But, one might ask, isn't this chorus of criticism little more than a modern restatement of the time-honored theme of paternalism in public policy? Critics may view a lottery ticket as a poor bet and a waste of money, but the many who play obviously derive some satisfaction from participating. In virtually every state where lotteries have been put on the ballot, citizens have shown their willingness both to legalize them and to play. If these people enjoy gambling, why shouldn't they have the opportunity? The economist's peculiarly nonjudgmental perspective on individual behavior is a useful benchmark here. It begins with the assumption that a voluntary act of consumer behavior is undertaken only if it makes that person better off. Excepting "children and madmen," consumers with adequate information are presumed to be good judges of their own well-being.[18] For the vast majority of people it would be hard to argue that playing the lottery is any more harmful or wasteful than, say, eating a candy bar or playing bridge. Prohibiting such a benign activity seems not only paternalistic but even a little absurd. As Dick Netzer has noted, "Editorial and other criticism of legal gambling smacks of nannying ordinary working and retired folks: we the affluent, who would not dream of playing numbers whether legal or illegal, long shots on the races or for jackpots at slot machines, don't want you, the unwashed, to enjoy your simple pleasures."[19] In the absence of strong evidence of addiction or poor information, therefore, the lottery can be viewed as a product that, for whatever reason, people enjoy. If in addition the product causes no great harm to others, there can be little objective basis for prohibiting it.

Viewing the lottery debate simply in terms of paternalism versus tolerance, however, misses the most prominent feature of lotteries as they currently exist. The states now offering lotteries do not simply make a product available in order to accommodate the widespread taste for buying a low-priced chance at a big prize. They seek to foster that taste. Lottery agencies are not merely acting out of a liberal respect for consumer sovereignty. They are engaged in a well-focused quest for increased revenues. The state lottery agencies have in fact evolved into a new breed of government agency created in the mold of the modern corporation with its eyes firmly fixed on the bottom line. With businesslike efficiency these state enterprises have combined their monopoly position, their high built-in profit rates, and the techniques of modern marketing to generate new revenues for state governments. But by choosing to stimulate rather than merely accommodate demand, they have thrust the state into an unaccustomed role, one that may be inconsistent with other functions of government. To succeed in increasing sales, lottery advertisements must either encourage existing players to buy more tickets or entice nonplayers to begin playing, neither of which is consistent with the traditional government policy of not inducing citizens to gamble. The manner in which the lottery agencies have advertised has also come into question. Some have charged that the agencies are less than forthcoming in explaining the low probabilities of winning or the manner in which prizes are paid out. Others are troubled by the message of lottery advertising. The columnist Andy Rooney asks, "How can we teach kids that hard work is the way to success if they hear radio commercials paid for by their government suggesting that the way to get rich is to bet money on a horse or a number?"[20]

There exists, in short, an undeniable Jekyll-and-Hyde quality to state lotteries. It arises in part from our ambivalence toward gambling itself. On the one side is the traditional view of gambling as a vice and the opprobrium directed toward those who overindulge. On the other is the wide acceptance of gambling in moderation as an innocent form of amusement. In the case of lotteries, this traditional ambivalence is accentuated by the policies of state government. In legalizing a widely popular form of gambling, the states are accommodating consumer preferences. But in their marketing efforts the states have raised a new set of questions. For most of the country the central policy question concerning lotteries today is no longer whether states should legalize them—voters in state after state have answered that—but whether their businesslike behavior can be reconciled with the public interest.

Why Study Lotteries?

We believe that now is a good time to step back and take a careful look at state lotteries and the public policy questions they raise. Based on their meteoric growth alone, lotteries represent a cultural phenomenon with few parallels in recent decades. Once legalized, they have quickly assumed a place in the popular culture. If for no other reason this spectacular emergence makes the lottery an object of special interest. But lotteries are interesting too for the light they shed on economic behavior. One of the most active areas of inquiry in economics over the past two decades has been the study of choices involving risk. In fact simple lotteries are often used to illustrate theoretical propositions in this literature because the lottery is a prototype for a wide variety of risky situations in life. To the extent that it is possible to study actual behavior in situations involving lotteries, state lotteries offer a ready laboratory for testing theories of risk-taking. What explains the popularity of lotteries as a form of consumer expenditure? Other possible applications to economic behavior would be a study of lottery winners to test hypotheses about consumption, saving, labor force participation, charitable giving, and bequests. How do people respond to sudden changes in wealth? More broadly, it is interesting to ask what implications the widespread popularity of lotteries might have for attitudes toward work and saving and perceived opportunities for upward mobility.

The second reason why lotteries are worth studying is that their operation has important policy implications. For the states that have not approved lotteries, these issues are clearly germane to debates over adoption. These questions would also be relevant to the consideration of a national lottery, which has been the subject of increasing attention in Congress. But what about states where lotteries already operate? As it is usually debated, the question has virtually always taken the form "Should we adopt a lottery?" Although this remains an issue for the nation as a whole and for the states that have not yet approved a lottery, it is for all practical purposes a moot question for the majority of states where lotteries are an established fact of life. Nonetheless it is a central argument of this book that all states—those with lotteries and those without—face important policy choices regarding lotteries. Even the states already operating lotteries must make choices about what kind of lottery to operate, choices that have not in most cases been the subject of serious debate.

To see the kinds of policy choices involved, it is useful to distinguish four aspects of lotteries as they are operated in the United States today: legalization, provision, marketing, and implicit taxation. Until New Hampshire approved a lottery in 1964, every state prohibited lotteries. The *legalization* of lotteries as an activity is thus a first step in the operation of any state lottery. As obvious as that may be, the shift from prohibition to legal status inevitably implies a level of approval that may be meaningful for its own sake from the standpoint of public policy. *Provision* is a second aspect of all state lotteries currently operating. In each case the state has made its own government agency the sole provider of lottery products rather than opening up the market to competition or allowing private firms to bid for franchises. The third aspect common to state lotteries is *marketing,* which includes the development of new lottery products as well as the advertising that has become a familiar feature in lottery states. And fourth, by channeling lottery profits to the state treasury, states subject lottery purchases to *implicit taxation.*

Beginning with New Hampshire the states have combined these aspects to create a class of government agency with no precedent. States have turned to market-oriented managers who are ready to advertise their products in order to increase sales. One could argue that by operating the lottery itself, the state sanctions gambling in a much more active way than it would simply by legalizing the activity. But when it markets lottery products, it solidifies the approval implied by legalization and operation. At the same time, however, the states have imposed relatively large implicit tax burdens on these products through their use of lottery profits to fund state programs.

Although the resulting formula has been followed by virtually every state that has adopted a lottery, there is nothing inherent in the operation of lotteries that dictates this particular combination. Once the choice has been made to legalize a lottery, decisions on the remaining three features are largely independent of one another. One could imagine a high implicit tax rate combined with private provision of lottery products or with low levels of advertising, for example. While the question of legalization is a live policy issue only in the states without lotteries (until a serious prohibition movement materializes), questions about operation, finance, and marketing are as relevant in lottery states as they are in states considering adopting lotteries. For example, states with established lotteries must decide what to do in the face of stagnant or declining sales. Should they restructure existing games? If so, should they seek to increase or decrease the chance of winning? Should they increase the percentage of revenues paid out in prizes? Should they consider more or different forms of marketing?

The relevant policy choice then is not simply whether or not to have a lottery but *what kind* of lottery to have. As will become apparent, basic questions about the role of government and the legitimacy of individual decisions enter into making this choice. In order to inform the public discourse on this topic, this book deals with the question of state lotteries at two levels. On a purely empirical level the purpose is to offer a comprehensive yet comprehensible analysis of the demand and supply of lottery products. This requires looking at the lottery games themselves, the factors motivating people to engage in this form of gambling, and the operation of state lottery agencies. On another level the book is about the policy choices—both explicit and implicit—involved in the operation of a public lottery. Although the book offers no policy recommendations, it does raise the questions that any policy debate should address and provides evidence for judging the likely effects of various decisions.

This book thus has two major purposes. The first is purely descriptive: to provide a reasonably comprehensive factual analysis of state lotteries and the demand for their products. All but the final chapter is thus basically empirical in nature. The book begins with an overview of lotteries in the United States, proceeds to an analysis of the demand for lotteries and their social effects, and then considers the important aspects of the provision of lotteries. In Chapter 2 we present some quantitative measures of lotteries in order to give an idea of the magnitude of the phenomenon. Chapter 3 describes the tension that has existed between the widespread popularity of lotteries and disapproval of lotteries by religious groups and spokesmen for good government. Chapter 4 describes the four major products sold by lotteries and notes the increasing importance of games that allow players to select their own numbers. Chapter 5 discusses the reasons why people gamble and the patterns they follow in selecting numbers to bet on. Chapter 6 examines who plays lottery games and how much they play. It then considers factors that may influence demand and notes the implications of these findings for the structure of lotto games and for advertising strategies. Chapter 7 looks at the effects of demand on players and nonplayers.

The book's second purpose is to provide a framework for considering the significant public policy issues related to state lotteries. The next four chapters examine in turn the four aspects of lotteries just discussed: legalization, provision, marketing, and implicit taxation. While these chapters are also basically empirical in nature, they are designed to be useful in the consideration of public policy toward lotteries. Chapter 8 deals with the politics of adopting a state lottery. Chapter 9 describes the structure and operation of state lottery agencies, noting the importance of marketing to their overall mission and their dependence on private firms that supply lottery products and advice on how to sell them. Chapter 10 focuses on lottery advertising as an instrument of the lottery's marketing effort. It includes measures of the amount of advertising and a description of the content of lottery ads. Chapter 11 examines the lottery in its role as revenue-raiser for the state. It examines the incidence of the implicit tax and compares the rate of implicit taxation with the rate of excise taxation on other commodities. The final chapter focuses on the policy choices open to states with lotteries as well as those still considering whether or not to adopt a lottery. Legalization is not a state's only important policy question regarding state lotteries. To highlight these other questions, we describe an alternative policy that states could pursue.

2.

Magnitudes

It's gone beyond a cycle. It's gone beyond a habit. It's
become a mania. These people are obsessed.

—Lottery retailer in Maryland, 1986

The Commission on the Review of the National Policy toward Gambling
began its final report in 1976 with these words: "Gambling is inevitable. No
matter what is said or done by advocates or opponents of gambling in all its
various forms, it is an activity that is practiced, or tacitly endorsed, by a
substantial majority of Americans."[1] What the Commission said about
America goes for the world in general: gambling is a worldwide activity that
is supported by widespread popularity and official sanction. In order to appreciate the rise of lotteries in North America during the last three decades
we must understand two things. First, lotteries are just one form of gambling.
Although lotteries certainly have distinctive features, their popularity and
growth have arisen out of the same soil that has nurtured gambling in general.
While the modern state lottery is a comparatively recent innovation, legalized gambling has had a firm foothold in North America for quite some time.
Second, like other forms of gambling, lotteries are popular around the world.
In legalizing lotteries the United States has been a follower, not a leader. It
is useful to begin a systematic study of lotteries by putting in perspective the
extent and growth of gambling in general and lotteries in particular. This
chapter looks first at the spread of legalized gambling in North America and
throughout the world and then focuses more specifically on the dimensions
of the lottery phenomenon in the United States.

As conventionally used, the term *gambling* encompasses activities in which
money or something of value is bet on the outcome of some uncertain con-
tingency. Public attention has traditionally focused on commercial gambling,
which involves bets placed with a firm or agency, as opposed to bets with
friends. It includes betting on horse races, in casinos, in charity bingo halls,

and on lotteries. There is, of course, illegal gambling as well, which constitutes a category in itself. And some activities, such as playing the stock market, are usually not studied as forms of gambling despite close resemblances. As a form of gambling, lotteries are distinctive in being dependent on chance, as opposed to other kinds of uncertain outcomes that might depend on a player's skill. Such skills enhance the probability of winning in bets on poker, horse races, or sports, whereas lottery outcomes are random and entirely independent of the player's abilities.[2] Gray areas exist in which skill may make some small difference, as in football pools that require a player to predict the outcome of numerous games.

Legal gambling exists in a variety of forms other than lotteries. It is informative to study such legal gambling for several reasons. First, because lotteries are just one form of gambling, any tide that lifts gambling also lifts the lottery boat as well. Thus lotteries cannot be examined in isolation from gambling in general. Second, other forms of gambling, where they are legal, provide ready substitutes for lotteries. While activities such as horse racing and casino gambling differ from lotteries in important ways, they nevertheless offer the potential gambler many of the same game characteristics available in state lotteries. Exactly what these are and the degree to which they are shared by lottery games are subjects taken up in later chapters. A third reason concerns the political economy of legalizing any form of gambling. As we shall see, most groups that oppose lotteries on moral grounds likewise oppose all forms of gambling. At the same time, many of the arguments in favor of legalizing lotteries apply with equal force to the legalization of other forms of gambling. It would not be surprising, therefore, if a proposed lottery faced quite a different political climate in a state where other forms of gambling were already legal in comparison to a state that permitted no legal gambling. By the same token the legalization of lotteries may increase the likelihood that other gambling will be legalized.

Major Forms of Gambling in North America

State and provincial governments in the United States and Canada have legalized most of the major forms of gambling available in the world today. By far the most common form is bingo (also called beano), which by 1986 was legal in every Canadian province and all but five U.S. states. Typically bingo is operated for the benefit of nonprofit organizations, with operations handled by private firms. Other than keno, a similar game traditionally played in casinos, and charitable instant lotteries, no other form of legal gambling comes as close to state lotteries in the pure dependence on randomly drawn numbers and the virtual absence of active player participation. Bingo and lotteries also have another feature in common: rapid growth. In the last decade five states have legalized bingo, a larger increase over the period than for any other form of gambling except lotteries.[3] Still, bingo as usually played today differs considerably from state lottery games. Not only do lotteries offer much larger prizes, but they also offer bettors greater convenience and more frequent drawings, albeit without the excitement of crowded halls, face-to-face play, and the periodic cries of "Bingo!"

The next most common form of legalized gambling is parimutuel betting, including betting on horse racing, greyhound racing, and jai-alai. In a parimutuel system winning bettors share the total prize pool in proportion to the amount bet.[4] The most familiar of these forms is horse racing, whether harness, quarter horse, or thoroughbred. In 1986 horse racing of some type was legal in thirty-six states and was operated in thirty of them and in all but two Canadian provinces. Dog racing was operated in thirteen states and jai-alai in four. The largest area of growth related to parimutuel games in the last two decades has been the emergence of legalized betting parlors, televised races, and legal bookmaking, but in general the parimutuel share of legal gambling has not grown rapidly in recent years. Several states allow telephone bets, and three have established legalized off-track betting parlors.

By 1986 casinos were legal only in the state of Nevada, in Atlantic City, New Jersey, and in three Canadian provinces, but these few locations manage to generate an impressive volume of betting. Card rooms were legal in eight states and slot machines for commercial purposes in four. Betting on sporting events was legal in only two states, Nevada and Montana.[5] Among the forms of gambling legalized for charitable purposes, one is especially noteworthy because of its similarity to a game commonly used by state lotteries. "Breakopen" games, featuring tickets that are opened to reveal a winning number, are sold in bars, bingo halls, and fraternal clubs in a number of provinces and states. In several nonlottery states the sales of these tickets in 1987 rivaled the sales of state lottery tickets in lottery states; North Dakota and Minnesota led, with per capita sales of $197 and $94, respectively.[6]

The two most significant forms of illegal gambling in the United States and Canada are numbers and, chiefly, betting with bookies. The latter consists of bettors making wagers on individual contests, with bookmakers setting odds or point spreads. Less common are sports cards or sports pools, in which players try to guess the outcome of a list of contests.[7]

In order to get an idea of the relative extent of the various legal forms of gambling, and the illegal ones as well, it is useful to examine two basic kinds of measures. One is survey data on participation by type of game. A 1974 survey conducted by the Commission on the National Policy toward Gambling revealed that 61 percent of American adults participated in some form of gambling. Nationwide 19 percent of adults played bingo, 14 percent bet on horses at the track, and 9 percent played slot machines or other casino games. In lottery states 48 percent of adults played at least once a year. Respondents reported much lower rates of play for illegal games, with 3 percent each citing numbers and sports cards. Overall, 44 percent of the adult population played some commercial games and 11 percent bet in illegal games, with 48 percent playing at least one of the two types of games. Another 13 percent of the population reported betting only with friends, yielding a 61 percent total participation rate.[8]

Additional information useful in determining the relative extent of various forms of gambling comes from data on expenditures. Two measures are significant. The first is the gross amount bet—the "handle." In the case of lotteries this corresponds to the total sales of lottery tickets; in the case of slot machines it is the total amount put into the machines. Because a portion of the amount bet is returned to players in the form of prizes, however, gross bets overstate the amount collectively "spent." A second measure of betting is thus the "takeout" that the house or the state removes before prizes are awarded. Takeout rates for lotteries in the United States have varied over the years from as low as 10 percent to over 50 percent in today's state lotteries. Neither handle nor takeout is an unambiguous measure of the quantity of betting, however.

Estimates are available for the amount of wagering on different forms of gambling, but it is readily acknowledged by those in the field that some of the estimates are quite unreliable. Table 2.1 presents estimates of the gross amount wagered in 1986 on major legal and illegal games in the United States, as calculated by Eugene Christiansen. By far the largest share of the total handle was accounted for by casino table games, at over $100 billion. Slot machines came second, accounting for about $29 billion. Given the low takeout rates for these games, these totals represent net expenditures "only" on the order of $2.6 and $3.2 billion, respectively. Looked at either way, these figures are huge when one considers the limited number of states where such gambling was legal: after all, casinos operated in only two states. Among legal games, lotteries and horse racing at the track had handles of just over $10 billion each, although the takeout for lotteries was considerably higher. According to Christiansen, the total handle for legal games in 1986 was $166 billion. This compares to an estimated handle of $32 billion for illegal games, $5.6 billion of which is attributed to illegal numbers games. But the possibility of error in these estimates is large, as shown by a comparison between these and earlier estimates for 1974 provided by the Commission on the Review of

Table 2.1.   Estimated gross legal and illegal wagering and revenue in the United States, 1986

Gambling revenue sources	Gross wagering (millions)	Percent increase from 1982	Gross revenue (millions)	Takeou rate (percen
Parimutuels				
Horses at track	$10,442	5%	$1,973	19%
Dogs at track	3,009	36	587	20
Jai alai	668	7	130	19
Off-track betting	1,949	14	454	23
Lotteries	12,480	205	6,334	51
Casinos				
Slot machines	28,504	98	3,153	11
Table games	101,438	17	2,591	3
Legal bookmaking	1,188	121	81	7
Card rooms	1,119	12	56	5
Bingo	3,600	20	920	26
Charitable games	1,789	49	545	30
Gambling on Indian reservations	286	NA	100	35
Total legal	$166,470	32%	$16,923	10%
Illegal gambling				
Numbers	5,550	27	2,831	51
Horse books	6,066	10	1,031	17
Sports books	19,203	32	874	5
Sports cards	1,486	32	892	60
Total illegal	$ 32,306	27%	$ 5,627	17%
Grand total	$198,777	26%	$22,551	11%

Source: Eugene Martin Christiansen, "The 1986 Gross Annual Wager," *Gaming and Wagering Business* 8 (July 1987), 14, and 8 (August 1987), 17.

the National Policy toward Gambling. In 1986 dollars those estimates were considerably smaller: $39 billion for legal games and $11 billion for illegal games.[9] It is worth noting recent growth in the games as shown in Table 2.1. According to these estimates, the fastest-growing segment of gambling in the

United States is none other than state lotteries, fed by the entrance of new states and the growth in per capita sales.

The Global Appeal of Gambling

Gambling is a worldwide pastime. Most countries legalize some form of gambling, the major exceptions being those governed under Islamic law. The forms of gambling vary surprisingly little throughout the world. Although some distinct forms certainly exist—hockey pools in Canada or boat races in Japan, for example—most of the common forms of gambling found overseas are also found in the United States, and the most widespread form of gambling is the lottery. Of 140 countries and territories that permitted some form of legal gambling in 1986, 100 had legalized lotteries. In many countries the lottery is a firmly entrenched social institution. The Philippines, for example, has had a national lottery since 1933, and in China a lottery was reintroduced in 1988 for the first time since the Communist revolution. Spain's El Gordo ("the fat one") becomes the country's center of attention when it gives out the equivalent of hundreds of millions of dollars in one drawing each year. And lotteries in the Soviet Union, which offer coveted washing machines, television sets, and automobiles as well as cash, sell more than a billion tickets each year.[10]

The next most prevalent form of legalized gambling is casino gambling, which in 1986 was legal in seventy-seven countries, and betting on horse racing, which was legal in seventy-three. Slot machines were permitted in fifty-nine countries, including parts of the United States. One form of betting that shares a number of similarities with lotteries is sports pools, in which players pick the winners of various sporting events. Like lotteries, this form of betting is carried out through a network of ticket outlets which are today frequently computerized. Widely popular in Europe and South America, sports pools are not common in the United States. Off-track betting was legal in forty-one countries and bingo in thirty-six, the United States and Canada permitting both. Of the remaining major forms of gambling, dog racing was legal in seventeen countries and jai-alai in five, including the United States. Legalized cockfighting (legal in eleven countries) was largely confined to Latin America, although its illegal form remains popular in parts of the United States.[11] If countries are ranked by the size of their economy, the prevalence of lotteries is equally striking. Of the ten countries with the largest economies, six had legal sports pools, seven allowed off-track betting, nine had legalized horse racing, and nine had government-sanctioned lotteries.[12]

One noteworthy lottery form virtually unknown in the United States is the interest lottery. In 1956 Great Britain issued a series of "premium savings bonds," low-interest government bonds that offered the opportunity to win large tax-free prizes in periodic drawings. Sweden created a similar series in 1973, but with winnings partially taxable. Sales of such bonds have remained modest since their introduction.[13] In the United States a variant of the interest lottery was proposed in 1941 to raise money for the war. Loan certificates were to be sold for $1.10, from which ten cents would be added to a prize fund and the remainder held as a savings bond.[14] In 1974 Maryland authorized an interest lottery program, but apparently no bonds have ever been issued under that authority.[15]

Another indication of the worldwide popularity of gambling comes in the form of survey responses about the way people spend their leisure time. In one international comparison of surveys of leisure activities the percentage of people mentioning gambling differed markedly by country. Within the group of countries surveyed gambling was mentioned most often in France (21 percent of respondents) and Britain (19 percent) and least often in Italy and West Germany (3 percent each). In the middle were Canada (12 percent), the United States (13 percent), and Australia (17 percent). One should be cautious, however, in using such survey results to indicate the percentage of people who gamble. For example, a survey in 1978 showed that 15 percent of Japanese bet on some form of racing in that year, yet only 7 percent of Japanese in the international survey mentioned gambling as a way in which they spent their time.[16]

Interest in lotteries and other forms of gambling is clearly worldwide. The lesson for the analysis of American lotteries is that lotteries are not cropping up in a field untouched by gambling. Rather, the way has already been paved.[17]

The Extent and Growth of Lotteries in America

To assess the significance of state lotteries, one must know something about how they compare in size with other ways of raising public revenue and other kinds of consumer expenditure. Because lotteries are associated with frenzied appeal and million-dollar prizes, it is often difficult for the casual observer to obtain a true sense of the scale of lottery play. Probably the most striking aspect of the U.S. lottery experience in the twentieth century has been the rapid spread from state to state. Legal in no state in 1960, lotteries had extended to twenty-eight states and the District of Columbia by 1988. Figure 2.1 is a map of lottery states in 1989, showing the period in which each state started its lottery. Beginning in New Hampshire in 1964, the lottery movement spread to New York and other northeastern states before jumping

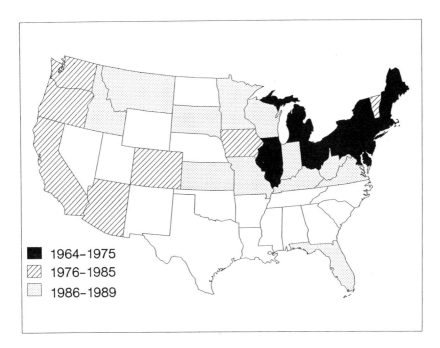

Figure 2.1. Lottery states by first year of operation

to the West and Midwest. By 1989 lotteries were operating in every section of the country.

This geographical spread has brought with it ever-increasing lottery sales. Table 2.2 summarizes the growth in the number of lotteries and their sales, from 1970 to 1988. As the number of states has increased, so too have national lottery sales. From two states in 1970, containing about 9 percent of the country's population, the number of lottery states (including the District of Columbia) had increased to thirty-three by the end of 1988, accounting for almost three-fourths of the population. Of these, as Table 2.2 shows, twenty-three operated throughout the 1988 fiscal year. What is remarkable about this growth in total sales is that it has come about less as a result of the rapid growth in the population of lottery states than as a result of growth in per capita sales. While the population of lottery states grew at an average rate of 12 percent a year between 1970 and 1988, per capita sales increased 16 percent a year, combining to produce an astounding annual growth rate in sales of 31 percent. Even if one omits the most active five-year period of growth, 1970–1975, the annual growth rates in sales are still impressive. Since 1975 total sales have increased an average of 21 percent a year and per capita

Table 2.2. Growth of U.S. lotteries, 1970–1988

Fiscal year	Number of established state lotteries[a]	Sales in 1987 dollars	
		Total (billions)	Per capita
1970	2	$ 0.1	$ 7
1975	9	1.1	20
1980	14	3.3	38
1985	18	9.4	97
1988	23	13.7	98

Sources: Annual reports of state lottery agencies for various years; Council of Economic Advisers, *Economic Report of the President;* U.S. Bureau of the Census, *Statistical Abstract of the United States; Gaming and Wagering Business* 9 (October 1988), 30.

a. Lotteries operating the entire fiscal year. Includes the District of Columbia in 1985 and 1988. See Table 2.3 for a list of the twenty-three state lotteries operating throughout the fiscal year and the note to the table for a list of the latest ones.

sales at 13 percent. Such growth rates have few precedents aside from hula hoops and videocassette recorders in their peak years.

What do these sales figures imply for a typical consumer? Are lottery bets a significant part of household budgets? By 1988 per capita lottery sales had reached almost $100 in lottery states. But since a portion of sales in most states is accounted for by out-of-state residents, this figure should be adjusted downward to reflect purchases by state residents only. And since minors are not permitted to buy lottery tickets, it is useful to convert the per capita figure into an average for households. When these adjustments are made, they imply an average household expenditure of roughly $240. While lottery purchases are by no means a large portion of a typical family's budget (amounting to only about 1 percent of total expenditures), they are sizable. They exceed the average outlays for prescription drugs and medical supplies and for reading materials. Households in lottery states spend fully two-thirds as much on lottery products as on alcoholic beverages and only slightly less than they do on tobacco products.[18] Of course households are no more uniform in their spending on lottery products than on other commodities, including alcohol and tobacco. Only a little more than half of the adults in lottery states ever play the lottery, so the averages for people who do play are higher than these figures indicate. In Chapter 6 we consider the degree to which lottery expenditures differ among households. Suffice it to say that on average, and in states where lotteries operate, expenditures on lotteries are on the same order of magnitude as for a number of familiar consumer items.[19]

Behind the enormous growth in total lottery sales large differences remain in expenditure levels within both the United States and Canada. Table 2.3 gives a breakdown of lottery sales in 1987 by state and province. Total sales were $12.5 billion in the United States and $2.5 billion in Canada. At $90 the average per capita expenditure in the United States was below the 1988 figure of $98 shown in Table 2.2, the difference being largely attributable to a surge in California's lotto sales in 1988. The per capita spending level varied markedly, from $33 in Iowa to $216 in Massachusetts. In general, the more established lotteries of the urbanized eastern states and provinces showed higher average levels of spending than the newer lotteries. Such per capita figures are gross measures of participation at best, in part because they assume that all sales are made to residents. Not only can travelers buy tickets, however, but some lottery states share borders with nonlottery states and consequently have larger effective markets for selling tickets. As a rough correction for this border effect, the fourth column uses an estimate of the population of bordering nonlottery states living within twenty miles of the state border. The resulting average of $85 per capita serves as a useful approximation of the average expenditure level of lottery state residents.

The last three columns of Table 2.3 show how the gross lottery proceeds are distributed. With very little variation the states and provinces return roughly half of their gross revenues as prizes; the 50 percent for prizes implies a takeout rate of 50 percent, reflecting a slight decline in takeout from the 51 percent for 1986 shown in Table 2.1. After prizes have been paid, lotteries must pay operating expenses, including commissions to retail sales outlets. As a percentage of sales, operating expenses vary considerably more than prizes, with the larger states enjoying lower expenditure ratios than the smaller states. After prizes and operating costs have been paid, the remainder is turned over to the state as net revenue. It is convenient and reasonably accurate to summarize the distribution of a dollar's worth of lottery betting as being divided into fifty cents for prizes, twelve cents for operating expenses, including retail commissions, and the remaining thirty-eight cents for net revenue to the state treasury.

As suggested by their widespread acceptance, lotteries in other countries enjoy similar levels of popularity. Although no publicly available data exist comparing total lottery sales in different countries, comparative data have been published for one of the world's major lottery games, lotto. Long popular in Europe, lotto has experienced rapid growth in the United States and Canada since 1975.[20] With per capita lotto sales of $36 in 1986, the United States had a relatively high rate of play, but it was by no means the highest

Table 2.3.   U.S. and Canadian lotteries by first year of operation: Sales and distribution of sales in FY1987 (in U.S. dollars)

Place	First year of operation	Sales			Distribution of sales (percent)		
		Total (millions)	Per capita	Adjusted per capita[a]	Prizes	Operating expenses	Net revenues[b]
New Hampshire	1964	$58.6	$ 55	$ 55	48%	17%	35%
New York[c]	1967	1,458.8	82	82	46	12	42
New Jersey	1971	1,116.9	146	146	50	9	41
Connecticut	1972	489.3	152	152	51	10	39
Massachusetts	1972	1,265.2	216	216	58	10	33
Pennsylvania	1972	1,338.5	112	112	48	9	43
Michigan	1972	1,006.3	109	103	49	14	37
Maryland	1973	760.5	168	139	48	8	44
Rhode Island	1974	57.9	59	59	48	16	36
Maine	1974	58.1	49	49	52	17	31
Illinois	1974	1,303.9	113	99	50	9	41
Ohio	1974	1,069.9	99	90	53	12	35
Delaware	1975	45.8	71	71	52	11	37
Vermont	1978	25.3	46	46	52	17	31
Arizona	1981	142.3	42	42	45	19	36
District of Columbia	1982	121.7	196	101	51	17	32
Washington	1982	193.9	43	41	45	14	40
Colorado	1983	113.3	34	33	50	19	30
Oregon	1985	100.3	37	35	51	18	31
Iowa	1985	98.8	35	27	48	21	31
California	1985	1,392.2	50	50	50	15	35

West Virginia	1986	70.6	37	30	43	24	34
Missouri	1986	174.1	34	28	45	20	35
Total (U.S.)		$12,462.3	90	85	50%	12%	38%
Loto-Quebec	1970	733.6	112	112	46	16	38
Western Canada	1974	350.4	77	77	46	15	39
Ontario	1975	922.0	101	101	47	15	38
Atlantic	1976	144.9	64	64	46	21	33
British Columbia	1985	327.0	113	113	46	16	38
Total (Canada)		$2,477.8	98	98	46%	16%	38%
Total (all lotteries)		$14,940.1	91	87	49%	12%	38%

Sources: Annual reports of state lottery agencies; *Gaming and Wagering Business* 9 (September 1988), 28–29, 9 (October 1988), 58; U.S. Bureau of the Census, *Statistical Abstract of the United States, 1988* (Washington, D.C.: Government Printing Office, 1987), p. xvii; U.S. Bureau of the Census, *County and City Data Book, 1983* (Washington, D.C.: Government Printing Office, 1983); *Corpus Almanac and Canadian Sourcebook, 1987*, pp. 5.2, 13.6. States that began operating lotteries in 1987 or 1988 were Florida, Kansas, Montana, South Dakota, Virginia, and Wisconsin. States that approved lotteries in November 1988 were Idaho, Indiana, Kentucky, and Minnesota.

a. Sales divided by state population plus estimated population in bordering nonlottery states within twenty miles of the lottery state's border.

b. Revenue from ticket sales equals sales minus prizes, commissions, and other expenses.

c. First lottery operated 1967–1975. A restructured lottery began again in 1976.

in the world. For example, four countries—Australia, Germany, Sweden, and Finland—had per capita sales over $50 in U.S. dollars. To be sure, these figures compare only lotto sales and therefore do not reflect the role of other major lottery games. When other games are included, for example, per capita lottery sales in Finland and Sweden come close to the level reached in the United States.[21] The United States is a comparatively recent entrant into legalized lotteries, but its level of expenditures is already on a par with that of countries that have been in the business for years.

The Lottery and State Finance

Not only are lotteries a consumer item, but they are also an instrument of public finance. Since the debate often begins with the question of a lottery's potential to generate state revenue, it is useful to compare lotteries to taxes and other such sources of revenue. But it is necessary to look beyond this function to a second, and distinctive, role of lotteries in public finance: they represent one of the major services produced by state government. This fact derives not only from the size of the typical lottery operation but also from the degree to which the state becomes identified with that product through its provision and marketing.

As a source of state revenue, lotteries are not "large"—certainly not in the sense of being comparable to state sales or income taxes. To show how lotteries compare to other sources of state revenue, Table 2.4 summarizes the major components of own-source revenue (that is, excluding intergovernmental grants) in lottery states in 1986.[22] By far the two primary sources of state revenue were the income tax and the sales tax, which together made up half the total for these states. Corporate taxes were next, contributing about 7 percent of the total. The remainder of state revenues came from a variety of sources, of which lotteries were a significant one. For example, lotteries, bringing in 3.3 percent of the total, accounted for more revenue than excise taxes on tobacco, alcohol, and parimutuel betting combined. Among excise taxes, only that on motor fuels brought in more revenue than lotteries. Lotteries are also by far the most profitable public enterprise operated by state governments. In 1986 lotteries generated over ten times the amount of profits yielded by state-owned liquor stores.[23] To be sure, their contribution differed from state to state, in large part owing to significant variations in per capita spending. In Maryland, for example, lottery revenues accounted for almost 6 percent of own-source revenues in 1986, and lotteries in New Jersey, Pennsylvania, and Illinois all contributed 4 percent or more of their revenues. But in some states the lottery's contributions were quite modest. One gauge of a lottery's usefulness as a source of revenue is to

Table 2.4.   Own-source revenues in lottery states, FY1986

Revenue source	Percentage of total own-source revenue[a]
Taxes	
General sales and gross receipts	23.2%
Selective sales and gross receipts	
Motor fuels	4.1
Tobacco products	1.7
Alcoholic beverages	0.7
Parimutuels	0.3
Other	6.1
Individual income	26.5
Corporation net income	7.1
License taxes	4.9
Property	1.3
Death and gift	1.2
Other	1.1
Charges	
Higher education	5.2
Hospitals	1.8
Other	2.3
Miscellaneous general revenue	
Lottery net revenue	3.3
Other	9.3
Total own-source revenue	100.0%

Source: U.S. Bureau of the Census, *State Government Finances in 1986* (Washington, D.C.: Government Printing Office, 1987).

a. Based on the eighteen states that had started lotteries by July 1, 1985.

calculate the increase in the state's sales tax that would be necessary to raise an equivalent amount of revenue. In only four of the fifteen lottery states with sales taxes in 1986 would the increase have been as much as 1 percent.[24] While lotteries are not a revenue source on the order of sales or income taxes, therefore, they do represent a significant source and one that is larger than most excise taxes.[25]

A lottery's contribution to its state's public finance cannot simply be measured by dollars of revenue. As we have stated, lotteries also play a major role as an *output* of government. In fact lotteries represent one of the largest such outputs purchased directly by state residents. This producer-consumer relationship further heightens the significance of the lottery as an activity of government. In operating a lottery agency a state provides a service in the same sense in which highways, public universities, and parks are services. Thus a lottery's expenditures must be counted along with those for other services provided by state agencies in any description of the output of state government. Table 2.5 presents a comparison of the major outputs of state governments, measured by direct expenditures of the state governments themselves or by private expenditures on outputs they sell to customers. Quantitatively, education and public welfare were the two most costly services that state governments provided in 1986, with per capita expenditures of about $240, and highways were next at about $125. After those three major categories came state lotteries, by virtue of expenditures on them by consumers, with a higher level of expenditure than for state hospitals and twice as high a level as for natural resources, parks, and recreation combined.

As odd as it may appear, therefore, lotteries turn out to be one of the main services produced by state governments. In terms of state products that citizens purchase directly, the lottery ranks second, right after higher education.

Table 2.5.   State expenditures and sales revenues, FY1986, selected functions

Expenditures and sales by function	Per capita
Total direct expenditures (50 states and District of Columbia)	
Education	$ 244
Public welfare	236
Highways	126
Hospitals	72
Health	54
Correctional institutions	41
Natural resources, parks, and recreation	39
Other	212
Total	$1,024
Direct sales	
State lotteries (23 states)[a]	$84
Tuition, fees, and expenses, state higher education[b] (50 states)	71
State liquor stores (17 states)	45
Utilities (15 states)	32
Hospitals (50 states)	27

Sources: U.S. Bureau of the Census, *State Government Finances in 1986* (Washington, D.C.: Government Printing Office, 1987), tables 7, 11, 19 and 21; annual reports of state lotteries; U.S. Bureau of the Census, *Statistical Abstract of the United States, 1987* (Washington, D.C.: Government Printing Office, 1986), p. 22.
a. Estimate, adjusted for out-of-state sales, Table 2.4.
b. Excludes auxiliary enterprises.

(Per capita spending on lotteries in fact exceeds the amount that citizens pay for tuition, fees, room, board, and books to state colleges and universities, but the total state expenditure for higher education is considerably more.) And lottery sales are much higher on a per capita basis than sales of liquor or utilities, where those are provided by the state. In assessing the role of state lotteries, it is thus useful to think of them as an output of state government. Like higher education, the states' single most important product, lotteries are highly visible and commonly associated with the state. States seldom promote the liquor or utilities they sell, but both lotteries and higher education are marketed, publicized, and implicitly endorsed by the states, each in its own way. Far from being an insignificant appendage to state government, lotteries have become a highly visible enterprise.

3.

The Fall and Rise of Lotteries

> You could scarcely imagine what a rage we have here for
> lotteries. 8,000 tickets sold in four days, in the
> Marblehead lottery . . . I wonder Secretary Hamilton
> does not hit upon a lottery.
>
> —Rev. Jeremy Belknap of Boston, 1790

State lotteries did not spring forth fully grown in the last two decades. Both gambling in general and lotteries in particular have long histories in this country and abroad. Lottery-like games and decision processes seem to be a universal phenomenon and have appeared in many forms throughout history. Lotteries have been used in law, from the election by lot of officials in Rome to the allocation of landing times in airports and the drafting of young men for military service in the United States in recent years. Americans enjoyed playing lotteries before the Revolutionary War; illegal lotteries have flourished throughout the twentieth century; and sweepstakes continue to be a favorite means of marketing consumer products. Despite their popularity, however, lotteries have not always been viewed as a respectable form of entertainment or finance. The total prohibition on them during the first sixty-three years of the twentieth century was by far a more sweeping condemnation than that placed on alcohol, tobacco, or many other forms of gambling. Yet attitudes did change, and gambling in the form of lotteries gradually began to lose its status as a vice. Although opposition remained, lotteries began to be viewed by a majority as an acceptable, almost respectable vehicle for raising public funds. In this growing acceptance of lotteries the pendulum of public attitudes was merely returning to a position it had occupied at times during the previous two centuries. But the nature of the modern lottery is indelibly shaped by the country's past experience and the depth of the enduring moral objections to gambling, as well as the games' widespread popularity.

For over two centuries tension has existed between acceptance and rejection of the lottery as a means of raising funds. Support for the lottery has been provided, first, by the continuing popularity of such games as a form of entertainment. A broad segment of the population has played lotteries where they were legal and similar games where they were not. A second source of support, based on civic responsibility, has arisen at various times among the ruling elite. Lotteries during the colonial and postrevolutionary periods, for example, were respectable instruments of public finance, sponsored by prominent citizens, approved by state legislatures, and subscribed to out of civic spirit as much as enthusiasm for the game. Since profit rates were low, there was little to be gained by commercial participation in their operation. The sponsors of lottery schemes volunteered their time to raise money just as prominent citizens do today for charity. In this century proponents have included those who see lotteries as a source of funds that can be used for worthy purposes. In the 1930s and 1940s philanthropists of the economic elite proposed lotteries for funding public projects. More recently civic leaders have boosted lotteries by suggesting that the revenues be used to support public education.

Opposition to lotteries has been based on two arguments: gambling is morally wrong, and lotteries have harmful effects. Moralists, of which the religious right forms only a part, base their opposition on grounds largely unrelated to the actual consequences of gambling. By contrast, reformers—from the social reformers of the nineteenth century to political liberals in the twentieth century—have worried about the harmful effects of gambling and disproportionate participation among minority groups and the poor. Opponents have also pointed to fraud and corruption as negative consequences of legalized lotteries.

This chapter documents the rise, fall, and resurgence in public acceptance of lotteries in the United States. It shows, further, that the same arguments for and against the lottery as a means of raising funds in colonial times can be heard today in the debate over state lotteries. In this light the widespread adoption of modern lotteries is seen less as a discovery of a "new" source of public revenue than as a victory of pragmatic considerations over long-standing reservations concerning the use of lotteries in any form. In the wake of profound shifts in social attitudes on many issues, the old arguments have increasingly been overcome by recognition that the enduring popularity of lotteries makes them an attractive alternative to tax increases.

Historical Roots of the American Lottery

The overwhelming impression one gains from studying the history of lotteries is that, in this respect as in others, there is indeed nothing new under the sun. Choosing by lot has been a method for making determinations at least as far back as biblical times, with the division of the land west of the Jordan among the tribes of Israel (Numbers 26:55). According to Proverbs 18:18, "The lot puts an end to disputes and decides between powerful contenders." Lots also appear in the literature and traditions of Greece, India, China, Japan, and Rome. The first real lottery, involving the payment of some "consideration" for the chance of winning a prize, probably occurred in Italy during the Middle Ages.[1] These first lotteries were conducted by merchants as a way of stimulating the sales of their products, often stale goods. Prizes were given in the form of merchandise. The first lottery offering prizes of money was held in Florence in 1530, with proceeds going to the state.[2] The Italians brought lotteries to France as early as 1533.[3] In England Queen Elizabeth I chartered the first government lottery in 1566, although private and illegal lotteries had apparently existed before.[4] The English brought lotteries to America in the form of an authorized drawing to support the Virginia Company's Jamestown settlement in 1612.[5]

The Colonial Period

In colonial America lotteries were a popular and common means of financing public projects. Lotteries run for private profit also existed but were never legalized. All of the colonies authorized lotteries at one time or another, and a few of them used the device on many occasions. In the decade 1766 to 1775, for example, Rhode Island authorized forty-three different lotteries; during the same period seven other colonies authorized a total of eighteen lotteries. The proceeds of most of these lotteries were devoted to projects of public infrastructure such as paving roads, constructing bridges and wharves, and erecting buildings, although the line between public and private was typically indistinct. Among the most prominent projects supported by lotteries in the colonial period were the rebuilding of Faneuil Hall and the construction of college buildings for Harvard, Yale, Princeton, and King's College (later Columbia). Other projects included churches and Masonic halls as well as libraries, lighthouses, and workhouses. During the Revolution lotteries were used to supply and support troops in the field, and after independence the device continued to be used for many of the same purposes.[6]

The lotteries themselves were typically drawings with a fixed prize distribution. Tickets purchased were simply stored together until the drawing to determine winners. The whole process was anything but quick. Usually it took months to sell the required number of tickets, and some schemes failed to do so and had to give refunds. The drawings themselves could take weeks, owing to the practice of drawing simultaneously from one container holding the tickets with the names of purchasers and another containing an equal number of tickets representing all prizes and "blanks." Organizers were usually public-spirited citizens who volunteered their services.[7] Most early lotteries returned about 85 percent of their proceeds in the form of prizes. Since tickets were generally sold without commission, the remaining 15 percent went to the beneficiary.[8]

Measured by the amount spent, lotteries were a very popular form of consumption indeed. Lotteries amounting to $106,000 were authorized in Rhode Island in 1774. If this is a good estimate of annual sales, it implies a per capita rate of expenditure of about $3. Equally affecting their widespread use, however, was the absence of other sources of public financing. Neither debt finance nor taxation appeared to be an attractive alternative for the financing of large capital projects. Capital markets were rudimentary, to say the least, before a national banking system had been firmly established. Bond issues were not used as a reliable source of public financing until well into the nineteenth century, and even then the possibility of default gave potential investors reason to be nervous. Taxes, of course, were a notoriously unpopular instrument of government policy throughout the colonial period and beyond.[9] At the same time, there was little organized opposition to lotteries as a means of raising money. To be sure, some were opposed on moral grounds, including Congregationalists in New England and Quakers in Pennsylvania. But it is evident from the number of religious organizations that benefited directly from lotteries that organized religion for the most part had no real objection to them. Instead, lotteries appear to have been viewed as more akin to charitable contributions for public purposes. According to one nineteenth-century authority the lottery was "not regarded at all as a kind of gambling; the most reputable citizens were engaged in these lotteries, either as selected managers or as liberal subscribers. It was looked upon as a kind of voluntary tax . . . with a contingent profitable return for such subscribers as held the lucky numbers. All the subscribers and managers contributed their influence to secure the sale of all the tickets, so as to insure the largest return for the object to which the funds remaining above the prizes drawn were pledged."[10] As with church raffles and bake sales today, the objectives were lofty, the organizers were volunteers, the customers were willing, and the hope was to raise as much money for the purpose as the law allowed.

Nineteenth-Century Lotteries

Lotteries retained much of their popularity into the next century, but their mode of operation changed, resulting in new problems, vigorous opposition, and finally abolition. The objective of nineteenth-century lotteries remained for the most part the funding of public projects. The rising need for construction and equipment in cities, roads and canals to support increased transportation, and schools to serve the growing population motivated most of the lottery authorizations in the early 1800s, although churches and other nongovernmental organizations remained prominent beneficiaries as well. Between 1790 and 1833, for example, Pennsylvania authorized sixty lotteries to benefit church groups, including Lutheran, Presbyterian, Episcopal, Reformed, Baptist, Catholic, Universalist, and Jewish congregations. Conspicuous by their absence were the Quakers, who had consistently opposed lotteries. For the most part, however, lottery proceeds went to state or local governments or to quasipublic projects. Authority over lottery offerings generally remained with state legislatures rather than with the federal government. The only exceptions to this rule—which has continued to hold in the twentieth century—were a lottery to support the Continental Army in 1776 and a series of lotteries approved by the federal government between 1792 and 1842 to fund projects in the District of Columbia.[11]

Sales. By all accounts lotteries were an exceedingly popular form of entertainment in the early nineteenth century. Not only does the implicit acceptance of the activity by major religious groups bear witness to its popularity, but such sales figures as exist also suggest relatively high levels of purchase. Two estimates of sales for 1832, apparently one of the peak years for lottery play, indicate the rate of sales during the period. A contemporary estimate of lottery sales in Philadelphia, then the country's largest city with a population of about 200,000, was $1.5 million, implying an annual per capita expenditure of $7.50 for the total population.[12] Also useful, though problematic, is a compilation of lottery authorizations for eight states during 1832 showing a total of $53.1 million.[13] Assuming that this represents the annual rate of sales for lotteries in these states, and assuming that these states represented all lottery offerings in the country, this figure implies a per capita sales figure of about $4.10, a rate about half that calculated for Philadelphia. Combining these data on income for the period suggests that lottery expenditures were over 3 percent of national income in 1832. This is an astounding figure, but one that must certainly be taken with several grains of salt, given the rudimentary nature of the monetary system and national income accounts.[14]

Privatization of lotteries. The distinguishing feature of nineteenth-century lotteries was the emergence of firms specializing in organization and marketing. The number of dealers selling tickets as a primary activity increased. These ticket brokers would often set up offices in various cities to sell tickets, at a commission, for the lotteries authorized in different states. Some of the early commercial banks arose from these brokerage houses, owing to their expertise with the numerous currencies then in circulation. At the retail level purchases took place in lottery shops, some of which were operated by national firms. An indication of the growth of both the lottery industry and the demand for its product is suggested by the number of shops in Baltimore and Philadelphia that sold lottery tickets. In Baltimore the number of such offices rose from 6 in 1820 to 13 in 1825, three of which were branch offices of national firms.[15] In Philadelphia the number of shops increased from 3 in 1809 to 60 in 1827 and 177 in 1831.[16] Advertising by lottery offices was as vigorous as it was common. Newspapers carried daily inducements to buy tickets, with slogans like "Now is the time to fill your bags!" Even the names of the shops, such as Kidder's Lucky Lottery and Dean's Real Fortune, were designed to appeal to the potential player. Another activity taken up by entrepreneurs was the management of the entire lottery enterprise. Soon it became more common for lotteries to be operated by such private firms than by the volunteers who had served this function in the early lotteries.[17]

Whether as a result of the entrance of private enterprise into the lottery business or as an accompanying trend, there was increasing evidence of fraud and dishonesty in the operation of lotteries. Drawings were sometimes delayed, and in some cases managers defaulted entirely on their obligation to award prizes. On other occasions unscrupulous operators added blanks to the prize box, thereby reducing the number of prizes.[18]

Growing opposition. Outrage at these abuses gained momentum among those who already opposed lotteries on moral grounds. From the days of colonial lotteries some religious leaders had spoken out against their operation. During the first three decades of the nineteenth century this opposition drew strength from the larger ferment of social reform in the United States, including movements for temperance, peace, women's rights, educational reform, prison reform, and the abolition of slavery.[19] Opponents offered three fundamental objections to lotteries: as a form of gambling they were morally corrupting; they were often operated dishonestly; and they created serious social problems, including economic distress and gambling addiction. In 1823 one opponent stated, "Public gaming by Lotteries so far from being less criminal than other species of that vice, is the worst of them all; for it abets and sanctions, as far as example and concurrence can do it, a practice which opens the door to every species of fraud and villainy; which is pregnant with the most extensive evils to the community and individuals." Another in 1818 charged that lotteries "spread a horribly-increasing mass of idleness, fraud, theft, falsehood, and profligacy throughout all the classes of our labouring population."[20] Some historians suggest that one motivating force for the opposition to lotteries was the rise of Jacksonian resentment of privilege, manifested in this case by the exclusive charters granted to lottery operators.[21] Lotteries thus joined banks as symbols of unjustified privilege.

These reformers prevailed, with states first and eventually the federal government stepping in to outlaw lotteries by the end of the nineteenth century. In 1833 Pennsylvania, New York, and Massachusetts all put an end to state-authorized lotteries. First the northeastern states, then the southern and western states abolished lotteries until, by 1860, only three states—Delaware, Missouri, and Kentucky—still allowed them.[22]

The Louisiana lottery. After the Civil War a few southern and western states had brief flings with lotteries,[23] but it was the history of one postwar lottery that had the most lasting impact on attitudes and legislation regarding lotteries. The Louisiana Lottery Company was authorized in 1868 in the midst of corruption and Reconstruction. Both the granting of its twenty-five-year charter and subsequent attempts to repeal it were accompanied by outright bribery of legislators. The Louisiana lottery was a veritable money machine, combining a monopoly position with a high profit margin. Its monopoly was reinforced in Louisiana by a strict crackdown on illegal lotteries. But the key to its success was national marketing, with over 90 percent of its revenue coming from out of state. The proportion of revenue it retained for expenses and profits (about 48 percent) was much higher than in earlier lotteries or contemporary foreign lotteries. Although other states moved to stop lottery play, first by ending authorizations and then by forbidding the purchase of out-of-state tickets, the Louisiana lottery continued to do a thriving business by mail. Following Kentucky's decision to drop its similarly run state lottery in 1878, Louisiana's was the only legal game in the country, although illegal lotteries continued to operate. Spurred by antilottery sentiment in the other states, Congress passed a series of increasingly effective restrictions on the use of the mails to conduct lotteries. In 1890 it prohibited all mail referring to lotteries and in 1895 all lottery activity in interstate commerce. This legislation effectively closed down the Louisiana lottery. By 1894 no state permitted the operation of lotteries, and thirty-five states had explicit prohibitions in their constitutions against them.[24]

Popularity under Prohibition

From 1894 to 1964 no legal, government-sponsored lotteries operated in the United States. The only way Americans could play lotteries during this period was to participate in church bingo or charity raffles where allowed, to bet in illegal numbers games where available, or to play foreign lotteries. By all appearances, interest in these forms of betting was high during the period of prohibition. The Irish Sweepstakes started up in 1930 and soon had a large clientele of Americans.[25] One Post Office official lamented in 1932, "The country seems to have gone lottery mad."[26] Several national surveys during this period confirm the widespread participation in lotteries. In 1938, for example, 13 percent of those interviewed nationally had bought a sweepstakes ticket, although this figure declined when the Irish Sweepstakes stopped operating during the war. A survey in 1944 showed that a quarter of all adults had bought a chance in a church raffle or lottery, and 7 percent had played illegal numbers or policy games. Counting bets on card games, elections, sporting events, horse races, slot machines, and punchboards, over half of Americans were gambling in some form.[27] Despite the official disapproval of lotteries, therefore, the interest in gambling in general and lotteries in particular remained strong, at least among a subset of the population. Before we look at the reemergence of legalized lotteries, let us examine the kind of lottery activity that existed during this interval of prohibition.

Illegal Lotteries

Illegal lotteries existed alongside official lotteries from at least the nineteenth century, and, until the reemergence of the state lotteries in the 1960s and 1970s, represented the only real alternative for the lottery aficionado. In the United States the two dominant illegal games have been policy and numbers. Policy, or "insurance," got its start in this country as a side bet in connection with drawings for authorized lotteries. In the midst of the lengthy drawings to determine the winners of early lotteries, the custom arose to make bets on whether a specific number would be drawn on a given day. In contrast to the relatively high-priced tickets for the official lotteries, these bets could be secured for pennies each. Policy was attractive, then, because chances were inexpensive and betting action could be accomplished quickly. By the time of the Louisiana lottery, lottery shops routinely offered policy bets as well as official lottery tickets.[28]

Operators of the illegal games gradually began to draw their own numbers and thus grew independent of public lottery operations. One of the common forms of policy was based on the selection of twelve numbers between 1 and 78, with bets being placed on various combinations of drawn numbers. Two Supreme Court cases around 1900 involved policy games in Covington, Kentucky, and their Cincinnati patrons.[29] Policy appears to have been especially popular in the black neighborhoods of Chicago, with thirty-eight shops, or "wheels," operating on the South Side in 1931.[30] One description of policy as played in Chicago's black neighborhoods around 1940 reveals a game of great activity, with many different games, or "pools," several drawings per day, and an elaborate system of shops, collectors, and "pick-up men." The most popular bet was to guess at three numbers that would be among the twelve picked, a bet that would pay off $20 for a dime's investment.[31] Many variations were available, including bets on one, two, or four numbers as well as bets based on two sets of numbers.[32]

In the 1920s the numbers game was introduced as an alternative to policy,[33] and it soon became the dominant illegal lottery game in New York and other cities in the Northeast. Simpler than the policy game played in Chicago, the numbers game typically was based on a simple three-digit number drawn daily. Any random number could be chosen, but the method favored in New York used payouts from local race tracks.[34] Players could bet on the numbers chosen in exact order (with a probability of winning of 1 in 1,000) or on combinations of the digits. Like policy, the numbers game offered its urban patrons the opportunity of placing small bets on a daily basis.

Beyond their quick outcome, low price, and convenience, ultimately the most attractive feature of policy and numbers games may be the ability of players to pick their own numbers. "Dream books," which purport to translate dreams, names, and life circumstances into bettable numbers, were used as early as the late nineteenth century. They were popular among black policy players in Chicago around 1940 and among black, Hispanic, and other numbers players in New York in recent years.[35] Players also used birthdays and other lucky numbers in betting. In New Orleans in the 1880s there were even trained parakeets in the business of picking numbers.[36]

Not surprisingly, quantitative measures of the extent of numbers play are difficult to derive. A survey taken in New York in 1972 showed that 24 percent of the adult population had played the numbers game, a third the percentage who had played state lotteries. Of those who played numbers, the estimated average weekly expenditure was over $8, or almost $20 in 1985 dollars.[37] Another study estimated that policy in 1970 employed fifteen thousand people in the Bedford-Stuyvesant area of New York, with an annual handle of $36 million.[38] Nationwide the handle for illegal numbers in 1974 was estimated to be $1.1 billion, which equals over $2 billion, or slightly less than $10 per capita, in 1985 dollars.[39] A more recent estimate of the handle for numbers is $5.5 billion, or about $25 per capita.[40] Whatever the national averages are, numbers play appears to be heavily concentrated in urban areas.

Bingo, Bank Nights, and Sweepstakes

Except for foreign lotteries, illegal lotteries offered the only true lottery games during the period of official prohibition. Imperfect substitutes did arise over time, however, in the form of charity bingo and legalized pari-mutuel gambling. It seems unlikely that any amount of official prohibition could stop the use of bingo and raffles by charitable and civic organizations if the state authorities did not move to shut down their operations. This appears to have been the case in New York. Although bingo was illegal until 1958, a commission investigating it in New York conceded that "the laws prohibiting the game as an unlawful lottery seemed more honored by violation than by observance and enforcement. Many highly respectable groups conducted bingo games in open violation of the law."[41] Bingo was legalized as early as 1937 in Rhode Island, 1949 in New Hampshire, and 1954 in New

Jersey. By 1973 thirty-four states had legalized it.[42] Thus a seemingly harmless alternative to illegal lotteries existed not only after legalization but apparently before it as well.

Another outlet for lottery enthusiasts lay in sweepstakes and other so-called chance promotions used to bolster sales. Originated by Italian merchants, such schemes became a familiar fixture in commercial marketing. Despite the legal abolition of lotteries in the United States in the first half of the twentieth century, chance promotions have apparently enjoyed consistent popularity, although their legality has required them to be distinguished from lotteries. During the depression, movie theaters swelled with patrons on "bank night," when prize drawings were held and winners, although technically they did not have to be in the theater for the drawing, had to present themselves within a few minutes. The legal status of such promotions hinged on the common law definition of three necessary ingredients for a lottery: chance, consideration, and prizes. The first and last were virtually always present, in that prizes were offered based on chance. The determining factor from a legal point of view turned on the issue of consideration, the cost borne by the entrant in order to play. Where "no purchase is necessary," consideration usually is not deemed to be present, although the case law in this area is replete with variations in contest rules and legal interpretations.[43]

The Rehabilitation of Lotteries in the Twentieth Century

The reemergence of state-sanctioned lotteries in the latter half of the twentieth century was not sudden. The introduction of the New Hampshire Sweepstakes was preceded by several decades of increasing public acceptance of gambling and support of numerous lottery proposals by respectable public leaders, and by gradually softening attitudes toward legalization. Although opposition to lotteries has remained alive all the while, their reemergence most of all bears testimony to the enduring popularity of lottery games.

The Resurgence of Legalized Gambling

Lotteries were not the only form of gambling under a cloud as the twentieth century began. One established form of commercial gambling, horse racing, was permitted in only three states in 1900: Maryland, Kentucky, and New York. New York later prohibited it, but gradually other states began to allow it once more as the parimutuel betting system came into general usage. By 1911 six states had legalized gambling at racetracks, and the number grew to twenty-one by the depression. In 1931 Nevada legalized gambling casinos, slot machines, and horse racing, to establish itself as America's gambling mecca.[44] These are the beginnings of what has been called the third wave of

legalized gambling in American history.[45] The first, from colonial times to
the early nineteenth century, and the second, the three decades following
the Civil War, both featured the lottery as a popular form of gambling. But
this time legalization appeared to be much more comprehensive. By 1963,
on the eve of New Hampshire's introduction of a lottery, twenty-six of the
fifty states had legalized horse racing.[46] The following two decades would see
even further expansion of legalized gambling. The number of states permitting parimutuel betting on horse or dog races increased to thirty-two in 1977
and thirty-six in 1986. Bingo had been legalized in thirty-eight states by 1977
and in forty-five states by 1986.[47]

Lottery Proposals

Despite their checkered nineteenth-century history, lotteries apparently continued to hold promise as an easy device for raising money to support worthy
causes. Here one sees elements of plutocratic leadership overcoming the
opposition of traditional elites, as in the civic-minded lotteries of colonial
times. The depression spawned a flurry of proposals for lotteries at the state
and federal levels. By 1934 lottery bills had been introduced in the legislatures of at least five northeastern states. The New York proposal, typical of
those in other states, would have directed lottery proceeds for unemployment
relief.[48] At the same time a group of lottery supporters, led by prominent
New York philanthropists, formed the National Conference for Legalizing
Lotteries, to push for lotteries at the state and national levels that would
support hospitals and other charitable causes.[49] At the national level Congressman Edward Kenney of New Jersey introduced a bill to authorize a
lottery to fund veterans' benefits and other federal expenditures.[50] Lottery
bills were defeated, however, at both the federal and state levels.[51] The Second World War brought new lottery proposals, including schemes offering
war bonds as prizes and one combining a loan instrument with lottery drawings.[52] More proposals aimed at tax reduction followed the war. Congressman
Paul Fino of New York introduced bills for a national lottery regularly from
1953 until the early 1960s.[53] In 1953 a state legislator in New Hampshire began
a decade of annual proposals for a state lottery.[54] And on the eve of New
Hampshire's adoption of a state lottery the New York City Federation of
Women's Clubs in 1962 endorsed a national lottery to benefit hospitals. One
delegate stated, "If we can find a way to raise revenue in an easy, pleasant
way, don't you think we should?"[55] Although they were outlawed in the
United States for over seven decades, therefore, lotteries retained a degree
of support for their use in funding worthwhile charitable and public goals.

Public Attitudes toward Lotteries

The public attitude toward lotteries is and apparently has long been one of fundamental paradox. On the one hand, lotteries have enjoyed sustained and widespread popularity. As we have seen, throughout the period of official prohibition illegal lotteries thrived in major urban areas, as did lottery-like marketing games and charity games such as bingo. When the question of state-operated lotteries began to be put to voters in the 1960s and 1970s, the verdict was stated emphatically in a series of majorities favoring adoption.[56] Yet on the other hand, there remained an abiding opposition to the legalization of lotteries.[57] The arguments used by opponents in the twentieth century bear a distinct similarity to those used in the nineteenth century and earlier. Before we turn to the shape of emerging lotteries and the patterns of lottery play, it is helpful to understand the climate of public opinion regarding government lotteries and, as a part of that examination, the kinds of moral arguments used by opponents of lotteries and gambling in general.

Opinion polls show that support for government lotteries has been strong for a long time and has grown steadily. As Table 3.1 shows, the earliest national Gallup polls, taken twenty-five years before the first twentieth-century American state lottery, showed that about half of all adults in the United States favored public lotteries of some kind. Although percentages varied with the year and the type of lottery suggested, every poll taken after 1938 found more supporters than opponents. After 1964 the support for lotteries began to grow, with those favoring state lotteries increasing from around 50 percent in 1963 and 1964 to 61 percent in 1975 to over 70 percent in 1982. By the mid-1980s support for a federal lottery was also high, with two national surveys showing at least 65 percent approval. This same growth in support is evident in a series of polls taken in Iowa between 1963 and 1984, summarized in Table 3.2. The percentage favoring lotteries there grew steadily from 25 percent in 1963 to 74 percent in 1985.

While the growth in acceptance of lotteries in this century is unmistakable, the reasons for the change are less clear. Certainly some of the thaw in opposition to lotteries could be due to the post-1960 experience with public lotteries in Canada and in several states. One reason to believe that familiarity itself may mollify opposition is the apparent rise in approval of lotteries in states following adoption. But the major share of the increasing acceptance of lotteries in the United States must surely be due to other factors, which might be contained under the rubric of the general liberalization of attitudes on social and moral questions in society. The "erosion of traditional (i.e., smalltown) American values"[58] is frequently referred to in analyses of social

Table 3.1. Opinion polls on government lotteries, 1938–1986

Year	Lottery level	Use of lottery revenues	Percent who—		
			Favor	Oppose	Have no opinion; no answer; not sure
1938	State	General revenue	49%	51%	—[a]
1941	Federal	National defense	51	38	11%
1941	State	Old-age pensions	45	41	14
1942	Federal	Cost of the war	54	37	9
1943	Federal	Cost of the war	49	42	9
1963	State	General revenue	51	39	10
1964	State	General revenue	48	41	11
1975	State[b]	General revenue	61	29	10
1982	State	General revenue	72	—[c]	—[c]
1984	Federal	Paying off the national debt	70	24	6
1986	Federal	Reduction of the deficit	65	30	5

Sources: For 1938–1964, George Gallup, *The Gallup Poll* (New York: Random House, 1972), pp. 103, 264, 320, 370, 1820, 1876; for 1975, Commission on the Review of the National Policy toward Gambling, *Gambling in America* (Washington, D.C.: Government Printing Office, 1976), pp. 71, 157; for 1982, Howard J. Klein with Gary Selesner, "Results of the First Gallup Organization Study of Public Attitudes toward Legalized Gambling," *Gaming Business Magazine* 3 (November 1982), 7; for 1984, Roper Organization, national poll, April 1984, Roper Center printout, USROPER 84-5, R60; for 1986, *Los Angeles Times*, national telephone poll, February 1986, Roper Center printout, USLAT.103.R57.

a. "No opinion" evidently omitted in calculating percentage.

b. Respondents were asked about a number of forms of gambling, including "buying lottery tickets." For those who lived in states where it was legal, the question was, "Would you like to see ——— continued or would you like to see it abolished?" For those who lived in states without that form of gambling, the question was, "Are you definitely in favor of legalizing it, do you tend to be in favor of legalizing it, do you tend to be against legalizing it, or are you definitely against legalizing it?"

Table 3.2.   Opinion polls on state lottery in Iowa, 1963–1985

| | Percent who— | | |
Date	Favor	Oppose	Are undecided
June 1963	25%	59%	16%
January 1976	44	42	14
December 1982	58	35	7
June 1983	52	40	8
January 1984	62	29	9
March 1985	74	18	8

Source: David Westphal, "Iowans Favor a Lottery, but Branstad Says 'No,' " *Des Moines Register,* February 7, 1984; David Elbert, "Iowa Poll Finds 74% Want Lottery," *Des Moines Sunday Register,* March 24, 1985.

change, and there is in fact evidence of significant change on a number of fronts. One study summarizing surveys over time on dozens of social issues—including abortion, divorce, women's rights, premarital sex, racial integration, homosexuality, and nonconformist religious views—concludes that Americans have become decidedly more liberal in their attitudes.[59] One indication of shifting social values may be the decline in church membership that occurred after the Second World War. The percentage of Americans who were members of churches or synagogues fell from 76 percent in 1947 to 67 percent in 1982, although it had risen to 71 percent by 1985.[60] Perhaps more striking was the apparent decline of religious influence in society. The percentage of people who claimed that religion was very important in their lives dropped from 75 percent in 1952 to 56 percent in 1984.[61] Similarly, the proportion of college freshmen who believe it is necessary to "develop a meaningful philosophy of life" fell by over half between 1967 and 1987.[62] If traditional values have lost ground, it is not at all clear what has taken their place. In 1970 Daniel Bell noted the rise of "a hedonism which promises a material ease and luxury" taking the place of traditional notions of the Protestant work ethic.[63] Whether or not this is true, it does appear that the prevalence of materialistic values has been rising steadily. Annual surveys of college freshmen show that the percentage who think that being "very well off financially" is an important goal increased from 44 to 71 percent over the last two decades.[64] While changes of this sort are difficult to document precisely, the rise in popularity of lotteries may be merely an indication of the extent to which society at large has become more permissive on social issues. The much-heralded return to traditional religious and social teaching in recent years seems not to have dampened the general enthusiasm for lotteries.

Marketing with Sweepstakes

An indication of the growing acceptance of lotteries is the apparent increase in the use of sweepstakes to market grocery products, magazines, and other consumer items. In 1985 U.S. firms spent an estimated $230 million on sweepstakes.[65] Sweepstakes are used to promote products from breakfast cereal to hamburgers to candy bars. One brand of beer based its appeal and name on the cash sweepstakes denoted on bottle tops offering prizes up to $1,000.[66] This kind of marketing appears to be on the increase.[67] Data from the state of New York, which requires that all such sweepstakes games be registered, suggest that the annual number of games increased more than tenfold between 1972 and 1986.[68]

Despite the obvious similarities between chance promotion schemes and government lotteries, significant differences remain. One natural result of the no-consideration requirement is that the cost of entering chance promotions is usually small. Such contests require only the purchase of a product, a visit to a store, or the price of a stamp to obtain an entry blank or ticket. While these out-of-pocket costs are low, inconvenience may be a factor, and such requirements tend to discourage multiple entries. In contrast, there is no barrier except cost to prevent a player from buying any number of state lottery tickets at one time. Another difference follows from this one: the probability of winning big prizes in commercial sweepstakes promotions is infinitesimal. For example, the stated odds of winning the grand prize in three contests run in 1987 were 1 in 35 million and 1 in 250 million to win $1 million (Oreo and McDonald's) and 1 in 192 million to win a sports car (M&M/Mars). All the same, game designers appear to devote as much attention to the prize structure of these marketing games as lottery managers do.[69]

It is worth noting that marketing games of this sort are regulated in a variety of ways. Several states require operators to register, and some call for the posting of a bond. In the case of chance promotions for retail food and gasoline products, the Federal Trade Commission requires promoters to post the exact number of winners and the odds of winning each prize as well as lists of actual winners following the contest.[70]

The Residue of Opposition

Despite the growing acceptability of state lotteries, objections remain. Moral, mostly religious, opposition, where it exists, is uncompromising. Most public arguments against lotteries, however, are based on qualms about the alleged harmful consequences of gambling in general and state-supported lotteries in particular.

Religious Objections

In stark contrast to the widespread popularity of lotteries is the persistence of a solid core of moral opposition to gambling that has probably been in existence as long as bets have been placed. In America the Quakers were early opponents, as were the prominent Congregational ministers Increase and Cotton Mather of Massachusetts. Religious groups were active in the antilottery movement of the nineteenth century.[71] Today that opposition to gambling continues to be part of the doctrine of mainstream Protestant churches in America, although in some denominations congregational autonomy precludes doctrinal dictums of any kind. Among the denominations on record against gambling are Methodists, Mormons, Baptists, and Lutherans.[72] Although gambling is not explicitly forbidden in the Bible, religious opponents charge that gambling is based on selfishness, that it undermines the stewardship of resources, and that, by relying on chance, it denies providential control over human life.[73]

While gambling is anathema to many Protestant denominations, it receives no blanket condemnation from the Catholic church. According to the *Catholic Encyclopedia*, "Gambling, . . . though a luxury, is not considered sinful except when the indulgence in it is inconsistent with duty."[74] Similarly, Jewish teaching permits gambling in some circumstances, but not for gain or in fundraising for synagogues.[75] These doctrinal differences are reflected in a survey of attitudes about the lottery in California conducted several months after its introduction there. Catholics and Jews were least likely to oppose the lottery, which is consistent with the positions on gambling just discussed. Among major Protestant denominations, non-Southern Baptists and otherwise unclassified Protestants were most likely to disapprove of the lottery. The latter group contains some mainstream Protestant denominations but appears to be composed largely of members of fundamentalist churches. Another aspect of religious attitudes toward lotteries revealed by the survey is that religious conservatives are much more likely than average to oppose the lottery, while self-described middle-of-the-roaders and those who do not pay attention to religious matters are less likely to be opposed.[76]

Concern for Harmful Social Consequences

From the earliest days of American lotteries opponents have placed far less stress in their public arguments on fundamental moral objections than on the presumed harmful effects of gaming. Ministers meeting in Boston in 1699, among them Cotton Mather, decried lottery schemes as "a plain cheat upon the people."[77] And in a resolution opposing a national lottery in 1942 the Atlanta Christian Council also stressed consequences over principle: "The verdict of history, both sacred and secular, emphatically condemns gambling, in whatever form, as a breeder of crime, a destroyer of character, and a source of poverty and debauchery."[78]

Likewise, most contemporary public statements against lotteries stress harmful consequences rather than uncompromising moral principles. This is true even of one religious spokesman's statement entitled "Moral Arguments against State-Operated Lotteries," which seems intended almost entirely to demonstrate that lotteries are a regressive form of taxation, that they appeal disproportionately to minority groups, and that they stimulate illegal gambling and contribute to compulsive gambling.[79]

Finally, let us note one objection that is not an issue in current opposition to lotteries: the corruption, fraud, and criminality that characterized the operation of many lotteries in the nineteenth century and other more recent forms of gambling. The infamous Louisiana lottery was only the most extreme of the many unsavory lottery operations of the last century, and their gross abuses were the single most important reason for the sixty years of prohibition. Opposition to lotteries in the 1960s contained warnings of similar consequences, pointing to criminal influences in casinos and legalized bingo. But after two decades of largely honest and efficient operation by state lottery agencies, this argument has all but disappeared.

Conclusion

Lotteries have been around for a long time. They have numerous precedents as a form of public finance, and they are similar to other games and activities common in the United States today. That lotteries exist is not surprising, given their history and worldwide popularity. That all U.S. lotteries are operated as monopolies by state governments is, however, striking. The reasons why states have kept provision of the lotteries to themselves rather than authorizing private firms to provide them can best be understood as a reflection of their history. In this country lotteries were begun largely as an informal means of financing public projects. Professional lottery operators soon emerged, and with them came increasing concern about fraud and the harmful effects of gambling. The potential for corruption in privately run lotteries was epitomized by the infamous Louisiana lottery. This operation and others like it in the nineteenth century were no doubt responsible not only for the restrictions on lotteries in state and federal law but also for the particular form that they have taken today.

PART II

The Games and the Players

4.

The Games People Play

The essence of a lottery is the purchase of a chance to win a prize, based on a random drawing. Although this seemingly simple formula can be expanded to include almost infinite variations, virtually all of the games used in twentieth-century lotteries are of four basic types: so-called passive drawings, instant scratch-off games, numbers, and lotto. Over the last two decades lottery agencies, with the assistance of lottery suppliers, have developed these four basic products by modifying existing games and introducing new ones.

In this process of product development the suppliers have gradually altered lottery products in ways that are aimed at increasing sales. Players have demonstrated their preference for games that allow them to participate and for games that offer big prizes. Players also appear to like having a variety of games to play. The lottery agencies have paid attention to these preferences and have sought to design products that will sell. Thus the evolution of the product line is as much a result of conscious product design as of consumer demand. Six basic trends are evident in the many changes in lottery products since 1964:

Tickets have become cheaper, especially in real terms.
The number of retail outlets has increased.
The size of grand prizes has increased.
Games have increasingly allowed bettors to choose their own numbers or otherwise have a sense of participation.
The frequency of drawings has increased, owing in part to an increase in the number of games offered.

The payout rate (prizes as a percentage of sales) has increased.

One technological change has been fundamental to several of these developments: the computerization of lottery retailing, which has made it possible for hundreds of retail outlets in a state to sell at high volume, operate various games simultaneously, some of them quite complex, and offer customers daily opportunities to bet. Such computerized systems also offer protection against fraud, which has been an important element in the public acceptance of lotteries.

Passive Drawings

The first game to be employed in twentieth-century American lotteries was little more than a raffle in which winning tickets were drawn from among all tickets purchased. In this passive lottery game players simply bought a ticket and waited for the drawing, usually held weekly. These lotteries offered little of the sense of participation typical of games that allow players to do something, however inconsequential, such as picking a number or scratching a card. Some states took this passivity a step further by selling books of tickets good for successive drawings, making weekly purchases unnecessary.

When New Hampshire ushered in the modern American lottery, it used a passive game based on drawings held considerably less often than once a week, originally twice a year.[1] This "first of the modern state lotteries" was in fact a near-replica of the colonial lotteries: purchasers wrote their name and address on a ticket, and the lottery agency made its drawings from the tickets sold and collected by agents. New York, which began operating its lottery in 1967, increased the frequency of drawings to once a month but continued to require the buyer's name and address on tickets.[2] This approach was soon made obsolete by the application of computer technology; then only the serial number of a purchased ticket had to be retained, and "drawings" consisted only of a random selection among those numbers. Both New Hampshire and New York restricted retail outlets, the former to racetracks and state liquor stores and the latter to banks and certain public offices. New Hampshire initially set the price of its tickets at $3, closely approximating the cost of an Irish Sweepstakes ticket, but the going price gradually dropped. New York reduced the price to $1, and New Jersey, which began operations in 1971, set it at fifty cents. The payout rates of early games gradually went in the other direction. New Hampshire's first games paid out an average of thirty-one cents per dollar bet. By 1971 New York was paying forty cents and New Jersey forty-five cents per dollar.

Far from beginning an inexorable march toward double-digit growth rates, these early lotteries were marked by lackluster sales and public uncertainty about the prospects for raising money in this way. Following a burst of enthusiasm over its introduction, the New Hampshire Sweepstakes suffered five years of steadily declining sales. In real terms sales did not regain their initial 1964 level again until 1975. By 1968 the lottery was running a poor second to horse racing in the state in terms of amount wagered.[3] In contrast to racetrack bettors, lottery players did not actually "play" the game, and they could not find out right away if they had won. By 1970 New Hampshire's lottery was averaging sales of $4.50 per capita and New York's only $2.60.[4]

It was not until New Jersey entered the lottery field, with computer-numbered tickets, a fifty-cent price, and modern marketing, that the revenue potential of state lotteries began to be recognized. But the sales potential for passive games remained limited. In 1985 only four American lotteries offered passive games, accounting for an inconsequential portion of total sales, but they remained a significant part of the Canadian product line, with 23 percent of sales in 1986.[5] They also appear to be making a resurgence of sorts in the United States as an addition to some lotto games. In one such "hybrid" game run by West Virginia, for example, lotto players can spend an extra dollar to play a passive game, with prizes for matching from two to six digits of a number printed on the betting slip.[6] The simple passive game, however, appears to have been left behind in the evolution of lottery games. Although the technology of selecting tickets had changed—from a barrel in a public house to a computer in a government building—little else about the passive games was different. Lottery players sought more involvement—more "play value"—and lottery suppliers were prepared to provide just that.

Instant Scratch-off Games

The first breakthrough in product design was the application of a printing technique developed for promotional sweepstakes: a ticket already printed with a combination of numbers, letters, or words hidden with a vinyl covering. The covering is rubbed off to show "instantly" whether the purchaser has won a prize. Tickets are winners if they, for example, reveal matching symbols, letters spelling a word, numbers adding to a particular total or a score exceeding that of a printed "opponent." The main technical requirement for instant games was a printing process that made it impossible to counterfeit tickets, to see through the rub-off layer to identify winning tickets, or to alter tickets once sold. The firm of Scientific Games, Inc., came forward with a product meeting those requirements, thrusting the company into prominence in the gaming industry. By 1982 all state lotteries were operating some form of instant game. These games have been especially useful for lotteries just starting up. Because they do not rely on a system of interconnected computer terminals, as the numbers and lotto games do, instant games can be run as soon as a network of retail agents is ready to sell the tickets.

Unlike the passive games, instant games bear the unmistakable mark of modern marketing. This new lottery product was carefully designed to appeal to consumers by providing two features unavailable in passive games: variety and simulated "play value." Instant lotteries have been characterized by the variety of different games used, each with its own theme and pattern for determining winners, and for the short duration of each theme. Games using themes such as Lucky Joker, Money Tree, Baseball, or Blue Hen Bucks are typically run for a few months each and then discontinued. For example, the Arizona lottery ran five separate instant games in its first fiscal year: Scratch It Rich, The Double, 3 of a Kind, The Prospector, and Pan for Gold. According to a New York lottery executive, "Our game designers are always looking for new themes."[7] Only one model appears to exist for the marketing of the instant game, and that is to operate one game with a given theme and prize structure for an allotted time, end it, and then introduce a new game. Occasionally games overlap, but more often they are separated by a hiatus of a few weeks. This formula was developed by John Koza of Scientific Games, who explained, "We have found that total annual sales will be higher if you leave the stage while everyone is still interested than if you wait until the audience gets restless."[8] Why lottery marketers have concluded that instant games, unlike other lottery games, require constant changing is unclear, but there has been no deviation from this procedure to date.

The other feature of instant rub-off games that we have noted is their simulated play value. As explained by Koza, the originator of the concept, the objective in designing instant games is to keep the player in suspense, believing he has a chance to win, as long as possible.[9] This can easily be accomplished through judicious ticket design. For example, if winning a game requires having three identical prizes or symbols out of six rubbed spots, printing tickets with two matching symbols creates the feeling of a near win. Koza calls such tickets "heartstoppers": "You have to make sure the game is not boring. Heartstoppers are one of the best ways of doing this."[10] The play value created by the designers of instant games is not unlike the suspense of opening a letter or a locked trunk. Immediacy is another factor in play value. Having to wait three months to discover if you have won is not as attractive as finding out on the spot.

Daily Numbers Games

Even as the first instant games were being introduced in Massachusetts and New Jersey, officials from both states were considering new games that would for the first time allow players to choose their own numbers. It was evident not only from the enduring popularity of the illegal numbers and policy games but also from the lotteries' own marketing research that consumers wanted a chance to pick their numbers. In order to capture this ready-made market the lottery agencies and their marketing advisers produced a computerized replica of the illegal numbers games. To understand the appeal of this new legal lottery we need to know how the illegal game works.

The Mechanics of Illegal Numbers

Two major illegal games grew up during the period when lotteries were prohibited. They became a fixture in the daily life of many urban neighborhoods, particularly in the Northeast. The first widespread illegal American game was policy, in which players make bets about which numbers will be selected from a larger field of numbers. In recent decades this has been the dominant game in Chicago's black neighborhoods. The numbers game, introduced as an alternative to policy in the 1920s,[11] consists of bets related to a three- or four-digit number and has been prevalent in New York. It was the numbers game that served as the model for the lotteries to copy. Policy was bypassed for the moment, although subsequent lotto games would bear a striking resemblance to this other illegal game.

In its most common form the illegal numbers game is based on a single three-digit number drawn daily. The most popular bet is to guess all three digits in exact order (the "straight" bet), but bets on one digit ("single action") and two digits ("bolita") are also common. In addition players can bet on all six combinations of their three digits, a bet known as a "box."[12] Daily bets are taken by collectors who, for a commission, sell door-to-door or take bets in a store, at a newsstand, or even by telephone. Bets may be made for several days in advance. To this convenience is added the possibility of making bets for amounts as small as a nickel, or even buying chances on credit. The success of any numbers operation depends on its credibility. The process by which the number is selected must be seen as honest, and all winnings have to be paid without delay. The first requirement is satisfied by any randomly drawn and verifiable number. In New York one of the principal methods of selecting the daily number for the illegal game was based on the handle at a given racetrack, and the other was based on the payouts of several specified races.[13] In policy, "wheels" serve the same purpose. As for the reliability of payoffs, illegal operators apparently go to some lengths to maintain a good reputation. One policy poster in Chicago stated in bold letters, "All hits paid promptly."[14]

Payout rates for winning picks in illegal numbers affect both the popularity and profitability of the game. Typical payoffs for a straight three-digit bet (with odds of 1 in 1,000) range from 500 to 1 to 600 to 1, except for some popular numbers such as even hundreds, triple digits, or lucky numbers such as 711. For such numbers payoffs are usually "cut," or reduced, to as little as 300 to 1 in order to protect the operators from the possibility of a disastrous liability should one of them be chosen. The typical payoff for the one-digit bet (with odds of 1 in 10) is 7 to 1 or 8 to 1, and for a two-digit bet (with odds of 1 in 100) about 60 to 1.[15] Out of the payoff a customary "tip" of 10 percent is paid to the runner. Thus if the stated payout on a straight bet were 600 to 1, the tip would reduce it to 540 to 1. Although they are supposed to be subject to income taxation, these winnings are effectively tax-free.

Legal Numbers: The Sincerest Form of Flattery

Legal numbers games have become a mainstay of most of the largest state lotteries, particularly in the Northeast. In format, payout rate, and even terminology these games are virtual carbon copies of their illegal counterpart. The central element they share is the opportunity for players to pick their own numbers. In the most common form players choose their own three- or four-digit number and receive a payoff if the number is selected. In planning its numbers game the Massachusetts lottery considered both a three-digit and a four-digit numbers game. The agency selected a game based on four digits because that was the form of the illegal game that was prevalent in the state. Like the illegal version, these games typically offer drawings six days a week. Likewise, states follow the illegal games in allowing a dizzying variety of bets, including straight, box, and two-digit bets. These options are illustrated in Table 4.1. Most states also offer four-digit games with similar variations. Offering longer odds and larger prizes than the standard three-digit version, the four-digit game has grown in popularity, although by 1986 sales were still only a quarter of three-digit sales. To boost the four-digit games some states have offered new games for players who bet on both a three-digit and a four-digit number.[16]

In their attempt to mimic the illegal numbers game lottery planners faced two issues related to prize payouts. The first was the choice of the payout rate. States considering the first legal numbers game felt they must at least match the rates offered by illegal games, which paid out at rates between 50

Table 4.1. Three-digit daily numbers games: Types of $1 bets

Type of bet	Description	Probability of winning	Illustrative bet	Winning combinations	Typical payoff[a]
Straight	Three digits in exact order	1 in 1,000	379	379	$500
Box					
6-way	Three digits in any order	1 in 167	379	379, 397, 739, 793, 937, 973	83
3-way	Same, for number with two identical digits	1 in 333	377	377, 737, 773	167
Front pair	First two digits in exact order	1 in 100	37-	370, 371, 372, 373, 374, 375, 376, 377, 378, 379	50
Back pair	Last two digits in exact order	1 in 100	-79	079, 179, 279, 379, 479, 579, 679, 779, 879, 979	50

Source: Lottery daily game brochures, various states.
a. Based on a fixed payout rate of 50 percent. Some states round the box payoffs down to $80 and $160, respectively.

and 60 percent of a "fair" bet (500 to 1 to 600 to 1 on a straight bet). Some experts proposed much higher payout rates, from 75 to over 80 percent, in order to discourage the illegal game.[17] In the end most states have chosen a 50 percent payout rate. The one prominent exception is Massachusetts, which set its overall payout rate on numbers at 60 percent and—because their research showed higher payout rates for three-digit bets—raised the payout rate on straight three-digit bets to 70 percent but gave only 50 percent on straight four-digit bets.[18] In short, the legal numbers game was designed to tap the illegal market by copying the most important features of the illegal game but offering a superior payout rate. While other states have continued the practice of aping the illegal game in design—or at least copying the first legal numbers game—they have not sought to offer higher payouts. Since most states do not compete against an established illegal game, most have not seen the need to pay any more than 50 percent.

Having selected an average payout rate, a lottery must choose a method of calculating prizes for actual drawings. One option is a *fixed* payout system, in which the lottery promises to pay a specified amount for a given bet. For example, the typical payout on a $1 straight three-digit bet is $500, exactly half the "fair" payout based on the probability of winning. This is the method used in illegal numbers games and is relatively easy for bettors to understand. This method, however, leaves the lottery vulnerable to huge losses if a popular number should be drawn (as the result of either a random draw or in the unlikely event of a fix), and lottery agencies are as skittish about big losses as their underground counterparts. Rather than "cutting" popular numbers, most lotteries using fixed payments protect themselves by placing a ceiling on wagers for any number.[19] An alternative method of calculating prize payments is a *parimutuel* system, in which all winning entrants share the prize pool.[20] If the average payout rate is 50 percent, a parimutuel game will average $500 for a winning three-digit straight bet, but unpopular numbers will tend to pay bigger prizes than popular numbers because there are fewer winners to share the prize. Although harder to understand than fixed payments, the parimutuel approach assures the agency that it will only have to pay a constant proportion of a day's sales in prizes. Of the two, the simplicity of the fixed payout combined with its use in illegal numbers has made it the method preferred by most game designers.[21]

Although these legal numbers games have been designed as replicas of the illegal version, some differences remain. The legal games offer no credit, nor do they allow bets of less than fifty cents. State games also lack the elaborate system of runners used in the illegal game, offering in its place a computer-based retailing network that is convenient as well as honest. Another theoretical difference is that winnings in the legal game can be taxed, but this distinction is immaterial in practice. Since federal withholding rules allow prizes up to $600 to be paid in cash with no withholding or reporting, players and lottery agencies alike understand that the Internal Revenue Service does not expect most winnings to be declared for income tax purposes.

Lotto

The most recent addition to the array of lottery games offered in the United States and Canada is lotto, a class of game with similarities to a variety of legal and illegal games, including bingo, policy, and the casino game of keno. As impressive as the growth in instant and numbers games has been, none of it could have predicted the explosive growth in lotto. Like the numbers game, lotto allows players to pick their own numbers using networks of computer terminals at retail outlets, but the possible variations in format it offers are much greater. Lotto players choose several numbers from a larger field, the size of each set determining the format of the game. The odds of picking all correctly are small and quite sensitive to format. A distinctive feature of most American lotto games is a jackpot that accumulates from drawing to drawing until a player wins. This has produced jackpots (measured as the sum of a series of annual payments) of over $100 million. Lotto games have been most successful in large states, for reasons that are discussed in Chapter 6. One result has been the joining together of small states to run multistate lotto games.

It is convenient to describe the format of lotto games by using three key variables. From a field of F numbers, the lottery agency draws D of those at each drawing. Players pick P numbers, and their winnings are based on their success in choosing the numbers drawn. A lotto game's format can thus be summarized as $P/D/F$. Any player whose picks are all drawn is a winner, but prizes are often awarded to players who have chosen one or two incorrect numbers.

Simple Lotto

On the basis of format lotto games can be divided into two major types. In the best known of the lotto games, referred to here as simple lotto, the pick and the draw amounts are the same, reducing the format to D/F. For example, one common format is 6/40, in which players choose six numbers between 1 and 40. The odds against picking just the right combination are enormous, but so too are the prizes. Table 4.2 illustrates several common formats of simple lotto used in the United States and abroad. The probability of winning is quite sensitive to the format. Among games drawing six num-

Table 4.2.   Simple lotto: Sample formats and odds

Format	Approximate odds of matching all numbers[a]	Format users, 1986
5/40	1:700,000	Rhode Island
6/30	1:600,000	Iowa, West Virginia
6/34	1:1.3 million	Delaware
6/36	1:1.9 million	Massachusetts, Tri-State
6/38	1:2.8 million	Oregon
6/39	1:3.3 million	Arizona, Missouri
6/40	1:3.8 million	Connecticut, Pennsylvania
6/42	1:5.2 million	New Jersey, Oregon
6/44	1:7.1 million	Michigan, Ohio
6/45	1:8.1 million	South Australia
6/48	1:12.3 million	New York
6/49	1:14.0 million	California, Ontario
6/56	1:32.5 million	Western Canada
7/35	1:6.7 million	Sweden
7/39	1:15.4 million	Finland

a. Where F = total possible numbers and D = numbers drawn, the probability of drawing D correctly is $1/C(F, D)$, where $C(F, D)$ is the number of possible combinations of F numbers taken D at a time, or $D!(F - D)!/(F!)$.

bers, for example, the chance of picking all six correctly is approximately halved for each addition of four numbers to the total field. Combined with the long odds of picking all numbers correctly, the "rollover" of prize money when no one wins creates huge jackpots, and it is these jackpots that have made lotto games so visible right from the start. Lesser prizes are typically awarded to players who correctly pick four or five of the six numbers. While the top prize in lotto games is always based on parimutuel calculations, these lower-tier prizes can be calculated straight (with a fixed prize going to each winner at each level) or on a parimutuel basis (each level of winners shares a percentage of the available prize pool).

The operation of a simple lotto game can be illustrated by showing how prizes are determined in an actual drawing. Table 4.3 sets out the prize calculation for Maryland's 6/40 game for a drawing in 1988. Of the 50 percent

Table 4.3. Calculation of prizes in simple lotto (format 6/40), Maryland, April 2, 1988 (sales for the week = $6,185,475; stated jackpot = $7,000,000)

	Number of correct picks		
	Six	Five	Four
Percentage of sales devoted to prize pool	25%	11%	14%
Prize pool			
From week's sales	$1,546,369	$680,402	$865,967
Rollover	1,523,043		
Breakage[a]		114	4,757
Total	$3,069,412	$680,516	$870,724
Number of winners	3	657	27,300
Prize per winner			
Paid immediately		$1,035	$31
Paid over 20 years	$2,333,333		

Source: Lotto prize calculation schedule, issued by Maryland State Lottery Agency, April 2, 1988.
a. Resulting from rounding off previous week's prizes.

of sales that the state returned as prizes, half was put into the grand prize and the other half was distributed among players who correctly picked five out of six and four out of six numbers. Because there had been no grand prize winners in either of the previous two drawings, the $1.5 million that had accumulated in the top prize pool was rolled over and added to the additional prize pool based on the current week's sales, which turned out to be another $1.5 million. At the beginning of the drawing week the lottery agency announced a jackpot of $7 million, which represented the sum of twenty annual payments it would guarantee to pay a single winner. (Based on its knowledge of market interest rates and its anticipation of sales for the week, the agency had calculated that it could, at a cost of about $3 million, buy an annuity that would make twenty annual payments totaling $7 million.) Jackpot amounts typically stated for lotto prizes are about twice the value of the money actually in the prize fund.[22] In this drawing three people correctly picked the six-number combination (in this case 5, 10, 12, 14, 24, 25), and each received twenty-year payments of $2.3 million. Like most other states Maryland devoted a significant portion of its lotto prize pool, half, to lesser prizes. Over 650 players picked five of the six numbers correctly, and they split 11 percent of the week's sales, each winning $1,035. Another 27,300 players got four numbers out of the six right, winning $31 each. In the case of these smaller prizes, the amounts were rounded down to the next dollar, with the remainder carried over to the next week as "breakage."

If there is one characteristic that sets lotto apart from other games it is the rollover feature and its potential to produce very large prizes. On the occasions when lotto games in large states have gone for several drawings without a winner, pushing jackpots to unusually high levels, the lottery has invariably become page-one news. A large jackpot stimulates sales and creates lines at ticket counters. To illustrate the effect of rollovers, Figure 4.1 presents the

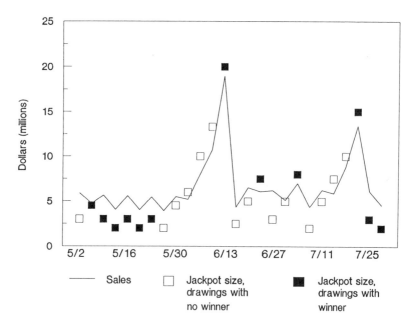

Figure 4.1. Lotto jackpots and sales for New York's 6/48 game, May–June 1987

(*Source:* New York State Lottery, unpublished data)

jackpot and sales for New York's 6/48 lotto game over a three-month period in 1987. An unusually long string of drawings without a winner produced a jackpot of $20 million in June. Then again in July four drawings with no winner produced a jackpot of $15 million. As the figure clearly shows, players responded to the increases in the jackpot by buying more tickets. When no one picked the winning combination, this increase in sales just served to add fuel to the fire by increasing the jackpot that much faster. The role of jackpot size in the demand for lotto is analyzed in Chapter 6.

Variants of Lotto

A recent development in game design in the United States is the gradual introduction of variants on the lotto theme in which the set of numbers drawn is larger than the set any player picks. Such variants of simple lotto are in this regard like bingo, where it is common to draw many more numbers than the four or five in a line required to win. Pennsylvania's Super 7, for example, featured a weekly drawing of eleven numbers from a field of eighty. Players picked seven numbers. In our notation this is a 7/11/80 format. If all seven are among the eleven drawn (odds are 1 in 9.9 million), the player wins all or part of a jackpot, with rollovers operating as in simple lotto.[23] Also like simple lotto, Pennsylvania's game awards lesser prizes for six or five correct numbers.

More complicated variants allow players to choose P, the number of picks they get. The model for this variant is keno, a casino game usually operated with a 15/20/80 format, in which players may pick from six to fifteen numbers. The illegal game of policy also bears a close resemblance. The more numbers picked, the smaller the odds and the larger the payoff. In this respect players determine the odds of winning, much as they do in choosing variants of the straight bet in numbers. New York was the first state to adopt this format, offering combinations of from three to ten numbers out of a field of eighty.[24]

The Evolution in Product Mix

Surely one of the most impressive trends in state lotteries since their emergence has been the dramatic change in the mix of games played. With the introduction of successive games the passive weekly game—the original mainstay of lotteries—has dwindled to the point of extinction. In its place instant games, numbers, and lotto account for a significant share each. This change in product mix is illustrated in Figure 4.2, which shows the combined sales for four states that began lottery operations in 1972, Connecticut, Massachusetts, Michigan, and Pennsylvania. Representing over 98 percent of

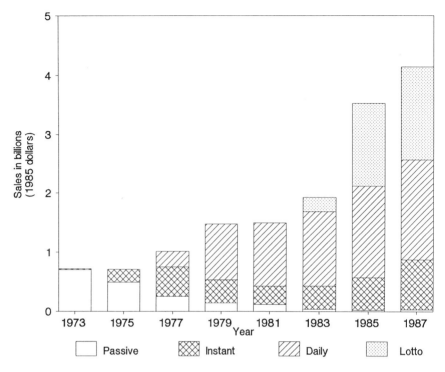

Figure 4.2. Lottery sales by game in four states
(*Source:* Annual reports of Connecticut, Massachusetts, Michigan, and Pennsylvania lottery agencies, various years)

sales in 1973, the passive weekly game in these states had dropped to 10 percent of total sales in 1979 and less than 1 percent by 1987. The instant game quickly claimed a sizable share of total sales shortly after its introduction in Massachusetts in 1974, and its level of sales remained more or less steady through 1981. The daily numbers game has grown in sales since its introduction in these states, with an average annual growth rate between 1977 and 1987 of 20 percent over and above inflation. But perhaps the most striking aspect of this figure is the stupendous growth in lotto. From a modest beginning following its introduction in New York in 1978, lotto grew at an annual rate of 60 percent between 1983 and 1987 and accounted for 38 percent of all lottery sales in these four states by 1987. For the United States as a whole, lotto represented 40 percent of sales by 1987, surpassing numbers (37 percent) and instant games (24 percent).[25] These trends no doubt reflect both developments in technology available to lottery agencies and consumer preferences. One interesting and surprising aspect of these sales figures is the apparent lack of "cannibalization": the introduction of new games appears not to have eaten into the sales of existing games, a point taken up again in Chapter 6.

New Frontiers in Game Design

There is every reason to believe that the lottery product mix will continue to change. As one lottery official told us, "You can't stand still in the lottery business."[26] Indeed, new lottery games appear to be constantly under consideration, spurred by what appears to be a steady apprehension that sales for the established games will stagnate. The lottery agencies, with the help of product designers, periodically augment their line with variants of the basic games. In recent years these have included so-called "niche" games, such as a form of lotto based on picking up to five cards from a deck of fifty-two, games based on casino games, and on-line games based on bingo. In one game, for example, a customer can play a variety of card games with different odds and be paid on the spot for a winning bet.[27] The agencies have also experimented with a new generation of betting machines that would allow players to bet without having to go through a retail agent. Some are little more than vending machines, ideal for busy areas such as airports and shopping centers. A more daring variant is video lottery games, often referred to in industry circles as PALM (player-activated lottery machines) or VLM (video lottery machines). These are similar to commercial video games, but winning is randomly preordained and not related to the player's skill. In effect these machines are little more than an instant game with light and sound. States have been slow to adopt video lottery games, however, perhaps because they bear an uncanny resemblance to slot machines, which are widely outlawed.[28]

But the hardware with perhaps the biggest potential for influencing future lottery sales is the machinery used for taking on-line bets. The current statewide networks rely on computer terminals located in retail establishments, but advances in communications technology are making other methods of placing bets feasible as well. For example, automated teller machines in banks can be adapted for use as self-serve lottery betting windows. Touchtone telephones might also be employed to place bets from home. Such developments could have a major impact on lotteries. Because they would make it possible to bet anonymously, these methods might appeal to those who do not want to be seen playing the lottery. This increased availability could significantly boost sales and could even open the door to a national lottery, in competition with state lotteries, without the necessity of installing a new network for placing on-line bets. And there is no technical reason for stopping at a national lottery: one marketing firm has proposed a worldwide lotto game using bank teller machines.[29]

In game design the next big step could well be in the direction of sports-related betting. Although such a move has been consistently opposed by organizations representing professional sports, the enormous popularity of sports in this country and the success of sports pools abroad make this a possibility that cannot be ignored. Based on successfully picking the outcomes of numerous contests, pools such as the European soccer pools involve some skill and thus are not strictly lotteries. Yet there is a vast capriciousness, making pools similar to lotto, only with greatly enhanced play value. The Delaware lottery in fact introduced a game based on professional football games in the 1970s, but the scheme failed because of poor planning. Since then the subject of legalized sports betting has seldom come up in the United States. It was proposed in 1984 by New York's Governor Mario Cuomo but nowhere undertaken.[30] Yet it remains a real possibility, as indicated by the British Columbia lottery's introduction in 1988 of a game based on professional football. This game combines the element of skill in picking outcomes and scores with a random number printed on each ticket.[31] One attraction of sports pools is the week-to-week variety that would be built into any sports-based game. According to one Delaware lottery official, "Sports betting would be ideal because you'd have new games each week. Each game is different and each betting sheet would be different."[32]

Sports betting presents two special problems, however. First, there may be financial risks for the state. A sports pool run on a parimutuel basis would protect the state by limiting prizes to a certain percentage of the handle. But any entry into bookmaking would be perilous because, as traditionally operated, sports books employ fixed payouts and variable point spreads, and any miscalculation of the latter would leave the state vulnerable to losses.[33] Second, established sports organizations have consistently opposed legalized sports betting. The National Football League attempted, unsuccessfully, to block Delaware's use of team names in that state's sports game, arguing that the association with gambling would damage the league's reputation.[34]

The Art of Lottery Design

The designer of any lottery must decide how many of what kind of prizes to award and how much of the gross revenue to return as prizes. It almost goes without saying that, other things being equal, players will be more attracted to games that distribute a higher percentage of revenues in the form of prizes. But the more that revenue is distributed as prizes, the less will be left over for the state. In their attempt to maximize net revenues lottery producers have devoted considerable attention to fine-tuning their games' prize structures. Lottery agencies have had less leeway in determining payout rates, since state laws typically set limits on them.

Prize Structure

In the case of passive and instant games, as with most traditional lotteries, there are no constraints on prize structure other than the total amount of prize money to be given away. A few big prizes can be awarded, or many smaller ones, or various amounts in between. By modifying the prize schedule game designers can influence several key variables, including the size of the largest prize, the probability of winning any prize, and the inequality among prizes. Other features such as the chance to win a prize in a second drawing may have value, at least to some players. Because our understanding of gambling behavior is still quite primitive, the influence of these various features of prize structure is not well understood.

While increasing the percentage of players who win may be attractive to players, it can be accomplished only by shrinking the average prize. The distribution of the prize fund itself is also a variable. A large grand prize may be attractive to players, but again it can be offered only by diluting the other prizes. One school of thought maintains that the best way to sell lottery tickets is to make winning seem possible, but this can be done only by producing many winners. The opposing view stresses the importance of very large prizes at the expense of a wider distribution of prizes. In a series of notes on establishing a lottery Alexander Hamilton appears to have favored the big-prize approach, noting, "Adventurers would as lieve lose altogether as acquire trifling prizes and would prefer a small chance of winning a *great deal* to a chance of winning little."[35] These issues were central to the design of prize structures for instant games. Typical of the early thinking was John Koza's support for a U-shaped ("concave") prize structure featuring one large prize and many small prizes. The latter, according to John Koza, makes "winning credible." "It is like two cherries in the slot machine. It feeds the action."[36] Pennsylvania followed this approach in the mid-1980s. As a percentage of all prize money in its instant games, prizes of $100 or less increased from 84 percent in 1985 to almost 99 percent in 1987.[37] Massachusetts took a different approach in 1979, which was followed by an increase in instant game sales. In response to information gleaned from consumer research that state's lottery agency reduced the number of nominal prizes, eliminated their top prize of $100,000, and increased the number of $1,000 and $10,000 prizes.[38] In part the decision to reduce the top prize was predicated on the large jackpots offered in the state's new lotto game.

To illustrate the kinds of structures that lottery designers have devised to deal with these choices, Table 4.4 compares several features of the prize distribution for five lotteries: one eighteenth-century lottery, one nineteenth-century lottery, and three contemporary instant games.[39] Take, for example, Maryland's 1986 Instant Baseball. Of over 23 million tickets printed, almost 3 million, or 12.5 percent, contained winning combinations of numbers. This high proportion of winners was made possible by putting over half of the prize pool into $2 and $5 prizes. At the other end of the prize spectrum the largest prize was $25,000, won by sixteen players, or one out of every 1.5 million. Winners were a quarter of all players in the old lotteries but are considerably rarer in the contemporary instant games. More striking is the amount of variation in the size of the grand prize. The $34,000 top prize in Maryland's 1825 lottery accounted for 22 percent of the total prize fund, while one of the $25,000 top prizes in the state's 1986 offering was only .2 percent of the total. Connecticut's Joker's Wild game illustrates the high-tier prize approach, while Ohio's Holiday Cash represents the opposite strategy of offering more medium-sized prizes.[40] Prize structures such as this show only a few of the infinite number of possible distributions, but they also serve to point up the fact that contemporary lottery operators face precisely the same dilemmas of game design that their predecessors did.

Payout Rate: Are Lotteries a "Sucker Bet"?

Probably the biggest contrast among the games shown in Table 4.4 is in the payout rate, ranging from less than half to 90 percent. Over the past two centuries payout rates in America have tended to fall, and these examples illustrate that decline. One historical study of American lotteries shows that payout rates for lotteries before 1790 clustered tightly around 85 percent while the rates for later lotteries were lower and more variable. While 75 percent or 64 percent would have been typical of English lotteries of the period, this was still lower than average for early nineteenth-century American lotteries.[41] The Louisiana lottery, of course, introduced much lower payout ratios—only slightly above 50 percent—a rate that has been retained so far in almost all modern state lotteries. The Ohio instant game shown in Table 4.4 is in a sense the exception that proves the rule. This game represented an experiment in game design to see if higher payout rates would induce more sales.

Lotteries are sometimes disparaged because their average takeout rate of 50 percent is considerably higher than that of any other form of legal gambling in this country. With payout rates of 90 percent or better available in casinos, legal bookmaking, and card rooms, the argument goes, only a "sucker" would

Table 4.4.   Summary measures of prize structures in five lottery games

	Faneuil Hall 1762	Maryland 1825	Maryland Instant Baseball 1986	Ohio Holiday Cash 1986	Connecticut Joker's Wild 1986
Gross receipts	$12,000	$24,000	$23,400,000	$20,000,000	$26,100,000
Total prizes	$10,800	$153,000[a]	$11,222,500	$14,999,600	$15,740,300
Payout rate[b]	90%	64%	48%	75%	60%
Percentage of players who win	25	26	12	9	18
Highest prize	$1,000	$34,000[a]	$25,000	$1,000	$1,000,000
Gini coefficient	.43	.71	.41	.73	.34

Sources: Table A.1; correspondence from Ronald Nabakowski of the Ohio lottery, September 11, 1986; Gaming and Wagering Business 7 (October 1986), 14.
a. Prizes after 15 percent state lottery tax is deducted.
b. Ignores income taxes.

play a game that returns just fifty cents on the dollar in prizes.[42] John Koza disputes not only this conclusion but also the comparison of these payout rates, arguing that the payout rate on lotteries may actually be *better* than in casino games if the tendency to bet repeatedly on casino games is taken into account. He illustrates this conclusion in the case of a slot machine paying out 95 percent. He asserts that the expected payout on fourteen successive plays is 49 percent, less per dollar than in the average lottery.[43] This statement is in fact true given certain assumptions, one being that all winnings are put back into the machine on the next turn.[44] But on any one bet the expected return per dollar is still ninety-five cents for slot machines versus fifty cents for lotteries. So which of these games is the "sucker" bet?

At first blush this example looks like just so much probabilistic sophistry. Koza does have a point, however, to the extent that slot players do tend to play repeatedly during one betting session, often immediately betting their winnings again. Similarly, few roulette players quit after one bet. After repeated plays the expected return for these casino bettors declines if winnings are played again. One might note, of course, that lottery winnings are likewise used to buy more tickets, thus reducing the expected return. The problem is that no comparison between games will be fully satisfactory because of the inherent differences in the nature of the games. Because bets are made and paid off so much more often in casino games than in lotteries, the gross amount wagered is not a comparable measure of the quantity of each type of betting. For similar games, and certainly for similar lottery games, though, the gross wager is a useful measure of play, and the takeout rate is a meaningful indication of the per-dollar cost of playing. If the comparison is between a numbers game paying out 50 percent and an otherwise similar game paying 60 percent, the latter is clearly the better bet.

5.

Why (and How) They Play

The Lottery, with its weekly pay-out of enormous prizes,
was the one public event to which the proles paid serious
attention. It was probable that there were some millions
of proles for whom the Lottery was the principal if not the
only reason for remaining alive. It was their delight, their
folly, their anodyne, their intellectual stimulant. Where
the Lottery was concerned, even people who could barely
read and write seemed capable of intricate calculations
and staggering feats of memory. There was a whole tribe
of men who made a living simply by selling systems,
forecasts, and lucky amulets.

—George Orwell, *1984*

Why is the lottery so popular? Consider the three-digit numbers game. A
dollar bet typically buys a 1 in 1,000 chance at a prize of $500. Those figures
ensure that all but a few regular players will be losers in the long run. And
whether a player wins or loses has nothing to do with his knowledge or skill;
novices have precisely the same chance of winning as experienced players.
What, then, explains the broad appeal of this game?

One answer is that for many people $500 is a lot of money, and an oppor-
tunity to purchase a chance to win $500 for just a dollar seems attractive to
those who do not have other ways of obtaining that much spending money.
A second answer is that the objective odds do not carry the same meaning
for players as for statisticians. A 1 in 1,000 chance is hard to grasp on an
intuitive basis, but players know that there is *some* possibility of winning.
And many believe that they can improve on it by using a lucky number or by
analyzing recent patterns of winning numbers or by studying dreams and
other portents. The numbers game does not offer just a .1 percent chance of
a prize through a passive drawing; it offers an opportunity to win by "predicting" the winning number correctly. The challenge is to beat the odds,
and many people believe they can do just that if they are sufficiently skillful
in playing the game.

Thus, part of the answer to *why* people play is suggested by evidence on
how they play. And to a remarkable degree the evidence on how they play
suggests that ancient superstitions and fallacious beliefs about numbers are
still thriving in this modern age. Interestingly, the lottery agencies do nothing
to educate the public on these matters; if anything they seek to encourage
magical thinking.

The chapter begins by considering aspects of lotteries that might explain their wide appeal. It then addresses the question of why people play by drawing on the literature of economics, psychology and sociology to sketch four illustrative types of lottery players, and concludes with a look at the patterns of play in lottery games that allow players to select their own numbers.

The Lottery's Broad Appeal

Typically in a lottery state half the adult residents play at least once in any given year, and two-thirds of this group play regularly. These statistics indicate a level of market penetration far exceeding those of other forms of commercial gambling, or indeed of most other forms of paid entertainment. This extraordinarily broad participation must arise from some combination of convenience, low price, advertising and promotion, and the universal appeal of winning a lot of money.[1]

Lotteries are the most widely and conveniently available form of commercial gambling in the United States today. Lottery tickets can be purchased as part of a normal shopping trip, often without even making a separate stop. They are sold in numerous retail locations and are available whenever the retailer is open for business. Because their low price makes them only a little more expensive than a candy bar, some marketers have come to regard player behavior as an example of impulse buying. Like candy bars and gum, the lottery display is often right next to the cash register, and one or two tickets can be added to the shopper's purchases at the last moment. While this judgment may be correct for instant games, it seems a less apt description of on-line games. Survey results illustrate the difference. Regarding the instant game, 73 percent of Californians surveyed said their purchase was a spur-of-the-moment decision while 24 percent followed a regular buying habit or planned the purchase beforehand. In contrast, evidence from Arizona on lotto shows that 56 percent of players planned their purchases while 44 percent decided on the spur of the moment. For the daily numbers game survey results from Massachusetts show that over a third of players always use multiple-day betting slips, confirming the impression that the clientele for that game includes a high proportion of faithful players.[2]

Obviously the fact that the lottery is cheap and convenient to play is not enough to guarantee deep market penetration. It must also be true that a large portion of the public is attracted by what the game itself has to offer. Lottery games lack some of the features that boost sales for other forms of gambling. There is no tie-in to a sports event as there is in parimutuel betting and bookmaking. No skill or knowledge is required to play the lottery, unlike in card games and sports betting. The lottery lacks the intense, continuous action and quick feedback of casino games and the excitement of competing head to head with other players at bingo. And the lottery is a poor bet in that it pays out a much smaller percentage of the handle in prizes than any other form of commercial gambling. What the lottery *does* offer, in addition to convenience, is a cheap chance to win some very large prizes and become a celebrity. Because lotteries are marketed to the masses, advertised heavily, and featured prominently in news stories, they have become a part of the popular culture. But they have also tapped into a subculture of belief, a phenomenon we describe later in this chapter, which has become one of the supporting pillars of demand for this commodity.

Each lottery game offers a probability distribution of prizes in exchange for a wager. A decision to play reflects a judgment that the prize distribution is worth the price of a ticket. This judgment may be well informed and carefully thought out, or it may be impulsive and ill considered. It may be made on the basis of scientific reasoning or superstitious belief. In any event, the chance to win money is the primary attraction of playing the lottery; the excitement of the process, and the social aspects of participation, are derived from this chance.

Four Types of Play

Economists and other social scientists have long been intrigued by gambling behavior and have given the subject considerable attention. In considering why people play lotteries it is necessary to review several alternative models of gambling behavior. Rather than simply outlining these models, we have incorporated them into four caricatures of lottery players: the investor, the plunger, the believer, and the participant. They differ in terms of two basic individual characteristics: the ability to perceive correctly the probability and prize structure of lottery games, and the preference for monetary as opposed to nonmonetary features of lottery games.

The Investor

A lottery ticket can be seen as one sort of risky financial asset. Given the method financial experts use to value such assets, are there circumstances in which it is a worthwhile investment?[3] The answer is a qualified yes.

Most lottery games pay out in prizes only about fifty cents for every dollar bet. For example, a typical three-digit numbers game pays $500 to the winning number, which on the average will be chosen by one in every thousand players. Such a gamble is called unfair by statisticians because the expected value of a bet is negative.[4] The law of large numbers ensures that anyone who plays such a game a sufficient number of times will be assured of losing money. This losing tendency is exacerbated by the federal income tax laws, which do not treat wins and losses symmetrically. Net gambling losses incurred during the tax year cannot be deducted from taxable income, but if the taxpayer comes out ahead for the year, the net gain must be added to taxable income.

In some cases, however, a lottery game offers the possibility of a favorable bet (that is, one with a positive expected value). A simple example is a lotto game in which the pot has been augmented by a series of rollovers. In a game with a 1 in 500,000 chance of winning, a pot that has grown past $1.5 million will create a relatively attractive betting situation to the well-informed gambler.[5] Of course, even in this case a bet will be favorable only if the bettor is virtually assured that if he does win, he will not have to share the jackpot with one or more others. He can help his chances in this regard by betting a combination of numbers that tend to be unpopular with other bettors.[6]

Herman Chernoff, a statistician at the Massachusetts Institute of Technology, performed a thorough statistical analysis of the numbers game in Massachusetts.[7] This game is the most generous in the nation, with a prize pool equal to 60 percent of the amount bet for each drawing. It is also unusual in having a parimutuel payoff system.[8] There is at least a logical possibility, then, of making money by "playing against the crowd," or playing numbers that are infrequently bet. Chernoff identified several numbers that were relatively unpopular, and he demonstrated that a betting strategy utilizing these numbers has a positive expected value and over the long run could be expected to yield a profit. Unfortunately this long run may be too long for the pocketbooks of some bettors.

It is true that, as a group, bettors tend to choose some number combinations much more often than others. For every sophisticated bettor like Chernoff who understands this fact and takes advantage of it, several others bet on some popular number that offers the prospect of a highly diluted prize if it hits. As a result, most lottery players place highly unfair bets in the statistical sense. That is the inevitable consequence of the state's paying out only 50 or 60 percent of the handle in prizes, and the reason why investment advisers do not encourage people to play the lottery.

Every rule has exceptions. Some people's financial affairs are such that the lottery *is* an attractive investment, despite the low payout rate. For example, it offers a largely invisible method of laundering small amounts of cash income from the underground economy.[9] And in some cases the state numbers game offers a convenient way for bankers of the illegal numbers game to lay off bets on numbers that are receiving heavy play. (Of course this method works only if the illegal game uses the same winning number as the legal game, as it does in at least one state.)[10] But for most people lottery bets are likely to be a losing proposition.

The Plunger

Consider the example of a man who is down to his last few dollars, owes $500 to a loan shark, and expects to be beaten up at the end of the day if he cannot pay. The numbers game may offer his only hope of salvation. This shows vividly that an "unfair" gamble may appeal to an individual who believes that winning a large amount of cash is his only means for escaping trouble or just the dreariness of normal life. In the words of one player in a poor neighborhood on Chicago's West Side: "I've dug so many holes for myself over the years that realistically, winning the lottery may be my only ticket out."[11] For such a person—who may be fully aware of the odds against him—even the remote chance of success offered by the lottery may be better than no chance and is worth the expenditure of a few dollars.

One aspect of gambling that has fascinated scholars is that it seems inconsistent with other behavior. Most people most of the time are averse to risk and will pay a premium (above the expected value) to reduce the financial risks that they face; hence the insurance market. A number of experiments have helped confirm the prevalence of risk aversion. For example, it has been found that most subjects, when given a choice between a 50 percent chance of making $1,000 and a sure thing of $400, will prefer the latter.[12] This choice indicates that the subjects are willing to "pay" $100 or more (in expected value terms) for the sake of avoiding the risk associated with the larger prize. Yet someone who buys a lottery ticket is giving up a sure thing (the price of the ticket) in exchange for a risky prospect that is worth less in terms of its expected value.

One explanation for this seeming inconsistency, related to the example of the man in debt to the loan shark, was first offered in a well-known article by Milton Friedman and L. J. Savage. They suggested that people may perceive a disproportionate benefit to a prize that is large enough to elevate their social standing, and be willing to pay a premium for a chance at that sort of change in their standard of living:

> An unskilled worker may prefer the certainty of an income about the same as that of the majority of unskilled workers to an actuarially fair gamble that at best would make him one of the most prosperous unskilled workers and at worst one of the least prosperous. Yet he may jump at an actuarially fair gamble that offers a small chance of lifting him out of the class of unskilled workers and into the "middle" or "upper" class even though it is far

more likely than the preceding gamble to make him one of the least pros-
perous unskilled workers. Men will and do take great risks to distinguish
themselves, even when they know what the risks are.[13]

Of course, spending a few dollars each week on the lottery is not a "great
risk" even for someone of meager means, and it may provide that person
with his or her only imaginable avenue out of an unsatisfactory economic
status.[14]

Friedman and Savage's explanation for why otherwise risk-averse people
may choose to gamble when the prize is large has intuitive appeal. Further,
it may explain why lottery games with relatively small jackpots appeal primarily to low-income players (for whom $500 may be enough to buy a quan-
tum improvement in standard of living, at least temporarily) whereas games
with million-dollar jackpots attract more middle-class players.[15]

There is a second reason why utility-maximizing individuals would take
bets that are not fair: players typically have incomplete information about
the probabilities and prize structures of the games and suffer from the usual
human limitations in the ability to evaluate such information in a consistent,
realistic fashion. One survey in Arizona, for example, found that very few
people knew the probability of winning a prize in the state's instant game.
Although there was in fact a 10 percent chance of winning cash, almost half
of the respondents in a survey thought the probability was closest to 1 in 500.
Nor do players appear to know the percentage of gross receipts paid out in
prizes. A California survey showed that only one in ten adults could correctly
state the payout rate, plus or minus 5 percentage points.[16]

The probability of winning a large prize in the numbers game, and especially in lotto, is infinitesimal. The four-digit numbers game offers a 1 in
10,000 chance of winning, while in the usual lotto format the odds against
hitting the jackpot are several million to one. These probabilities are well
beyond the realm of experience gained from playing the game, and as a result
players cannot be expected to have much intuition about their chances. For
example, someone who spends $20 per week on a 6/49 lotto game for his or
her entire adult lifetime would still have a chance of less than 1 in 200 of
winning a jackpot.[17]

Two scholars who have studied the psychology of choices involving risk
are Daniel Kahneman and Amos Tversky. Their work suggests reasons why
some lottery players might tend to overstate the probability of winning. They
present experimental evidence showing that subjects who are asked to make
decisions about gambles involving very small probabilities tend to make er-
ratic choices. Two general tendencies are evident: placing too much weight
on a low-probability event on the one hand and, on the other, ignoring it

entirely. In addition, people appear to assign higher probabilities to events if they know of actual occurrences of the event.[18] In the case of the lottery a player has vivid evidence that winning the jackpot is possible, since new winners are announced every week and they receive a good deal of publicity. Lottery agencies reinforce this impression in their advertisements by frequently featuring winners.[19] The logic is on the order of "Someone has to win the jackpot; why shouldn't it be me?" Once convinced that a low-probability event is in the realm of the possible, people tend to behave as if it were much more likely than it actually is. Kahneman and Tversky spell out the implication of this cognitive bias: "Consequently people are often risk-seeking in dealing with improbable gains and risk averse in dealing with unlikely losses. That contributes to the attractiveness of lottery tickets and insurance policies."[20] In sum, the plunger is someone who judges a lottery ticket to be a worthwhile investment because the subjective value placed on winning a large prize is out of proportion to the amount of money involved, or because he has an exaggerated perception of the likelihood of winning.

The Believer

Because random drawings are the basis for all honest lotteries, every possible outcome has the same chance in each drawing. A player, then, has no valid method for increasing the probability of winning, except by betting more numbers, and has no information relevant to predicting the winning number. But many lottery players believe otherwise. According to the psychologist Ellen Langer people have a tendency to deny the operation of chance even in situations that are entirely chance-determined, such as lotteries. This tendency, which she calls the "illusion of control," is exacerbated in games that allow players to make choices. She has demonstrated through several gambling experiments that this illusion is heightened if subjects are asked to make choices or in some other way participate actively in a task, even if their efforts have no effect on the outcome.[21] After all, in most of the range of human experience choices can be improved by skillful application of knowledge. So perhaps it is not surprising that there is a widespread belief in techniques that purport to better the objective odds of choosing winning numbers. Some of the manifestations of this belief are commonplace. For example, many people believe that certain numbers are lucky for them.[22] But other manifestations seem anything but ordinary. Part of the lottery's clientele is immersed in a culture of superstition that attaches significance to certain numbers. In its modern form this culture is guided by a collection of seers, numerologists, and pseudoscientists who constitute the lottery's analogue to stock market analysts. Alien as it is to scientific calculation, and irrelevant as it is to the actual outcome of lottery drawings, this culture of belief must be taken seriously in assessing the demand for the products sold by state lotteries.

Dream books. One of the most common artifacts of this culture is the "dream book," a cheaply printed list of objects and occurrences that might appear in dreams, as well as birthdays, holidays, and names, each with the number or numbers believed to correspond with it, sometimes accompanied by an explanation. For example, the *Prince Ali Lucky Five Star Dream Book* gives the following numbers: apples, 416; bugs, 305; grave, 999; priest, 001; February birthday, 212; the name Judith, 557.[23] The divination of the future through the interpretation of dreams is one of many kinds of fortune-telling, and it has a special link to the history of numbers gambling in America. One bibliographic review noted that dream books were already in circulation during colonial times, and that the first dream book to provide guidance on linking events in dreams to specific numbers was published in 1862.[24] Studies of the modern numbers game in northern cities found that this type of book played a prominent role, and was linked to a kind of sorcery known as "hoodoo," which originated among American slaves: "Of those books now used in Harlem, the most popular include Rajah Rabo's Dream Book, the Three Witches Dream Book, Aunt Sally's Dream Book, The Harlem Pete Dream Book, and the Black Cat Dream Book. In some, the numbers are assigned in keeping with well-known hoodoo symbolisms, such as 769 for death or 369 for fecal matter, while in others the assignment seems essentially random."[25] The content of the word lists is related to occurrences in the daily life of the ethnic groups for whom the books are written. For example, a study of the New York City numbers game noted that a Spanish-language dream book made frequent reference to "oppression, revolution, the Catholic Church and its saints, birth and the family, tradition and homelands," and that the dream books aimed at the black community were concerned with common problems of life in the ghetto.[26]

How and how often dream books are used, and by whom, are questions that cannot be answered with any precision. Much that has been written about their use in illegal numbers games deals with blacks, but there is no evidence on usage by race. As to the methods for using dream books to bet, there is equally little to go on. One runner in New York's illegal numbers game in the 1940s viewed them as only one device to aid in the selection of numbers: "Well, some play by hunches, dreams, or numbers on a car or transfer ticket. Some go to Spiritualists. They are obtained for the most part, though, from dreams and hunches. You watch the 'book' your dream falls in most and play in that 'book.' Some people are lucky and some are not."[27] Similarly, according to a former policy writer on Chicago's South Side, most players used "the book": "It tells you everything, but there's an art in using it."[28] Without doubt even the most credulous of dream book users must soon find that discretion is necessary. Not only will most bets end in disappointment, but different books give different numbers for the same dream objects or other items. Of three dream books we consulted, none gave the same numbers for any of six items used for comparison. Death, for example, was assigned numbers of 148, 461, 512, and 418.[29] July 4 was 776 in one and 417 in another.

Dream books have easily made the transition from illegal numbers games to state-sponsored betting and have remained widely available. They appear to have resisted the influences of rational thought in twentieth-century America. They thrive in even the most erudite of environments, as evidenced by the busy lottery outlet in Harvard Square, whose dream books include *Prince Ali Lucky Five Star, Original Real Lucky 13*, and *3 Wise Men*.

Lottery advisers. Probably more important than dream books are the national circulation weekly newspapers. Publications such as *The National Enquirer, Globe, Sun, National Examiner*, and *Weekly World News*, which have a combined circulation of over 8 million, carry numerous ads and articles purporting to help individuals improve their odds of winning the lottery.[30] More specialized publications include lottery-oriented newsletters and books. Many of these advisers claim to employ the ancient arts of astrology, numerology, and dream interpretation.

Readers of the weekly pulp newspapers are provided with lottery advice from a number of different perspectives. The *Globe* is an especially fruitful source in this regard. For example, issues published during the summer of 1987 carried astrologer Katherine Singer's "Astroguide," with several "winning" numbers for each day of the month; they ran articles on numerology with titles like "Your Telephone Number Is Your Secret Hot Line to Good Fortune" and "Your Zip Code Could Put You on Easy Street"; and they provided for each state lists of numbers that were "overdue" as well as those that had won the most times. The *Globe* and other such newspapers run advertisements offering guidance on choosing numbers, with extravagant promises of results. One ad that ran in the *National Examiner* and the *Globe* depicts Gail Howard, the lottery editor of *Gambling Times* magazine, with the headline "She Wins Lottery 72 Times!!" For $13 the reader can be sent her special report that "can VASTLY INCREASE YOUR CHANCES OF WINNING ANY U.S. OR CANADIAN LOTTERY *EVERY TIME YOU PLAY. (The minimum winning edge is always over five hundred percent!)*" The ad includes testimonials from people who have won using Howard's system as well as kudos from "a professor at a major Eastern university who teaches statistics."[31]

For people who want to work out their own systems, a variety of computer software is available that facilitates analysis of patterns in previous sequences of winning numbers and keeps track of the player's bets and the outcomes. A product offered by Entertainment-on-Line, Inc., will, among other things, "produce EXPERT trend charts to identify those HOT and DUE numbers!"[32] There is an amusing similarity here to the approach of stock market analysts known as "chartists," who provide guidance to investors based on previous patterns in market prices.

The voluminous advice available on how to improve the odds of choosing winning numbers finds a receptive audience among lottery players who are willing to believe that effort and skill will be rewarded in this endeavor as in most others. The effect is to give believers an exaggerated sense of the value of a lottery ticket, and thus to stimulate play, especially in the on-line games in which players choose their numbers.

The Participant

Quite apart from hopes of prizes and the evaluation of probabilities, some people may simply enjoy the nonmonetary aspects of playing the lottery. For some there may be excitement in scratching off the coverings on instant tickets. For others the lottery is an experience that can be shared with friends. Players can discuss the merits of alternative methods for choosing numbers and in some cases join together to form betting pools, as in the celebrated case of the group of workers at a printing factory in New York who shared a $40 million lotto jackpot in 1986.[33] In some urban neighborhoods the daily numbers game may play a role like that of the old illegal game, "furnishing much of the content of casual conversation, imparting a temporal structure to the day, and offering a sense of participation in a community-wide institution."[34]

So while it is possible to play the lottery in isolation, for many it becomes a basis for social interaction. Of course, as we noted in Chapter 4, lottery games are notoriously low on play value in comparison to other forms of betting, but lottery suppliers diligently attempt to make their products more interesting to play. In addition, many lottery advertisements tout the excitement of playing the lottery. When players in California were asked whether they played the lottery more for fun or for the money, almost equal numbers cited each reason, although those with incomes below $30,000 were 25 percent more likely to cite money than fun, while the reverse was true at upper incomes.[35] What is amusement to the affluent may seem more like an investment to those less well off.

A related motivation is the possibility of enhancing one's reputation with peers and even achieving fame if the win is big enough. As one psychologist has observed, "Interestingly, and for many people I have surveyed, the most secretly alluring feature of the lottery is a chance for celebrity status. If you triple your money in the stock market, how many people know about it? But if you win the lottery, you end up on TV."[36]

The four types characterized as the investor, the plunger, the believer, and the participant are not mutually exclusive. The investor is a rare species among lottery players and is in a class by himself, but the style and motives attributed to the others are commonplace and overlapping. For example, most players enjoy some of the social aspects of lottery play that appeal to the participant. And many believers may share the plunger's dream that a big win will bring a quantum leap in social standing.

Which Numbers Do They Play?

One of the easiest ways to observe the effects of skill orientation in lottery play is to look at the patterns of play in games in which players choose their own numbers. Such patterns are interesting for their own sake, for what they reveal about the enduring mystical power of certain numbers. In addition, the existence of such patterns—whatever their origin—has implications for the operation of lottery games and the success of alternative betting strategies. It is useful to begin simply by describing the betting patterns.

Perennial Favorites and Flashes in the Pan

When given the chance to choose their numbers, lottery players do not bet uniformly. Some numbers, as we have said, are simply more popular than others. And some enjoy a brief moment in the sun followed by a return to obscurity. What patterns can be discerned?

Events and dates. One time-honored method of choosing numbers in lottery games is to bet on a number associated with a well-known event. Illegal numbers banks were flooded with bets on 715, for example, when Hank Aaron was on the verge of breaking Babe Ruth's record of 714 home runs. When one Cleveland numbers banker received a sentence of from six to sixty years in prison, the number 660 was played heavily (and won). Players in the Italian lottery traditionally bet heavily on numbers associated with the pope at the time of his death. Following the death of Pope John XXIII, for example, the numbers 3, 7, 49, 23, and 81, corresponding to the date of death (June 3), the time (7:49), the number after his name, and his age received heavy play. In 1976 an episode of a popular television series showed a woman who dreamed of and bet on the number 652 and won. The next day witnessed a flood of bets on that number: betting in New Jersey was over ten times the average daily rate, and the number was "sold out" in Maryland.[37] In Illinois betting on the number 2880 in 1982 was halted after hitting the agency's limit of $5 million; 2880 was the lot number of Tylenol capsules that had been laced with cyanide.[38]

Similarly the date often becomes the basis for numbers bets. For example, of the thirty-six occasions on which numbers in the Maryland lottery reached the agency's maximum allowable sales level during a two-month period in 1986, five corresponded at least roughly to the date (for example, 6686 for June 6, 1986; 711 for July 11; and 1313 for June 13). One, a 1776 bet on July 4, provides a historical twist to the date motif.[39] The date appears to influence betting often. We examined betting on three-digit numbers corresponding to the date of the month during October 1986 in the Maryland numbers game (101 to 109) and found that bets approximately doubled for each number on the matching date.[40]

Personal lucky numbers. For most popular numbers there are no such obvious reasons for betting. Articles on winners and other players reveal that they have used such numbers as their children's birthdays, their address, their favorite ballplayer's uniform number, a number from a dream book, or simply their "lucky number." The motivations for playing numbers such as these are personal, idiosyncratic, and generally not newsworthy, but they appear to constitute the basis for much of the number selection observed in numbers and lotto games. Numbers based on celebrated events are of little empirical importance, yet they serve as the exception that proves the rule, in the sense that they represent events that have taken on a personal meaning. In contrast, most numbers are based purely on personal circumstances or beliefs. As a whole the pattern of play on numbers has two important characteristics. First, because the numbers themselves are based on the circumstances of individual players, the pattern of betting tends to be highly stable over time. Second, people appear to have much in common when it comes to personal lucky numbers. Combined with the tendency to choose convenient combinations, this commonality results in a markedly uneven distribution of bets across numbers. Let us begin by looking at what numbers are bet most often.

Table 5.1 displays the most popular and least popular numbers played on three days in the Maryland three-digit numbers game during the fall of 1986.[41] Each of the seven most popular numbers is a triple, led by 333 and 777. Both 3 and 7 are traditionally viewed as lucky numbers, and triple numbers evidently are as well. As we have noted, the number 769 traditionally signifies death. Among the least popular, four numbers begin with a zero and another four begin with an 8. As an indication of the relative popularity of these numbers, the table also gives the relative amount wagered on each number, counting all varieties of bets. These amounts differ dramatically, by a factor

Table 5.1. Most and least popular numbers in Maryland's three-digit daily game, autumn 1986

Number	Bets relative to the average[a]
Most popular	
333	9.93
777	9.18
555	7.02
444	6.11
888	5.15
666	5.11
999	5.09
769	5.06
101	4.65
419	4.21
Least popular	
096	0.27
788	0.27
076	0.26
855	0.26
878	0.26
968	0.25
884	0.25
887	0.25
086	0.25
092	0.23

Source: Calculated from unpublished data provided by the Maryland state lottery agency.

a. Ratio of bets on a number to the average bet (total amount bet divided by 1,000 equals average bet per number). Based on the lottery's potential liability as a percentage of the pool for three days: September 4 and October 3 and 28, 1986. Liability is a weighted sum of all bets on a number, including straight bets, boxes, and combinations, and averages 50 percent, corresponding to the 50 percent payout rate in the state's lottery.

of over 40. It is worth noting that these differences would have been even greater had the state not stopped taking bets on number 333 on each of these three days.[42]

Another way to illustrate differences in the frequency of play among the numbers is to group them by hundreds. Data for the same three days of the Maryland three-digit game show that, even at this high level of aggregation, the rates of play differed markedly. Numbers between 100 and 399 received more than the average amount of play (39 percent, well above the 30 percent that would occur if all numbers were played uniformly), and numbers between 400 and 799 receive about the average amount of play. In contrast, the numbers beginning with zero, 8, and 9 are played much less often—less than two-thirds the average rate. It is interesting to note that this distribution is remarkably similar to the pattern of betting in New York's illegal numbers game, in which numbers beginning with 1, 2, or 3 also tended to be popular.[43]

Numbers of convenience. In the three- and four-digit daily games most people seem to be able to come up with numbers to bet on. But choosing six different numbers appears to be a daunting prospect for many lottery players. One solution is to have the computer pick a number, and indeed most lotteries offer this option. Another popular approach is to choose a set of numbers easily suggested by the design of the betting slip itself. Combinations based on rows and diagonals are among the most popular combinations bet. A striking illustration of this effect was a listing, published in the *Boston Globe* on January 28, 1986, of the most frequently bet lotto combinations in the Massachusetts 6/36 lotto game. The most popular combination consisted of the numbers making up the diagonal beginning at the top left of the betting slip (1, 8, 15, 22, 29, 36), and the second most popular combination was the other diagonal. Columns on the betting slip accounted for six of the next seven most frequently bet combinations. Perhaps it should not be surprising that such convenient combinations dominate the betting in a game that strains the average player's imagination by requiring him to select so many different numbers.

Unevenness of play. As a result of the tendency of players to choose convenient or otherwise popular numbers, a disproportionate amount of betting is concentrated on a relatively few combinations. This is true even for games that allow players the option of having a combination selected for them randomly. As an illustration, consider the pattern of betting in Maryland's 6/40 lotto game on one day in August 1986, a day on which some 60 percent of all bets were made using the state's random selection option.[44] On that day about 5 million bets were placed (two for each dollar ticket purchased), but those bets included only about 2.6 million of the 3,838,380 possible combinations of six numbers between 1 and 40. Thus only 69 percent of all possible combinations were bet. (This percentage is the "coverage" that lotto designers watch closely, since it equals the probability that there will be at least one winner; 100 percent minus the percentage is the probability of having a roll-over.) But even among those combinations that were bet, a relatively few received the lion's share of the attention. Out of the almost 4 million combinations, fewer than 70,000, or about 1.8 percent, were bet as many as five times; these most popular combinations accounted for 11.6 percent of all bets. The most frequently played one-third of possible combinations accounted for over 70 percent of total play.[45] The story is much the same for numbers betting, as is shown clearly in Figure 5.1. In Maryland, for example, the most popular hundred numbers accounted for almost 30 percent of all bets, or about three times the average rate.[46]

In games with fixed payoffs for winning combinations, such as Maryland's three-digit daily numbers games, this unevenness in play among number combinations would be no more than an interesting oddity of gambling behavior. But in games with parimutuel payoffs the size of prize winnings for players who select such popular combinations can be dramatically less than the average. For example, on the one day we analyzed the most popular

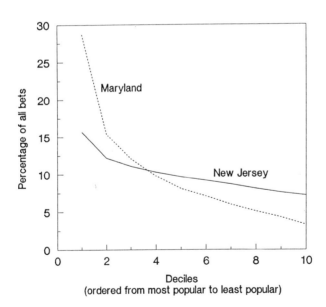

Figure 5.1. Concentration of betting in the three-digit numbers game, Maryland and New Jersey

(*Source:* Maryland and New Jersey lottery agencies, unpublished data)

combination in Maryland's 6/40 lotto game was 1-2-3-4-5-6. Bettors played this familiar combination 3,207 times, well over 2,000 times the rate for the average combination. If this combination had been drawn, each of the winners would have taken home a "jackpot" of just $193.50! For this reason lottery players are well advised to choose unpopular combinations whenever prizes are determined on a parimutuel basis. Of course lottery agencies also know that popular combinations are not a smart bet. Their policies regarding information about popular betting combinations are discussed later in this chapter.

Gambling Behavior as Revealed by Choice of Numbers

It is clear that lottery players do not think all numbers are created equal. Rather some numbers are imbued with special meaning and others are simply familiar, and these are the numbers that most players choose. Some players are content to or prefer to let a computer pick a number for them, but for the majority the number itself takes on a meaning that indelibly distinguishes it from any other. Although all numbers share vital characteristics such as frequency of drawing, ease of betting, and objective probability of winning, each number is a distinct "product." To an economist accustomed to studying consumer behavior, a preference for 777 over 092 is no less rational than preferences for colors, tastes, or fragrances. At the very least it indicates that for most players lottery tickets are not merely a financial asset with a given risk and expected return but a more complex commodity which offers as one component some statistically defined payoff. Yet granting that number combinations are not perfect substitutes for one another from the viewpoint of the consumers does not mean that the conventional utility-maximization model is irrelevant to gambling behavior. In particular it is interesting to examine two hypotheses that arise from an application of conventional consumer theory to the choice of number combinations. These relate to the effect of payout ratios on the demand for specific numbers and the perceived independence of the probability of a number's being drawn over time.

Payoff and the "price" of a number. Economic theory would suggest that, whatever the basis of demand for a product, the quantity demanded of it will tend to fall as its price increases. The difference in the method of determining the payoff for winning numbers in legal daily numbers games provides a unique opportunity to test whether lottery players behave in this way. Where the payoffs to winners are fixed, such as $500 for a straight three-digit bet, the cost of buying a dollar's worth of expected value—one measure of price— is the same for all number combinations. But in a parimutuel system, in which the amount of the payoff depends on how many people bet on the winning number, popular numbers will have lower payoffs, and correspondingly higher prices, than unpopular numbers. The logic of the economic model of consumer behavior implies that a bettor who would be indifferent between two numbers in a fixed-payoff game should prefer the unpopular one in a parimutuel game.

To see whether this price effect takes place, we compared the distribution of bets in two legal numbers games, one using fixed payouts and one using a parimutuel system. The distribution of bets under a fixed payout regime was obtained by averaging data from the Maryland lottery on bets by number for three days in 1986. We were unable to obtain similar data for a state using parimutuel payoffs, so we inferred the popularity of a large set of numbers by collecting data on the payoffs for winning numbers in the New Jersey three-digit game over a twenty-three-month period, during which time over 450 of the 1,000 possible combinations won at least once.[47] All other things being equal, if players are sensitive to the payoff, the effect of a parimutuel payoff system would be to flatten the distribution of betting across numbers. The most popular numbers under a parimutuel system should account for less of the total play than under a fixed payoff system. Figure 5.1 compares the distribution of bets by decile of frequency in Maryland and New Jersey. The figure does in fact reveal a marked difference in betting patterns between the two states. In Maryland, the fixed payoff state, the one hundred most frequently bet numbers received 29 percent of all bets. The average number combination in this decile was over eight times more likely to be bet than the average number in the decile of least frequently bet numbers. By contrast there was much less variation in play in New Jersey, the parimutuel state. There the ratio of average proportion of bets on the most popular to the least popular numbers was only about 2.3 to 1. This result does not prove that bettors are sensitive to price, of course, but it is suggestive. For these differences to be due to non–price-related effects, differences in preference for specific numbers would have to have been significantly more uniform in New Jersey than in Maryland, and there is no evidence to suggest that this was so. The possibility that price effects influence the quantity of betting is discussed further in Chapter 6.

The gambler's fallacy. One often-noted misconception about the laws of probability is the notion that the odds that a random event will occur vary over time depending on whether the event has occurred recently. Specifically, the "gambler's fallacy" is the belief that an event based on independent random chance is less likely to occur if it has just happened, when in fact the probability is always the same.[48] Since a lottery is based on independent random drawings, it would be incorrect to assume that the probability of drawing any given number drops after it has been drawn. Yet there is evidence that lottery players are in fact subject to this misconception. One lotto player in New York, for example, used a device with numbered balls to choose a combination. She bet all of the numbers indicated except 37, which had recently been a winner, and bet 47 instead.[49] The gambler's fallacy also seems to be enshrined as part of the belief system taught by lottery advisers. Among the most commonly available sorts of data is the historical record of hits for each number. A national magazine, for example, carries lists of numbers that are "due." One inexpensive publication sold next to dream books in the Boston area not only showed the number of times each three-digit number had been chosen since the beginning of the lottery but also gave the number of hits in the illegal numbers game since 1927.[50] While such publications do not prove that bettors shy away from numbers that have recently won, they certainly could be used for that purpose, and they would be of no use to anyone who treated the probabilities for a given number as a constant. More to the point is the analysis of various three-digit numbers given in the *3 Wise Men Dream Book*. Under 444 it notes: "A little below its Law of Averages rating lately."[51]

In order to see whether lottery players are subject to the gambler's fallacy, we examined betting on numbers that were drawn in Maryland's three-digit daily game. What we found was strong evidence that the gambler's fallacy is alive and well in its effect on lottery betting patterns. During a one-month period in 1986 betting on a number dropped by almost a quarter on the day after it was drawn and by over half on the second day. In all but one case the proportion of betting on a number fell after it was drawn.[52] (One explanation for the greater drop on the second day is that some people bet their numbers for more than one day at a time, so changes do not register right away.) An examination of betting on fifty-two winning numbers over a longer period in 1988 showed that the amount bet on a number had dropped in every case by the second day after it was drawn. As much as a month after a number was drawn betting stayed low in almost 90 percent of the cases, but betting returned just about to normal after three months. Despite the attempts by lottery officials to ensure random drawings, therefore, players do not appear to believe in the laws of chance.[53]

Lottery Agencies and the "Mystique" of Numbers

What do the lottery agencies do in the face of this behavior? One possible response would be to publish the frequency with which various numbers are bet, showing the effect on payoffs of betting on popular numbers. Instead the policy followed by virtually all lottery agencies is not to reveal the distribution of bets by number. Nor do lottery agencies inform players that playing popular number combinations in parimutuel games will tend to reduce their expected winnings. The only information on numbers that is typically made available are the winning numbers and, occasionally, tabulations of numbers that have been drawn. Iowa's 1987 annual report, for example, showed the frequency of drawings for each of the thirty-six numbers in its lotto game, revealing that the number 25 had been drawn on nineteen occasions while 36 had come up only twice. While this kind of information is of no use to bettors as long as the drawings are random, it may appeal to those who believe that some balls have a better chance than others of being drawn or to those who act in accordance with the gambler's fallacy.[54]

Instead of providing information that would be helpful to bettors in parimutuel games, the lottery agencies appear to be interested in encouraging rather than dispelling the fallacy that numbers are important for their own sake. While most have introduced a random selection option for on-line games, they continue to foster player loyalty to personal lucky numbers. The Iowa lottery's annual report states:

> Picking numbers for the LOTTO game is an exercise in individuality that many players take very seriously. While some are content to let the LOTTO Terminals pick their numbers for them and others just randomly select numbers that catch their fancy, many LOTTO players put a lot of thought into the process. Some pick numbers that have very personal meanings, anniversary dates and birthdays, while others play their "lucky numbers" or numbers that coincide with the dates of historic events. One Jackpot winner even used the birth date of her cat to win the big prize.[55]

Similarly, the West Virginia lottery gives explicit advice in the directions it provides for filling out the betting slip for its lotto game: "Mark any six (6) numbers between 1 and 36 on the bet slip. (Hint: Use birthdays, anniversaries, or other favorite numbers.)"[56] The Connecticut lottery distributes a wallet-size card with a schedule of prize payouts on one side and a page devoted to "favorite numbers" on the other, with spaces for license plate number, birthdays, anniversary, address, weight, and other personal numbers.[57] And an ad in California showed six sports jerseys with numbers on the backs and told how a recent lotto winner had won by using the uniform numbers of six of his sports heroes. The ad instructed, "Mark your six lucky numbers on the Play Slip. This is how our winner of $10.7 million did it."[58]

Because many on-line lottery players ascribe special significance to the numbers they play, lottery agencies may see that it is to their advantage to encourage bettors to play personally significant numbers on a regular basis. Advertising the low expected payouts on popular numbers might have the effect of undermining such devotion and hurting sales. For the same reason agencies may use random selection options to expand the player base. A consultant working for GTECH, a supplier of lottery computer software, advises agencies to introduce the random selection option only after the hard-core demand by regular players has solidified: "GTECH believes that it is important to allow players to become interested in the 'mystique' of the numbers, with the result that they want to play the same numbers every week. It is because of this effect that GTECH normally recommends against Quick Pick for new lotto games. After sales level off, Quick Pick should be intro-duced so that incremental revenues may be realized."[59] By minimizing the disadvantages of playing popular numbers and by suggesting ways to choose numbers lottery agencies have been able to capitalize on widespread beliefs about the personal or supernatural significance of numbers and in the process maximize the sales potential for their on-line products.

Conclusion

The mystique of numbers is an important element in explaining the popular-ity of the lottery. Games that allow players the chance to choose their number create an opportunity to apply effort and skill, no matter how illusory, toward the end of beating the odds. This skill orientation is not universal, of course, but it is common enough to deserve serious attention. Among the implica-tions are the following. First, the objective probability distribution of prizes will have less relevance to a player with a skill perspective.[60] Second, those who believe they have a valid system for choosing numbers will presumably bet more than if they lacked that confidence. And third, winners will be perceived as people who in some sense earned their prizes.[61] As Victor Hugo observed in *Les Misérables:* "Prosperity supposes capacity. Win in the lot-tery, and you are an able man. The victor is venerated."

6.

The Demand for Lottery Products

That the chance of gain is naturally over-valued, we may
learn from the universal success of lotteries . . . The vain
hope of gaining some of the great prizes is the sole cause
of this demand.

—Adam Smith, *Wealth of Nations*

Who plays the lottery, how much do they play, and what factors affect their participation? Questions such as these underlie the empirical analysis of the demand for any consumer product, and the lottery may be examined in much the same way. First among those interested in the demand for lottery products is, not surprisingly, the state lottery agencies. As we shall see in greater detail in Chapter 10, these agencies use modern methods of marketing to increase their sales. Knowledge of the market and the factors that influence demand are essential ingredients in any marketing strategy. Not only do marketers need to know who buys their product, but they also aim to distinguish heavy users from occasional users and determine how the product's price or promotion affects demand. One question that often arises in discussions of lottery marketing is whether lottery purchases constitute "impulse buying"—irregular purchases determined on the spur of the moment.

But there are good reasons other than the mercantile interests of marketing to examine the demand for lottery products. One is the pragmatic concern of states that may be considering whether or not to adopt a lottery: how much revenue can a state expect to collect from a lottery? Another application for the empirical study of lottery demand is in assessing the distributional incidence of the revenue burden of lotteries. As we discuss in Chapter 11, lotteries levy an implicit tax on players, and the incidence of that implicit tax corresponds to the distribution of lottery expenditures.

In this chapter we explore the diversity of lottery participation. We first develop a picture of high concentration in the context of broad participation. Then we demonstrate that some population groups play more often than others on the average. Of special concern is whether minorities and low-income groups are especially active in lottery play. Finally we examine the variables associated with high levels of lottery expenditures and analyze specifically the demand for lotto games.

The Curious Majority, the Intense Few

Most adults who live in lottery states have played the lottery at least once, but the real market for the lottery consists of those who play on a regular basis or who might be enticed into playing regularly by the offer of a new game or a more effective sales pitch. As with most products, a small percentage of lottery customers are so active (relatively speaking) as to account for the bulk of all sales. This group is of special interest to those responsible for marketing lotteries, as well as to those concerned about the financial hardships caused by excessive gambling.

In 1986 the average expenditure on lottery tickets was slightly over $110 per adult in lottery states, which works out to about $2 per week. But the $2 bettor is not at all typical of lottery players. Rather, the distribution of lottery play is concentrated among a relatively small fraction of the public who spend much more than that. In this respect the lottery is like most other commodities. First of all, not everyone plays the lottery. In any given week only about one-third of all adults play; over the course of a year participation broadens to encompass one-half or more of the adult public. Among those who do play, the top 10 percent of players in terms of frequency account for 50 percent of the total amount wagered, while the top 20 percent wager about 65 percent of the total. Interestingly, the degree of concentration among players (as indicated by these percentages) does not depend on the time interval under consideration. Measures of concentration are virtually identical for three surveys that asked respondents to report lottery expenditures for some period preceding the interview: a one-week period (Maryland, 1984), a two-month period (California, 1985), and a twelve-month period (all lottery states combined, 1974).

The distribution for the California survey is depicted in Figure 6.1, which illustrates the importance of heavy players in determining total lottery sales. Half of the survey respondents said that they had purchased a lottery ticket in the preceding two months. Within this group the median expenditure was a modest $12, but those players who bet that amount or less accounted for only about one-seventh of the total handle. The top 10 percent of players reported spending more than $50 and accounted for over half the total.

How does the distribution of lottery play compare with the distribution of

The 10% of the adult population who bet most heavily accounted
for 65% of the total wagers

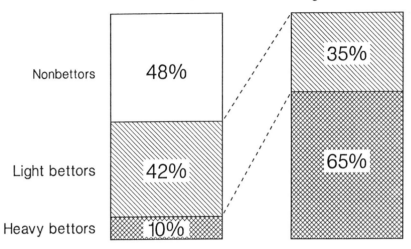

Figure 6.1. Concentration in lottery wagers, California, March 1986
(*Source:* Calculated from unpublished data from *Los Angeles Times* Poll,
no. 103, March 1986)

expenditures for other commodities? One rule of thumb of marketing, the
"law of the heavy half," holds that the top 20 percent of consumers of any
commodity account for 80 percent of total purchases.[1] If this is indeed a law,
then lotteries are in violation, since the most active 20 percent of players
account for only 65 percent of lottery play. Still, the qualitative outcome is
the same: a relatively small minority of all consumers are responsible for the
bulk of total expenditures.

While expenditures on lotteries are somewhat less concentrated than this
"law" would suggest, expenditures on other sorts of commercial gambling
are more concentrated. A survey conducted by the University of Michigan
Survey Research Center in 1975, *Gambling in the United States,* provides the
most complete available account of self-reported gambling participation in
the United States. Thirty percent of the national sample reported having
participated in some form of commercial gambling, legal or illegal, in 1974
(not including state lotteries). The top 20 percent of these players (about 6
percent of the sample) accounted for fully 93 percent of the total reported
wagers, and the top 10 percent of players wagered 84 percent of the total.
To what extent this is due to differences in the availability of the various

forms of commercial gambling is unclear. Whatever the explanation, the state lotteries have considerably broader participation, and less concentration of play among participants, than other forms of commercial gambling. There is, however, one form of illegal gambling whose distribution of play appears to resemble that of its legal cousin quite closely. Calculations based on data from a 1972 study of the illegal numbers game in New York City show that the degree of concentration among participants of the illegal game was quite similar to that in Maryland's three-digit legal numbers game in 1986.[2]

A commodity that has much in common with commercial gambling and lotteries is alcohol, and it is illuminating to compare this distribution across the adult population. Drinking and gambling are both subject to special legal controls and have been broadly condemned in religious teachings. The dominant modern view is that moderate indulgence in either of these activities is acceptable, but the potential exists for excess and abuse and must be curtailed through special regulations. The distribution of alcohol consumption reflects both the moderate nature of "normal" drinking, and the potential for trouble. Most adults in the United States abstain (33 percent) or drink moderately (57 percent). The remaining 10 percent of drinkers average about ten drinks each day and account for about half of total alcohol consumption.[3] Thus, the degree of concentration of drinking is much the same as the concentration of lottery play, and the basic implication is the same for both alcohol and lotteries. Most participants indulge lightly; the majority of the "action" involves the relatively small group at the top of the distribution.

For lotteries, as for alcohol and other commodities, the relatively heavy participants are of special interest. From the perspective of the state lottery agencies, since this is the group that accounts for most of the revenues, maintaining the interest of the heavy players is essential to the financial health of the lottery. Because of the predominance of regular players in total lottery sales, one lottery marketing consultant has disputed the common belief that lottery demand is based on impulse buying.[4] On the contrary, he says, for many lottery players—especially the big spenders—purchases are planned and are made regularly. Upon such distinctions depend crucial choices about how best to market the product. Finally, from the perspective of lottery critics, the heavy players are the ones at greatest risk from the hazards associated with gambling: the feeding of self-destructive compulsion and the temptation to neglect other financial obligations for the sake of pursuing the dream of wealth.

The concentration of lottery play is also of interest because of its effect on public perceptions. The typical lottery player may quite rightly be perceived as someone who spends a few dollars a week or less. For this player the lottery is surely a harmless diversion. What is not so easily understood from casual observation is that the typical player is not the source of the typical revenue dollar.

Who Plays

The focus here is on the readily observable characteristics of individuals and groups: age, gender, race, income, place of residence, education, family status. We do not explore the more subtle dimensions of human diversity, such as personality characteristics or attitudes, although these may well be instrumental and have been studied extensively by those whose job it is to market lottery products. But the politics of the question "Who plays?" is dominated by socioeconomic concerns, especially the pattern of play across income distribution. As it turns out, several socioeconomic characteristics are highly correlated with lottery play, but income is not one of them.

At least three measures of lottery involvement may be used to measure the play of a given population group. The first is the participation rate: the percentage of group members who bought at least one lottery ticket during a given period of time. Second is the average expenditure by members of the group—the total expenditure over some period of time divided by the number of people belonging to the group. Third is the prevalence of heavy players within the group—the percentage of group members who spent a relatively large amount over the specified time period. In practice these three measures are closely related, in the sense that groups that rank relatively high on one measure are also high on the other two. For example, dividing the adult population of California into four groups by educational level, we find that the group with the highest average expenditure (those who did not complete high school) is also the group with the highest participation rate and the highest concentration of heavy players. While it is logically possible that certain groups might attain a high average expenditure level despite a low participation rate (that is, if those who did participate were all heavy players), this possibility is not observed in practice.

We obtained information on the characteristics of players from a number of different sources. Most important were household surveys from Arizona, California, Maryland, and the nation at large that included questions about participation in state lotteries. We also have used information based on household surveys taken in Massachusetts and New Jersey and a national household survey of gambling made in 1944, and we have examined lottery data aggregated by zip code for California and Maryland.[5] In analyzing who plays lotteries it is informative to begin by examining simple two-way classifications that compare the rates of play for members of various demographic groups. We have also analyzed these data using multivariate analysis techniques that control for the effects of other characteristics, but in general we have found that the simple tabulations give a good qualitative picture of the patterns of lottery play.

Differences by Socioeconomic Group

Figure 6.2 compares the rates of lottery play among various population groups based on a survey taken in California in 1986, at a time when only instant

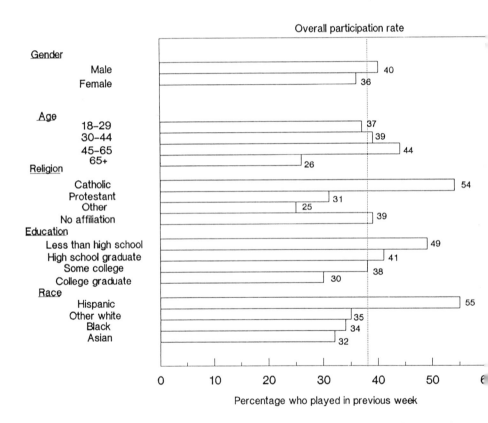

Figure 6.2. Lottery participation rates for one week, California, March 1986

(*Source:* Calculated from unpublished data from *Los Angeles Times* Poll, no. 103, March 1986)

games were available in that state. For each group the figure shows the participation rate, measured by the percentage of people who played in the previous week. In the entire adult population 38 percent bought at least one ticket during the week. The discussion here presents a number of generalizations which are illustrated by the patterns in Figure 6.2, but which are based on a number of other sources of information as well.

Gender. Men gamble more than women as a rule, but the difference is small in the case of lotteries. The national surveys of gambling in 1975 found that 68 percent of men participated in some form of gambling, compared with only 55 percent of women. In California the difference in lottery participation is small, as shown in Figure 6.2. A survey in Massachusetts also found similar participation rates for men and women in all three lottery games.[6] Generally the gender difference in amount played is more notable than the difference in participation rates, with men having a definite edge.

Age. The pattern of lottery participation by age is an inverted U, with the young (eighteen to twenty-five) and the old (sixty-five and over) playing less than the broad middle range. Heavy play is most prevalent in the middle years as well. Interestingly, this pattern is a departure from the age profile of gambling in general, which shows the highest rates of gambling among young adults and a steady decline in participation with age.

Religion. In lottery play as with gambling in general the biggest religious difference is the markedly higher rates of participation among Catholics. Previous surveys of gambling have shown that participation rates for Catholics are half again as large as those of Protestants, and the differences for lottery purchases shown in Figure 6.2 are similar. Roman Catholic dogma is tolerant of moderate gambling, and Catholic churches, unlike Protestant ones, have long used bingo nights as a fund-raising device. Lottery play among those not affiliated with organized religious bodies falls between rates for Catholics and those of other religious groups.

Education. Anytime a lottery critic calls the lottery a "sucker bet" or decries the exploitation of uninformed citizens the role of education in lottery play is being questioned. Indeed there is no more clear-cut correlation with lottery participation: lottery play falls with formal education. Figure 6.2 shows that the proportion of adults who participate drops from 49 percent for those with less than a high school education to 30 percent for those with a college degree. Yet this clear association contrasts sharply with that for gambling in general. In national surveys conducted in 1944 and 1975 gambling was shown to *increase* with education. Whatever the role of education in the ability of players to assess objective aspects of betting, it is clear that lotteries appeal to a less well educated clientele than most other forms of gambling.

Occupation and employment status. Another way to gain a picture of who plays lotteries is to examine how play breaks down by occupation and employment. Among six broad occupational categories in the California survey lottery play was most common among laborers (including both skilled and unskilled), with a participation rate of 46 percent. Right behind are service and protective and clerical workers. Among the occupations showing the lowest rates of play were advanced professionals, although even among them the participation rate was over 25 percent. Retired people and students played the least.

Race and ethnic group. Racial and ethnic classifications are, of course, loaded with social and political significance in almost any context, for better or worse. In the case of lotteries the social significance is enhanced by the history of the daily numbers game. As we saw in Chapter 4 the daily numbers games developed by state lotteries were copies of illegal numbers games that had operated for decades. Blacks, and to a lesser extent Hispanic groups, considered policy and numbers "their" games, and with good reason. These illegal games had thrived in minority neighborhoods for decades, providing a source of cheap entertainment, employing hundreds of residents as runners and bankers, and ultimately becoming a fixture of the cultural landscape.[7]

Although the evidence is somewhat mixed, it appears that in the United States blacks and Hispanics play more than non-Hispanic whites. Figure 6.2 shows that in California Hispanics played considerably more than other whites but that the rate of play for blacks was similar to that for non-Hispanic whites. Betting at least $5 per week was twice as common for Hispanic adults as for others. Similarly, a survey taken in Arizona showed a higher rate of play for Hispanics than other whites. While only 9 percent of other whites in that state reported playing the lottery at least once a week, the rate for Hispanics was 28 percent.[8] The available survey material for northeastern states suggests that blacks play more than whites in that region.[9] Calculations based on a survey taken in Maryland in 1986 reveal that some 43 percent of whites had played the lottery within the previous month, but among blacks the comparable figure was 68 percent. The size of this racial difference depends on the type of lottery game, and is largest for the legal version of the numbers game. In Maryland blacks participated in the three-digit numbers game at a rate over twice that of whites, 61 to 24 percent, whereas the difference for lotto was only 54 to 38 percent.[10] A survey in New Jersey produced similar findings, showing blacks and Hispanics playing numbers games at a rate twice that of the population in general and lotto at a rate 30 percent higher than average.[11] This preponderance of blacks and Hispanics in the daily numbers game also closely parallels the racial pattern of play in New York's illegal numbers game.[12] Given the importance that has been attached to racial differences in lottery play, one must ask whether differences such as these can be explained by other observable differences. We turn to this question in considering the last of the demographic variables to be discussed.

Income. The relationship between income and lottery expenditures is of particular interest owing to the frequent charge that lotteries are played disproportionately by the poor. In fact there has been more research on this question than on almost any other related to lotteries. The preponderance of the evidence suggests that there is little systematic relationship between income and the amount spent on lottery play. Absolute expenditures appear to be remarkably uniform over a broad range of incomes. This uniformity is noteworthy since spending, say, $10 per week on the lottery represents a much greater financial commitment for a household with an income of $10,000 per year than for one earning $40,000 per year. Yet we find no consistent differences in participation or play over this range, with the possible exception of daily numbers games, whether or not other household characteristics are taken into account.

Figure 6.3 depicts the patterns of lottery play by income using data from the 1986 California survey. Most of the respondents lived in households with

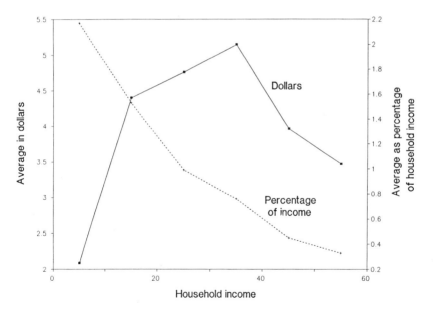

Figure 6.3. Household weekly expenditure on lottery, California, March 1986

(*Source:* Calculated from unpublished data from *Los Angeles Times* Poll, no. 103, March 1986)

incomes in the range of $10,000 to $60,000. Over this range average play does not differ much. As a *percentage* of income, however, average play declines over the entire income range, as shown by the dotted line in Figure 6.3. While the average person in the lowest income class spent 2 percent of his household income on lottery tickets, those with incomes above $40,000 spent less than 0.5 percent on tickets. The expenditure pattern evident in this table is consistent with several previous studies of lottery expenditures, most of which were based on weekly passive lottery games.[13] It is also consistent with the patterns that emerge when expenditures are estimated by counting the number of winners by zip code (see Table 6.1). Using data for Maryland and Massachusetts we found that, with one exception, the estimated average level of expenditures bore no consistent relationship with the average income by zip codes. The exception was lotto games with comparatively large jackpots, for which expenditures tended to rise with income.

Of the various data sets we analyzed there was just one showing the poorest respondents playing more than others. A 1984 Gallup survey in Maryland (see Table 6.2) found that respondents with incomes below $15,000 (about 15 percent of the sample) played more than those with higher incomes— indeed more than twice as much. Whether this difference is valid or an artifact of the special difficulties involved in surveying poor neighborhoods is not clear. The less error-prone data on winners by zip codes, found in Table 6.1, does not provide much support for this result.

On the basis of a number of data sets for different states and years, we conclude that there is no strong and consistent pattern of lottery play across income categories. Indeed, the upper and lower ranges of the middle class play at about the same rate on the average. Income patterns differ somewhat among games, with lotto having a relatively strong appeal to upper-income households and numbers to lower-income players. The most definitive finding is that as a *percentage* of household income, lottery expenditures decline steadily as income rises.

In sum, members of certain groups are more likely to play lotteries and to play them heavily: males, Hispanics, blacks, the middle-aged, Catholics, laborers, and those with less than a college degree. One question that arises in the interpretation of such results is whether or not these factors remain significant when the others are taken into account. Does income have an effect, for example, when education and race are accounted for? In order to examine the independent effects of race, education, and other individual characteristics, we estimated multivariate equations explaining average weekly expenditures based on the survey of Maryland residents. Largest and statistically most significant among the explanatory variables is race, with blacks

		Number of winners	Median household income for zip code, 1980				
Winners in two states	Item		Under $10,000	$10,000 to $15,000	$15,000 to $20,000	$20,000 to $25,000	$25,000 and over
Maryland							
Upper-tier winners, 1/86 to 8/86, and lotto jackpot winners, 1/84 to 8/86	Number of zip codes	—	34	116	150	99	99
	Game:[a]						
	4-digit numbers	211	1.34	1.01	.92	1.31	.74
	Instant	66	1.85	1.48	.90	1.20	.48
	Lotto	581.5[b]	1.00	.72	.89	1.12	1.20
Massachusetts							
Lotto jackpot winners, 12/82 to 3/86	Number of zip codes	—	28	113	227	135	67
	Game:[a]						
	All lotto	425	.47	.90	1.01	1.24	.89
	Lotto when jackpot exceeded $5 million	123	.24	.85	.90	1.60	.71

Sources: Calculated from unpublished data on winners' residences provided by the Maryland and Massachusetts state lottery agencies and from Claritas Corp., *REZIDE, 1980: The National Encyclopedia of Residential ZIP Code Demography*, sec. 2 (Arlington, Va., 1983).

a. Ratio of share of sales to share of households, by game.

b. Ticket shared with nonresident. All winners of shared tickets with only one zip code shown were assumed to reside in the same zip code. Otherwise, shared tickets were prorated among zip codes.

Table 6.2.   Determinants of lottery expenditures: Average weekly expenditures in the preceding month, Maryland, 1984

Bettor characteristics	Estimated coefficients and standard errors		
	Full sample	Whites	Blacks
Education			
High school graduate only	−2.79	−4.93*	1.36
	(1.98)	(1.98)	(5.19)
College graduate	−8.34*	−11.24*	0.62
	(2.08)	(2.08)	(5.55)
Age			
25–39	1.70	.51	5.15
	(1.68)	(1.70)	(4.39)
40–54	3.81*	1.73	11.61*
	(1.84)	(1.83)	(4.90)
55–69	3.59	3.44	3.62
	(2.10)	(2.02)	(6.67)
70+	−2.43	−2.25	−8.61
	(3.67)	(3.37)	(13.59)
Race			
Black	10.20*	—	—
	(1.48)		
Hispanic and other nonwhite	−3.12	—	—
	(4.34)		
Income			
Under $10,000	4.50	0.90	25.02*
	(2.55)	(2.60)	(6.94)
$10,000–15,000	0.89	1.14	10.02
	(2.33)	(2.53)	(5.50)
$25,000–50,000	0.85	0.48	5.55
	(1.67)	(1.60)	(5.14)
$50,000 and more	−1.25	1.05	4.48
	(2.02)	(1.92)	(6.67)
Refused to say, don't know	−1.59	−2.02	6.71
	(2.12)	(2.10)	(5.86)
Male	3.14*	2.59*	7.45*
	(1.16)	(1.12)	(3.46)

Table 6.2. (continued)

	Estimated coefficients and standard errors		
Bettor characteristics	Full sample	Whites	Blacks
Percent urban in county	.036	.020	.128
	(.023)	(.021)	(.084)
Intercept	6.72	−0.10	−23.8*
	(3.18)	(3.05)	(10.4)
Log likelihood	−2485.8	−1797.1	−619.9
Mean of dependent variable	3.73	2.71	8.79
Proportion nonzero	.500	.455	.725
	1,051	847	182
$F(z)$	.444	.420	.548

Source: Calculated from unpublished data from survey conducted by the Gallup Organization, Inc., Gallup Study GO 84190, November 1984.

Note: Method of estimation was Tobit. Standard errors are in parentheses. Asterisks (*) denote statistics 2.0 or greater in absolute value. The derivative of the expected expenditure with respect to any right-hand variable is equal to the estimated Tobit coefficient multiplied by $F(z)$.

spending an average of about $4.50 more than whites, other characteristics being the same. This racial difference is so large in this data set that we estimated separate equations for blacks and whites. (The estimated equations are given in Table 6.2.) Lottery expenditures for whites and blacks alike tend to fall with education. This effect is significant only for whites, with the difference between college graduates and those who did not complete high school being almost $5 per week. A similar pattern with smaller differences is observed for blacks, but owing to the small sample the coefficients are estimated very imprecisely. Regarding age, the estimates imply that expenditures on lottery products are lowest for the elderly and highest in the prime earning years of twenty-five to fifty-four. Males spend more than females: the estimates imply a difference of about $1 for whites and $4 for blacks. Surprisingly, expenditures do not vary significantly between urban and rural counties once income, race, and other characteristics are held constant.

The estimated effects of income reflect the patterns previously discussed. Among those who report their income, expenditures are lowest in the $15,000-$25,000 income group, other factors being equal. The highest expenditures are recorded at the under-$10,000 level in the entire sample, a pattern that the separate regressions suggest is limited to black respondents; for whites, there are no significant differences in play by income category.

Other Gambling

The demographic categories used here to describe lottery players give a useful but incomplete picture of who plays the lottery. There are also less readily observable characteristics that affect whether people play regularly, such as personality (do they like to take chances?) and associates (do their friends gamble?). One obvious indicator is the extent of participation in other forms of commercial gambling. People who participate in other kinds of gambling are more likely to play the lottery, and to play it heavily, than people who do not. But the introduction of a lottery does not simply provide those who already participate in commercial gambling, whether legally or illegally, with a new game. Lotteries also recruit a great many people into commercial gambling. The participation rates in state lotteries far exceed participation rates for other forms of commercial gambling.

The most complete survey of gambling participation ever conducted was the 1975 *Gambling in the United States.* A total of 1,735 respondents were interviewed, of whom 907 lived in states that operated lotteries in 1974. Questions were asked concerning participation in all aspects of commercial gambling, both legal and illegal. Overall, 58 percent of lottery-state residents reported gambling at some time during 1974, compared with only 27 percent of residents of nonlottery states. Most of this difference was due to the much higher rates of lottery play by residents of lottery states: comparing the two groups by participation in commercial gambling other than the lottery, we find the lottery state residents "ahead" by a margin of only 34 percent to 23 percent.

These differences are dramatic and strongly suggest that the introduction of a state lottery brings a large fraction of the adult population into commercial gambling. To confirm this conclusion it must be demonstrated that the observed differences in commercial gambling are not the result of other differences between residents of lottery and nonlottery states. Hence, we conducted a multivariate statistical analysis (probit) of participation in commercial gambling for the entire sample, which included variables for sex, race, religion, frequency of church attendance, household income, age, education, the size of the respondent's city of residence, and whether or not the respondent lived in the South. Controlling for all these variables, we found that the likelihood of participation in commercial gambling was still heavily influenced by whether or not the respondent lived in a lottery state. For example, a person with the socioeconomic characteristics associated with a participation probability of 27 percent if living in a nonlottery state had a participation probability of 52 percent in a lottery state. Thus we conclude with considerable confidence that the lottery is a powerful recruiting device, which in 1974 was responsible for inducing about one-quarter of the adult population who would not otherwise have done so to participate in commercial gambling.

The national data do confirm, however, that people who participate in other forms of commercial gambling are more likely than average to play the lottery, if given the opportunity. Indeed for respondents from lottery states, lottery participation was twice as high among gamblers as among those who did not participate in other commercial gambling (74 percent as opposed to 36 percent). We can sum up these results this way: the lottery has an especially strong appeal to established gamblers, but it also creates new ones.

One indication from *Gambling in the United States* is that most commercial gamblers do not specialize in a single type of gambling. Even within the confines of the lottery many players will regularly buy tickets for two or more types of games. To demonstrate the overlap in play among various lottery products we report findings from surveys in Massachusetts and New Jersey. Lotto is very popular in Massachusetts, and, according to one survey commissioned by the state lottery agency, almost everyone who bought lottery tickets played lotto. Overall, 62 percent of adults played at least one game. About half of these played lotto exclusively, and the remainder played lotto in combination with one or both of the other games (numbers and instant games). As might be expected, those who play more than one game usually bet more than those who dabble in only one. For example, those who play only lotto bet an average of about $12 per week, but those who combined lotto with numbers bet an average of $31, and those who played all three bet over $42.[14] The heavy players who account for such a large share of total lottery wagers thus tend to diversify their portfolio of lottery games.

A New Jersey survey affirmed the predominance of lottery players who play more than one game. For example, 22 percent of the population played the numbers game, but among lotto players 43 percent also played numbers.[15] The survey reveals the degree of overlap between participation in the lottery and in other forms of commercial gambling, reinforcing the results reported in *Gambling in the United States*. In general, those who play the lottery are more likely than average to bet on bingo or horse races. And, according to this survey, lottery players are much less likely than average to use cents-off coupons in stores, whereas they are more likely than average to participate in giveaway games. Between the prudent coupon-clipper and the let's-take-a-chance sweepstakes player, there is little doubt who will be in line to buy lottery tickets.

Conclusion

The socioeconomic variables by which social scientists classify people—sex, race, age, religious background, education, income, profession—provide a useful framework in which to understand observed patterns in lottery play. But even when such readily observed characteristics are accounted for, there remains considerable diversity. Ultimately the question of personality enters: some people simply find gambling a more engaging activity than others. When the state introduces a lottery, residents who are already betting on the horses or bingo or the illegal numbers game tend to become regular customers. But the lottery also finds a large following among the majority who had not previously been spending money on commercial games and whose taste for gambling needed the stimulus of the lottery in order to be awakened.

Of course whether and how much someone plays the lottery is not simply a function of circumstances and taste. Also important is the nature and quality of the products being offered by the lottery. In the next sections we consider the determinants of lottery sales which are under the control of the state agency, including the types of games offered, the payout rate, the prize structure, and the amount of advertising.

Influencing Demand

In fiscal 1986 Massachusetts lottery revenues were $193 per capita, the highest in the nation. The lottery with the lowest sales that year was neighboring Vermont, at $23 per capita. Both states had well-established lotteries, offering all three of the major games—lotto, numbers, and an instant game. How can this eight-to-one disparity in per capita sales be explained? What can Vermont and other states with relatively low sales learn from Massachusetts, Maryland, and other states whose lotteries have been sales leaders?

We have described the socioeconomic patterns of lottery participation. Much of the interstate variation in lottery sales is the result of differences in these factors, which are determinants of the gambling propensity of the resident population. For example, 84 percent of Massachusetts residents live in urban areas, compared with only 34 percent of Vermont residents. In Massachusetts sales also are enhanced in comparison with Vermont by the relatively high percentage of residents who are Roman Catholics and/or members of ethnic groups in which participation in commercial gambling has traditionally been high. Such factors help explain the large interstate disparities in sales,[16] but this sort of explanation is not very helpful to the lottery manager seeking to increase sales. Presumably this manager is not in a position to proselytize for the Catholic church or encourage rural residents to move to the city.

A number of actions that *are* available to lottery managers are potentially effective in stimulating sales. First, expanding the product line by introducing a new game will increase total sales. Second, increasing the payout rate on existing games will probably increase sales, and a carefully considered restructuring of the prize offerings may also help in this respect. Third, for the game of lotto an increase in the population base (through joining a consortium of states) will increase sales by making it possible to offer larger jackpots.

Expanding the Product Line

The typical pattern for states that began operating a lottery during the 1980s was to start with the instant game and then introduce one of the on-line games (numbers or lotto) several months or even years later, with the other following after an additional interval. There is a natural concern that introducing a new game will detract from sales of existing games—for example, that given a chance, players may redirect some of their instant game expenditures to playing lotto. If this were to happen, the increase in overall lottery sales would be somewhat less than the sales of the new game. In technical terms the concern is that the several types of lottery games are *substitutes* for one another, just as are, say, different brands of cigarettes. This concern is plausible, especially since most lottery participants play more than one game, given the opportunity. But the evidence clearly indicates that the standard lottery games are not substitutes for one another. Indeed, sales of an existing game or games are unaffected by the introduction of a new one.

Figure 6.4 depicts sales trends for four states that introduced new games during the 1980s. In each case it appears that the sales trend in existing games was unperturbed by the introduction of a new one. Patterns for other states help confirm this remarkable result. In particular, we checked sales trends for numbers and instant games in thirteen states around the time they introduced a lotto game. In each state we compared the average growth rates for the two-year periods before and after the introduction of lotto. In nine of these states the growth rate *increased;* in only four did the growth rate decrease, as would be expected if lotto were a substitute for the other games.[17] Based on this evidence we conclude that the introduction of lotto in a state does not reduce sales of other games; expenditures on lotto come from increased play and new players. The three major games are thus not substitutes for one another.

Another type of evidence provides further support for this conclusion. Lotto sales tend to vary widely from drawing to drawing, depending on the size of the jackpot (as determined by the number of consecutive rollovers from previous drawings). Figure 4.1 in Chapter 4 illustrates this effect. If lotto and other games were substitutes, then the run-up in lotto sales when

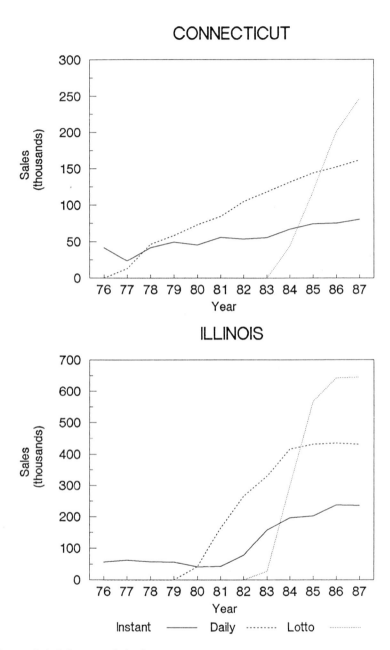

Figure 6.4. Sales trends in four states

(*Source:* Annual reports of state lottery agencies, various years)

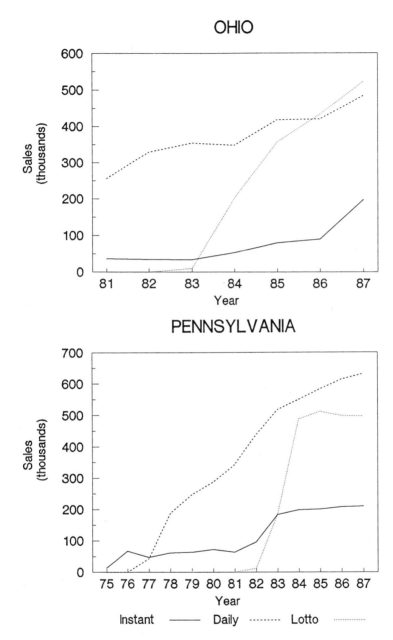

Figure 6.4. (continued)

there is a large jackpot would depress sales of other games. An analysis of Massachusetts numbers sales data for eighty-five consecutive weeks was conducted to test for this possibility; it revealed that the size of the lotto jackpot, which had an enormous effect on lotto sales, had *no* discernible effect on sales of the numbers game. The additional betting on lotto was "new" money.[18]

The evidence presented here is limited to the three major games currently offered. In the future, as new games like keno and sports pools are developed and widely introduced, the pattern may change. But at present the three available games are remarkably independent of one another. For states that do not offer all three games, expanding the product line is virtually guaranteed to increase sales.

Increasing the Payout Rate

Much has already been said about the low payout rate offered by the lotteries. Most states pay about 50 cents in prizes to every dollar of revenue, and in about half the states the authorizing legislation would have to be amended in order to increase this rate. The uniformly low payout rates are likely to persist until persuasive evidence is produced that a higher rate would increase net revenues to the state treasury, and available evidence on this subject is not especially persuasive one way or the other.

The basic issue here is analogous to the attention paid in the field of public finance to the relationship between a tax rate and the amount of tax revenue collected. During the early years of the Reagan administration the economist Arthur Laffer became famous for his claim that lowering the federal income tax rates would increase federal revenues. In the case of the lottery the analogous assertion is that an increase in the payout rate would increase sales by so much that net revenues would increase, despite the reduction in net revenue per dollar of sales.

It would be surprising indeed if an increase in the payout rate did not increase sales somewhat. Given a higher payout rate, the lottery game designers could increase the lotto jackpot or the numbers prize, thus enhancing the appeal. Alternatively, designers could increase the number or size of small prizes in lotto or instant games, thus giving more players the experience of being winners and encouraging them to continue playing. In short, a larger payout rate would give the designers new options for creating attractive prize offerings, which would in turn generate increased action from players whether they evaluated a game on the basis of actuarial science or on instinct.

Interestingly, one common pattern of lottery play—reinvestment of winnings—virtually ensures a sales increase from a higher payout, even if players' evaluation of the game does not change. In a poll conducted for the *Los*

Angeles Times in March 1986 respondents who reported having won money in California's instant game were asked, "When you win, what do you usually do? Do you put the cash in your pocket or do you reinvest your winnings by buying more California lottery tickets with the money you have won?" Only 14 percent reported taking the cash; the rest said they reinvested the winnings (73 percent) or did both about equally (12 percent).[19] If more prize money is paid out, then more will be reinvested, at least for the instant game. The virtually inevitable result is that an increase in the payout rate will increase sales. But the question remains whether the increase would be sufficient to increase net revenue to the state.[20]

This question cannot be answered from the available data. For example, take the case of the numbers game. As of 1986 every state but one offered a payout rate of 50 percent. The exception was Massachusetts, with a payout rate of 60 percent. It is true that Massachusetts' per capita sales were relatively high: 36 percent higher than Connecticut's, for instance, and the difference was greater still compared with other neighboring states. But Massachusetts also has much higher instant game and lotto sales per capita than its neighbors, and for those games its payout rate is no different from theirs. It is thus not feasible to infer what proportion of Massachusetts' numbers sales are due to its high payout rate.[21]

The game of lotto offers slightly more interstate variation in payout rates. In fiscal 1986 nineteen states offered lotto. While most of these had a payout rate of 50 percent, five had lower payout rates. A regression analysis of sales data for lotto did yield a coefficient estimate significantly greater than zero for one specification. Indeed, the point estimate was large enough to suggest that an increase in payout would increase net revenue, although the coefficient was estimated imprecisely enough to leave considerable statistical doubt about this conclusion. Other variables included in this specification were population, per capita income, and percent urban (all positive and significant) and percent black (small and insignificant). Other specifications yielded smaller coefficient estimates on payout rate.[22] Given the multitude of plausible specifications and the small number of observations, this approach does not yield confidence-inspiring estimates.[23]

From the point of view of a lottery agency, increasing the payout rate is an expensive tactic for stimulating sales. (For example, the unit cost of increasing the payout rate by 2 percentage points is equivalent to more than doubling the advertising budget in most states.) While it seems likely that the tactic would be effective in increasing sales somewhat, it is not clear that sales are sufficiently responsive to the payout rate that net revenues would increase. At the level of payout rates currently being offered, an increase in the rate would produce an increase in net revenues only if sales were increased by more than 2 percent for each percentage point hike in the payout rate.[24] In particular, increasing the payout rate from 50 percent to 60 percent would increase net revenues only if sales increased by more than 30 percent as a result.[25] Given currently available evidence, there is no persuasive basis for predicting whether that much of an increase would be likely to occur.

Modifying the Prize Structure

Most players do not care about the payout rate per se; indeed, very few lottery participants even know the payout rate of the games they play. Players *are* concerned about the prizes offered by a game, and presumably different players focus on different aspects of the prize structure—the likelihood of winning some prize, the size of the top prize, or the likelihood of winning a prize that is above some minimum magnitude. While players may not have an accurate impression of the prize structure, they can form some sort of impression from personal experience (and the experience of their acquaintances) in playing the game and from advertising and promotional material. The primary objective in designing a prize structure for a game is to create as favorable an impression on the market as possible within the financial limits of the game. The reason why we expect an increase in the payout rate to increase sales is that the payout rate defines the budget for the prize structure, which if increased would allow changes that would make the prize structure more attractive to at least some potential players. Put another way, the success of a game depends not just on its payout rate but to a large extent on how the payout is structured into prizes.[26]

This point is illustrated with a case study from Ohio. In November 1987 the Ohio lottery introduced a new instant game, Holiday Cash, with an unprecedented payout rate of 75 percent, compared with the normal 50 percent. Holiday Cash sales averaged about $4 million per week during the first month, which was about double the sales rate for the two previous instant games introduced by the Ohio lottery. At first glance this appears to be evidence that sales are highly sensitive to an increase in the payout rate. Subsequent history casts doubt on that interpretation, however, since the two games introduced after Holiday Cash enjoyed sales just as high, despite the fact that these games offered the traditional 50 percent payout rate. Why did sales persist at the new level after the payout rate reverted to the old level? One possible explanation is that Holiday Cash introduced a new prize structure along with the high payout rate. The new structure eliminated prizes above $1,000 and increased the number of smaller prizes. Subsequent games continued to emphasize lower-tier prizes. So it would appear that the new prize structure found a larger market than the old, even with the payout rate at the old level.[27]

Game design is an inexact science at best, but lottery agencies have been quite active in experimenting with changes in prize structures for instant games and lotto. Ohio provides another interesting example, in this case a lotto format experiment. Prior to February 1986 Ohio offered a twice-a-week drawing for a 6/40 lotto game that placed only 43 percent of the prize pool into the jackpot. That month the agency introduced a new 6/44 game, with 70 percent of the prize pool in the jackpot. The two games ran side by side for over a year, with one weekly drawing for each. In April 1987 the old game was dropped in favor of a twice-a-week drawing of the new game. What the agency had learned from this experiment was that the new game had about the same sales as the old when there was no rollover, but that the new game had more rollovers (as one would expect from the format) and as a result generated higher total sales.

The prize structure is an important feature of lotto and instant games, and, unlike in the case of the payout rate, lottery agencies have felt free to experiment. Given the diverse motivations for and styles of playing the lottery (discussed in Chapter 5), it is perhaps not surprising that designing prize structures that will maximize public appeal remains more a matter of trial and error than science.

Increasing the Population Base

For the game of lotto bigger is better. Small states are unable to mount a lotto game that attracts much public interest because the jackpots are inevitably small compared to the multimillion-dollar bonanzas generated in California and New York. As a result, multistate lottery consortiums have formed in order to offer a lotto game that, by combining the populations of several small states, rivals the games of the largest states. The first such consortium was the Tri-State (Maine, New Hampshire, and Vermont). The second was LottoAmerica, initiated in 1988, including the District of Columbia and five widely scattered states with a combined population of about 12 million. The states in both of these consortiums have enjoyed a considerable jump in lotto sales since joining together. Explaining the peculiar economies of scale for lotto requires more than a sentence or two.

Lotto is a parimutuel game, with the jackpot set equal to a percentage of the amount bet (typically about 25 percent). If there is no jackpot winner in a drawing, the money in that jackpot rolls over into the jackpot for the next drawing, as described in Chapter 4. When several players win, the jackpot is divided among them. The explanation of why the population base is important to lotto sales but not sales of other lottery games hinges on the role of the jackpot in attracting lotto action.[28] An example may help explain how this works.

Suppose state A has an adult population of 10 million and state B has only 100,000. Given equally attractive games, we assume that lotto purchases in both states will average $1 per capita at each drawing. In state A the initial jackpot is then worth $2.5 million, compared with only $25,000 in state B. If both states set the probability of winning at 1 in 100,000, then there will be an average of one hundred winners in state A and one winner in state B, with the average prize per winner the same in both states. Given these rules, the games in the two states do not appear to differ much. State A, however, has the option of reducing the probability of winning to, say, 1 in 10 million, in which case there would be only one winner on the average. Under these rules, which state has the more attractive lotto game?

Compared with state B, state A offers one hundred times the jackpot but a much lower probability of winning—1 percent of state B's probability. For reasons discussed in Chapter 5, most players prefer state A's game to state B's. The prize in state A is the stuff that dreams are made of, and in case anyone is not paying attention, the lottery agency will focus its advertising on the magnitude of this jackpot. Yet the correspondingly large difference in probabilities between the two states has little influence on potential players. The failure of intuition to grasp such probabilities, or the belief that the chance of winning is influenced by effort and skill, ensure that probability has less meaning to the average player than to an actuary. As long as most drawings produce a winner, the prospect of winning will be equally credible in both states.

Our statistical analysis of lotto sales data confirms that the number of sales per capita is driven by the size of the jackpot and is quite insensitive to the objective probability of winning that jackpot.[29] Under these circumstances, then, a large population base can generate a more attractive lotto game than a small one. Of course it is these large lotto jackpots that produce much of the folklore of the lottery as well. For a small state that wishes to be part of the lottery action, joining a lotto consortium is a sensible move.

The "Inevitable" Decline in Interest

The conventional wisdom regarding lotteries is that after they have been around for a while, the public loses interest.[30] Maintaining sales requires the introduction of new games or new versions of old games. As in Alice's experience through the looking glass, it is necessary for the lottery agencies to run very fast just to hold their ground. In the words of one observer: "Two considerations motivate the constant search for new ways to dress up the lotteries' ancient arithmetic. The first is the hope that a new combination of price, prize, and gimmick will attract new players. The second is the inevitable decay of a consumer product that . . . is not unlike the hula hoop or Coca Cola, and closer to the hula hoop than Coca Cola."[31]

Is waning interest inevitable? Certainly it is true that new lotteries in the mid-1980s experienced a surge of interest when first introduced, which dissipated quickly. California sold over $120 million in instant game tickets during its first week of operation but by the end of a year was down to about $20 million per week. After this honeymoon period is over, however, the pattern is not one of further decay, as is suggested by the statement just quoted, but rather of more or less steady growth. The introduction of a new game, notably lotto, creates a surge in total sales, but even in the absence of such innovations it appears that growth is the norm in all three types of games. The sales trends in Figure 6.4 support this conclusion.

Perhaps the impression of declining interest is created in comparison with an expectation of very high growth. Per capita sales in lottery states increased at an annual rate of 14 percent in real terms between 1975 and 1985. To sustain this sales trajectory, in which sales double every five years or so, would require major innovations in product and marketing techniques. Recent history suggests that in the absence of such innovations, sales will grow at a moderate rate. Consumers are not going to lose interest in the lotteries anytime soon.

Conclusion

Lottery managers are very much concerned with increasing their "profits," the net revenue that remains after prizes and other costs of doing business are paid. In most circumstances achieving growth in profits requires increasing sales. Recent experience indicates two methods that have enjoyed universal success—adding lotto to the product line and (for smaller states) joining a consortium of states to expand the population base for lotto games. One cannot be so confident about the effects of changing the prize structure of an existing game or changing the payout rate.

The state agencies have been remarkably timid about experimenting with payout rates. Their reluctance may result from the fact that this is a costly strategy for increasing sales on a per unit basis. And while it is certainly to be expected that increasing the payout rate on a game from, say, 50 to 60 percent would increase sales, there is no persuasive evidence that it would stimulate sales enough (more than 30 percent) to increase net revenues. Perhaps if the competition were to increase among states for cross-border sales, the standard 50 percent payout would no longer be tenable.[32]

In addition to the modifications in product line, product design, and payout discussed here, lottery agencies seek to increase demand through marketing and promotion efforts and by increasing the number of outlets. These mechanisms are described in Chapter 10.

Finally, the various methods for increasing sales may also influence the distribution of sales across different population groups. Introducing or expanding the game of lotto brings in more middle-class players, just as the numbers game brought in more minority players. The lottery has a vast and varied market. The contour lines of growth of this market depend in part on the detailed choices of the lottery agencies.

7.

Winners and Losers

And now that I have told of gluttony,
I'll take up gambling, showing you thereby
The curse of chance, and all its evil treat;
From it proceeds false swearing and deceit,
Blaspheming, murder and—what's more—the waste
Of time and money.

—Geoffrey Chaucer, *The Canterbury Tales*

What are the consequences of state lotteries? Previous chapters have examined the demand for lottery products in terms of the motivation to play and the empirical patterns of participation. These patterns tell us what kinds of people are attracted to playing the lottery and thus who are the direct beneficiaries of its creation. Their decision to play indicates that to them the value of the prizes offered and of the process of participating exceeds the cost. Most of these players end up losing money, of course, but that could also be said of other forms of entertainment. Of greater significance is the fact that some people are tempted to gamble more than they can afford, with unfortunate results. At the other end of the spectrum are the big winners, the lucky few who actually realize the dream of riches. Through them the lottery redistributes and concentrates wealth.

Operating a lottery redistributes business activity as well. By becoming lottery outlets small retail shops may gain business at the expense of larger stores. Also, state lotteries have been accused of cutting into other legal forms of gambling, although that claim is not supported by available evidence. More likely is the possibility that the illegal numbers game is losing out to its legal counterpart. The day-to-day decisions about whether and how much to play made by millions of individuals have wide-ranging social ramifications. Indeed the lottery itself—by giving official sanction to gambling, by involving so much of the public, and by bringing so much attention to winners—has far-reaching effects on cultural values. By offering an effortless avenue to wealth, however unlikely, the lottery offers hope to those who might otherwise despair, while perhaps also undermining the commitment to more arduous avenues to success. By encouraging people to gamble in one context, it may encourage other kinds of gambling as well, and may exacerbate the problems some people have in exercising self-control over their gambling. The lottery has a long history of controversy. It is not our objective to perform a comprehensive evaluation of its costs and benefits. Our more modest goal is to describe some of the principal effects of state lotteries and to summarize what is known as well as what remains uncertain about these effects.

How the Lottery Affects Players

For the vast majority of players the lottery is a social activity of minor significance. It involves little expense and offers the small pleasures of trying one's luck, participating in a public event, having something to talk about with friends, and occasionally winning a few dollars. But for the several thousand winners of jackpots worth a million dollars or more, the lottery has undoubtedly made a profound difference. And for still others the lottery has been a cause of financial hardship.

The Benefit of Participation

Is the lottery a waste of money, as Chaucer says about gambling in general? Such a judgment suggests that the lottery should be evaluated simply as a financial asset. But if it is instead viewed as a form of recreation, on a par with dining out or going to the movies, then this judgment is more difficult to defend. As we saw in Chapter 5, playing the lottery offers the pleasures of participation and the excitement of discovering whether one is holding a winning ticket.[1] But beyond this, the lottery supports the dream of a better life.

Like the movies, the lottery offers recreation heavily laden with fantasy. It encourages escape from the everyday demands of job and family to a transformed life. According to Edward C. Devereux, Jr., one of the most thoughtful students of lottery play, it provides a "little window of hope and escape" from the workaday world:

> Although escape is still not a legitimate expectation, the possession of a lottery ticket gives a stamp of authenticity to the hope for escape. The lottery represents a tiny hole in the "closed system" of toil and budgeting, a "safety valve" through which the repressed wishes crowd for escape. This is why the stories of lottery winners make news of never-failing popular interest. The story of a working girl suddenly rich is Cinderella brought to life and made dramatically real.[2]

Of course it is troubling that the fantasy is sustained to such a large extent by ignorance and delusion. The lottery player who believes she has a real chance of winning the California lotto jackpot because *someone* has to win is like a man who buys a worthless remedy for baldness. In both cases the subjective value of the product depends on misinformation. Such cases are the stuff of debates over paternalism and consumer sovereignty. Is the individual's belief that buying the product will make her better off sufficient grounds for concluding that she is in fact better off? If so, the broad participation in the lottery is sufficient to demonstrate that it improves the quality of life for a large segment of the population. Or is there some external standard that can and should be applied in defining welfare? In this case one could argue that the lottery's popularity should be discounted because it stems to a degree from delusions and misunderstandings about the random process that determines who wins.

Outcome Distributions

Most players lose money on the lottery. To illustrate this sobering truth we used a simple computer simulation. For each of three possible betting patterns a random-number generator simulated the outcome of five years of regular play for a thousand hypothetical players using that pattern. The results are summarized in Table 7.1. Pattern A involves betting $2 each day on the daily numbers game—$1 on a straight three-digit number (paying $500 for an exact match) and $1 on a six-way box (paying $80 for three specified digits to appear in any order) of a different number. Over a five-year period (six days each week) the player makes wagers amounting to $3,120. In only 2 percent of these trials did the bettor end up ahead for the five-year period, with the luckiest of the thousand bettors ahead by a net total of $1,520. The other 98 percent of trials produced a net loss, including one trial in which the bettor lost $2,960 on his $3,160 wager. About 58 percent lost half or more of their wager.

The second pattern that we simulated involves a more modest wager of $2 each week on the three-digit numbers game—$1.50 on a three-way box (paying $250) and fifty cents on a front pair (paying $25) of a different number. Using this pattern bettors came out as winners more often (nearly 18 percent of the time) than under pattern A, but the percentage losing half or more of their total wager was still substantial (50 percent). Pattern C reflects the betting of a regular instant game player who buys five tickets each week for a representative instant game with a 50 percent payout. We used the prize distribution for Maryland's Instant Baseball game for the sake of illustration. As shown by Table 7.1, the results for Pattern C are nothing short of dismal,

Table 7.1.   Simulations of three betting patterns in 1,000 trials

Betting pattern[a]	Total amount wagered	Percentage of trials with net gain after 5 years	Greatest net gain	Greatest net loss	Percentag losing more tha half of wager
A	$3,120	2.0%	$1,520	− $2,960	58.1%
B	520	17.6	855	− 520	49.9
C	1,600	0	− 326	− 1,067	62.9

a. Betting patterns defined as:

A: $1 per day on straight bet (three digits in exact order, paying $500) and $1 per day on a six-way box (three different digits in any order, paying $80) six days per week for five years.

B: $1.50 one day a week on a three-way box (any combination with one repeated digit; for exampl 112, 121, 211, paying $250) and fifty cents one day a week on a front pair (for example, 34-, paying $25).

C: $5 each week on an instant game with a distribution of prizes identical to Maryland's Instant Baseball game: of 23,400,000 tickets there were 16 prizes at $25,000 each; 468 at $1,000; 8,658 at $50 46,800 at $25; 173,160 at $10; 542,880 at $5; and 2,152,800 at $2.

with none of our thousand hypothetical players winning the grand prize of $25,000 (with odds of about 1 in 1.5 million). In fact every player lost more than he won.

Although none of these patterns of play is intended to mimic the behavior of actual lottery players, they are consistent with the survey data on lottery play. Each of the three patterns shows a wide range of outcomes in a thousand trials, but few of them involve a net gain over the five-year period. In a majority of trials our hypothetical bettors ended up losing over half the amount wagered.

The Big Winners

A few lottery players not only win but win enough to join the ranks of the wealthy. Most of the huge prizes are awarded in lotto, the most prominent game of the 1980s. The winners of the multimillion-dollar jackpots become instant celebrities. They embody the dream shared by everyone who bets on this longest of long shots. Who are they, and what is their experience?

For some the notion of instant wealth may be reminiscent of the 1950s television series "The Millionaire." In each show a life was transformed (for better or sometimes worse) by the tax-free gift of $1 million from an eccentric philanthropist.[3] Adjusting for inflation, $1 million in 1959 had the purchasing power of about $4 million in 1987 dollars, which is in turn equivalent to a lotto jackpot announced as worth $12 million, after discounting for tax liability and for the fact that payments are typically stretched out over twenty years. Only a handful of lotto prizes during the 1980s were worth as much as those cashier's checks in "The Millionaire." Adopting the more modest standard of a prize worth $1 million after taxes at today's prices implies an announced jackpot of $3 million, and there were about 240 winners in that category in 1987.[4]

The public is understandably fascinated by stories about the big winners. The mass media provide a steady flow of such stories, telling how they won, how winning changed their lives, whether they have any regrets. The sociologist H. Roy Kaplan provided the first systematic study of these winners, based on interviews with thirty-three of the first thirty-seven people to win $1 million in the New Jersey lottery.[5] Some interesting generalizations emerge from this and subsequent work.

The question of *how* or *why* a person won may strike the scientist as foolish. Someone wins by chance, choosing the right lotto combination or buying the winning ticket in a million-dollar drawing. Lottery winners are simply a random sample of players, weighted by expenditure (that is, someone who plays $20 a week is twice as likely to show up in this sample as someone who plays only $10). But this sort of dispassionate answer is not what makes news. Many winners have a "system" for playing the lottery, and these systems are duly reported. And winners are often compelled to find some sort of explanation or meaning for winning. Kaplan heard a number of such explanations, including dream portents, premonitions, and divine intervention. All told, he found that one-third of winners reported religious or psychic experiences that led to their winning.[6]

Winners also tend to make predictable plans for spending their winnings. A spokesman for the Massachusetts lottery who has presented hundreds of winners with their first checks reports that these people typically say that the money is not going to change them; that they plan to take a trip to Disney World (if they have young children) or to Hawaii; and that they hope to buy a new car.[7] Whatever the details, winners enjoy greater opportunities and reduced anxiety about their finances.

But winning can have its problems. Kaplan found that the fame accompanying a big win can create a variety of difficulties: "The instant fame and fortune promised in the glossy lottery ads said nothing about the endless phone calls from well-wishers and pranksters; the countless letters from strangers; and the threats, intimidations, harassment, loss of privacy, and broken relationships with family and friends which often accompany such celebrity status."[8] Winners are the object of envy and greed on the part of relatives, friends, co-workers, and even total strangers, and often find it necessary to quit their jobs and hide from their fame. A reporter for the *New York Times,* after pursuing interviews with some of the million-dollar winners in New York State, concluded that "if there was a common denominator, it was that the first thing most of them did was get an unlisted phone number."[9]

While others envy them, winners are wont to complain that their take is much lower than expected. (Annuity values are typically about half the advertised magnitude of the prize, and taxes take a big bite out of each annual check.) While in some states lottery prizes are exempt from state income taxation, they are never exempt from federal taxes. Inheritance taxes pose a special problem because they are assessed on the annuity value of the remaining payments at the time of the winner's death and must be paid in a lump sum. In addition, before paying out the prize, state agencies may check to determine if winners have unmet financial obligations or are wanted by the law.

> No state is as thorough as California in checking out lottery winners. Every winner who gets a check mailed—that is, every winner in excess of $100—has his or her name run through a computer to compare against the records of 100 different state and local agencies. Whether the winner has any arrest warrants outstanding, whether he or she owes any back federal, state, or local taxes, whether he or she has any back child support or alimony payments due, whether they have received welfare or unemployment payments that might now be recovered, whether there are unpaid student loans or even unpaid traffic tickets becomes immediately apparent.[10]

As luck would have it, two of the first eleven big winners of the California lottery were identified as illegal aliens and were persuaded by the authorities to return home, no doubt leaving forwarding addresses for their annual checks.

In a way the most remarkable finding about the big winners is that they continue to play the lottery. Kaplan reports on the basis of a survey of million-dollar winners in Ohio that on the average, play by men increased from $15 to $16 per week and by women from $7 to $11 per week. Only 18 percent of respondents reported that they rarely or never played anymore.[11] For most big winners, then, achieving the dream does not satisfy the wish.

Perhaps the last word on big winners is owed to the leading expert, H. Roy Kaplan: "Despite their trepidation, the harassment, tax problems, and conflicts with friends and relatives, no one regretted having won or wanted to give the money back."[12]

Losers

Most lottery players lose money, but some lose enough over a long enough period to cause a considerable reduction in their standard of living. By spending much more than they can afford on lottery tickets they suffer, and so do their creditors and dependents. In extreme cases this excessive gambling may lead to or exacerbate criminal involvement, loss of employment, and suicidal despair.

These big losers do not receive the same public attention as the big winners, but there are occasional accounts in the popular press. This letter to Ann Landers tells one story:

> I have been married to "Jim" for 28 years. We have four grown kids and I have always worked to help out with the bills. I've earned a rest and I would love to stay home but I can't. Why? Because my husband spends half of his paycheck every week on lottery tickets . . . If it weren't for the lottery I would have decent furniture, carpets and draperies. He tells me I am lucky he doesn't drink or smoke or chase women. Maybe so, but I feel cheated.[13]

Or consider this confession at a Gamblers Anonymous meeting by a former player of bingo and the lottery:

> Not only did I work two jobs, my wife wasn't well and she had to work. I'd stop at a gas station where they sold lottery tickets. The guy'd stay open for me until I got there. I'd buy $20 worth of lottery tickets and he'd put it on my credit card as a purchase or car repair. You couldn't put lottery ticket purchases on a credit card. I would get my bill each month and pay $200 or so, and the total bill would stay the same or rise some each month.[14]

These stories of middle-class problems contrast with Leo McCord's experience. A resident of one of the poorest ghettos in Chicago, he played the lottery as a form of escape. He started out at $5 a day while he was working but increased his play to as much as $15 a day, even after losing his regular job. "You name it, I did everything short of robbing somebody so I could play." "Everything" for him included collecting pop bottles and working odd jobs. He eventually quit after a friend of his had difficulty collecting a large lottery prize.[15]

Each of these cases involves someone who is judged—by himself or someone else—to be spending more money on the lottery than is appropriate, given his financial circumstances. There is a tendency to label people with costly gambling habits "compulsive gamblers," a term which suggests that their gambling is due to mental illness. (Ann Landers' reply to the letter just quoted was that "Jim" was a compulsive gambler and should be encouraged to seek help.) More generally, the creation of new compulsive gamblers is sometimes identified as the primary social cost of the rapid growth in legal commercial gambling. For example Arnold Wexler, an official with the National Council on Compulsive Gambling, has warned that owing to state lotteries "we are breeding a society of gamblers—and some of them are going to be compulsive gamblers."[16] This definition of the problem represents success for those who have sought to medicalize excessive gambling by defining this form of deviant behavior as a disease.

In recent years the association of certain patterns of excessive gambling with compulsion was given a scientific basis with the publication in 1957 of a treatise by Edmond Bergler entitled *The Psychology of Gambling*.[17] Bergler argued that some gamblers are driven by a masochistic unconscious wish to lose money which causes them to lack control over their gambling. The first in-patient treatment for compulsive gambling was started in 1972 in a Veterans Administration Hospital in Ohio; the same year the National Council on Compulsive Gambling was formed to promote the medical model. A major achievement for this group was the adoption in 1980 by the American Psychiatric Association (APA) of a newly defined diagnosis of pathological gambling. The essential features of this disorder are "a chronic and progressive failure to resist impulses to gamble, and gambling behavior that compromises, disrupts, or damages personal, family, or vocational pursuits."[18] The APA classifies pathological gambling as a disorder of impulse control and offers diagnostic criteria that are modeled after those for abuse of alcohol and heroin and other forms of drug dependence.[19]

A gambler who is led to seek help for his or her problem is most likely to end up attending a meeting of Gamblers Anonymous (GA), which since its start in the late 1950s has grown to over five hundred chapters in the United States and Canada. GA is modeled in almost every respect on Alcoholics Anonymous, including the goal (total abstinence), the twelve steps to cure, the use of first names only, and the parallel group (GamAnon) for relatives. Members admit that they have lost control of their gambling and that they are suffering from a progressive illness.[20]

Once the "problem" is made synonymous with compulsive gambling, it seems natural to attempt to estimate the number of people who suffer from it. One widely noted estimate was offered by the Commission on the Review of the National Policy toward Gambling on the basis of a national survey of gambling participation conducted in 1975. The conclusion was that .77 percent of the adult population (about 1.1 million people) were "probable" compulsive gamblers and another 2.33 percent were "potential" compulsive gamblers. A separate survey of Nevada residents produced an estimate that the prevalence of "probables" there was much higher (2.62 percent) than for the nation as a whole, and concluded: "Not only is the incidence of compulsive gambling higher in Nevada than in the national sample, but the ratio of probables to potentials is as well. This is consistent with the hypothesis that widespread availability of gambling in a legal form leads a portion of those classified as potential compulsive gamblers to actualize their potential compulsion."[21]

More recent polls conducted in Ohio, the Delaware Valley, and New York State in 1984 and 1985 produced estimates of the prevalence of "probable pathological gamblers" between 1.4 percent and 3.4 percent.[22] These estimates are higher than those from the 1975 national survey (as is, of course, the volume of commercial gambling), but differences in scope and definition preclude any firm conclusions about the growth of pathological gambling during the intervening decade. Indeed there is a good deal of debate concerning reliable procedures for diagnosing pathological gambling, and still more about how to measure the prevalence of this disease in a general population.[23]

This concern about the prevalence and treatment of pathological gambling reflects the success of the campaign to medicalize this behavior, attributing the cause to disease and stressing the importance of providing sufficient resources to permit treatment. This perspective has been challenged on the grounds that it detracts attention from the financial problems surrounding excessive gambling. First, the presumption of permanent loss of control has led to a usually fruitless effort to help the gambler become and remain abstinent, rather than attempting to help him manage his money better in gambling situations. More important, the effort to single out a relatively small group as "the problem" creates the impression that gamblers can be neatly divided into two groups ("sick" and "healthy"), whereas, as Henry Lesieur notes, "sociological explanations of pathological gambling tend to recognize that rather than being a state, pathological gambling is the end on a continuum which includes social gamblers at one end and suicide attempters at the other."[24] Another expert has suggested that the terms *pathological* and *compulsive* be replaced with the term *problem gambling: "Problem gambling* is a more accurate term, and is defined as the losing of excessive amounts of money through gambling. (The individual gambler's financial situation, of course, determines how much is 'excessive.') This definition eliminates psychiatric overtones and focuses on the area of greatest concern to gamblers and their families—excessive monetary loss."[25] A study published by the British Home Office proposed the use of the labels *moderate* and *immoderate* gambling, to be distinguished not in terms of craving or loss of control but rather by the social problems engendered by the behavior.[26]

These social problems range from neglect of family responsibilities, to extensive indebtedness to friends, commercial lenders, and loansharks, to criminal activities (embezzlement, employee theft, even street crime) undertaken to repay debts or gain funds for additional gambling. Problem gamblers risk losing family and employment, and there is an elevated likelihood of suicide.[27] Of course gambling is not unique in causing difficulties of this sort. Heavy use of alcohol or illicit drugs is an obvious case in point. Indeed it is logically possible that severe financial problems could result from excessive indulgence in any expensive activity, including stamp collecting, shopping for clothes and jewelry, or taking long vacations from employment. Gambling is simply one more temptation to live beyond one's means, but the social costs it engenders should not be ignored simply because it is not unique. We can be sure that the availability of gambling opportunities will have the effect of impoverishing some dependents, raising the cost to all of us of obtaining a personal loan, and increasing the volume of criminal activity.

But how much does the introduction and promotion of state lotteries contribute to these social problems? The direct effect is probably quite small. First, the total wager for lotteries, $13 billion in 1987, is small compared to the overall addition to consumer indebtedness during that year of about $80 billion. Second, lottery play lacks some of the attributes that are thought to be conducive to excessive gambling: continuous action, short payout interval, substantial demands on the knowledge and decision-making skills of the player, and availability of credit.[28] It is a "soft" form of gambling, whereas casino and sports betting are "hard." Nevertheless, far more people participate in the lottery than in any other form of commercial gambling, and some of them obviously do bet beyond their means. Lesieur believes that the best available data on this matter come from the 800-GAMBLER hot-line tabulations in New Jersey, a state where nearly every form of commercial gambling is available. During one period 17 percent of those who called this hot line indicated that excessive lottery expenditures were their problem, or part of their problem.[29]

A direct test of the influence of gambling on social problems would require data on social indicators such as personal indebtedness and bankruptcies, crime rates (including crime in the workplace), and rates of divorce and suicide. Even given such data for an extended period (before and after the introduction of the state lotteries), we would still face the difficult problem of controlling for changes in availability of other forms of gambling and other relevant factors. Satisfactory studies of this sort are not yet available.[30]

We are left with only a smattering of evidence on how the lotteries affect the volume of gambling-related social costs. For some people who feel themselves to be in trouble with their gambling, the lottery is the primary or only form of involvement. Most other problem gamblers also play the lottery, but to a lesser degree than other forms of play. Some of these people may have been introduced to commercial gambling through the lottery. More gener-

ally, the visibility and promotion of the lottery and the widespread participation in commercial gambling that it engenders may help create a climate
that supports and encourages gambling. Those whose circumstances and in-
clinations place them at risk of being lured into a pattern of excessive gambling may be more likely to do so if gambling is omnipresent in their social
and cultural environment.[31]

Conclusion

Some states have recognized that their introduction and promotion of a lottery will have harmful consequences for some players and that some effort
should be made to redress this harm. For example, by law Iowa earmarks .5
percent of gross lottery revenue to assist individuals and families in difficulty
because of gambling. A recent performance audit for the Pennsylvania lottery concluded that a program of this sort should be created and that financing
it should be considered a cost of doing business.[32]

While it seems appropriate for the states to take seriously the harmful
consequences of the lotteries and other forms of legal gambling, there is an
open question about what sort of program would do the most good. Support
for medical treatment of those labeled pathological gamblers is of unproven
effectiveness. A public campaign to educate the public might be somewhat
more effective, especially if it were not undermined by the lottery's promotional advertising.

One conclusion can be stated with assurance: the enormous and continuing
growth in legal commercial gambling of all kinds will result in a corresponding
increase in the number of people who are losing more money than they can
afford. Lotteries share the responsibility for this problem.

Commercial Interests

A lottery causes substantial redistribution of wealth among individuals, in
effect taking money from the great majority of players and concentrating it
on the relatively few. But the lottery may also be viewed in the context of
commerce, where it also creates winners and losers. About 5 percent of the
lottery handle is retained by the retailers who sell the tickets, and 5 percent
goes for administration and operating expenses, much of it paid to private
contractors. The retailers and contractors who receive the lottery's business
presumably profit and can thus be counted as winners. Firms such as Scientific Games and Southland Corporation (owners of the 7-Eleven convenience
store chain) have been active supporters of lottery adoption campaigns (see
Chapter 8). The lottery also affects other forms of gambling. Legal commer-

cial gambling interests in states without lotteries have opposed adoption for fear of losing business, although the evidence suggests that this fear is probably not justified.

Retailers

Among the redistributional effects of introducing a state lottery one of the most visible is the business it provides certain industries. One obvious group of beneficiaries is the suppliers of lottery products, a relatively small number of national firms that design games, produce tickets and computer software and equipment, and offer marketing advice. Chapter 9 discusses the role these firms play in the operation of state lotteries.

Other businesses may benefit from lotteries at the retail end. The liquor stores, convenience stores, newsstands, and grocery stores that sell most lottery tickets have certainly seen an influx of customers in the form of lottery players. Commissions from selling lottery tickets, averaging a nickel per ticket, constitute a modest increase in the revenues of most stores.[33] But does selling lottery tickets make a store more profitable, owing either to the lottery commissions or to a concomitant increase in retail sales? The answer appears to be yes. An executive of Southland Corporation explains why his 7-Eleven stores are lottery retailers:

> I make a profit on every transaction, but that's not the reason. In an industry where rent is frequently in excess of 5% and labor always in excess of 12%, it would take some extremely creative accounting to believe that selling a product with a 5-6% profit will pay [its] way.
> The reason I want to have a lottery machine in [my] stores is because I believe that it brings traffic through the door; customers who will spend money on other, more profitable products.[34]

The principal advantage of having a lottery machine may, in fact, be defensive: *without* the machine a store may lose business to others with one.

Of the major types of retail firms selling lottery tickets, those most likely to be affected are convenience stores. Their locations and hours of operation make it easy for a bettor to place a bet. In addition, their nonlottery business stands to gain at the expense of their major competitors—grocery stores, drugstores, and gas stations. In order to prove whether lottery sales in fact give a boost to convenience stores, we examined the relationship between these sales and convenience store business by state from 1979 to 1983. We found that increases in lottery sales were associated with both increases in per capita convenience store sales and the share of food sales accounted for by convenience stores.[35] These findings provide some support for the notion that lotteries pull in customers for nonlottery products. Liquor stores may benefit for similar reasons.

As the fortunes of some industries rise, those of others decline. By and large these adjustments are small and diffuse. Even when they are noticeable, as in the case of lottery suppliers or retail merchants, the primary effect is one of expansion of output rather than permanently higher profits. This expansion is simply the private market manifestation of the increase in economic resources devoted to lotteries.

Commercial Gambling

In some states the campaigns for adopting a lottery have been opposed by existing commercial gambling interests concerned that gamblers would spend their gambling dollars on the lottery rather than betting on the horses or playing bingo. One journalist, writing about the first day of the Florida lottery, noted that its "corner-store convenience and the state government's boosterism" spelled trouble for the state's racetracks, "which are bracing for business declines."[36] A more optimistic view holds that the lottery is not a substitute but rather attracts a new clientele to commercial gambling and draws additional money from existing bettors. Some of those who are initiated into gambling by the lottery may even graduate to more sophisticated forms of gambling such as betting on races.[37]

Is the lottery a complement to or a substitute for other forms of gambling? The National Study of Gambling (NSG) remains the most comprehensive study of its kind. We conducted a multivariate analysis of the survey data, using as a dependent variable the participation and level of play in all forms of commercial gambling excluding lotteries. One conclusion we drew is that the prevalence and level of betting on all other forms of commercial gambling combined were not affected by the lottery. Survey respondents living in lottery states bet the same amount on the average as other respondents with the same socioeconomic characteristics. It should be noted that the survey was conducted in 1975, before the introduction of on-line games; the result might be different now. But at that time at least, lottery expenditures were not detracting from other forms of play.[38]

The plausibility of this result is supported by the finding reported in Chapter 6 of independence among the principal types of lottery games. If lotto sales are independent of instant game and numbers sales, then it is certainly possible that lottery sales as a whole are independent of racetrack and casino betting. Before turning to the direct evidence on those forms of gambling, let us consider the effect of lotteries on a more obscure but quite important form of play: charity games.

As of 1987 the sale of charity game tickets by nonprofit organizations was legal in a number of states, including sixteen of those operating a lottery. These tickets are quite similar to instant game tickets in appearance and in the type of "action": the player pulls tabs on the ticket to reveal symbols which indicate the prize, if any. Prizes are paid on the spot in cash. Only a few states keep good records of charity game sales. Remarkably, in 1985 these games outsold the lottery in two of the states (Washington and New Hampshire) and came close in a third (Maine). The only analysis of growth patterns in charity games has been made for the trade association representing charity game ticket manufacturers. It is nevertheless persuasive in concluding that charity games and instant games do not cut into each other's sales, despite the apparent similarity between the games.[39]

Betting at racetracks has been stagnant or declining in many states, but that trend appears to be due to factors other than the lottery, since the decline is not limited to states with lotteries. Two studies of the thoroughbred parimutuel handle report that the introduction of a lottery does reduce racetrack betting, but both studies have significant flaws that leave the issue in doubt.[40] Unlike parimutuel betting, casino betting increased during the 1980s, despite concern among Nevadans that the introduction of the California lottery would curtail this growth. The California lottery opened for business for the last quarter of 1985. The annual growth rate in taxable gaming revenues was about 8 percent from 1983 to 1985, and increased slightly to an average of 8.8 percent for the subsequent two years.[41] While this evidence is by no means decisive, it supports the conclusion that the lottery had little or no effect on casino play.

Illegal Gambling

While it appears that the lottery is not cutting into revenues from other forms of legal commercial gambling, it is possible that it has caused a reduction in one form of illegal gambling—the numbers game. The evidence on this issue, although inconclusive, is worth reviewing.

Historically the public concern with regard to illegal gambling has stemmed from the widespread belief that the profits are enormous and go to support other more harmful activities of organized crime. According to two experts on illegal gambling:

> For a quarter-century, from the time of the Kefauver Committee in 1950 to about the mid-1970s, illegal gambling played a prominent role in accounts

of organized crime's power in America. Senator Kefauver asserted that organized crime dominated illegal gambling, including bookmaking, casinos, and numbers and that control of illegal gambling was central to the income and power of organized crime . . . Similar statements were made by other official bodies.

In 1970 the Nixon administration launched a campaign against organized crime with the creation of a number of Organized Crime Strike Forces, which for five years were predominantly concerned with gambling.[42] This intense effort at the federal level was in marked contrast to local efforts; local anti-gambling enforcement typically received very low priority although the police nonetheless shared the federal law enforcement officials' concern.[43]

The repeated assertions that illegal gambling was highly lucrative and monopolized by organized crime were challenged in a federally funded study conducted by Peter Reuter and Jonathan Rubinstein, published in 1982[44] and in a report the following year published by the Internal Revenue Service.[45] After carrying out a long-term study of bookmaking and numbers in New York during the late 1970s, Reuter and Rubinstein concluded that the numbers game was not controlled by any single operator or group but rather that it was quite competitive. The average "bank" in New York was small, handling $2 million of wagers and netting just $50,000. In their opinion the market could not be effectively monopolized unless a single police department had sole jurisdiction and was thoroughly corrupt.[46]

The Internal Revenue Service report in effect gave official sanction to Reuter and Rubinstein's conclusions. Based largely on the National Study of Gambling survey conducted in 1975, the report estimated that illegal gambling generated revenues of $3 billion from a handle of $15.7 billion. Both of these figures were less than one-third the estimates published four years earlier by the IRS.[47]

Whether or not the concern about organized crime was valid during the 1970s, it did serve as justification for introducing new forms of legalized gambling. The introduction of legal numbers games, beginning in the mid-1970s, was hailed as a means of undercutting their illegal counterpart, on which they had been closely modeled.[48] While some evidence suggested that the introduction of the lottery had little or no impact on illegal gambling before 1975,[49] it was entirely plausible that the numbers game would be different. Given the alternative of a legal numbers game, why would bettors stay with the illegal version?

More than a decade later we know that the illegal numbers game has not disappeared in the face of legal competition. Some players continue to use the illegal version because placing bets is more convenient, the numbers retailers are willing to extend credit, and the minimum bet is smaller.[50] It has frequently been asserted that another reason why the illegal game retains its customers is that it offers a higher effective payout. But this claim is not well founded. For example, Reuter and Rubinstein report that the New York City game typically paid $600 on a $1 straight three-digit bet, which certainly appears more attractive than the $500 payout on the state game. But this difference is eroded by several practices and problems unique to the illegal game. First, winners are expected to tip the retailer 10 percent, so the net prize is actually only $540 for a $1 bet. Second, payouts on popular numbers are cut to a fraction of the normal level. And third, there is always a chance that a winner will not be paid at all, given the uncertainties of doing business in the underworld.[51] It is true that the tax laws may give an edge to the illegal game, since illegal winnings are readily concealed. But the state lotteries also make it easy to evade taxes on prizes of less than $600 by not reporting these to the federal authorities. In some states the practice of running computer checks on winners' names may push welfare recipients and people wanted by the authorities toward the illegal game. With that exception, the illegal game has no clear edge on payoffs. Convenience, flexibility, and credit preserve it in the face of legal competition.

It is ironic that in two respects the introduction of legal numbers may have strengthened the illegal version. First, the state lottery supplies intense advertising and promotion that may encourage numbers play generally, regardless of whether it is legal or illegal. And second, the legal game has provided illegal operators with a solution to the problems of how to choose and publicize the winning number each day. Illegal operators now take bets on the state drawing, thus assuring their customers that the drawing is not rigged and enabling them to find out the winning number each day simply by watching the televised drawing.[52] Furthermore, if the illegal game is being run on the state's drawing, then the illegal numbers banker who is holding too many bets on a popular number can protect himself by "laying off" some of them at his local lottery outlet. Then, if the number hits, he can pay off his customers with his winnings from the legal game.

So *has* the illegal numbers game lost business as a result of the widespread introduction of legal games? Unfortunately there are no reliable data for measuring this trend. The most widely disseminated estimate of the illegal numbers handle, published in the trade journal *Gaming and Wagering Business,* is generated each year by use of a formula rather than by direct observation.[53] The formula specifies that an increase in legal numbers play will be associated with an increase in illegal play. While this formula was first promulgated by the Internal Revenue Service,[54] it is not based on evidence that a positive relationship does in fact exist between legal and illegal play. Indeed a smattering of proof, mostly anecdotal, suggests that the true relationship is negative, that in some regions, at least, the illegal game may have been undercut by the legal one.[55] Whatever the truth of the matter, it is clear that the early hopes for the legal numbers game as a means of eliminating crime have not been realized. Even if the illegal numbers game were to vanish, it is hard to imagine that the power of large criminal organizations would be much diminished. The revenues from the drug rackets far exceed any that illegal gambling ever provided for organized crime.[56] Rather, the impetus for eliminating the illegal numbers game now comes from concerns that it is depriving the legal game of sales. A headline in the *Chicago Tribune* tells the new story: "State Lottery Losing Millions to Illegal Rackets, Police Say." The illegal game is just another form of tax evasion when there is a heavily taxed legal game in place.[57]

The Lottery and Social Values

While the lottery redistributes the economic pie in various ways, it may also change the quality of life over the long run. Many would argue that the public's fascination with the lottery and other forms of gambling undermines the values that contribute to economic productivity, thus making us all losers.

Commonly held beliefs about work, self-determination, patience, and the importance of material well-being represent a capital stock of great importance to economic growth. If members of the next generation are persuaded that the way to get ahead is through education, hard work, and deferred gratification, then our old age pensions are secure. But if they come to believe that success is a matter of luck, or that there is no point in working hard when an effortless play of the lottery can have the same effect, then the whole society suffers. A 1984 Gallup poll found that 20 percent of Americans agreed with the statement that the only way to get ahead is by playing the lottery.[58] For some that may be an accurate assessment of their circumstances, but whatever its truth, it surely is a view that encourages passivity and economically unproductive behavior.

It is of course difficult to determine whether the lottery is eroding the work ethic. But there is no question that children are exposed to much celebration of the lottery on television, with all the implied lessons about instant, effortless wealth. And gambling among children is increasing, with a sizable percentage playing the lottery on a regular basis.

Every state lottery law prohibits the sale of lottery tickets to minors, presumably on much the same basis that alcoholic beverages and tobacco products are restricted to adults. But minors are in fact able to buy lottery tickets. When he came to California to speak out against the adoption of a lottery in

1984, Arizona Governor Bruce Babbitt called the ban on sales to minors unenforceable, saying that lottery tickets were "part of the culture" at the public school his children attended.[59] A study in Delaware reported that several retailers were observed selling tickets to children under eighteen.[60] Comparative data on play by children in different states are not available, but some survey information does exist on gambling by high school students. It indicates that a majority of high school students have gambled for money and that where legal, lotteries have become part of that gambling. A survey of high school juniors and seniors in New Jersey found that 45 percent had played the state lottery or the illegal numbers game and that 13 percent did so weekly. A similar study of tenth through twelfth graders in Quebec found that 39 percent had played the lottery in the last year. Both studies identified pathological gamblers among these students.[61]

One possible response to such findings is that lottery play by teenagers, regrettable as it may be, represents no more than a redirection of a proclivity that already existed. The main question is whether state lotteries cause an increase in the amount of gambling by minors. If gambling behavior by the young is like that of adults, lotteries are not a substitute for other forms of gambling but in fact tend to increase participation. To our knowledge only one study exists that can shed light on this issue. Two surveys of ninth to twelfth graders were conducted in a group of high schools in southern California in 1984 and 1987. Since the California state lottery did not begin until 1985, differences in gambling behavior between the two years could reflect the introduction of the lottery. The survey results show that gambling among high school students increased sharply over the period. Of those who reported gambling in the second survey, 40 percent had played the lottery, more than for any other form of gambling.[62]

These results clearly indicate that some minors are playing state lotteries, although it is difficult to judge how many. Enforcement of minimum age requirements probably differs among states and among retailers within states. To the extent that children are playing lotteries, those who are concerned about the social effects of lotteries may have more to worry about than was previously thought. This concern would be heightened if the availability of legal lotteries has led to an increase in the total amount of gambling by minors.

Conclusion

Some of the lottery's effects are baldly redistributional: many lose so that a few might win. For the most part the amounts lost are not great, and in fact the voluntary nature of participation suggests that even most of the "losers" get something over and above the financial return out of playing. Yet the easy normative conclusions of welfare economics are clouded to the extent that lottery players make purchases based on poor information or incorrect calculations. Especially troublesome is the spectacle of problem gamblers, whose excesses create serious economic hardships.

The lottery can be seen as a risky experiment to determine whether a system that allocates rewards on the basis of luck will undermine a parallel system that allocates rewards, at least in part, on the basis of effort and skill.[63] Unfortunately the answer, if one ever becomes clear, may not emerge until after it is too late to reverse the process.

PART III

The Government's Business

8.

State Politics and
the Lottery Bandwagon

The people want it.

—Governor John W. King of New Hampshire, 1963,
commenting on the proposal for a state lottery

For the first six decades of the twentieth century lotteries were prohibited throughout the United States. New Hampshire broke the ice in 1963, and first New York and then the rest of the Northeast followed by the mid-1970s. During the 1980s states in every region adopted lotteries, and by 1988 two-thirds of the nation's population lived in states that were actively promoting the sale of a commodity that had been illegal twenty-five years earlier. The cautious start and increasing momentum of the adoption bandwagon makes an interesting story, one that has often taken the form of the public demanding what their most respected political and religious leaders did not want them to have. With the growth of the lottery business has come a change in the politics of adoption, as lottery suppliers and other commercial interests have become increasingly instrumental in the effort to expand the domain of lotteries. But the basic concerns and conflicts of these campaigns have remained the same, as has the basic fact of political life in a democracy: an idea with broad popular support cannot be resisted forever.

Two pairs of forces have been at work in these adoption campaigns. On the side of the lottery are its popularity and its potential to generate revenue for the state. Opposition takes the form of moral objections to gambling as well as concerns about the lottery as a revenue source. Among the latter are objections that the lottery takes advantage of the poor, that it encourages excessive gambling, and that it is an inefficient way to raise public revenue. The politics of adoption can be characterized as a holding action by lottery opponents, a minority attempt to fend off legislation that would allow the majority to have its way. Although the majority eventually wins in most states, opponents have been remarkably successful in at least delaying adoption in a number of cases.

The story begins with the widespread popularity of the lottery itself. This appeal is not abstract. People simply want to play the game. Voters, given the chance to decide for themselves, have almost always approved state lotteries. Whatever the social and cultural forces that underlie popular attitudes toward gambling, its appeal is central to an understanding of the politics of adoption.

If the lottery issue were to be decided in the statewide equivalent of a town meeting, then the majority would rule quickly and easily. But in the decision-making processes of representative government the will of the majority is not implemented so easily. Lottery bills, like any others, can be tied up in legislative committees, sidetracked by parliamentary maneuvering, or, if finally passed by both houses of the legislature, vetoed by the governor. This system of multiple hurdles, which in most states works similarly to the federal legislative process, was intentionally designed to protect minority interests and resist quick adoption of faddish innovations.[1] The history of the struggle to adopt a lottery in most states includes a string of failed efforts before eventual success. But once in place, no lottery has yet been seriously challenged or threatened with termination.

Despite the apparent widespread support, state lotteries have not figured prominently in elections. A dramatic exception occurred in Kentucky in the 1987 Democratic gubernatorial primary, when a dark-horse candidate, Wallace Wilkinson, won the nomination over former governor John Y. Brown and several other candidates apparently because of his energetic support for a lottery. Still, numerous other elections have demonstrated that favoring a lottery does not guarantee victory any more than opposing it ensures defeat.

The second force on the side of the lottery is the state's need for revenue. Although lottery revenues may not be large in relation to the entire state budget, projections of lottery revenues have been a prominent feature in debates over adoption. Voters may see the lottery as a way to forestall tax increases, although they may be deluded about how much money a lottery can raise. Consider this statement by Jack Gordon, the sponsor of a lottery bill in the Florida Senate in 1985: "There is no question in my mind that a personal income tax would be a more efficient way of getting money. The question is, who is going to pass it? Not me . . . Every time we talk about a tax, people say try a lottery. So we should get that out of the way."[2]

Campaigns for lottery adoption have stressed that the lottery will act as a "painless tax" that can be put to good use in supplying state services. In many cases this promise has been made specific by earmarking lottery revenues for some designated expenditure such as education. A vote for the lottery, then, can be represented as a vote for better schools. While proponents stress such high-minded objectives, the bulk of public support doubtless stems from a fact that is scarcely mentioned in the adoption campaigns: people simply want to play.

As we have seen, opposition to lottery adoption comes from religious groups that view gambling as immoral, as well as from civic-minded spokesmen who see a lottery as inconsistent with principles of good government. Many political leaders have argued that it is not in the public interest for government to promote gambling or to become dependent on lottery revenues. They typically stress such drawbacks as the fact that lottery revenues vary from year to year and come from what amounts to a highly regressive tax, and they note the inappropriateness of the state's encouraging people to gamble.

These battle lines have been evident from the first debates over adoption. Increasingly, however, a new element has acted as a catalyst for change: the active lobbying of firms involved in the sale of lottery products. During the 1980s the campaigns for lottery adoption became increasingly well funded and organized, with most of the funding coming from the private companies that supply lottery tickets and computer equipment. This business grew from nothing in 1970 to a quarter of a billion dollars in 1986,[3] and the suppliers' ability to act effectively in the political arena grew correspondingly. These companies have hired lobbyists to persuade state legislators to vote for adoption, and in some cases they have supported petition campaigns to place lottery referendum measures on the ballot in states where legislatures were not willing to do so. Another economic interest group that has been increasingly active is the convenience store chains, whose retailers stand to profit from the increased business associated with an influx of lottery customers. These private interests have been successful in a number of instances. Several case studies of adoption campaigns help illustrate how private financial interests have combined with popular support to overcome the opposition from religious groups and political leaders.

The Politics of the Earliest Lotteries

In contrast to recent lottery adoptions, the first lottery states were moving into unknown territory. Let us see how these pioneers proceeded.

New Hampshire

From the perspective of twenty-five years the adoption of the first modern lottery in the United States seems highly noteworthy. But, like many firsts, this lottery did not swagger in the knowledge that it would become the leader of a long procession. On the contrary, it was unsure of itself and of the demand for its product, and wary of the potential effect of federal lottery laws on the out-of-state sale of tickets.

In understanding the politics of lottery adoption in New Hampshire in the early 1960s the primary fact to consider is that the idea of a lottery was neither alien nor brand new. Lottery bills had been introduced in the state legislature as far back as 1937, and in 1955 one of these was passed, only to be vetoed by the governor. Indeed the idea of government-run lotteries had been discussed in the Northeast since the depression. Massachusetts had considered lottery bills in 1941 and 1950, and the legislatures of Rhode Island and Vermont were debating the issue in 1963. There were also proposals for national lotteries, among them New York Congressman Paul Fino's regular bills in Congress. In addition, by 1963 New Hampshire and the rest of the Northeast had considerable experience with commercial gambling in general. Like most of the other states in the region New Hampshire had already legalized horse racing. The legalization of bingo in New York and New Jersey during the 1950s and the intense debate over off-track betting in New York heightened the general awareness of legalized gambling. "It was in the air" is perhaps too loose a way to describe the attitude toward legal gambling in the Northeast in 1963, but the prospect of a legalized sweepstakes was certainly not seen as out of the bounds of political feasibility. While lotteries and legalized gambling were not universally embraced in New Hampshire, the idea had gained a certain familiarity.[4]

A second piece of the puzzle was New Hampshire's peculiar revenue structure. The state took New England's traditional reliance on property taxes to an extreme, adding only scant state supplement to locally raised revenues. Having neither a sales tax nor an income tax, the state gained over half its revenue from excise taxes on tobacco, horse racing, and alcoholic beverages.[5] New Hampshire ranked lowest in the nation in state aid to education. Demographically the state was distinctive in other ways. New Hampshire had a relatively high proportion of foreign-born population, and the percentage of Catholics (over a third) was well above the national average.[6] Although it was viewed as a bastion of conservative Yankee puritanism, the state was in fact more mixed than the stereotype suggested.

The legislative debate in 1963 featured arguments that would continue to be used in adoption struggles for decades to come. Supporters emphasized the revenue that a lottery would bring in. Not only could it stave off a long-resisted state sales tax, but it could be used to help the state's schools. Moral opposition, stressing traditional values, was led by such groups as the New Hampshire Council of Churches and the Christian Civic League. Other opponents warned that the lottery would invite organized crime. To the surprise of many, the lottery bill passed both houses of the state's Republican-controlled legislature. Governor John King, a Democrat, who as a legislator had twice voted for lottery bills, deliberated for days and then made his announcement to a packed legislative session. Noting that the bill had received support from both parties, the governor said he was satisfied that a majority of the people wanted a lottery. He sounded a populist note: "I am unwilling to set myself up as a Solomon or a Caesar in the holy assumption that my views are more intelligent or discerning or moralistic than those of our people." Indeed, there were still hurdles to be cleared before the bill would become law. The legislature had to authorize funds to operate the lottery, and the scheme would not be activated until a referendum in 1964, in which towns could vote to exclude the sweepstakes by local option.[7] In signing the bill, the governor joined supporters in expressing confidence that the state could operate the lottery "on a high plane," in the same way in which the state's liquor stores were run. The plan called for tickets to be sold only at racetracks and the state-run liquor stores, with only two drawings a year.

One dark cloud that hung over the adoption deliberations in New Hampshire was the degree to which federal gambling laws would restrict a state lottery. In addition to the antilottery laws that had been passed in the last century in order to close down the Louisiana lottery, an excise tax on wagering had also been levied. The Internal Revenue Service had announced its intention to apply the tax to the new lottery, but the state sidestepped the plan by basing drawings on horse races, which were explicitly exempted from the wagering tax.[8] Laws restricting interstate transport of tickets or lottery advertising were also a source of concern, given the state's evident desire to sell tickets to citizens of neighboring states. The uncertainty was so great that authorities even had to seek a ruling on whether the lottery referendum could be discussed on television during the 1964 campaign. The federal government eventually allowed the state to use the mails for advertising but forbade their use for ticket purchases. New Hampshire's lottery scheme thus faced obstacles unknown to lotteries in the 1980s. Yet the federal regulations were anything but damaging to the state's marketing objective: in the first year of operation 80 percent of New Hampshire Sweepstakes tickets were sold to residents of Massachusetts, New York, and Connecticut.[9]

New York

Adoption in New Hampshire paved the way for New York State to follow. The lottery was placed on the political agenda in 1965 by legislators searching for sources of revenue that would not bear the stigma of a new tax. (The sales tax had been raised 2 percent in 1964 at Governor Nelson Rockefeller's request.) Legislative leaders proposed a constitutional amendment to create a lottery modeled closely on New Hampshire's, with proceeds earmarked for state aid to public schools.[10] Legal commercial gambling was already well established in New York in the form of bingo and parimutuel betting on horse racing. State law required two separately elected legislatures to endorse the lottery amendment: it sailed through both houses of the legislature in 1965 and again in 1966 and was placed on the ballot for public ratification. Meanwhile, other states toyed with the lottery idea but rejected it. Between 1963 and 1965 legislatures in Florida, Rhode Island, Vermont, Connecticut, Maine, and West Virginia voted down lottery bills.

In the campaign leading up to the referendum in New York opponents were more visible than supporters. Both the Republican and Democratic candidates for governor were opposed, with only the Liberal party candidate, Franklin D. Roosevelt, Jr., in favor. Governor Rockefeller called the lottery "the most retrogressive taxation you can get." The fifteen-member Board of Regents, the governing board of the state public education system, voted unanimously to oppose the lottery, saying, "We believe that attempts to support public education by the lottery involve serious moral considerations and, in our opinion, are inconsistent with the goals of education." And the *New York Times,* which had earlier editorialized in favor of the lottery on the grounds that as long as gambling was going to exist anyway, it might as well be subject to taxation, came out against the amendment because of concerns about the earmarking provision: "In the long run this would work to the disadvantage of education, because future legislatures might consider that this source of income guaranteed to education all the funds it needed." But on November 8, 1966, 61 percent of the voters said yes to the lottery, and the second largest state in the union was set to launch its first public lottery since the nineteenth century.[11]

The Proliferation of Lotteries

In the early 1970s lotteries spread throughout the Northeast and parts of the Midwest. New Jersey began lottery operations in 1970 and had been joined by ten other states by 1975. From Michigan to Maryland to Maine a total of 36 percent of the nation's population lived in lottery states. After a lull of several years, during which Vermont was the only new entrant, another wave began rolling in 1980 that had engulfed most of the country by the end of the decade. There were three adoptions in 1980 (including the first western states, Arizona and Colorado), one in 1982, five in 1984, five in 1986 (including the first southern state, Florida), and two in 1987. By 1988, 66 percent of the population lived in lottery states.

An interesting aspect of these adoptions is the number that were ultimately decided at the ballot box. Because the antilottery sentiment of the nineteenth century had resulted in constitutional bars against lotteries in most states, referenda or initiatives were often required to bring about the necessary changes in state constitutions. In some cases legislatures were only too happy to pass the buck to the voters rather than take full responsibility for bringing a lottery into being. Table 8.1 summarizes the outcome of these votes. In state after state voters gave ringing endorsements to government-run lotter-

Table 8.1. Public votes on state lottery adoptions, 1964–1988

Year	State	Percentage in favor	Year lottery began
1964	New Hampshire	76%	1964
1966	New York	61	1969
1969	New Jersey	81	1971
1972	Michigan	73	1972
	Iowa	67	1985
	Maryland	77	1973
	Washington	62	1982
1973	Rhode Island	76	1974
	Maine	72	1974
	Ohio	64	1974
1976	Vermont	72	1978
1980	Arizona	51	1981
	District of Columbia	64	1982
1981	Colorado	60	1983
1984	Oregon	66	1985
	California	58	1985
	West Virginia	66	1985
	Missouri	70	1986

Table 8.1.   (continued)

Year	State	Percentage in favor	Year lottery began
1986	Idaho[a]	60	1989[b]
	Kansas	64	1987
	Montana	69	1987
	North Dakota	45	—
	South Dakota	60	1987
	Florida	64	1988
1987	Virginia	57	1988
1988	Idaho[a]	52	1989[b]
	Indiana	62	1989[b]
	Kentucky	61	1989[b]
	Minnesota	59	1989[b]
	North Dakota	42	—

Source: See Table A.7. Connecticut, Illinois, Massachusetts, and Pennsylvania enacted their lotteries without holding a public referendum.
a. A legal challenge to the 1986 vote necessitated a second referendum in 1988.
b. Projected.

ies. Of the nearly thirty referenda on lotteries since 1964, only a handful have failed, and three of those proposals—California in 1964, Nevada in 1968, and Colorado in 1972—would have authorized private firms to run lotteries, turning most of the proceeds over to the states. The only state to turn down a state-run lottery is North Dakota, where voters said no in 1986 and again in 1988. In the twenty-seven winning referenda the average level of support was 65 percent. This success is all the more striking when compared to the outcome of votes on other forms of gambling over the same period. While commercial gambling has expanded since the 1950s, neither casinos, slot machines, horse racing, nor dog racing has had the lottery's success at the ballot box. Among other forms of gambling only bingo has made as strong a showing in popular referenda as lotteries.[12] About the same pattern of popular sentiment was found in a 1975 national survey assessing attitudes toward the legalization of various kinds of gambling. Bingo received the strongest support, with 68 percent favoring legalization, followed by horse racing (62 percent), state lotteries (61 percent), and dog racing (49 percent). Casinos and slot machines were favorably rated by only 40 percent of adults.[13]

By 1975 thirteen states from Michigan to Maine to Maryland had initiated a lottery. Why did the bandwagon get started in this region? And why have the southern states been slowest to join? While it is not possible to give an unchallengeable answer to these questions, several statistical patterns seem relevant.

Table 8.2 divides the forty-eight continental states into three groups: states that approved a lottery before 1980, states adopting lotteries between 1980 and 1988, and states that were lottery holdouts as of June 1988. The table characterizes each group according to several characteristics that seem relevant to adoption. First, it is noteworthy that other forms of commercial gambling were already legal in the early adopting states of the Northeast; as of 1963 all but one of these states allowed parimutuel betting at racetracks, and all but one had legalized bingo. In other words, these states had already accepted commercial gambling as a legitimate activity and thereby demonstrated the political impotence of groups that objected to gambling on moral or other grounds. By comparison, only half of the states in the third column had legalized parimutuel betting at the time the lottery movement was starting up.

Much of the organized opposition to lotteries and other forms of commercial gambling comes from religious groups. As Table 8.2 shows, religious affiliation has a marked correlation with the date of adoption. The early adoption states average 33 percent Roman Catholic and only 2 percent Baptist, while nonadoption states average 11 percent Catholic and 19 percent Baptist; the remaining states fall in between on both measures. As we noted in Chapter 3, Catholic teaching does not specifically condemn gambling, and in fact one traditional fund-raising tool of Catholic churches has been bingo. By contrast Baptists, here the sum of Southern and American Baptists, are among the Protestant denominations that are firmest in their condemnation of gambling.

Finally, the three groups of states differ markedly with respect to political ideology. Several suggestive measures are included in Table 8.2. First, an index of conservatism based on the outcome of the 1972 presidential election shows the negative association between conservatism and date of adoption. Three indicators of conservatism with respect to social regulation—the adoption of Prohibition by 1919, the existence of antisodomy laws, and the use of corporal punishment in schools—all tell the same story.

We might expect that the timing of lottery adoption would also be influenced by the need for additional state revenues. From the beginning lottery supporters have stressed the importance of the lottery as a new and badly

Table 8.2. Comparative characteristics of states with and without lotteries

Characteristic	States adopting lotteries 1963–1979[a]	States adopting lotteries 1980–1988[b]	States without lotteries as of Jun 1988[c]
Legalized gambling			
Horse racing, 1963 (percentage of states)	93%	50%	30%
Bingo, 1976 (percentage of states)	93%	86%	55%
Religion[d]			
Catholics (percentage of combined states' population)	33%	17%	11%
Baptists (percentage of combined states' population)	2%	6%	19%
Political ideology ranking[e] on scale of 1 (most conservative) to 50 (least conservative) (average of states)	40	27	14
Conservative attitudes			
Statewide liquor prohibition in 1919 (percentage of states)	29%	79%	85%
Antisodomy laws (percentage of states)	21%	43%	75%
Paddling permitted in school (percentage of states)	50%	93%	100%

Sources: For political ideology, George Rabinowitz and Stuart E. MacDonald, "The Power of the States in U.S. Presidential Elections," *American Political Science Review* 80 (March 1986), 65–87. F legalized gambling, Council of State Governments, "Research Brief: Legalized Gambling," 1977. F percentage of Catholics and Baptists, Bernard Quinn et al., *Churches and Church Membership in th United States, 1980* (Atlanta: Glenmary Research Center, 1982). For others, "Paddling: Still a Sore Point," *Newsweek,* June 22, 1987, 61; Thomas A. Bailey, *The American Pageant* (Boston: D. C. Heath, 1961), p. 746; *New York Times,* July 1, 1986.

a. Connecticut, Delaware, Illinois, Maine, Maryland, Massachusetts, Michigan, New Hampshire, New Jersey, New York, Ohio, Pennsylvania, Rhode Island, Vermont.

b. Arizona, California, Colorado, Florida, Iowa, Kansas, Missouri, Montana, Oregon, South Dakota, Virginia, Washington, West Virginia, Wisconsin.

c. Alabama, Arkansas, Georgia, Idaho, Indiana, Kentucky, Louisiana, Minnesota, Mississippi, Nebraska, Nevada, North Carolina, North Dakota, New Mexico, Oklahoma, South Carolina, Tennessee, Texas, Utah, Wyoming. (Alaska, Hawaii, and the District of Columbia are omitted owi to incomplete information.)

d. Religious percentages are weighted by 1983 state population; other percentages are unweighte

e. Ranking based on predicted outcome of 1972 presidential election. See Rabinowitz and MacDonald, "The Power of States in U.S. Presidential Elections."

needed source of funds to support state services. It is reasonable to suppose that this argument would be most influential in states that are in the direst financial straits. To test this proposition we constructed an indicator of fiscal need for each state. This indicator presumes that need is a relative matter, and that the sense of need will depend on how current state revenues compare with those of earlier years. Our indicator, then, is the percentage change in per capita total state revenues (adjusted for inflation) between the current year and the two preceding years.

The results of this effort do not lend much support to the fiscal crisis theory. As shown in Figure 8.1, total state revenues per capita (adjusted for inflation) had been growing in the two years preceding lottery authorization in all but four of the states. In one-third of the states revenues had grown more than 14 percent during that period. So most of these are not cases of fiscal starvation. Compared to other states at the same time, 41 percent of adopting states were experiencing above-average rates of revenue growth at the time

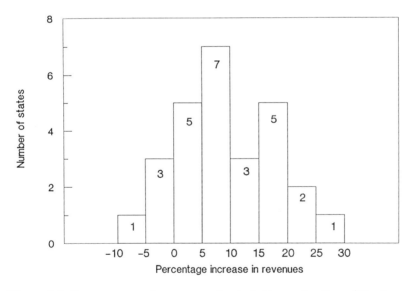

Figure 8.1. State revenue increases prior to lottery adoption. (The horizontal axis indicates the percentage increase in real per capita revenues during the two years prior to the public referendum or vote of the legislature that led to initiation of the lottery.)

(*Source:* U.S. Bureau of the Census, *Statistical Abstract of the United States,* various years)

of adoption. So at least by this measure there is no evidence that need increases the chance of success for a lottery adoption campaign.

One more aspect of the lottery diffusion process needs comment: lotteries appear to be contagious, with states following the lead of their neighbors. This pattern is not unique to the lottery. A well-known study of the diffusion of innovations across the United States found a strong regional pattern to the diffusion process. Jack Walker studied eighty-eight innovations occurring over a hundred-year period, ranging from professional licensing to anti–age-discrimination statutes. He found a consistent pattern of some states (including New York, Michigan, Massachusetts, and Colorado) acting as pace-setters in adopting innovations, each with a group of followers, mostly nearby, that appear to be influenced more by the pace-setting neighbor than by states in other regions: "In all cases . . . the likelihood of a state adopting a new program is higher if other states have already adopted the idea. The likelihood becomes higher still if the innovation has been adopted by a state viewed by key decision makers as a point of legitimate comparison. Decision makers are likely to adopt new programs, therefore, when they become convinced that their state is relatively deprived, or that some need exists to which other states in their 'league' have already responded."[14]

In terms of the specific politics of lottery adoption, regional influence is enhanced by the fact that a lottery in one state will attract players from neighboring states. Until Indiana and Wisconsin established their own lotteries, for example, Illinois lottery outlets had numerous customers from those neighboring states; for those out-of-state players who did not want to make the trip themselves, "runners" ensured that Illinois tickets were available in the state office buildings in Indianapolis and from certain bus drivers in Madison. Thus when one state adopts a lottery, the effect is to undercut arguments against adoption in neighboring states. Since their residents can now play (albeit inconveniently), and do, moral concerns and public interest arguments seem moot. And if state residents are going to play the lottery anyway, why should the neighboring state enjoy the benefits? Hence the dominoes begin falling in the region. Governor John Carlin of Kansas, grumbling about the new lottery in Missouri, explained his change of heart this way: "I've never backed a lottery before. But not having one when your neighbor has one is like tying one hand behind your back."[15]

There is a broader sense in which the early lotteries influenced the politics of adoption in the other states. The pioneering states demonstrated for all to see that it was possible to run a lottery that was both financially successful and largely free of corruption, thus setting to rest two major procedural concerns. Walker makes the general point about state innovations: "Uncertainty and the fear of unanticipated consequences have always been formidable barriers to reform. Proponents of new programs have always had to combat the arguments of those who predict dire consequences if some innovation is adopted."[16] No dire consequences flowed from the early lotteries, and the path was cleared for the lottery bandwagon to begin rolling.[17]

The Politics of Adoption in the 1980s

Although regularities emerge from examining the pattern of lottery adoptions across the country, it is impossible to appreciate the variety of adoption politics without taking a closer look at the peculiarities and forces at work in individual states. The politics of adoption has changed markedly since the early days of New Hampshire and New York. Today the lottery is a known quantity, but one still seeking acceptance where it has been outlawed. In order to capture the complexity of the political forces involved in current adoption campaigns, we look at the political debate in three states, each of which captured national attention in the 1980s. Despite the differences, it is possible to see the tension between popularity and revenue needs on the one side and the objections derived from good government concerns and moral principles on the other. In these states the catalyst for change was not the introduction of a lottery by a neighboring state so much as a gradual erosion of antigambling sentiment and the political efforts of forces within the state as well as one force from outside the state: the lottery industry.

California: The Campaign of the Carpetbaggers

In typical California style, the battle over whether to institute a statewide lottery was carried out on a grand scale as the rest of the country watched. The final decision came in November 1986, in one of that year's numerous statewide ballot initiatives, but the issue itself had been around for two decades. In 1964 the American Sweepstakes Corporation succeeded in placing on the ballot an initiative that would have given it an exclusive ten-year franchise to run a statewide lottery. Promoted as a means of helping schools and fighting communism (by lessening the state's reliance on the federal government), the proposal would have turned over a hefty 65 percent of gross sales as revenue to the state. The private firm operating the lottery would get another 13 percent of sales. The remaining 22 percent would not all have gone for prizes, since the proposal stipulated that the cost of tickets and the salaries of commissioners be paid out of this remainder. Californians had little to compare this scheme with other than New Hampshire's nascent state-run sweepstakes, so it is hard to know how voters would have regarded a payout rate of 20 percent or less.[18] While American Sweepstakes pushed for the proposal in radio and television ads, the scheme attracted a long list of prominent opponents, including Governor Pat Brown, the superintendent of public instruction, the head of the state board of education, and most of the state's newspapers, religious organizations, and law-enforcement groups. The governor opposed the proposal on the grounds that it would be costly to administer, that it "trades on human weakness," and that its primary aim was private profit. Other opponents claimed that it would invite crime and corruption.[19] The opposition proved overwhelming, and the proposal went down to defeat, winning only 31 percent of the vote.

Over the next nineteen years five new lottery proposals surfaced, but none had sufficient support to make it onto the ballot. The fourth of these was introduced as a bill into the legislature in 1978, the year of Proposition 13. Opposed by religious groups, law enforcement officials, and the horse racing industry, the bill failed to win a simple majority in the lower house, much less the two-thirds majority required. By 1982, however, the legislature seemed ready to take seriously the idea of a lottery. In the wake of a recession and limitations imposed by Proposition 13 the state faced a shortfall in revenues of some $2 billion. Governor Jerry Brown followed his father in opposing a lottery, but several legislators, including one gubernatorial candidate, had emerged as outspoken advocates. Typical of their view was one legislator's remark, in reference to the fiscal crisis, that "people probably would rather solve it in this manner, which is somewhat recreational, than by increased taxes." By 1983 the lottery had become part of the agenda for political debate, along with off-track betting, which was being promoted by the racing industry. Both forms of gambling found wide support among voters. A statewide poll showed that an overwhelming majority, 77 percent, favored a state lottery, and 60 percent favored off-track betting. A bill to set up off-track betting and a racing-based lottery passed the lower house, but the opposition and a promised veto by Governor George Deukmejian effectively killed the bill.[20]

Given the lottery's apparent popularity among the voting public, one way around the difficulties of getting a lottery bill through the legislature was by way of the popular initiative. This was the approach taken in 1984 by a prolottery coalition led by Scientific Games, Inc., a company that supplies lottery products. As in previous initiative efforts in Arizona and Colorado, the company's representatives wrote a lottery proposal and financed a petition drive to put the proposition on the ballot. In addition to the sheer cost ($1 million) of obtaining the necessary signatures, three other features of this proposal are worth noting. First, the lottery's net revenues would be earmarked for education. Unlike in Arizona, where Scientific Games had advised against earmarking because of fear that the legislature would not want to be restricted in the use of lottery revenues, in the case of California the company felt that earmarking for education would increase the plan's chances.[21] Second, the lottery proposal required the lottery to begin operations within 135 days after the vote, a period that was remarkably brief considering the size of the state. Third, the proposal required suppliers to make elaborate financial disclosures, including past tax returns for principal officers. Scientific Games was already producing lottery tickets for other states and had already made financial disclosures because its parent firm, Bally Manufacturing Corporation, was required to do so in its application for a gambling license in New Jersey; thus the company was in a unique position to meet these last two requirements.[22] The prolottery campaign organization took the name Californians for Better Education, raised a total of some $2 million, mostly from Scientific Games, and won the endorsement of the school boards of San Francisco, Oakland, and San Diego.[23]

In addition to the governor, those on record in opposition to the lottery included a coalition of mostly Protestant religious leaders, the state's attorney general, the superintendent of public instruction, the state Parent-Teacher Association, an association of police chiefs, and the Los Angeles school board. Governor Deukmejian criticized the lottery as an inefficient way to raise public revenue, a burden on lower-income individuals, and a revenue source with limited potential. The attorney general warned that the lottery would promote gambling through its ads and criticized parts of the plan that would exempt the lottery agency from certain bidding and contract requirements normally imposed on state agencies. He called the proposal a "sweetheart deal" with Scientific Games, saying, "It's not Californians for Better Education; it's really Scientific Games for itself, out to make a buck." Religious opponents decried the use of gambling to raise public revenue, but other religious leaders, including the Catholic bishops, remained neutral. Opponents also questioned the effectiveness of the earmarking provision, claiming that there would be no way to prevent future legislatures from taking lottery revenues into account when allocating funds for education. Opponents even brought in Arizona Governor Bruce Babbitt to denounce Scientific Games and the lottery's influence in his own state.[24]

One issue hardly mentioned in this or any other state's debate over adoption was the popularity of lotteries: many people simply want to play. As in referenda in other states, the outcome of the California vote showed solid support for a lottery. The initiative won majorities in all but one of the state's fifty-seven counties; overall, 58 percent voted in favor. Although the margin was comfortable, the approval rate was considerably lower than the 77 percent indicated by the poll taken in 1983.[25] The reason for the apparent decline in support is impossible to determine. One possible influence was the charge that the initiative was inspired by outsiders, or "carpetbaggers," motivated by profits. It was a difficult accusation to counter, as one Scientific Games representative made clear: "If lotteries are your only business, then you expand your business by legalizing lotteries, selling out of the country, or by increasing participation in lotteries."[26]

Florida: The Confederacy Falls

It is not surprising that the first southern state to adopt a lottery was Florida, populated as it is by transplanted northerners. When the state voted on the lottery amendment in November 1986, it passed easily, with favorable majorities in every region of the state, even the Panhandle, which is typically southern in having a high concentration of Baptists and conservatives.

The context for this successful lottery campaign included a well-established commercial gambling industry, with bingo and state-regulated parimutuel betting on horse racing, dog racing, and jai alai. The major related political controversy during the preceding decade had been over the introduction of casino gambling to revitalize the "Gold Coast," Miami Beach and environs. This proposal had gained momentum in 1976 with the successful campaign in New Jersey to authorize casinos in Atlantic City. A petition drive succeeded in putting a casino amendment on the Florida ballot in 1978. The opposition to this amendment was led by Governor Reuben Askew, who believed that it was unethical and counterproductive for the state to encourage people to gamble. His rhetoric could have been applied equally well to the lottery: "What kind of a community and state do we want to live in? Can government build economic strength by catering to people's weaknesses? Should government try to exploit the people? Is this any way to lead?"[27] The casino initiative was defeated overwhelmingly, in part reflecting public concern about the influence of organized crime in the casino business. But a petition drive placed another casino amendment on the ballot in 1986, this time to permit local option in deciding whether to legalize casinos, and a multimillion-dollar campaign was launched by some of the Gold Coast hotels to persuade the voters to take a chance on this form of gambling.

The lottery issue had been less vivid than the casino question in Florida, although there had been some interest. Florida was growing rapidly during this period, and a high percentage of the newcomers were moving from states with established lotteries.[28] A statewide poll conducted in 1983 found majority support (56 percent) for a lottery,[29] although a petition campaign to put a lottery amendment in the 1984 ballot failed to collect enough signatures. The following year lottery supporters renewed their efforts under the leadership of a new convert to the lottery, Education Commissioner Ralph Turlington.

In early 1985 most of the political elite continued to oppose the lottery, including Governor Bob Graham ("Government should not be in the business of pandering to people's worst instincts"). But Turlington announced his support in February saying, "I know of no other realistic proposal to secure the economic margin for educational excellence in the near future, and for that reason, I am pledged to this program."[30] Lottery amendment bills came before the legislature, but these ultimately failed in committee votes. Turlington began collecting signatures to place an amendment on the November 1986 ballot through the petition process.

Ralph Turlington was an experienced politician, having been elected to public office a total of sixteen times in thirty-five years, and his lottery petition effort was the capstone of his career. His constant theme was the role of the lottery in supporting education—a theme that won his campaign the endorsement of both of the state's major teachers' unions and other education groups. But to collect the 343,000 signatures needed to place the amendment on the ballot he needed money and manpower, and those came primarily from the private interests that stood to benefit from the lottery. By August 1986 he had raised nearly $500,000, about half of which came from lottery ticket vendors and equipment manufacturers. It was the first time that all eight major suppliers of lottery equipment contributed to a single campaign. The other major source of support was the convenience store chains, which expected to gain a large share of the retail action if the amendment passed. The chains contributed money to the petition drive and, perhaps more important, distributed lottery petitions to customers.[31] By the end of August Turlington's campaign had collected valid signatures from nearly 400,000 registered voters, and the amendment was on the ballot for November.

Turlington succeeded in convincing the public that the lottery would be a bonanza for public education in the state. A newspaper poll conducted in August 1986 found that over half of the respondents believed that the lottery would pay for a "major portion" of the total state budget for education. While this phrase is a bit vague, it seemed likely that these people would be disappointed by the reality of lottery finance.[32] Turlington's prediction in 1986 was that the lottery would raise $350 million annually in state revenues; the state education budget at the time was fifteen times that amount.[33]

Opposition to the lottery came from Protestant church groups and from existing commercial gambling interests. But their organization spent only $65,000, and they were in any event faced with an impossible situation, given polls in 1985 and 1986 that consistently found public support running at about two-thirds of the adult population.[34] On November 4 the lottery amendment was approved by a 63.5 percent majority, with strong support from all parts of the state.

In the meantime a much more lavish campaign was raging on the casino issue. An extraordinary $4 million was spent to promote the local option amendment (mostly raised from five South Florida hotel owners), while opponents raised $2 million from a variety of sources. Most of these millions were spent on television spots, with the predominant issues being the effect of casinos on crime and on economic growth.[35] As it turned out, the result in November 1986 was the same as in 1978—a crushing defeat for the casino amendment by more than a two-to-one margin. The lottery was presumably viewed by voters as relatively innocuous in comparison to casino gambling.

Virginia and the "Genteel Lottery"

Virginia is more southern in the traditional sense than Florida, and the story of its adoption campaign is also worth telling. The state's eventual decision to adopt a lottery followed two decades of debate over commercial gambling. In 1969, as part of a comprehensive reform of the state constitution, a legislative group proposed abolishing Virginia's ban on lotteries, a provision that was interpreted as also outlawing raffles, bingo, and parimutuel betting. Both the governor and the legislature favored repeal of the provision because it opened the door to betting on horse racing. A lottery was not on their agenda. A constitutional amendment removing the prohibition and leaving to the legislature the decision on what forms of gambling to authorize was placed on the ballot in 1970. With strong support from the Norfolk area, the Washington suburbs, and the state's other eastern counties, the measure passed with 63 percent of the vote.[36] In light of this support it seems surprising that opponents of commercial gambling were so effective during the next two decades.

As advocates of parimutuel betting pointed out, horse racing was part of Virginia's heritage and was legalized and taxed in the neighboring states of Maryland, Kentucky, and West Virginia. But parimutuel betting bills failed repeatedly until 1978, when a bill was passed authorizing a public referendum on the issue. The debate was marked by a well-financed campaign by opponents, including the Reverend Jerry Falwell and other fundamentalist religious leaders. The opponents outspent their proracing rivals and won the vote 53 percent to 47 percent, with the eastern section of the state again giving the strongest support to the gambling measure.[37]

With parimutuel betting laid aside, attention in the 1980s turned to the issue of a state lottery. Especially for those Virginians who lived near the Maryland border it was hard to ignore the excitement the lottery had created. One colorful illustration of the lottery's appeal was the success of a Maryland ticket retailer located on a pier in the middle of the Potomac River only a few feet away from an eastern Virginia community. This outlet became Maryland's busiest, selling some $3 million worth of tickets a year by 1986.[38] A small band of persistent legislators from the eastern counties introduced a series of progambling bills beginning in 1982, pointing to the revenue possibilities. In the words of a reporter one lottery advocate "invokes visions of sugar plums. He invariably carries documents that deal with the uplifting effect of lotteries, past and present." But opposition to legalized gambling remained firm. Governor Charles Robb came out against a lottery in 1984. The *Richmond Times-Dispatch* compared gambling to prostitution, and in one legislative hearing a clergyman invoked Sodom and Gomorrah. A poll of 140 political leaders in 1987 showed that opponents outnumbered supporters by three to one. Only once between 1982 and 1987 did any lottery bill get out of committee for a full vote in either house of the legislature.[39]

Yet popular sentiment appeared to be much more favorable to a lottery, and legislators found it increasingly difficult to resist a referendum. As one legislator said, "I'd rather give [the voters] the option of voting for or against the lottery bill than give them the option of voting against me because I didn't support the lottery." So when the governor signaled in 1987 that he would sign a bill calling for a referendum, the legislature promptly went to work. The lawmakers started with much the same lottery bill that had been introduced in previous sessions and then debated one major modification: limiting the agency's advertising. The bill passed by the House banned advertising designed to induce people to play, allowing only information about odds, prizes, and other details about the games. In support of such a limit was evidence from Illinois suggesting that its lottery agency had devoted a disproportionate amount of advertising to black neighborhoods in an effort to increase sales.[40] A proponent of the advertising limit also saw a more general danger in lottery ads: "If kids see those ads on TV, they'll grow up thinking it's okay to buy [lottery] tickets. I don't think children ought to grow up thinking they're being good Virginians by buying tickets."[41] Lottery supporters opposed this restriction as reducing the proposal to a "genteel lottery" with limited revenue potential, but the full legislature voted to keep it in the final bill, along with an exemption of the first $5,000 in prize money from state income taxation. The legislature, with at least twice the number of lottery opponents as supporters in each house, but with all of its seats up for reelection, overwhelmingly endorsed the lottery referendum.[42] Such was the power of popular sentiment—at least perceived popular sentiment—in favor of a lottery.

The public debate over the referendum pitted an almost anonymous pro-lottery group, Virginians for the State Lottery, against an assortment of former governors, religious leaders, and a coalition of business executives.

included leaders of three major denominations, the Southern Baptists, Methodists, and Catholics.[43] Apparently wanting to avoid the notoriety that had accompanied the California campaign, lottery firms in general and Scientific Games in particular kept a low profile during the Virginia debate, though they did provide financial support. Of the $230,000 raised by the prolottery group, Scientific Games contributed 45 percent. The second biggest contributor (22 percent) was Southland Corporation, whose 7-Eleven stores hoped to have a major share of the state's ticket retail business. The bulk of other contributions came from lottery suppliers.[44] The industry's reluctance to appear to be running the prolottery campaign was illustrated by a short-lived controversy that arose when one long-time advocate in the legislature asked to be paid as a consultant in the campaign and was promptly dropped. Last-minute contributions by Scientific Games and Southland helped pay for sound trucks that drove through black neighborhoods on election day imploring, "Say no to Jerry Falwell. Say yes to the lottery."[45] The results showed 57 percent in favor, about the same margin as in California. The state's mountainous western counties opposed the lottery but were overwhelmed by the more populous urbanized counties in the east. In contrast to the California referendum, black voters in Virginia went decisively for the lottery. An analysis of the election results suggests that, other things being equal, support for the lottery increased with the proportion of the county's residents who were black. A difference of 20 percentage points in a county's black population raised the vote in favor of the referendum by over 6 percent on the average.[46]

Conclusion

Given the broad-based popular interest in the lottery, it is a wonder that the adoption bandwagon has not rolled more smoothly and quickly. But state government legislative processes, like those of the federal government, include a number of hurdles that must be cleared before a proposed innovation can become law, providing plenty of opportunity for minority interests to stage an effective opposition campaign. In the case of lotteries, this opposition has often been led by some of the most prominent and respected public figures in the state.

To a large extent the opposition has been motivated by concerns about morality and the principles of good government. Numerous state political leaders have spoken forcefully against lottery adoption, and they have received some organized support from Protestant church groups. There is, however, not much of a constituency for good government concerns about regressive taxation and the appropriateness of the state encouraging people to gamble.

The first lotteries appeared in the Northeast, where fundamentalists are few and a well-established commercial gambling industry was already in place. The success of these early lotteries transformed the politics of lottery adoption in other states in three ways. First, they demonstrated the possibility of running a profitable operation that was largely free of corruption, and apparently also free of serious political pitfalls to incumbents. Second, the national publicity given to the large jackpots and lucky winners in the lottery states intensified public interest. A new lottery in a neighboring state further undercut the opposition because so many residents crossed the border to play. Third, the lotteries engendered large profits for private suppliers and retail outlets, which became increasingly active in lobbying and grass-roots political activity. By the 1980s private interests were providing the resources necessary to translate unorganized majority support into effective political action.

Supporters have used the need for additional state revenues as the principal argument in favor of adoption. The lottery is presented as an alternative to fiscal starvation or, worse yet, an increase in taxes. In most cases the proposed lottery has dedicated the revenues to some specific state activity, thereby focusing perceptions of its purpose and consequences. In four states successful adoption campaigns came in a time of declining revenues, but fully half the adoptions occurred in states with above-average rates of revenue increase. Thus the objective fiscal circumstances of the state do not appear to have much influence on whether or when states adopt lotteries.

The overt content of the lottery adoption campaigns has stressed different aspects of the public interest. Proponents tout the importance of increasing state services and avoiding tax increases, while opponents argue that government should not be in the business of encouraging people to gamble. Ultimately the majority who want a chance to play the lottery has had its way in most states. Whether it is viewed as a social disease or a triumph of popular democracy, the lottery bandwagon had brought most of the nonsouthern states into line by 1988.

9.

The Suppliers

If you're going to have a lottery, you might as well have
one that's successful.

—Iowa Governor Terry Branstad, 1987

Governor Terry Branstad had opposed a lottery in Iowa and had vetoed two lottery bills. But when passage became inevitable in 1985, he threw his support behind a lottery that would earmark revenues for economic development. After the lottery's inauguration Branstad supported its use of marketing to increase revenues. This shift and shifts like it in other states epitomize the environment in which state lottery agencies have been born. The typical history of the lottery issue in any state is cleanly demarcated at the moment of the lottery's approval. Once approved, the lottery virtually ceases to be a political issue. The intensity that frequently marks the debate over adoption is quickly forgotten, and what attention the lottery does get from politicians usually centers on such matters as the amount of revenue being raised for the state and who is receiving licenses to sell tickets. Even former lottery opponents appear to want the lottery to be "successful," to raise as much revenue for state programs as possible. So control is handed over to managers who are rewarded for achieving and maintaining high revenue levels. To gain this objective these managers use state-of-the-art business methods to control costs and stimulate the demand for their products.

State lottery agencies are unique governmental creatures, existing somewhere between private industry and state politics. They are state agencies operated with the assistance of private vendors to develop and market lottery products and retailers to sell them. They use sophisticated techniques of marketing and computer operations, all directed to one purpose: the maximization of net revenues. Although they are state agencies they operate largely outside the realm of state government as quasi-independent enterprises. The laws setting up the lotteries dictate certain practices in the interest of financial prudence and accountability, but these laws are seldom a serious constraint on the agency's attempts to maximize state revenues. The lottery's managers seek to maintain public confidence in the integrity of its operations while at the same time stimulating the demand to play. But the agencies are not capable of supplying lottery products by themselves. They must turn to private suppliers to develop and produce the various lottery games. Because several large firms have become the major suppliers of lottery products, the lottery industry has become central to the story of state lotteries. This chapter begins by outlining the major provisions of state lottery laws. It then turns to the motivations of agency managers and the peculiar structure of supply in this industry.

The Legal Framework

The legacy of the political struggle over adoption is a law that spells out how the lottery agency is to be organized and operated. Lottery laws in the United States are conspicuous in their similarity, although this might not be surprising in light of the practice of newly adopting states to look to established lotteries for models and guidance. Probably the most fundamental element of state legislation is the provision for a state monopoly in the operation of games. Although state agencies use retailers to sell their products to the public, no state allows competition in the operation of lottery games. Also common to all the laws are provisions to ensure integrity and accountability in operating the lottery. The laws differ, perhaps superficially, in the amount of autonomy given to the lottery agency, the constraints placed on its operation, and the distribution of agency net revenues. State laws also include various provisions that have the effect of ameliorating possible harmful effects of lotteries. Finally, some of the laws offer explicit statements of purpose which offer insight that is useful in assessing the performance of the lotteries.

Autonomy

Most state lottery laws set up an agency outside the existing bureaucracy, and this gives the lottery agency a degree of autonomy not accorded the typical state agency. Usually a commission is appointed by the governor, with broad authority over questions such as the types of games to be offered and ticket prices, but day-to-day operations are under the supervision of a director, who is also appointed by the governor. Like many boards of directors in other organizations, the commissions often appear to have little to do other than give their stamp of approval to decisions already made by management. In Washington State, for instance, commission members have questioned their own usefulness, in that "they were being asked to confirm planned games which were firmly established due to long lead times involved."[1] Whatever the power of the commission, this arrangement probably has the effect of insulating the lottery from some of the pressures of partisan politics. In several states the lottery is part of the state department of revenue, but there is no evidence that this organizational difference has had any effect on performance or the degree of actual autonomy.[2] Whatever the organizational design, most agencies undergo annual budget reviews of some kind.[3] In terms of operational detail, the lottery laws are written with an understanding of the agency's dual role of purchaser and seller. There are provisions for the purchase of services from vendors and for the selection of retail agents to sell the tickets to the public. These agents receive a fixed percentage of their sales of tickets (usually 5 percent) plus various extra payments for sales of winning tickets in some states.

Monopoly

Fundamental to all existing lottery legislation is the establishment of a state agency as the monopoly provider of lottery games. Although a number of lottery states allow lottery-like charitable games to operate, none allows any competition for its standard lottery products. This was the model adopted by New Hampshire, and it has been followed without exception throughout the United States. Lotteries in Kentucky and the Canadian provinces are operated by public corporations, and legislation in at least one nonlottery state has been introduced to allow lotteries to be run by a nonprofit organization. Another possibility is for a state to award a franchise to a private company to run a lottery, with revenues collected in the form of a franchise tax.[4] None of these models has generated much support in the United States, nor has there been serious discussion of allowing competition among operators. The monopoly form appears to be a structural response to the corruption associated with the nineteenth-century lotteries and the hint of organized crime surrounding other kinds of gambling in which private firms are licensed to operate. Together with the elaborate accountability requirements contained in the lottery laws, government monopoly appears to be aimed at ensuring as completely as possible the incorruptibility of the games.

Accountability

Every state lottery law provides explicit safeguards against corruption. As amply demonstrated by the history of gambling in general and state lotteries in particular, nothing undermines the public support for any form of commercial gambling more than the perception that it is being operated dishonestly. Not only do the laws provide for competitive bidding and financial reporting—requirements common to all public agencies—but they also pay special attention to the uprightness of retailers and suppliers. Licenses are not granted to anyone with connections to organized crime or illegal gambling.[5] Illinois explicitly warns against the use of the lottery "as a cloak for the carrying on of organized gambling and crime."[6] The lottery laws mandate background checks of retailers and suppliers, and many also impose elaborate disclosure requirements on contractors. A notable example is California, whose law requires potential suppliers to disclose information on activities in the gambling industry, criminal convictions, financial distress, political contributions, and income tax returns for officers of companies printing tickets.[7] Additional measures to ensure a clean operation include prohibitions against lottery play by agency employees and stipulations about the disposition of unclaimed prizes.

Distribution of Revenues

Virtually all state lottery statutes specify how the sales revenues are to be allocated, as shown in Table 9.1. Most commonly a minimum percentage (usually 45 or 50 percent) is specified for prizes. Proportions for administrative costs and net revenue vary widely; this may be due to the variation in operating costs by size of state.[8] In most cases the percentage limits set for administrative expenses appear not to present major problems for the lottery agency, although an exception was Missouri, where a crisis developed over that state's unusually low limit of 10 percent.

In about half the states the net revenue from lotteries simply goes into the general fund. Laws in the other half earmark lottery revenues by specifying their use as state expenditures. As indicated in Table 9.1, education is the most common destination specified when funds are earmarked. Other categories include economic development, transportation, distribution to local governments, parks and recreation, and programs for senior citizens. This last category, used and publicized by the Pennsylvania lottery, is the narrowest adopted by any state as its major expenditure category. A few other states have specified even narrower uses, but only for part of the lottery's revenue. For example, Iowa sets aside .5 percent for a gamblers' aid fund. Illinois provided for the proceeds of one game to go to the University of Illinois Athletic Association. In Maryland proceeds from several games have been earmarked for the construction of new sports stadiums in Baltimore.[9]

One effect of earmarking may be to increase expenditures for the function

Table 9.1. Statutory provisions for distribution of lottery revenues

State	Mandated distribution as percentage of sales			Directed use of revenues
	Prizes	Administration	Net revenue	
New Hampshire[a]				Education
New York[b]	40%[c]	15% max.	45% min.	Education
New Jersey			30 min.	Education and state institutions
Connecticut	45 min.			General fund
Massachusetts	45 min.	15 max.		Cities and towns, arts
Pennsylvania	40 min.			Senior citizens
Michigan	45[c]			Education
Maryland[d]				General fund, stadium project
Rhode Island	45[c]		30 min.	General fund
Maine[a]	45[c]			General fund
Illinois			40 min.	General fund, education, and other human services
Ohio	45[c]		30 min.	Education
Delaware	45 min.	20 max.		General fund
Vermont[a]	50 min.			General fund
Arizona	47.5[c]	20 max.	32.5 min.	Transportation
District of Columbia[d]				General fund

State				Use
Washington	45 min.	15 max.	40 min.	General fund
Colorado	50 min.		50 min.	Construction, conservation, parks, and recreation
Oregon	50 min.	16 max.		Economic development
Iowa	50[c]			Economic development, gamblers' aid fund
California	50 min.	16 max.	34 min.	Education
West Virginia	45 min.	15 max.	40 min.	General fund
Missouri[e]	45 min.			General fund
Kansas	45[c]		30 min.	General fund
Montana	50	20 max.		Education
South Dakota	45[c]		30 min.	General fund
Florida	50[c]		35 min.	Education
Virginia[f]		15 max.		General fund
Wisconsin	50 min.	15 max.		General fund, property tax relief

Source: State laws.

a. Prize pool for Tri-State Lotto is 50 percent. Administrative costs are limited to 15 percent.

b. Prize pool for numbers game not more than 50 percent.

c. "As nearly as practicable," or words to that effect.

d. No percentage distribution set by law.

e. Before August 1988 prizes could be no more than 45 percent, administrative costs were limited to 10 percent, and net revenues had to be at least 45 percent of sales.

f. Law sets a limit of 10 percent for administrative costs, excluding sales commissions; an estimated 5 percent for commissions is included in the table.

named, but such an effect is by no means assured. Since lottery proceeds are only a fraction of the total expenditure for education, for example, earmarking could easily be offset by reduced appropriations in that area. California is one state that seems to have recognized the possibility that earmarking revenues for so broad a category as education might not automatically ensure increased support. In its statement of intent the California statute states that lottery revenues "shall not be used as substitute funds but rather shall supplement the total amount of money allocated for public education in California." The law requires each school district to place lottery revenues in a separate lottery education account.[10] Still, there is no way to prevent future California legislatures from taking for granted this source of revenue when considering educational appropriations. Evidence of the effect of earmarking on expenditures is discussed in Chapter 11.

Another possible effect of earmarking is the creation of support for the lottery, and this is a possibility that has not escaped the attention of lottery supporters. Edward J. Powers, the first director of the New Hampshire lottery, advises lottery proponents to consider earmarking as part of any lottery proposal:

> It seems preferable from the lottery viewpoint to earmark the funds for a special purpose. By doing this, the benefits derived can be more readily measured and recognized. For example, it is very impressive to read in the annual report of the Pennsylvania Lottery of the $267 million distributed as tax rebates and free transportation for senior citizens, with appropriate photographs.
>
> Another benefit of earmarking is the creation of a support group for the lottery. The legislation in Colorado established the beneficiary as parks and recreation. This immediately provided an incentive for these state employees, their families and their vendors to work for public approval. The group was very effective in obtaining a favorable vote from the people.[11]

A Pennsylvania revenue official concurs: "One of the secrets of the Pennsylvania lottery is having targeted the proceeds. And having the public know where the money goes really seems to help ticket sales."[12] Other states have found that one effective theme to use in advertising is that lottery revenues are used for worthwhile purposes, and this theme has more appeal where revenues are earmarked.[13]

Taxation of Winnings

For lottery players and agencies alike, one of the most visible constraints imposed by law relates to the taxation of lottery winnings.[14] The federal income tax subjects all lottery winnings to ordinary income taxation, although the cost of all tickets purchased may be deducted against winnings, as in the case of any income from gambling. In contrast, about half the states have exempted winnings from state income taxation.[15] In practice, however, neither federal nor state taxation has any real significance except for winnings subject to withholding, a category that begins at $600. In designing their games lottery agencies are acutely aware of this threshold. For example, the decision to award a fixed top prize of $500 in a numbers game means that winnings will effectively be exempt from taxation, while allowing the prize to vary on a parimutuel basis would mean that some winners would be subject to withholding. Some agencies set the amounts for lotto second prizes at under $600.[16] An official for the Missouri lottery stated, "We know players are very adamant that they don't want a ticket valued at over $599." Because of the supposed negative impact of such withholding on lottery sales, lottery proponents in Congress have introduced legislation calling for an increase in that threshold or eliminating withholding altogether.[17]

The Lottery's Objective

Before turning to the management of the lottery agencies, let us examine the lottery laws to see what official guidance legislatures have given as to the aim of the agency. In the various debates over the adoption of lotteries virtually the only justification ever given by proponents is the raising of revenue, although other motivations may well exist. This emphasis on revenue is clearly reflected in the statutes setting up state lotteries. When a purpose is stated, it always refers to revenue for the state, sometimes specified as to type of expenditure program. Though surely more grandiose than the typical statement, California's law provides this kind of justification: "The People of the State of California declare that the purpose of this Act is support for preservation of the rights, liberties and welfare of the people by providing additional monies to benefit education without the imposition of additional or increased taxes."[18] Several states explicitly call on the lottery agency to maximize net revenues. Delaware's legislation charges the agency simply to "produce the greatest income for the State."[19] The enabling legislation in other states calls for the maximization of revenues subject generally to some constraint. Michigan's law, for example, states, "The lottery shall produce the maximum amount of net revenues for the state consonant with the general welfare of the people."[20] In Arizona net revenue is to be maximized "consonant with the dignity of the state."[21] Washington and Vermont call for a combination of the "dignity" and "general welfare,"[22] and West Virginia requires its lottery "to be operated so as to produce the maximum amount of net revenues to benefit the public purpose described in this article consonant with the public good."[23]

While revenue maximization is close to a universal goal, some of the lottery laws have imposed constraints on the extent to which the agencies can use marketing to achieve it. Limits on advertising are the most common form of restraint. Iowa and Arizona limit advertising to 4 percent of total sales, which appears to pose a genuine constraint on their spending. California's 3.5 percent limit, however, is quite high relative to ratios for other large states and seems to do little to hold its spending down. More common are limits placed on total administrative costs, as shown in Table 9.1, but it is clear that these limits are seldom binding. Some states place qualitative limits on lottery advertising. Three states require that the odds of winning be advertised, and others require that odds be listed on tickets.[24] But surely the boldest attempt at limiting a state's revenue-raising ability was the short-lived stipulations in the Missouri law that restricted ads to factual information about the games and forbade advertising "in a manner to induce persons to participate" in the lottery. What force this requirement might have had, however, was surely blunted by the law's definition of *induce* to mean "false or fraudulent persuasion."[25]

Other provisions of lottery laws appear to be intended to soften the possible negative effects of lottery operation. No state allows minors to play, for example. The sale of lottery tickets is prohibited in certain places: universities and schools in New Hampshire, and in Georgetown and the federal enclave in Washington, D.C., for example. Some states prohibit the use of casino gambling themes in the creation of lottery games, and most do not permit agents to make sales of lottery tickets their only business—a provision that may protect the interests of existing retail merchants as well as prevent the emergence of unseemly gambling shops. Resale of tickets for profit is similarly prohibited in most states. As devices to sanitize the unsavory aspects of the lottery, such measures were no doubt meant to moderate the entrepreneurial spirit of lottery managers. Whether they can be effective in this way is unclear.

Enter the Managers

Once the state legislature has crafted a lottery law, it is up to the governor and the governor's appointees to bring the lottery into being. What kind of person does the governor appoint to direct this new agency, and what instructions does the governor give the new appointee? In a clear effort to assure a reputation for integrity, the first three lottery states hired former FBI personnel as directors.[26] But the trend in the last decade has decidedly been in the direction of individuals with business, public management, or marketing experience. While security remains an ever-present concern, the pressure to increase revenues has focused attention on management and marketing skills. Of twenty-seven state lottery directors in 1987, two were former police officials, another twelve had previously held government positions within the state, eleven had worked in state lotteries or the lottery industry, and two had come from business. While the market for experienced lottery managers has expanded, states appear reluctant to hire from out of state in filling the director's position.[27]

To judge from their public statements and their actions, all lottery directors feel pressure to maintain, if not to increase, existing levels of revenues. To accomplish this task they have been encouraged to use marketing. Most annual reports of lottery agencies contain a statement from the director expressing the intention to maintain advances in sales through enlightened management and marketing. For example, 1987 annual reports from Iowa, California, Arizona, and the District of Columbia, respectively, included the following statements from directors:

> The key to future success will be diversification. In the year to come we will be involved in the formation of a multi-state lottery, the country's first coast-to-coast game. By offering this product, as well as our current Iowa LOTTO game, the Lottery will be able to expand its player base and thus increase over-all sales.
>
> Meeting our sales goal will require marketing innovations and production creativity.
>
> We are proud to have set yet another record—our revenues were $142 million, topping our original estimates of $130 million and beating the previous year's all-time high of $121 million.
>
> We attribute this success to the continued popularity of "The Pick," the stabilization of the instant games, and the introduction of several changes in our marketing approach.
>
> As we look to 1988 and beyond, we will meet the challenge of keeping customer interest high . . . Our mutual objective is to maximize sales and profits.

In most states the pressure for lottery revenue is relentless. When sales dip, legislators want to know why. Where revenues are earmarked, those affected by possible spending cuts are quick to raise the alarm. In 1987, for example, two established lotteries came under intense scrutiny when sales appeared to level off. In Michigan, the governor appointed a task force to examine lottery operations when sales increased by less than the projected amount. Virtually all of the group's twenty-nine recommendations concerned possible improvements in the marketing of lottery products, ranging from the redesign of numbers games to an increase in the payout rate. In Pennsylvania, the study took the form of a detailed performance review which produced numerous findings related to operations, finance, and marketing. Significantly, neither report questioned the objective of revenue maximization but rather applied principles of management and marketing to the achievement of this goal. Even routine budget review documents underline the importance of revenue. One such document used in the Missouri finance department plainly states the objective: "To adequately fund a state-operated lottery which seeks to maximize revenue to the state and provide a variety of lottery games to the people of the state."[28] A performance audit of the Washington lottery in 1986 took the agency's objective to be: "To produce the maximum amount of revenue to the state general fund."[29] In this atmosphere of high expectations a lottery director's main fear is that the lottery will be a failure. There are two principal ways in which this can happen: fraud and indifference. A third threat, controversy, is also a potential danger for the lottery, but it is a political danger, not one that would manifest itself in anemic sales.

Fear of Fraud

Credibility is central to the success of any commercial gambling enterprise, and state lotteries are no exception. If players do not believe that drawings are fair, that cheating is punished, and that prizes are calculated correctly, they will be disinclined to risk their money. While fraud certainly poses a threat to an agency's fiscal integrity, this is minor in comparison to the danger of undermining public confidence, to say nothing of political support. As we have seen, the abuses of the nineteenth-century lotteries constituted a major reason for their abolition in most states before the Civil War, and the flagrant corruption associated with the Louisiana lottery created a distaste for lotteries that lasted for half a century. So it is probably not an overstatement to conclude, along with one lottery official, that "the most serious threat to the lottery industry is the likelihood of fraud by employees, contractors, and consultants."[30]

In spite of the numerous security and accountability provisions included in state lottery laws, the short history of twentieth-century American lotteries shows that fraud and the appearance of fraud are ever present. Probably the most ignominious example was the 1981 "666 scandal" in Pennsylvania's numbers game drawing, in which all the Ping-Pong balls other than those numbered 4 and 6 were injected with liquid to make them heavier and less likely to be selected.[31] The perpetrators, including the television announcer for the drawings, were quickly found out. In 1988 an employee of Pennsylvania's lottery computer vendor printed a ticket with the winning numbers after a $15 million jackpot drawing, but again the fraud was uncovered.[32] Occasionally players attempt to collect on altered instant tickets, but such fraud does not appear to amount to more than a continuing nuisance for security officers.[33]

A bigger threat is posed by any perception that the lottery itself is crooked. In New York the governor closed down the lottery in 1975 after revelations that in seventeen out of the thirty-eight weekly drawings in the state's passive game the lottery had drawn and announced numbers of tickets they knew had not been sold.[34] Less damaging yet still a threat to credibility are misleading advertisements or suspicions that drawings are not entirely random. In 1983 the Illinois lottery continued to advertise a $100,000 grand prize in an instant game two weeks after the last such ticket had been sold. At the same time it was reported that residents of Chicago had won a suspiciously small share of top prize money, given the proportion of tickets purchased there.[35] Even corruption unrelated to the games can be damaging. Allegations that lottery contracts and retail licenses have been obtained through bribery cannot help the lottery's reputation.[36]

From the beginning the modern lotteries have taken pains to be attentive to matters of security and credibility, in no small part owing to security requirements in the state lottery laws. Agencies have been especially careful to assure citizens of the randomness of their drawings, for example by using elaborate mechanical devices subject to periodic checks.[37] They have also used their annual reports to respond directly to complaints that some communities appear to have more than their share of winners. An Iowa annual report presented a map showing the percentage of sales and winners for each county.[38] But it is the computer, both as threat and enforcement tool, that dominates the modern lottery's obsession with security. On-line lottery games are an obvious security risk because their operation depends not only on the access of many retailers to a central computer but also on trained computer experts who work for the agency. Separate telephone lines are used exclusively for lottery transmissions from retailers and elaborate security measures are built into the programs that operate on-line games. Whether or not agencies operate their own computer, most rely on programs written by vendors to provide the basis of their accounting and security systems.[39]

Measures have also been devised for instant games to guard against fraud. Forgery is clearly one risk with instant tickets, but the likelihood has been reduced by printing identifying numbers on tickets so that retailers can easily verify legitimate winning tickets. Such numbers raise problems of their own, however, in that employees of companies supplying the tickets could obtain numbers corresponding to winning tickets. To reduce the chance of this, at least one supplier sends its instant tickets through two printing runs, one to print the numbers used for play and one to affix separate identifying numbers.[40]

Fear of a Flop

The lottery director's second major fear is that customers will become discouraged or bored or simply lose interest. This is not an idle fear. The sales history of practically every lottery shows an initial burst of sales followed by a decline. In Illinois, for example, sales rose by 27 percent from the first year to the second and then dropped by 53 percent over the next three years. The most financially successful lotteries have been able to regenerate their sales with new products and active marketing, but success is by no means guaranteed.

Delaware offers two graphic examples of how a lottery game can flop. The state's first lottery in 1975 failed miserably when it introduced a six-digit numbers game allowing bettors to choose their own numbers. Sales in the first week were less than two-thirds of the anticipated level, and when they fell to 15 percent by the fifth week, the game was suspended. Over the course of the game no player won either the first or second prize by picking all six or the first five numbers correctly. The state sustained a loss of $470,000, more than double the game's total sales.[41] A second game was a form of sports betting, not strictly a lottery. Based on picking the winners of National Football League games, this game ran into different kinds of problems. Not only did the NFL sue the state, claiming that the game would tarnish the sport's reputation, but the game itself fell apart when its projected payouts differed from the Las Vegas betting line and the state had to refund almost $100,000 in bets.[42]

A more recent example of a lottery in trouble is Missouri's. The enabling legislation at the time contained the most severe restrictions on advertising and expenditures in the country. After an initial period total operating expenses (including commissions to retailers) were to be limited to 10 percent of sales, although only one state the size of Missouri has been able to keep expenses much below 15 percent. When it began selling instant tickets in 1985, the lottery enjoyed the flush of initial interest characteristic of recent start-ups, followed by the usual decline in succeeding weeks. Contrary to the pattern in most other states, however, sales continued to decline, and the introduction of a lotto game in 1986 failed to reverse this trend. Many Missouri residents continued to be attracted to the larger jackpots offered in Illinois. By 1987 the lottery made draconian cuts in its budget, including a 75 percent reduction in advertising. It lobbied the legislature for relief,[43] and in

1988 the voters approved a package of changes including the elimination of the limits on expenses (previously 10 percent of sales) and on the payout rate (previously 45 percent) as well as an end to the disclaimer that had been required on all advertisements that ads were not designed to "induce" people to play.[44]

Business Orientation and the Revenue Imperative

In light of the agency's relative independence from the rest of state government and the clear signal that the state wants maximum revenue from its lottery, lottery directors have chosen to run their agencies, in the words of one former director, "like a business as much as possible. This is the only way to maximize revenues."[45] Their agencies have been organized along the lines usually followed by producers of consumer products, typically broken into divisions for operations, sales and marketing, and finance. Much of the day-to-day work of the agency is routine, of course, and consists of awarding prizes, issuing press releases, sending checks, corresponding with retail agents, and carrying out the various security checks mandated by law. The agency can increase the net revenues it contributes to the state either by cutting costs or by increasing sales. While cost-cutting offers the possibility of modest gains, the real potential for increased revenues certainly lies in boosting sales. For that reason, almost all of the important management decisions made by lottery directors are marketing decisions.

What actions can the director take to increase sales? Within the limits imposed by most lottery laws several means exist. They range from making nuts-and-bolts adjustments in distribution schedules to devising innovative advertising campaigns. While advertising is discussed more fully in Chapter 10, it is useful to give a few examples here of specific changes that have been undertaken or considered by different lottery agencies. One aspect of on-line games open to change is the frequency of drawings. In its four-digit numbers game Pennsylvania conducted only three drawings a week, in contrast to the daily pattern of other states' four-digit games. A legislative report on the lottery suggested that increasing the frequency of drawings for the game would increase sales. Another suggestion, made in a report on the Michigan lottery, called for separating the drawing time for lotto from that for the numbers games. Since most bets are placed in the two hours before the drawing, the reasoning went, spreading out the drawings would increase players' opportunities to bet, and thus boosting sales. More directly, managers can increase the number of retail outlets or use field representatives to motivate retailers to sell more lottery tickets.[46]

One other variable at the command of most lottery managers is the payout rate, the percentage of gross revenues returned in the form of prizes. In 1987 state lotteries had an average payout rate of 50 percent, which is equal to the median payout of fourteen European lotteries during the 1970s.[47] Although some state laws permit no flexibility in this regard, a number of lottery agencies have been able to adjust the payout rate in an effort to increase sales. Massachusetts, with an average rate of 58 percent in 1987, adopted the high payout rate as an explicit strategy. On the whole, state lotteries have increased their payout rates over time. Beginning with New Hampshire's initial rate of 31 percent, the average payout rate rose to 46 percent by 1975 and 49 percent by 1986 to 50 percent by 1987. Spurred in part by robust sales in Massachusetts, other states have considered raising their payout rates, at least on instant games. The report on the Michigan lottery suggested an increase in payout rate from 45 percent to 55 percent and suggested that net revenues would increase as a result, although no definitive estimates of the responsiveness of sales to payout rate have yet been produced.[48] In 1986 Michigan did increase the payout on its instant game to 55 percent.[49] Ohio offered an even larger boost for one of its instant games in 1986 with a payout rate of 75 percent.[50]

Instant Games: The Massachusetts Miracle and Iowa's Take 5

It is instructive to consider in more detail the ways in which lottery agencies have used the marketing instruments at their command in the effort to increase sales. Two leading products, instant games and lotto, provide illuminating case studies. In the case of rub-off instant games Massachusetts has become something of a legend among lottery agencies for its dramatic increase in sales during the 1980s. Introduced in 1973, instant games were a sizable but stagnant part of the Massachusetts lottery offerings in 1983, accounting for sales of roughly $50 million. Three years later that total had climbed to $300 million, and the state's per capita sales on instant games were over three times the national average, quickly establishing the Massachusetts lottery agency as the guru of instant games. The changes made in 1983 became a checklist for other lotteries to emulate. First, Massachusetts altered the prize structure of the games, putting more prize money into smaller prizes and completely eliminating prizes over $10,000. Second, the payout rate was increased to 65 percent, well above the previous rate of about 50 percent. Third, the agency introduced new instant games more frequently and allowed more than one game to be sold simultaneously, in contrast to the previous one-at-a-time sequence. Fourth, the lottery expanded point-of-sale promotional signs in retail outlets and increased the size of the tickets in the belief that instant game sales are based on impulse buying. Fifth, the method of ticket distribution was changed. Previously retailers had had to go to banks to obtain tickets. Agents often ran out of tickets and were reluctant to open new packs at the end of the week because reimbursement was based on fully sold packs only. Under the new system retailers obtained tickets directly from the lottery's own couriers, reimbursing the lottery only after the tickets were sold, and squads of sales representatives paid frequent visits to check on ticket supplies and promotional material. Sixth, the lottery used coupons in newspapers and direct mailings to recruit new players.[51] While it is unclear what changes or forces were responsible for the dramatic increase in the state's instant sales, Massachusetts' experience with this product is a good example of the variety of instruments subject to the control of lottery agencies in their quest for more revenue.

An especially unvarnished attempt to increase instant ticket sales was Iowa's "Take 5" experiment. In its first instant game of 1987 the Iowa lottery arranged for two retail chains to offer packages containing five instant tickets in addition to the individual dollar tickets sold at cash registers. Because the packages were displayed so as to be both visible and accessible to customers, they contributed to the promotion of the product and made it more convenient to buy multiple tickets. But the biggest impact was on the price-per-quantity dimension: by bundling tickets in this way, the lottery created a "king size" product. The result of this test was a significant increase in ticket sales. Over the six-week course of the game total instant lottery sales in the experimental retail chains increased 17 percent more than the statewide average. The purchase of single tickets declined in these stores, but purchases of the multiple-ticket packages more than made up for the decline.[52] Merely repackaging the product proved to be a significant stimulus to increasing purchases among established players.

Fine-Tuning Lotto Games

Lotto offers a second example of management decisions designed to increase sales, but in this case the focus is less on questions of packaging and distribution than on the design of the game itself. The structure of lotto games is in fact open to almost limitless variation, and success depends in large part on the judicious matching of game design and player interest. Players appear to be attracted by large jackpots, as we note in Chapter 6, so populous states start with a considerable advantage. For any given population base large jackpots can be amassed only by making winning less likely and rollovers more common. But if a winner is chosen too infrequently, players appear to lose interest. A happy medium, then, might be to have a winner about half the time, with occasional strings of two or three successive rollovers to build interest. The variable that determines this frequency is "coverage," the percentage of all combinations that are selected by at least one player. The higher the coverage rate, the less often rollovers will occur. The three most important determinants of the coverage rate are the format (6/40, 6/48, and so on), the number of bets per dollar, and the state's population. As shown in Table 4.2, the format determines the statistical probability of picking the winning combination of numbers. For a 6/40 format, it is 1 in 3.8 million. But allowing two different bets per ticket doubles this probability. The bigger the state, the longer the odds the lottery agency can afford and still have occasional winners. The tension between frequency of winning and size of jackpot is especially acute for lottery agencies in small states since they can provide large jackpots only at the cost of infrequent hits. For example, tiny Delaware could offer a 6/48 lotto game as California does, and if people kept buying tickets the game would produce jackpots just as large as California's. But winners would be few and far between. More than likely players would become discouraged as week after week passed with no winner. This was apparently the problem with the first Massachusetts lotto game, introduced in 1978 with a 6/49 format. Not until it failed did the state come back with its successful 6/36 version. For this reason the idea of regional lotteries has growing appeal, especially for smaller states. Yet, as unlikely as it may seem, there is concern that lotto jackpots may become too large, with players or the public being put off if jackpots become "obscenely" large. The lottery agencies have in fact experimented with their lotto games and changed formats or introduced a second game offering longer odds and bigger prizes. Some lotteries have sought to limit the size of jackpots. Tri-State Lotto placed a cap on the top prize, with any excess going to second-tier prizes. At one time the Canadian 6/49 game reduced the proportion of the prize pool going into the jackpot when the pool exceeded $7 million from 45 percent to 15 percent.[53]

Other variables can also be manipulated to increase or decrease coverage. For example, the frequency of drawings influences the number of tickets sold per drawing, which in turn affects the chance that there will be a winner for any one drawing, and thus the coverage rate. In addition, the lottery agency may offer players the option of betting on a randomly drawn combination. Many players, primarily those who play infrequently, appear to like this option. In Pennsylvania as many as 45 percent of the bets in the state's lotto variant Super 7 game used the random pick when the jackpot was large.[54] Because of the distinctly nonrandom way most players choose their numbers, games that do not offer the random selection option typically have less complete coverage of all possible number combinations, thus reducing the probability that there will be a winner.[55]

It is possible to illustrate the effect of these various features by comparing the coverage rates for two similar lotteries in Connecticut and Maryland. Both states used the same 6/40 format, both offered the random pick option, and their lotto sales were within 10 percent of each other. The Connecticut lottery, however, did two things that reduced the coverage rate on its game: it held two drawings a week, to Maryland's one, and it allowed only one bet per dollar, to Maryland's two. As a result, Connecticut's coverage rate was about 40 percent while Maryland's was 70 percent. At these rates Connecticut could expect to have two successful rollovers more than three times as often as Maryland.[56] Because rollovers in their game were rare, Maryland officials in 1986 expressed some regret over their decision to introduce the random-pick option.

Moderation in Revenue Pressure

The managers of the state lotteries thus appear to be an unusual combination of public official and private business executive. As a group they pay careful attention to the design and promotion of their products, showing an almost single-minded devotion to their common goal of revenue maximization. In this behavior they appear to be responding directly to the incentives given them by the statutes that established the lotteries and by the leadership in their states. But is this revenue imperative really so one-dimensional? Is it moderated by other concerns? In fact, the years of modern lottery operation by U.S. states provide little evidence of other objectives moderating the demand for ever-increasing lottery revenue.

As we have noted, a few states include explicit limitations, such as the "subject to the dignity of the state" provisos, in clauses concerning revenue, but it is difficult to prove that such phrases have had a palpable impact on operating decisions.

In Colorado the legislature consistently limited its lottery's product line to instant games during the 1980s, and Arizona's law limited the number of drawings to one, and then two, per week, effectively excluding daily numbers games. Less formal actions by the governor or the legislature, through its budgetary review procedures, have been aimed at controlling lottery marketing. For example, the use of instant games in Maryland was effectively limited in the early 1980s by Governor Harry Hughes's opposition to the proliferation of lottery games. In 1981 Hughes took the unusual step of reducing the number of instant tickets that could be sold.[57] At about the same time the state budget office criticized a specific lottery ad they felt was inappropriate, and a report sponsored by the state budget office faulted the lottery's single-minded focus on revenue maximization, recommending in-

stead that the lottery's marketing objective explicitly recognize the importance of controlling costs, providing entertainment, discouraging illegal
gambling, creating revenue for lottery retailers, minimizing the gambling
connotation in its games, and avoiding hard-sell tactics and "exploitation of
the poor."[58] There is evidence in other states of concern about the appeal of
lottery products or advertising to low-income groups. The Pennsylvania report calling for more frequent drawings in the four-digit numbers game raised
a cautionary flag about its possible appeal to compulsive gamblers and the
poor.[59]

By and large, however, these kinds of limitations have been the exception
rather than the rule. It is quite possible, of course, that managers work under
significant implicit constraint on their activities. If there is a sufficiently powerful sentiment for moderation in marketing, a lottery director may not need
a report or an executive order to tell him to tone down an ad campaign, for
example. A statement by the director of California's lottery suggests that
nonrevenue concerns weigh heavily in that state's marketing: "I am com-
mitted to keeping a proper balance between maximizing revenue for schools
and exercising moderation in our marketing and sales strategies."[60]

The Structure of Supply

Whatever their objectives, these lottery managers immediately find themselves faced with providing a specific set of consumer products. Two specific
features distinguish the supply of lottery products from that of many other
consumer goods and certainly from most other activities of state governments. First, the state lottery agencies without exception end up operating
in between an industry of lottery product specialists and the army of small
retail outlets licensed to sell their products. The state lottery agency in effect
becomes both franchisee and franchiser. It is a franchisee of the producers
in the sense that it has the exclusive right to sell lottery products within its
own borders; it is a franchiser in that it grants licenses for retail outlets.[61] This
arrangement has significant implications for the role of private industry in
the political economy of state lotteries. And second, there are economies of
scale in the provision of lotteries with implications for the operation of lotteries at the state, regional, and national levels.

Vendors and Retailers

A newly created lottery agency has the authority to sell a product but not the
ability to produce it. Like other government agencies faced with the problem

of providing a specific commodity or service that they are not equipped to create—such as highway construction or military weapons systems—lottery agencies have turned to private firms specializing in the design and production of lottery products. Especially in a lottery's early years it is clear that the expertise of lottery specialists is invaluable to the running of a modern state lottery operation. An evaluation of the performance of the Oregon lottery revealed, for example, that vendors were especially struck with the inexperience of lottery agency employees during the initial months of operation.[62]

Lottery suppliers provide agencies with game design, computer services, tickets, and marketing advice. Game design is a critical first step in creating a lottery agency that will generate revenue for the state. As we showed in Chapter 4, lottery games can be quite complex to set up and operate. Without judicious design they could leave the state vulnerable to costly payouts or fail to interest people in playing. In the early days the state agencies themselves—notably in New Jersey and Massachusetts—worked alongside private companies devising the formulas that would become the standards for instant games and on-line games. But most of the states setting up lotteries in the 1980s, especially the smaller states, had little capacity or incentive to craft their own lottery games when proven products could be bought off the shelf and used right away.

Vendors also provide computer services, including the machinery and programs that are vital for running lottery games and doing the necessary accounting. While a few larger states own and operate their computer systems, most agencies contract this specialized work. The specifications from a New Jersey request for bids demonstrate the level of sophistication needed in these computer operations. Bidders were expected to install and maintain the system's computer equipment, including over three thousand terminals in retail outlets, each with the capacity to record bets and read betting slips optically; provide computer programs capable of handling bets for three different on-line games, including twenty-two betting combinations for the two numbers games; produce seventeen sets of regular reports on betting activity, collections from retailers, and accounting totals; and quickly make all necessary repairs, with penalties for downtime exceeding 1 percent of total operating time.[63]

Lottery agencies must depend on tickets printed by firms specializing in the business in order to meet the demanding specifications for accuracy and security required by instant games. And state agencies typically hire private firms to carry out marketing, although this function is performed to some extent within the agencies as well. Conventional advertising agencies are the primary supplier of this service, but several firms in the lottery industry also offer marketing advice.

A list of the major contracts of several lotteries illustrates the degree of dependence on private firms. In 1988 Michigan hired Webcraft Games to supply instant game tickets, Syntech International to manage on-line games and terminals, an advertising agency to handle its advertising and public relations, and an accounting firm to oversee its drawings. Arizona bought its instant tickets from Scientific Games, a subsidiary of Bally Manufacturing, and its computer services from GTECH, and likewise used an advertising agency and an accounting firm. The amounts spent on these services can be sizable. For example, in 1988 the Maryland lottery was paying about $14 million a year to various contractors, or about 2.2 percent of its sales. The lottery's major contractors were Control Data Corporation ($7.3 million per year) for computer equipment and the maintenance and operation of on-line games, a Baltimore advertising agency ($4 million), and Webcraft Corporation ($1.4 million) for instant tickets.[64] Smaller agencies are comparatively more dependent on suppliers. Oregon's payments to contractors in 1988 amounted to some $7 million a year, or about 5.5 percent of their total sales.[65] The largest items were for the on-line system ($4 million) and instant game tickets ($1.3 million).[66] Typical contracts for both instant and on-line games yield the supplier about 2 percent of gross sales of on-line games, although the ratios vary depending on the size of the state and services delivered.[67] Based on 1987 total U.S. sales of $12.5 billion, this percentage would imply total payments to contractors on the order of $250 million.[68]

At the other end of the hierarchy of lottery supply are the retail agents who operate the terminals and sell the tickets. Their primary business is anything but lotteries. Still, these retailers play a crucial role in the marketing of lottery products, as we shall see in Chapter 10. Working on commissions that average 5.5 percent of sales, these retailers have the potential of bringing in significant amounts of revenues from selling lottery tickets. In 1987 the typical retailer with a terminal made roughly $9,000 in commissions, and in five of the largest states the average was more than $15,000.[69] It is not hard to see how these agents can quickly become a sizable interest group. In some states they have become a vocal one as well, lobbying for increases in the commission rate and opposing the licensing of additional agents. In Michigan, for example, the lottery agency considered doubling the number of terminals in the state. But retailers, backed by research showing that such increases would decrease the average retailer's volume, opposed the move.[70] On this question the interests of the lottery agency and those of established retail agents appear to have been in conflict.

Economies of Scale

The provision of lottery products is subject to economies of scale: that is, a state that sells twice as many tickets as another will usually not have costs that are twice as high. The reason has to do with the large, relatively fixed costs associated with running a lottery, such as the computer system, marketing, and most administrative functions. The resulting economies of scale translate into a decided cost advantage for large states. As Figure 9.1 illustrates, operating costs for state lottery agencies as a percentage of sales in 1986 tended to fall as sales increased. While these points do not indicate the *minimum* cost of operating at each scale (and thus do not prove the existence of economies of scale), they do suggest the difficulties posed by a restriction on operating expenses, such as Missouri's limit of 10 percent, given the scale of lottery sales likely to be achieved in that state.[71]

A footnote to this discussion has to do with a peculiarity of lotto that has definite implications for the prospects for the success of lotteries in small

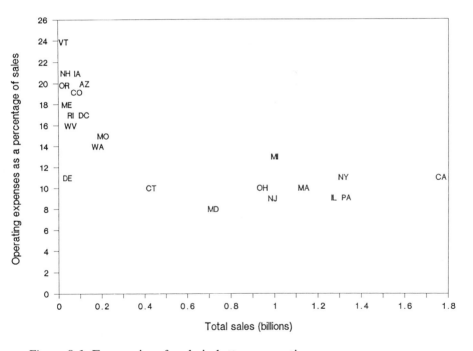

Figure 9.1. Economies of scale in lottery operations

(*Source:* Annual reports of lottery agencies, fiscal year 1986; *Gaming and Wagering Business* 8 [September 1987], 21)

states. Because demand appears to be affected by the absolute size of prize jackpots, large states have a decided advantage in generating high per capita sales (see Chapter 6).

Consequences: The Political Economy of Lottery Supply

In their ultimate organizational aim lottery directors may differ little from the heads of many other state government departments: the goal is growth for the agency, and the minimum requirement is survival.[72] What sets the lottery agency apart is the accepted means for achieving this growth. States have brought lottery agencies into being in order to raise as much revenue as possible and have placed few restraints on their pursuit of this aim. The successful director is one who can use marketing to increase sales without involving the lottery in controversy and corruption. These incentives, added to the distinctive aspects of supply, serve to distinguish lottery agencies from other government bureaus.

Like any government department, the lottery agency exists only by virtue of its political support, and all indications are that lotteries are now widely accepted in states where they operate. The typical lottery agency has three basic sources of political support. First, thanks to overwhelming endorsements in referenda and legislative votes, lotteries can claim broad popular support; the conversion of governors who were once opponents is an obvious indication. The solidity of this approval can be observed less in surveys of popular opinion, though there are some of those, than in the implicit acceptance of the lottery.[73] Although clearly widespread, this support could nevertheless be vulnerable to swings in opinion if the lottery were implicated in political controversy or fraud. A second source of support for any state lottery is, of course, the retailers who have come to depend on the commissions they earn from selling lottery tickets, not to mention the bonuses some states award to retailers who sell winning tickets. Lottery suppliers can also become beneficiaries of a state lottery agency. In Michigan and Illinois the lottery agencies came under pressure to award contracts to in-state lottery suppliers. In both cases the effect on employment in the state was a prominent issue.[74]

In states that earmark their revenues there is a third source of support: the favored programs and their beneficiaries. Just as these groups can be instrumental in the adoption drives for lotteries, they also serve as a large and responsive group of lottery defenders. Nor has the significance of this support been lost on the lottery agencies. Most of the states that do earmark their revenues also publish details showing how the lottery money was spent. For example, a booklet published in Arizona includes descriptions and photographs of projects funded by the lottery, including traffic signals in Scottsdale and a portable rock crusher in Chino Valley.[75] In Iowa lottery funds paid for a new faculty position in entrepreneurship at the University of Northern Iowa and a nature trail in Blackhawk County.[76]

What consequences arise from the mandate of lottery managers and the unique characteristics of the supply of lottery products? First, the lottery agencies have been honest, in the sense of being free of the taint of corruption, and have thwarted all but a few serious attempts at fraud. While isolated instances of bribery have occurred in connection with contracts, and some individuals have attempted to falsify tickets, the agencies themselves have kept themselves free from the unsavory connotations associated with nineteenth-century lottery operators. In this respect lotteries are no different from most agencies of state government.

There is a second consequence, however, that sets the lottery apart. In its highly unusual objective function—its aim to maximize net revenues for the state—the lottery agency is much more akin to a private business than to an arm of government. Moreover, remarkably little sentiment exists in most states to place any significant limitations on the pursuit of lottery revenue. No matter how much opposition the lottery may have faced in the debate over adoption, its continued existence ceases to become an issue of serious debate. Nor do its methods of marketing come under scrutiny in most states. Of nearly sixty lottery-related bills introduced in state legislatures in 1988, only one would have placed any restriction on the generation of lottery revenues—by requiring that the odds of winning be stated. Another proposal would have gone in the opposite direction, lifting restrictions on advertising. The bills introduced in the various lottery states suggest that the bulk of political concern has been with the details of lottery operation and the distribution of revenue.[77] This political climate gives lottery managers wide latitude to apply the methods of modern marketing, as we shall see in the next chapter.

A third consequence of the conditions of supply is that the private lottery industry has become an exceedingly influential player in the operation of state lottery agencies. Because of their expertise in the development and operation of lottery games, state lottery agencies are heavily dependent on these private suppliers, especially in the lottery's early years. For their part, the companies cannot fail to see that their interests lie in the continued development of new lottery-related products as well as in the expansion of lotteries to the remaining states. It is not surprising, therefore, that these firms have been major contributors to campaigns for the adoption of state lotteries. The real significance of the lottery industry becomes evident, however, only after a lottery is in place. Then it becomes an ally for the state lottery agency to turn to in meeting its growing appetite for sales. Lottery producers have worked with agencies to develop video lottery machines, which are akin to slot machines, as well as dispensers of instant tickets. Bally, which is a major producer of gambling machines, supplied video machines for a trial period in Illinois.[78] Whether in marketing existing games, reconsidering their design, or developing new games, the lottery industry stands ready and willing to help the agencies in their relentless push for increased sales. The industry's role here is not unlike that of the weapons industry in military appropriations at the federal level.[79]

A fourth characteristic is the acute sensitivity to certain topics that makes lottery agencies on the whole markedly less open than most public agencies. Where they are not constrained by freedom-of-information laws, the agencies are usually reluctant to release information they fear could damage their public support. Although the lottery agencies provided a great deal of information for this book, they tended to balk at responding in two areas. Most notably, the agencies are for the most part quite reluctant to share information they collect in their marketing surveys about who plays their games and how much they play. One reasonable conclusion is that this reluctance stems from sensitivity to charges that lotteries are regressive and are played disproportionately by minority groups and the poor. Another topic that tends to give the agencies pause concerns the details of their marketing strategies. Some agencies will allow their marketing plans to be released, but most do not. In both cases the agencies may give as their reason for not releasing information that it is the property of the advertising agency that did the work, but this seems a technicality at best. In the matter of openness to public inquiry, most lottery agencies resemble private corporations more than agencies of state government.

Appendix   1988 Survey of State Lotteries

In February 1988 we sent a survey to budget officers in each lottery state, requesting a written response or answers by telephone, along with additional material if available. Replies were received from all states. In some cases the questionnaire was filled out entirely by the budget office; in others it was referred to the lottery agency for some or all questions.

1. Is the lottery part of your department or a separate agency?

2. Is the lottery subject to periodic budget review? What does it consist of? Are there, for example, regular budget hearings?

3. Are there such budget reviews or hearings that I could obtain copies of? (If so, please attach.)

4. How many retail outlets are authorized to sell lottery tickets? How many of those have computer terminals?

5. Does the lottery offer incentives to retail outlets in addition to commissions based on sales (for example, payments based on sales of winning tickets)?

6. Is there a policy governing the *total number* of such outlets? If so, what is it?

7. Is there information on the amount of commissions earned for each retail outlet in the last fiscal year? Could I obtain a list?

8. How many employees does the lottery agency have? Full-time? Part-time?

9. Is there a publicly available list of the major contracts currently in effect for the lottery? (Specifically: lease or purchase of terminals and computer hardware and software; with television stations for broadcast of winning numbers; with ticket vendors). If so, could you send me a copy?

10. Are winnings subject to state income tax (where there is a state income tax)?

11. Are winning lottery numbers broadcast on a regular television show? Which station?

12. Does the lottery agency pay for this time?

13. Are there studies of the effectiveness of lottery advertising? In other words, do lottery sales increase when advertising is increased?

14. If your lottery net revenues are earmarked for specific purposes, do you have a list of expenditures made possible by these revenues? For example, what specific programs for the elderly (Pennsylvania) or compulsive gamblers receive how much?

15. Are there bills pending in the current or last legislative session concerning the lottery? If so, on what issues?

10.

The Sales Pitch

It was Saturday night. I took my change
Down to the store for the lotto game.
I got two chances at a buck a pair,
And by 7:05 I was a millionaire.

—Washington State lottery advertisement, 1987

Imagine a state government office where marketing directors and "brand managers" discuss television markets, penetration ratios, and product life cycles.[1] Welcome to the marketing department of the typical state lottery, an office that has more in common with Procter and Gamble than with almost any other kind of state agency. No aspect of state lotteries so vividly illustrates the distinctiveness of this new state function as the marketing they employ to sell their products. As Chapter 9 illustrates, the lottery agencies have found it convenient to act in many ways more like a business than a conventional government agency. One lottery director put it succinctly: "To survive and prosper, it is essential that lotteries practice the business techniques of the private sector, particularly in the area of marketing."[2] Probably the most significant aspect of marketing by lotteries is the very fact that they are marketing their product at all. They do so not as an afterthought but as a deliberate policy. Unlike virtually every other operation of government at any level, but very much like most suppliers of consumer products, lottery agencies pay attention to details of product design, pricing, and promotion. This marketing is motivated by the lotteries' objective of maximizing revenue and is made possible by their unusual degree of independence. In this enterprise the state agencies work closely with the private firms that act as wholesalers of lottery products and consultants on all aspects of lottery operation. With the help of these specialists and experienced advertising agencies, the lotteries have set about to increase their revenues by stimulating the demand for their products.

The adoption of modern marketing techniques by state lotteries has had its critics. Some have charged that lottery advertising misleads consumers by giving insufficient information on the size of prizes and the odds of winning. California's attorney general opposed the state's lottery, saying, "People look to the government to be honest and straightforward and not to be using suckering kinds of techniques." Others are generally uneasy about the propriety of the state's encouraging people by whatever means to gamble. For example, Governor George Deukmejian of California, an opponent of the lottery, said, "I don't think it's good for the state or good public policy to go out and push and urge people to gamble."[3] Still other lottery critics have charged that agencies aim lottery advertising at minority groups and the poor. For reasons such as these marketing has become an issue in adoption debates in a few states, and several lottery statutes reflect attempts to curtail advertising in some way (see Chapter 9).

This chapter examines the promotion of lottery products. It begins by discussing how the lottery's overall objective of revenue maximization affects marketing strategy. The parallels between lottery marketing and the marketing of other consumer goods are then described. The literature on marketing consumer products yields clear implications for strategies effective in selling lottery tickets, including the targeting of certain groups in the population. We then turn to advertising, the most visible manifestation of marketing, discussing both the amount and content of lottery advertising. Throughout we mean to address the question of whether advertising is essential to running a modern lottery.

Selling More Tickets: New Users versus More Usage

Once a lottery's overall objective of maximizing revenue is established, the most important fact of life influencing its marketing strategy is its monopoly position as a supplier of legal lottery games. While there are certainly substitutes for its products—including illegal gambling, the legal lottery games in other states, and other legal gambling, as well as the entire range of goods and services that compete for the consumer's dollar—each lottery is the sole producer of legal lottery games within its state's borders. It cannot increase sales by increasing market share, as most businesses can, so it must turn to enlarging the size of the market itself. Marketing theory teaches that this can be done through "new users, new uses, or more usage."[4] Since the second option is largely ruled out with lottery products, the market can be expanded by increasing the percentage of people who play or the amount that current players bet.

Of these two strategies for increasing sales lotteries appear to favor stimulating more usage among confirmed players rather than recruiting new ones. New Jersey's lottery director stated the essence of this approach: "We're taking an infrequent user and trying to convert him into a more frequent user."[5] It is also possible to discover some lottery agencies' objectives in "media plans," which contain formal statements of marketing goals. One of the most explicit statements of purpose is contained in the media plan for the Iowa lottery:

> Our broad objectives for Lottery Media are:
> 1. To geographically cover the state with media advertising to make Iowans aware of both the Instant Game and Lotto.
> 2. To target our message demographically against those that we know to be heavy users, while encouraging purchase among light or non-users.
> 3. To combine appropriate media using the strength of each medium selected to reach the most people with the most impact.
> 4. To time media to coincide with purchase cycles or ticket sales.[6]

Similarly, Maryland's stated goals include "consistent weekly purchases by current Lottery players," "cross play of the various Lottery games by current players" (that is, encouraging regular players of one game to participate in another), and "increased purchases by occasional players."[7] In each case more usage is the dominant strategy for increasing lottery sales.

Still, the new-users approach is sometimes employed as well. While in "well-done lottery promotions, you don't exhort people to bet," an Illinois official stated that the aim of their promotions is to "broaden the base of the players" rather than to increase the average size of bets.[8] One common practice to increase the number of players has been to advertise lottery tickets as Christmas gifts. A tactic used in Illinois was to send letters to residents of high-income areas inviting them to play lotto by mail and to buy subscription books of tickets.[9] Another way to attract new users is by introducing new games, although new games are aimed equally at stimulating crossover play by established players of other games.

Needless to say, there is no reason for lotteries to follow either strategy to the exclusion of the other. To maximize sales using a limited marketing budget, the agency must allocate its resources according to the standard budget allocation rule from the economic theory of the firm: expenditures on various aspects of marketing ought to be undertaken so that an additional dollar spent in any of these aspects would have the same impact on sales. This rule is relevant not only to the agency's choice between new users and more usage but also to its choice between radio and television advertising and between informational and thematic advertising. Because marketing costs money, sales can be increased most economically by creating loyal customers. As the Maryland lottery's advertising plan states, "All advertising programs for the Lottery must develop regular participants of the games, not casual impulse sales."[10]

Applying the Principles of Modern Marketing

In their efforts to boost sales lotteries have borrowed freely from the private sector, adopting state-of-the-art marketing techniques commonly used to sell consumer goods. Although unprecedented for a government agency, the use of these marketing techniques is a logical consequence of the lotteries' revenue-maximization objective, their administrative independence, and the nature of the product they provide. Lottery managers have discovered that the methods used to sell soap and cookies are easily adaptable to lottery products. Principal among these methods is an approach called target marketing, which provides an overall strategy for lottery marketers to follow. Marketing theory also teaches sellers to be attentive to the "four P's": product, price, place, and promotion. Lotteries have taken these principles to heart, and the result is a virtually brand-new class of public sector activity.

Target Marketing

Although it is nowhere formally stated, all of the marketing activity engaged in by lotteries suggests that they follow a general approach called target marketing, as distinct from mass marketing. In the language of marketing theory, mass marketing entails a producer designing and selling a product to an entire market. By contrast, target marketing requires the seller to distinguish among market "segments," deciding which ones to enter, and designing products for sale to specific segments. In practice this approach requires sophisticated market research methods to identify characteristics and preferences of the various segments. After collecting information on the purchasing patterns and other behavior and attitudes of people in various classifications, target marketing then divides consumers into groups according to geography, class, personality, and behavior.[11]

The evidence that lotteries follow this approach is abundant. Media plans frequently speak of "targeting" certain groups, as in Iowa's aim to "target our message demographically against those that we know to be heavy users," an approach that is referred to in marketing as "heavy-use target marketing."[12] Lotteries or their advertising agencies regularly obtain marketing data from focus groups, discussion groups used to test new ideas and learn about subjective perceptions of lottery products.[13] Lottery marketers also regularly conduct surveys in person or by telephone. Sometimes referred to specifically as "segmentation" studies, such surveys provide information on the demographic characteristics of players and nonplayers. The Arizona lottery, for example, used data collected from winners to infer socioeconomic characteristics of players. They found, for example, that games involving future drawings were more attractive to older people than to younger ones. According to that state's marketing analysts, "Maximal lottery revenues are dependent upon knowing the socio-demographic profiles" of players and nonplayers alike.[14]

Segmenting the population. The question of how to segment the population—always a significant issue in target marketing—takes on special meaning in the marketing of lotteries. Consumers can, of course, be divided in any number of ways, for example by the amount of lottery play or by conventional demographic classifications such as age, race, or income. One variant of conventional demographic breakdowns is a geographic classification system, such as one that stratifies by neighborhood type. This scheme was applied in New Jersey in 1982 using a survey of households. For each lottery game the neighborhoods with the highest relative rates of participation could be identified. For example, the neighborhood type with the highest rate of participation in daily numbers games is described as "black neighborhoods, older population, old rental housing." The neighborhood type with the highest rate for instant games was "older population, lower middle income, Eastern Europeans, Northeastern U.S."[15] Because market segments are easily identifiable as geographic areas, a segmentation method such as this has obvious advantages in designing a marketing strategy.

One issue of political sensitivity that has arisen in connection with market segmentation and target marketing is the use of minority groups as focal points for marketing lottery products. Given the history of numbers play among urban blacks and the striking differences in participation rates for various ethnic groups, it would be surprising if any lottery marketer was unaware of these differences in play. Following the usual practice in other industries, some lotteries have even devised separate marketing strategies for blacks and Hispanics.[16] Lottery ads in Spanish are commonplace in California, New York, and other states with sizable Hispanic populations. The targeting of minority groups, however, especially poor minority groups, has been a controversial issue in some states, most notably in Illinois, which saw a boycott of its lottery motivated by charges that it devoted special attention to sections of Chicago populated by poor blacks.[17] This charge was the subject of a special report sponsored by the state government. The report noted that, while it was briefly the practice of the Illinois lottery to target blacks, mainly through the use of outdoor advertising, the lottery had abandoned such marketing practices by 1986. Moreover, a painstaking comparison of advertising within the state failed to show any tendency to advertise disproportionately in minority or poor areas.[18]

The VALS typology. One popular way to classify consumers departs from traditional demographic groupings altogether. "Psychographic" classification schemes are based instead on consumers' attitudes and behavior. One

of the most widely used of these is the Values and Lifestyles (VALS) typology.[19] In the VALS system individuals are classified into one of nine distinct
"lifestyle" groups according to certain socioeconomic characteristics based
on their answers to a series of attitudinal questions. Most numerous are the
Belongers, constituting over a third of U.S. consumers. These are middle-
class individuals, loyal to traditional institutions and values. "Archie Bunker
is a Belonger."[20] Achievers, representing almost a quarter of the population,
are successful, affluent, and satisfied. Emulators, another 10 percent of the
population, are an ambitious lot who look to the Achievers as models of
material success but are considerably less well off. Together these three groups
are referred to as "outer-directed." Of the remaining groups the largest are
the Societally Conscious, a group of successful "inner-directed" people distinguished by their concern with social issues.[21] With this classification as the
starting point, marketing strategies can then be formulated.

   The lottery consultant John Koza illustrates how this kind of segmentation
may be used in marketing strategies for lotteries. His discussion focuses on
the Belonger group. According to Koza, the reason why such socially conservative individuals participate in lotteries as much as they do (their participation rates for the lottery games shown in Table 10.1 all indicate above-
average play) is that lotteries are government-sanctioned. "Belongers are
not inherently attracted to gambling activities—a fact that is consistent with
their generally conservative social attitudes. The key is the element of authority and legitimacy inherent in a *state*-operated lottery. If the government
says 'it's OK,' then it's OK." Koza notes that Belongers tend to exhibit
regular and predictable purchasing behavior and thus are attracted by so-
called continuity features, which require regular and repeated participation,
built into products or promotions. Thus games that require collecting all the
letters to spell a word, for example, or subscriptions of lottery tickets would,
like cents-off coupons, appeal to the Belonger group.[22]

   If reliable, such information is obviously useful in designing a marketing
strategy to increase lottery sales. Table 10.1 gives information on participation in lottery games and other activities for four of the VALS classes. The
table shows, for example, that Belongers bet more than average in each of
the lottery games but less than average with bookies. The Societally Conscious, by contrast, gamble considerably less than average. Straightforward
application of heavy-user target marketing would thus recommend ads aimed
at Belongers and Emulators. The characteristics of classes might also be used
in product design and promotion. For example, active promotion of ticket
subscriptions might increase sales to the Belonger group. Koza states: "An
opportunity certainly exists here, if pursued with sophisticated marketing
techniques that effectively aim the effort at the targeted market and carefully

Table 10.1.   Lottery players according to four VALS classifications

Characteristics	VALS Classification			
	Belonger	Achiever	Emulator	Societally conscious
Percentage of population	35%	22%	10%	8%
Median age	52	43	27	39
Average household income, 1979	$17,300	$31,400	$18,300	$27,200
Participation index for selected activities[a]				
Cents-off coupon	127	96	90	104
Betting with a bookie	61	69	158	52
Participation index for lottery games[a]				
Daily numbers	136	69	150	39
Instant games	114	96	129	62
Lotto	109	94	148	54

Sources: Arnold Mitchell, *The Nine American Lifestyles* (New York: Macmillan, 1983), p. 232, table A.1; John R. Koza, "Who Is Playing What," *Public Gaming* 12 (May 1984), 17ff.
   a. Participation index is calculated as the ratio of "regular players" in group as a percentage of all regular players to people in this group as a percentage of population, all multiplied by 100. Based on a survey of 1,876 New Jersey residents in 1982 (see Koza, "Who Is Playing What").

tailor the 'consumer benefit' message to the particular 'values' sought by this group."[23]

   To what extent theories of this sort actually manifest themselves in the kinds and amounts of marketing directed at various groups is another question. One way to see target marketing at work is to consider the radio stations the lotteries choose for their ads. A schedule of radio ads for the New York lottery over a two-week period in 1987 suggests which groups the lottery was trying to reach. Measured in terms of lottery ads per station, the formats of the stations used most frequently were "easy listening," country-and-western, and black music. Relatively few lottery ads were placed with diversified format, foreign-language, "oldies" and "middle-of-the-road" music stations, and none were aired on educational or classical music stations.[24] That lottery ads tend to be aimed at those who already play the most is also confirmed by surveys conducted by the Maryland lottery in 1985. Figure 10.1 measures exposure to advertising according to the percentage of people who had seen or heard *any* Maryland lottery ad within the previous month. Among the categories examined, the largest differences were by age, with those seventy and older least likely to have seen lottery ads. Blacks were more likely than whites to have noticed ads, and those who watch television during some daytime and nighttime hours more likely than nonwatchers. Finally, lottery players reported seeing ads more often than did nonplayers, although perhaps players simply notice such ads more often. To the extent that players do in fact see ads more often than nonplayers, the Maryland lottery appears to be succeeding in one of the essential aims of target marketing—to focus the bulk of the marketing dollar on creating more usage among those who already play.

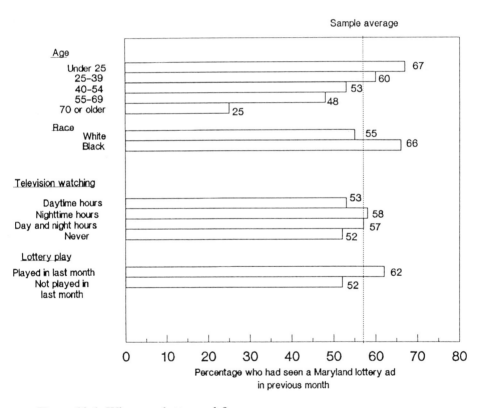

Figure 10.1. Who sees lottery ads?

(*Source:* Calculated from unpublished data from survey conducted by the Gallup Organization, Inc., Gallup Survey GO 84190, November 1984)

The "Four P's" of Lottery Marketing

Let us now turn in more detail to the "four P's": product, price, place, and promotion.[25] This typology provides a useful way to examine the methods used by lottery suppliers to sell their wares.

Product design. Some features of lottery products are inherent in the commodity, such as the fact that only a relatively small proportion of participants can win big prizes. But a number of aspects are subject to the control of the producer, and by manipulating these characteristics, lottery suppliers can "position" their products to appeal to various market segments. Four such product characteristics are the play value, prize structure, variety, and complexity of games. Perhaps least amenable to manipulation is play value, the simulated sense of player participation. Games that allow players to pick their own numbers offer more play value than games that do not. But, as we saw in Chapter 4, the designers of instant rub-off games have attempted to add play value to an otherwise passive game by inserting the elements of choice and suspense in variations of the game.

No single attribute can adequately describe the prize structure of a lottery game. Moreover, there is little consensus regarding the characteristics of lottery prizes that appeal most to consumers. About all that one can conclude from the discussion of prize structures in industry publications is that a prudent lottery agency will provide a mix in order to appeal to different players. Thus the introduction of lotto, with its huge grand prizes, has resulted in a restructuring of prizes for instant games, increasing the number of moderate prizes at the expense of the large prizes previously offered in instant games.[26] Similar considerations came into play in determining the format of lotto. Research in Washington showed that neither players nor nonplayers knew the odds of winning the state's lotto game and that concern over the odds was dominated by the awareness of large prizes, findings that are quite consistent with the statistical evidence cited in Chapter 6. As a consequence, the state changed from a 6/40 to a 6/44 format.[27]

Lottery suppliers inject variety into their product lines by supplying different games with different attributes, by offering variants to the basic bet in their numbers and keno-type games, and by keeping their instant games in a constant state of flux. Except for the inherent week-to-week variation in winning numbers, number of winners, and size of lotto jackpots, there is little inherent variety in lottery operations. Lottery suppliers make up for this in daily numbers games by offering the same kinds of bets traditionally available in the illegal numbers game. The suppliers have sought additional novelty in the design of their instant games, which have come to offer variety with a vengeance. As we saw in Chapter 4, these games are distinguished by the frequency with which new themes, new rules, and new prize structures are introduced. The packaging and graphic design of instant games is another source of variety.

The obverse of variety is complexity. Like other products, lotteries are less favorably received when consumers do not understand how they work. Some of the lottery games, notably passive and instant games, are quite simple and thus easy for most consumers to play. Only when extra drawings or combinations of tickets are involved do these games become very involved. For example, Washington decided to add a "stub" game to its instant game to allow for the possibility of very large prizes as well as a second chance to win, reasoning that the barriers this complication would create for new players would be worth the increase in interest among core players.[28] Still, the designers of instant tickets are careful not to use too many rub-off spots for fear that the game may become too confusing. Conventional wisdom holds that most players can manage games with three winning spots, but four is too many.[29] Simple lotto requires some explanation for first-time players, but it is reasonably accessible to most adults.

The daily numbers games and lotto variants offer almost boundless potential for complexity. Under either the three- or four-digit versions of the numbers game, the permutations of allowed bets would seem to intimidate all but the most dedicated aficionado. But because these games were designed to mimic an established game with a faithful following, the target consumers were assumed to be already knowledgeable. Complexity also appears to be a challenge in the design and marketing of new keno-type lotto games. For example, a 6/15/52 format game introduced in 1984 in Western Canada and British Columbia suffered poor sales in its first two years owing to its complexity and to players' mistaken notion that the odds of winning were smaller than for the 6/49 Canadian game.[30] While complexity seems to be anathema in generating new business, it may well be useful for maintaining the interest of old users.

Price. As obvious as it might seem, the concept of price is not easily defined for lottery products. In order to ascertain the price of any product, it is necessary to define units of quantity. Lottery products, however, vary in a number of specifics, such as the frequency of drawings, the size of the top prize, the probability of winning any prize, and the expected value of all prizes. As we have shown, no single variable can adequately measure the prize structure or indeed the characteristics of a lottery game, including the game's expected value. It seems natural to define price in terms of the expected value of prizes, for example as the cost of purchasing a prize distribution with an expected value of fifty cents. By this definition, an increase in the numbers game payout vote from 50 percent to 60 percent would imply a "price" reduction from $1.00 to $.83, corresponding to a 20 percent increase in the "quantity" offered by a standard bet. But comparisons among games are problematic because the products are qualitatively different; numbers and lotto are like apples and oranges.[31]

It is evident that state lotteries have been attentive to the payout rates of their products, but state legislation often allows lottery managers little room to maneuver. As we have seen, most statutes specify payout rates or set minimum rates. Lottery management in some states has the flexibility to vary the payout rates among games, especially with regard to daily numbers games, in which states face direct competition from illegal numbers. In order to make their legal games competitive, these states increase the payout percentage above the rate applied to other games. For example, Washington pays out 50 percent of its daily numbers revenues in prizes, compared to 45 percent for its instant and lotto games.[32] Massachusetts established a payout rate of 60 percent for its daily numbers game, and it further differentiated payouts among the various betting options, although it is not clear that players are very much aware of such differences. As we have noted, players generally appear to be ignorant about basic parameters of the lottery games in which they participate.

Lottery operators have also varied the face-value ticket price. New Hampshire began in 1964 with a ticket selling for $3 (well over $10 in 1988 dollars), but the going price for passive games eventually dropped to 50 cents following New Jersey's adoption of a lottery.[33] The $1 price for the instant game introduced by Massachusetts in 1974 was set to differentiate that game from the preexisting passive game.[34] That price has been copied by every subsequent instant game operator, a coincidence that may be explained by a combination of the dollar bill's convenience as a denomination, the success of the Massachusetts game, and the fact that there have been only a couple of major suppliers of instant games.[35]

Place. Where are lottery products sold to the public? How convenient is it for people to buy tickets? These are the questions the traditional marketing concept of place raises in the case of lotteries. The most common types of retail outlets for lottery sales are convenience stores, supermarkets, liquor stores, drugstores, and newsstands, although some lotteries also use shops or kiosks devoted exclusively to the sale of lottery tickets.[36] The role of these various establishments differs by state, owing in part to restrictions on the kinds of businesses that may sell tickets, but states are remarkably uniform in the density with which they distribute such outlets throughout the population. In 1988 the ratio of vendors to population varied from 4.3 per 10,000 in Michigan to 13.5 per 10,000 in Maine.[37] The optimal density is by no means obvious. On the one hand, there is evidence that for some games sales rise as agent density increases,[38] which is not surprising in light of the long lines that sometimes form at popular lottery outlets. Yet on the other hand, retailer loyalty is likely to fall as the number of franchises is increased, a problem that has its parallel in almost any franchising relationship.

There is little reason to doubt the sentiment of lottery managers that the success of any lottery's marketing strategy depends to a considerable extent on the enthusiastic cooperation of its retail agents. These agents can vary greatly in effectiveness of sales effort. Their ability to maintain an inventory of tickets and their willingness to make immediate payments for small winning tickets are two of the most influential factors cited by lottery managers. In order to improve effectiveness in this regard lottery managers have offered as special incentives an additional percentage commission for sales of winning tickets, hired field representatives to visit retailers, and tried to simplify bookkeeping requirements in connection with lottery sales.[39] In general, enthusiastic participation at the place of sale is a central component in the fiscal performance of any lottery. A cashier who asks, "Would you like a lottery ticket with that quart of milk?" may have a significant role in determining a lottery's success in maximizing sales.

Other factors affecting the convenience of lottery purchases are under the direct control of state lotteries. One of these is the computer equipment used to take bets. The easier the computers are to work, the shorter the lines will be in retail outlets and the more cooperation can be expected from retailers. Many potential problems can be bypassed altogether, however, simply by selling tickets through vending machines, referred to in the industry as player-activated terminals. Such machines have been used in high-traffic areas such as airports and large retail stores.[40]

Convenience of purchase especially affects that segment of demand based on impulse buying. As we saw in Chapter 5, impulse purchases seem to be most prevalent in instant games. Indeed, marketing experts agree that instant games are a classic impulse item. A Missouri executive estimated that as much as 80 percent of instant ticket sales were attributable to spontaneous buying. For such purchases conventional marketing practice calls for attractive packaging, convenience, and heavy point-of-sale advertising. According to a Missouri official, such advertising "is vital to stimulate impulse sales."[41] Agencies have found that clear plastic dispensers of instant tickets, placed next to the cash register, increase sales, as do five-ticket packs of tickets hanging above the counter.[42]

Promotion. The fourth of the "four P's" subject to control by the lottery agencies is promotion, which includes advertising, sales promotion, publicity, and personal selling. The last of these is the exclusive responsibility of retail agents and is thus highly dependent on the enthusiastic cooperation of those agents. The first of these, advertising, is of such importance in lottery operations that it is treated separately in the following section.

Sales promotions refer to short-term incentives designed to encourage purchases.[43] As is the case with consumer goods, one of the most useful such devices is coupons, which are thought to be a particularly good way to introduce lottery games. For example, Iowa sent a free lotto ticket to each household in the state at the game's outset.[44] To introduce its keno-type lotto game in 1987 New York offered the sort of "buy one, get one free" promotion familiar to all grocery shoppers.[45] A study of the effectiveness of coupons by the Massachusetts lottery revealed that 30 to 35 percent of the free ticket coupons for the instant game that were mailed out or included in newspapers were redeemed.[46] This compares with a redemption rate of about 4 percent for the coupons routinely used for ordinary household products.[47] Over a third of the redemptions were by new players, and over a third of those new players continued to play the lottery after the promotion ended. As a result, about 5 percent of the coupons distributed resulted in the addition of new regular players.[48] If these results are generalizable, it appears that coupons hold much potential for boosting demand by creating new users.

In other ways as well lottery promotions resemble the methods used to sell margarine and soap. For example, Maine offered discounts at McDonald's to those who bought instant tickets. Another promotion consisted of an inexpensive change in the state's instant game prize distribution intended to alter consumer buying habits: offering free tickets as prizes and then gradually eliminating them over time. Marketers reasoned that consumers would become accustomed to playing more tickets per week and would continue to purchase at the higher level after the promotion ended. Other promotions may involve the retailer directly. In a campaign to increase its four-digit numbers game, Michigan promised customers a free four-digit ticket if a retail agent forgot to mention the product. Agents were compensated and further encouraged to promote four-digit tickets by receiving one instant ticket for every five four-digit tickets sold.[49] A marketing experiment in Pennsylvania showed that aggressive promotion by the lottery's district sales representatives increased sales.[50]

Favorable publicity is both free and effective, so marketing managers are always looking for a friendly news story. Imagine how delighted most companies would be if their main product were featured on television news shows and newspaper front pages. For lotteries this kind of publicity has become routine. Lottery drawings and winners are, after all, news, so this is hardly surprising. But the promotional value of this publicity is high nonetheless. In tacit acknowledgment of this fact, all lotteries employ public relations specialists who make sure that big winners are photographed and interviewed. Reunions of winners are organized and publicized as well.

Beyond this kind of routine coverage, states have been energetic in staging sometimes extravagant media events to publicize the launching of new lotteries. The publicity effort of the California lottery is illustrative. In the final days before its inauguration, the director visited all of the media markets in the state and made himself available for interviews. The kickoff itself was marked by extravaganzas in four cities, featuring balloons, fireworks, celebrities, and marching bands. The lottery followed up in the early months of operation with a publicity program to feed information on winners to local newspapers.[51] Similarly, the Missouri lottery spent $400,000 on opening-day activities, including hot air balloons, fireworks, and a laser show.[52]

Lottery Advertising

Advertising—promotional messages paid for by the seller—is undoubtedly the most visible form of promotion engaged in by state lotteries. In addition to the familiar television and radio spots, states use newspaper and magazine ads, billboards, posters, and so-called point-of-sale displays in retail stores. Television takes the largest share of lottery advertising budgets, as it does in most industries. In 1988 television accounted for an estimated 57 percent of budgets allocated to specific media. Radio had the next largest share, with 16 percent, followed by point-of-sale ads (11 percent), print ads (7 percent), and transit signs and billboards (5 percent).[53] Because of the lottery's unique position among state agencies, lottery advertising has become one of the most widespread forms of information disseminated by state governments. For better or worse, most state citizens see lottery ads far more often than virtually any other message put out by the state. A survey completed in 1986 showed that 92 percent of adults in Arizona had seen lottery ads on television.[54] The Maryland survey summarized in Figure 10.1 shows that those most likely to be aware of lottery ads are young adults, blacks, television watchers, and those who play the lottery. Because lottery advertising has become a ubiquitous part of state government, it is useful to examine its role as a marketing tool and the messages it contains.

Amount of Advertising

Before we consider the nature and use of lottery advertising, let us get a sense of the quantity of that advertising. We know that lottery agencies advertise, but how much in comparison to other comparable goods and services? One simple way to answer that question is to calculate the agencies' advertising expenditures as a percentage of their total costs of production (prizes plus administrative expenses). Advertising budgets are occasionally tabulated in trade publications and listed in annual reports. But it is not clear to what extent the salaries of in-house marketing and public relations personnel are included in such figures. Nor do advertising budgets reflect the value of free time for nightly drawings traded by television stations in exchange for the boost in audience.[55] In our survey of lottery agencies we found that a majority of agencies paid nothing to have their drawings televised.

Subject to these important qualifications, Table 10.2 shows that lottery agencies devote about 2 percent of their costs to budgeted advertising expenditures. For the sake of comparison the table also gives information on American corporations' advertising as a percentage of all business expenses. For all corporations the comparable figure was 1.1 percent, about half the ratio for lotteries. Manufacturing and retail industries also spend less than lotteries. Perhaps the closest comparison is offered by amusement and recreation services at 3 percent, and public utilities, which operate under similar conditions of monopoly, at 0.6 percent. Among corporations in comparable industries, therefore, only amusement and recreation services have a higher rate of budgeted advertising expenditure. If the value of traded television time were added, lotteries might well exceed that industry's percentage too.

Table 10.2.   Advertising as a percentage of business expenses for lotteries and selected industries

Type of enterprise	Advertising as percentage of—
Lotteries, 1988	Prizes plus operating expenses
United States	2.0%
Canada	2.2
U.S. corporations, 1984	Total expenses[a]
All industries	1.1%
Manufacturing	1.5
Retail trade	1.7
Amusement and recreation services	3.0
Transportation and public utilities	0.6

Sources: For lotteries, *Gaming and Wagering Business* 9 (September 1988), 32 (1988 sales and advertising); 9 (October 1988), 30 (1988 government revenue for U.S. lotteries); Table 2.3 (1987 ratio of government revenue to sales for Canadian lotteries). Prizes plus operating expenses calculated as sales minus government revenue from sales. For corporations, U.S. Internal Revenue Service, *Statistics of Income, 1984: Corporation Income Tax Returns* (Washington, D.C.: Government Printing Office, 1987), table 2, pp. 23ff., figures for active corporations.

a. Total expenses are total business deductions, including taxes other than corporate income tax.

Another way of comparing advertising figures is to use data based on expenditures on various media rather than total advertising budgets. In 1984 lotteries in ten of the largest states placed ads in television, radio, newspapers, magazines, and outdoor signs worth an estimated $23 million, or about 27 cents per capita. By contrast, the per capita advertising figures for some of the most heavily advertised consumer products were roughly ten times as great (for example, beer at $2.43 and domestic passenger cars at $2.86).[56] But comparisons such as these ignore the extensive free publicity given to lottery drawings. In Detroit the state's weekly lotto drawing had a remarkable 30 percent share of the television market.[57] If one looks instead at government and political advertising for comparison, in 1984 lotteries were advertised on a per capita basis about half as much as all federal programs put together, but more than the combined Reagan and Mondale presidential campaigns (16 cents).[58]

Such national data may obscure advertising by governments on the state level, so it is useful to compare the amount of lottery advertising to that of other messages state government presents. The data in Table 10.3 are based on records of television advertising in major metropolitan markets. The amount of advertising by state government agencies—including lotteries—

Table 10.3.   Lottery share of total television advertising by state agencies, selected television markets

State	Television market	Percentage of all state advertisements devoted to lotteries
California	Los Angeles	100%
Illinois	Chicago	93
Massachusetts	Boston	100
Michigan	Detroit	77
New Jersey	Philadelphia and New York City	38
New York	New York City	47
Ohio	Cleveland	100
Pennsylvania	Philadelphia	61
Average		74%

Source: Calculated from unpublished surveys of advertising by Broadcast Advertisers Reports, Inc., "Brand Schedules by Parent Company," for the broadcast months of January 1987 (Boston, Detroit, and Cleveland) and October 1986 (other listed cities).

was measured for eight markets. Five of the eight states were running promotional advertising during the sample months; in the other three the only television advertising done by the state was for the lottery. Taken together, the time devoted to lottery ads was about three-fourths the total amount for state advertising. Undoubtedly states communicate messages to their citizens in other ways, but at least as far as television is concerned, a major component of that communication is in the form of enticements to play lottery games.

Within the overall category of lottery advertising it is obvious that the various lottery products do not receive equal exposure. Lotto games, which accounted for about 40 percent of U.S. lottery sales in 1988, received about the same share of lottery advertising allocated to individual games (36 percent). But instant games, owing to the practice of constantly introducing new games, consume proportionally higher levels of advertising. While instant games brought in only 26 percent of sales in 1988, they accounted for half of the advertising attributable to specific games. By contrast daily numbers games were allocated only 10 percent of advertising, much less than their 33 percent share of sales.[59] In this respect the legal numbers game is surely the "cash cow" of state lottery games.

Timing of Ads

As with any consumer product, advertisements for lottery products are timed for maximum impact on sales. Two distinct approaches to the timing of lottery advertising are evident. The first is "front-loading," which calls for heavy advertising at the introduction of a game. An illustration is the case of Ohio's SuperLotto game, introduced in 1986. The media plan developed to introduce this game called for a three-part campaign. First, a "teaser" campaign of about two weeks would "create awareness and stimulate excitement." An introductory blitz, intended "to firmly implant the creative message, as well as generate maximum awareness and repeat exposures," would follow, using a high concentration of ads. The final phase was to be essentially a maintenance dose emphasizing the size of jackpots, a factor identified as important to players. Expenditures during the intensive introduction were to be three times those allotted to the maintenance phase. With instant games this approach usually manifests itself in bursts of advertising every eight to ten weeks at the beginning of each new game. For example, Massachusetts spends most of an instant game's advertising budget on thirty-second spots when the game is introduced and the remainder on ten-second spots.[60]

The second approach to timing advertising, and one that may be used along with front-loading, is to schedule advertisements to coincide with paydays and the typically high levels of consumer spending that accompany them; thus the reference to "purchase cycles" in Iowa's statement of marketing objectives. Using this approach Washington succeeded in "saturating the airwaves every other Thursday and Friday" in promoting their instant games.[61] The advertising plan for Ohio's SuperLotto game was very plain:

> *Schedule heavier media weight during those times of the month where consumer disposable income peaks.* In general, schedule heavier media weight during the traditional pay periods of the first and fifteenth of each month. We recommend that promotional "pushes" be targeted as early as possible in the month. Government benefits[,] payroll and Social Security payments are released on the first Tuesday of each calendar month. This, in effect, creates millions of additional, non-taxable dollars in the local economies of which the majority is disposable.[62]

In order to discover to what extent plans such as these are manifested in the actual pattern of advertising, we studied the timing patterns of televised lottery advertisements in eight sample markets, using unpublished data based on round-the-clock monitoring. Stations in these markets carried ads for all eight state lotteries during the sample months. One pattern that was examined was the distribution of ads by day of the week. Any "pulsing" throughout the week might have been expected to correspond to paydays, usually Fridays, or to days on which lotto drawings occur, usually Wednesdays and Saturdays. In addition, since many bets are placed on Monday for the entire week, that day might be a reasonable time for concentrating ads. In fact, no one pattern was followed by all the states. In two relatively more ads appeared on Monday. Two others emphasized Wednesday, and two others Saturday. Taken together, the eight states tended to concentrate their ads at the end of the week, as shown in Figure 10.2. Sundays received by far the least advertising, with rates about three-fourths the average. The data provided no evidence of other systematic timing patterns, however. In particular, there appears to be no systematic attempt to time ads to correspond to specific days other than around Fridays.

Content of Advertising

After they have done their research, positioned their products, and identified their potential customers, what messages do the lottery marketers use in their advertising? In order to study the themes, we gathered a sampling of ads from various states. Requests were sent to seventeen of the largest lottery states and the District of Columbia. Thirteen of those lotteries or their advertising agencies responded, and 282 advertisements, not counting dupli-

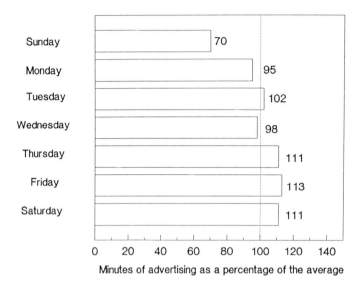

Figure 10.2. Distribution of lottery ads by day of the week

(*Source:* Broadcast Advertisers Reports, "Brand Schedules by Parent
Company," broadcast months of October 1986 and January 1987,
unpublished tables provided by Broadcast Advertisers Reports, Inc.)

cates, were collected.[63] Television ads accounted for 36 percent of the sample,
below their 54 percent share of lottery ad budgets. Radio accounted for 18
percent of the ads, which approximated that medium's 17 percent share in
lottery ad budgets.[64] We classified the ads by medium and principal message.
Where more than one theme appeared, a judgment was made about the ad's
primary message. Information contained in the ads about prizes and the odds
of winning was also noted.

Information. Table 10.4 summarizes the content of this sample of lottery
advertisements. Eight primary messages were identified, four of them largely
informational and the rest basically thematic in character. Informational ads
included announcements of a new lottery or lottery game ("Coming soon. A
new angle on fun," from California's introduction of lotto), and direct appeals to buy tickets ("Watch it grow! Play Lotto 6/49," also from California),
including the traditional incentives of free samples and coupons. Ads of this
sort accounted for 40 percent of the ads in the column labeled "other" (including newspaper, point-of-sale, and billboard advertising). Information on
rules of the game, prize structure, and odds of winning was carried in all of
the media but was concentrated in brochures. Virtually all the brochures in
the sample gave information about the games as their primary message,

ble 10.4. Content of lottery advertising

imary message	Percentage of total advertisements in—			
	Television (N = 101)	Radio (N = 50)	Brochure (N = 36)	Other[a] (N = 95)
formational				
Direct sales appeal[b]	13%	18%	11%	43%
How to play	5	14	83	16
Previous winners	1	2	0	5
Public benefits; where the revenue goes	4	0	0	12
ematic				
Fun, excitement of playing	15	6	3	2
You could win; winning could change your life	33	24	3	18
Wealth, elegance	2	10	0	0
Jackpot growing; money	28	26	0	4
Total	100	100	100	100
formation on odds	12	12	72	13
formation on prize nounts	51	46	81	53

Source: Samples of advertisements collected from thirteen state lotteries, 1987.
a. Billboards, posters, point-of-sale displays, and newspaper and magazine ads.
b. Introductory, play the game, coupon, free tickets, and gift suggestion.

although a number of them also urged people to play the game or mentioned the benefits to the state. Over 40 percent of the ads in the sample contained some information about how to play a lottery game. A few ads were designed to tell about former winners, with most giving their names and the amounts they had won. One memorable print ad from California used a winner's story to suggest a method for picking lotto numbers: it pictured numbered jerseys from various sports along with an explanation of how one sports fan had won the jackpot by using the numbers of six of his sports heroes.

Although many ads did feature a reminder of where the lottery revenue goes, only a few were devoted solely to that purpose. Maryland, though, put out a series of ads detailing some of the benefits resulting from lottery revenues, featuring services as diverse as the state education fund and a drug abuse program. One of the most dramatic of these was a television spot depicting a little boy wandering away from his family's campsite in the woods. In the gathering darkness the frightened boy wanders through the woods crying for his mother and father while the worried parents describe their son to police officers. A state police helicopter spots the boy with a searchlight, and a voice-over points out that the state lottery contributed $300 million in funds for public service, part of which was set aside for this police helicopter. As a sobbing mother is notified that her son is safe, the ad intones: "The Maryland State Lottery pays off in ways you may not even know about." So striking was this ad that it gained notoriety both in and out of the state. According to the state budget examiner's report, the ad has been criticized as "misleading gimmickry that does not articulate the impact of Lottery revenues on the State Treasury."[65] The ad's subsequent screening for Virginia legislators apparently built support for restrictions on advertising in that state.[66]

Although our tabulation of primary messages does not reflect the fact, many of the ads in the sample used generic or institutional themes, including slogans designed especially for that state's lottery, often referring to the special use to which lottery revenues are put. In most cases such themes are not the primary message of ads, so they do not appear in the tabulation, but they do seem to be an integral part of the lottery's total marketing strategy. Some slogans contribute generally to a "feeling good" statement about the lottery as an institution: "It's working for Arizona" and "Thanks to you, everybody wins" (District of Columbia).[67] Others refer more specifically to the public uses for lottery funds: "Lottery proceeds benefit Ohio schools," "Our schools win, too" (California), and "Benefits senior citizens" (Pennsylvania). Apparently there are marketing advantages to be gained from communicating a lottery's funding purpose. Lottery marketing research suggests, for example, that such ads appeal especially to those who might otherwise oppose or be unfamiliar with gambling—the inner-directed VALS types. A marketing strategist from Scientific Games states: "In Colorado, the revenues were earmarked for parks and recreation. We found that the inner-directed groups participated much more in Colorado because they felt that by buying a ticket, they were making a meaningful contribution. One Colorado man we interviewed said: 'When I buy a lottery ticket, I feel like I win either way.' "[68] To emphasize the worthy purposes to which lottery funds are put, at least two states have featured their governors in televised lottery ads.[69]

Thematic ads. Most lottery advertising on television and radio eschews both serious messages and the hard sell. Like current advertising of other products, the typical lottery ad uses humor and soft-sell techniques. To this they add a heavy dose of fantasy. Although one can identify several dominant themes in this advertising, it seems clear that the best lottery ads, like the best ads for other products, are meant to convey some of their most important messages with subtlety and indirection. Thus a California television spot showing a rural storekeeper putting up the lottery logo, with his dog on the porch and a school bus reflected in the window, evokes images of a whole-some America. Similar themes in ads for consumer products are thought to speak to the traditional values of Belongers.[70] Other ads based on fantasies of wealth and a transformed life may appeal to Emulator and Achiever groups.

It was possible to identify several themes in this advertising. First is that playing the game is in itself fun and exciting. Massachusetts named its first weekly lottery in 1972 The Game to highlight the aspect of fun.[71] In Maryland emphasis on the fun of playing has been a hallmark of television and radio advertising.[72] An Arizona radio campaign also touted the fun of its games, proclaiming in song, "It's the Pick / It's a Kick / Come in and try your luck / You can't buy more excitement for a buck." The theme of excitement is suggested by spies in District of Columbia ads and in Washington State by a motorcyclist who rides his bike out of airplanes for a thrill, when he discovers that the lottery offers excitement with better odds. Part of the reason for this emphasis on fun appears to be a desire to dispel unsavory connotations as-sociated with gambling, particularly illegal gambling.

A second theme is the dual message that anyone can win and that winning can change your life. A Michigan television spot begins with a man saying he has a better chance of being struck by lightning than winning the lottery. Sure enough, a lightning bolt hits him, after which he says, "One ticket, please." An Oregon ad shows an elderly man sitting in front of a general store muttering that nobody ever wins the Oregon lottery. In the space of thirty seconds three winners emerge from the store, after which he goes in to buy a ticket.[73]

The ads embellish this theme by giving graphic examples of how winning can transform one's life. The District of Columbia ran a series of before-and-after ads that exemplify this appeal. In one such print ad the "before" picture shows a bedraggled man, face covered with stubble, hair matted down, wear-ing glasses and sloppy clothes. In the "after" picture he is clean shaven, well groomed, wearing a tuxedo but no glasses, conspicuously holding a copy of a theater program. The ad proclaims, "Just One Ticket . . . and It Could Happen to You." A radio spot from Washington State is a musical testimon-ial from a successful lotto player: "And now I walk the streets of paradise / Just like the fella on 'Miami Vice.' " A Michigan ad showing a woman run-ning through her office after she had won advises, "Of course, you're going to have to figure out what you're going to tell your boss."

Closely related are ads that bypass the process of winning altogether to focus on the wealth and luxury that are the reward of successful lottery play. A California television commercial for an instant game called The Good Life touts the advantages of wealth with images of an elegantly dressed couple dancing, a woman walking expensive dogs, a red carpet being unrolled, and a couple on a yacht. A Michigan ad puts it simply: "The rich. Join them."

A fourth group of thematic ads builds on the fantasy of winning by focusing on the money itself. Ads show coins being minted, gold bars being stamped, or armored cars delivering vast sums of cash. One popular image is the bank vault. A series of television ads in Michigan show a vault in a science-fiction setting with the money inside throbbing and growing out of control. Oregon based one series of ads on the trials and tribulations of "Bob," the official whose job it is to count the lotto jackpot. Poor Bob never gets out of the vault because the prizes are so immense that he can never stop counting. To reinforce the message that prizes consist of money, and lots of it, lottery ads often mention the size of a game's top prize. Half of the ads we saw mentioned a specific sum.

This characterization of advertising content is necessarily incomplete, based as it is on a relatively small sample and an imprecise classification of dominant messages. Hardest to quantify are the repeated appeals to fantasy. While numerous ads portrayed wealth, leisure, and gracious living, others appealed to the taste for excitement, romance, and fame. Other fantasies were more prosaic. One California ad showed a series of dreams that winning might make possible, from a carefree retirement to establishing a father-son business. Another aspect worth noting is the tendency for ads to portray wholesome surroundings and people who are younger and more affluent than the typical lottery player. Not only may this tendency be an attempt to recruit new players, but it also appears to reflect the effort by marketers, first noted by Vance Packard, to build into products the traits consumers would like to see in themselves.[74]

Evidently some of the brightest talent in product marketing has been employed by the state lotteries in their efforts to sell more tickets. The advertisements produced for this purpose are among the most clever and appealing shown on television today. But it is perhaps as useful to make note of what is omitted from these ads as to discuss what they contain.

Do Lottery Ads Mislead?

Critics have charged that lottery advertising systematically gives short shrift to certain details about the games. Take, for example, the statement of the jackpot available for a given lotto drawing. As we have seen, these grand prizes are typically paid out over a twenty-year period, but the stated prize is the simple sum of the payments, not the present value, which might be only about half as large. Some critics have urged agencies to make clear that a prize of such magnitude will be awarded only if there is a single winner; otherwise the prize money will be divided. Still another criticism of current practice is that agencies do not emphasize that such jackpots are subject to federal and sometimes state income taxation.[75] The result of these practices, say critics, is a consistent overstatement of the true value of prizes.

But the practice that has raised the most objection is the lotteries' presentation of odds. John G. Cross, who has noted the difficulty of obtaining the necessary information to calculate a statistic as basic as the payout rate, charges lottery agencies with systematic "obfuscation."[76] A state commission studying the Illinois lottery also concluded that information on odds was difficult to obtain.[77] These criticisms would apply to the advertisements examined in the present study. Among the ads we looked at, statements about the odds of winning or the payout rate were conspicuous by their absence. For example, only 20 percent of all the ads in the sample gave any information on the odds of winning, and this figure drops to 12 percent for the two most prominent media, television and radio. Where such information was given, it usually applied to the probability of winning *any* prize, as opposed to the grand prize. In contrast, over half the advertisements in the sample mentioned the dollar amount of prizes—almost always the grand prize. Bolstering this emphasis on prizes over probabilities, the ads give a distorted impression of the probability of winning with their frequent portrayal of players who have won large prizes. Two-thirds of the television ads in the sample that showed any past or present lottery players showed at least one who was a winner. For all the media represented in the sample this ratio was over 70 percent.

In their defense lottery officials argue that there is not enough time in most radio and television ads to give much information on odds or prize structures.[78] In Missouri, where a statement including the payout rate and a disclaimer was required by law, the message merely flashed on the screen. Some states do require prominent statements of prize structures, the odds of winning, or payout rates. Whether or not elaborate statements of odds are feasible, it is instructive to note that in the case of sweepstakes under the jurisdiction of the Federal Trade Commission advertising must disclose the odds of winning all prizes as well as other facts about the games.[79] Applying these standards to lottery advertising would necessitate a dramatic shift in current industry practice.[80]

Combined with the themes of wealth, excitement, and transformation that run through the ads, the emphasis on winning makes for compelling copy. Consider this print ad from Oregon:

PLAY MEGABUCKS NOW
AND YOU COULD BE A WINNER
THIS SATURDAY NIGHT.

Imagine this.
You pick up a Megabucks play slip now.
Choose 6 of the 42 numbers available.
(Or ask for "Quick Pick" and let the machine pick 'em for you.)
Then, on Saturday night, you sit down to watch the Megabucks show.
Your ticket is clutched tightly in your hand.
The numbers are picked.
Your numbers!
And suddenly, your life has changed.
Suddenly, you're rich.
Could it happen?
Absolutely!
But, you have to do more than just imagine.
You have to play.[81]

What are the consequences of this kind of advertising? While no one can be sure, it seems likely that all this attention to prizes and winning at the expense of information on the odds (1 in 5.2 million in the case of the ad just cited) increases players' "subjective probability" of winning. As Amos Tversky and Daniel Kahneman argue, the perceived probability of a very unlikely event tends to be increased by tangible examples of the event.[82] Extensive coverage of winners and dramatized examples of winning coupled with the virtual absence of information on the probability of winning a grand prize— these are the essential ingredients in lottery promotion. Whether or not they lead to misperceptions that increase the demand for tickets, they hardly represent a balanced description of lottery games.

Lottery Advertising and the Inducement to Gamble

Lottery advertising presents a policy dilemma because the objective of revenue maximization conflicts with the widespread distaste for encouraging people to gamble. As we have seen, increasing lottery revenues requires either the recruitment of new customers or the stimulation of betting among existing customers. But blatant inducements to gamble, like inducements to drink or smoke, are commonly seen as offensive, if not unethical. In its 1971 code of conduct the National Association of Broadcasters stated that advertising legal lotteries was acceptable "provided such advertising does not unduly exhort the public to bet."[83] Several states have attempted to restrict lottery advertising. Laws passed in Missouri, Virginia, and Wisconsin all include limitations on the kinds of ads that may be run, forbidding ads that "induce" people to play the lottery. In addition, Missouri originally required a disclaimer to appear in all ads ("This message is for informational and educational purposes only. It is not intended to induce any person to participate in the lottery or purchase a lottery ticket"), but this requirement was dropped in 1988 after several years of disappointing sales.

What does inducement consist of? One answer was given by the broadcasting industry in 1975 when the National Association of Broadcasters refined its earlier admonition against "undue exhortation" by spelling out what kinds of lottery advertising were and were not acceptable. It stated that lottery ads could present such basic information as how the lottery works, the cost of tickets, prize distributions, winning numbers, and factual information about actual winners. As to what was not acceptable practice, the code was explicit:

> In order to avoid approaches which do, or have the capacity to, unduly exhort people to bet, commercials for legalized lotteries may not:
>
> 1. Indicate what fictitious winners may do, hope to do or have done with their winnings.
>
> 2. Use unqualified or inaccurate language regarding potential winners/winnings. (e.g., "There's a pot of gold for those who buy lottery tickets"; "Buy a ticket and be a winner.")
>
> 3. Utilize approaches which praise people who buy lottery tickets or denigrate people who do not buy tickets.[84]

Although the entire broadcasting code has subsequently been struck down as anticompetitive, these standards are revealing as a direct statement of industry mores. Given the numerous lottery advertisements demonstrating the changes in one's life that winning could make possible and the occasional lighthearted jabs made at nonplayers, it is clear that lottery advertisers feel no obligation to adhere to such standards.

Conclusion

Lottery products are marketed in much the same way as hundreds of other consumer products. Some ads are primarily informational, but most are whimsical, or humorous "soft-sell" presentations that are thematic rather than precisely factual. Winning and fantasies associated with winning play an important part in this advertising, while information on the odds of winning is less conspicuous. One possible if unproven effect of this advertising policy is that consumers' perceptions of the chance of winning might be systematically distorted. Another possible effect is an undermining of the credibility of state government in general. Michael Schudson has argued that much advertising is characterized by "persistent, underlying bad faith."[85] To the extent that the puffery that is taken for granted in commercial advertising becomes a part of government messages, the credibility of government in other areas may be damaged as well. And to the extent that lottery advertising fails to come up to standards of disclosure that apply to commercial sweepstakes, the likelihood of skepticism about the aims of government increases.

It has now become conventional wisdom that a lottery must market aggressively to be a "success."[86] This assertion raises at least two questions: how to define success and how to determine the impact of advertising on that measure. If one adopts the view implicit in the lottery policy of most states that success is judged purely in terms of net revenues, the question becomes simply what effect advertising has on lottery sales. Unfortunately there is as yet no evidence that can satisfactorily answer that question, although it seems likely that advertising can increase the demand for lottery products. In light of the possibly undesirable effects of lottery advertising, however, an argument certainly exists for considering more than the lottery's net revenues in assessing the amount and nature of lottery advertising.

PART IV

Lotteries as Public Policy

11.

A "Painless Tax"?

A LOTTERY is a Taxation,
Upon all the Fools in Creation;
And Heav'n be prais'd,
It is easily rais'd,
Credulity's always in Fashion:
For, Folly's a Fund,
Will never lose Ground,
While Fools are so rife in the Nation.

—Henry Fielding, 1732

Revenue is the raison d'être of contemporary state lotteries. In every case where states have adopted this institution, potential revenues and what can be done with them have been the principal selling points. Yet according to proponents, the lottery is unlike other sources of revenue; here, they say, is a "painless tax" because it is paid only by the willing. They are fond of quoting Thomas Jefferson, who is said to have portrayed the lottery as an ideal fiscal instrument, one exacting payment solely from those who choose to play. In fact, Jefferson was not altogether enthusiastic about lotteries.[1]

Opponents of lotteries have adopted the language of taxation and charged that lotteries rank poorly according to conventional criteria for judging taxes. For example, lotteries are said to be a relatively inefficient source of revenue owing to the high ratio of administrative costs per dollar raised. Lotteries have also been compared unfavorably to conventional taxes because of their alleged instability and limited revenue potential. But the charge that has stung lottery proponents the hardest—if the vigor of their response is any indication—is that lotteries are regressive. Lotteries are seen as "preying on the poor," whether wittingly, by marketing heavily in poor areas, or unwittingly, simply by offering a product that appeals to poor people. Yet there remains a sense of unease in this argument, as illustrated by the exasperated insight of one Maryland state senator who opposed the lottery: "Lotteries place an inordinate burden on the poor to finance state government. But the poor are willing suckers, and it's hard to defend a group that doesn't want to be defended."[2]

A useful beginning point in this assessment is to return to the four aspects of state lotteries outlined in Chapter 1. As operated in the United States today, lotteries entail legalization, provision, marketing, and implicit taxation. The lottery's profits, derived as they are from a state-owned enterprise, are no less useful than revenues that are labeled taxes, so it is altogether appropriate to label them implicit taxes. Although the formula for lotteries has varied remarkably little—state operation with about half of sales returned as prizes—nothing is inherent in a lottery that mandates a certain rate of profit. Once a lottery is established, the implicit tax can be raised or lowered in the same way as conventional taxes. So it makes sense to judge the implicit tax in the lottery by the standards by which other taxes are measured.

Economists at least as far back as Adam Smith have laid down criteria for "good" taxes. Smith suggested several standards for judging taxes, including equity, certainty, convenience, and economy in collection.[3] Tax analysts today take much the same approach. In this chapter we assess the implicit lottery tax, first in terms of the objective the lotteries themselves have adopted: revenue. Viewing the lottery chiefly as a revenue machine makes it essential to examine the amount of revenue the lotteries bring in, the reliability of that revenue, and the administrative costs required to raise it. If, however, revenue is not the state's only objective in operating a lottery, it becomes necessary to consider other criteria as well. Thus we turn to two concepts of conventional tax analysis, equity and efficiency.

The Lottery as a Revenue Machine

If the states are in the lottery business for the money, then the obvious question is, Just how much money are they adding to the state treasuries? Sales per capita in lottery states increased by a factor of ten between 1975 and 1988, which is an impressive accomplishment, even after discounting for the doubling of the price level during that period. On the average, 38 percent of these sales are profits transferred to the state treasury. Despite these impressive numbers, the overall impact of lottery revenues on state finance is small compared with income and sales taxes; in 1986 lottery profits accounted for little more than 3 percent of the total revenue raised by the states that have lotteries. In only a few states did the net revenues from the lottery amount to more than would a percentage point increase in the state sales tax.

Of course, the lottery has been much more successful in some states than others, with the top states scoring an order of magnitude higher in per capita sales than the bottom. Lotteries as revenue sources rank anywhere from fourth (in Maryland, behind income, sales, and motor fuel taxes) to fifteenth (in Maine, New Hampshire, and Vermont).[4] We have seen that the level of per capita sales differs markedly among states, owing in part to the availability of various types of games, marketing, and the social and economic characteristics of the state. While it is reasonable to expect that per capita sales in some of the newer lottery states will rise as more games are introduced, it seems unlikely that rural states such as Colorado and Vermont will ever observe betting at the levels experienced in urbanized states such as Maryland and Massachusetts.[5] In the case of lotto, the fastest-growing game of the 1980s, the small states have found themselves at a disadvantage in generating consumer interest because the jackpots are inevitably smaller than those in large states such as California and New York. The larger jackpots made possible by multistate lotto consortiums have lessened this disadvantage. Still, it seems doubtful that overall lottery sales can continue growing at double-digit percentage rates for long. Maintaining high growth rates requires the introduction of new types of games, such as those styled after sports cards or slot machines. Such games may offend public sensibilities sufficiently that they will be prohibited by state legislatures. But if the revenue imperative carries the day, then the state lotteries may continue to grow for some time to come.

If revenue is the objective, then an accurate accounting of lottery performance must take into account the effect of lottery sales on other sources of state revenue. Sales tax revenues decrease, for example, to the extent that people purchase lottery tickets out of income that otherwise would have gone toward consumer expenditures subject to tax. But a lottery generates a slight increase in income tax revenue if winnings are not exempted from state income taxation. The appendix to this chapter presents a simple model illustrating the effect of the lottery on other tax revenues. Under the assumptions made there, other revenues decline so that the lottery's net contribution is slightly less than the amount it transfers to the treasury. This sort of interaction between lottery sales and other sources of state revenue has only rarely been considered in previous estimates of the revenue impact of lotteries. One such study done for the state of Idaho also took into account the effect of expenditures being directed out of state. The study estimated that the net contribution of an Idaho lottery would be reduced to some 86 to 90 percent of apparent net revenues owing to declines in other taxes.[6]

Another possible interaction deserves consideration. Over the long run the operation and promotion of the lottery may depress the rate of economic growth in the state and thereby reduce revenues from income and sales tax. To the extent that the public comes to view the pursuit of a big jackpot as an easy avenue to wealth and substitutes lottery play for education, savings, and entrepreneurial efforts, the economy as a whole may suffer. Advertising that encourages people to believe that they have a real chance to win big may exacerbate this problem. But while this effect is plausible, there is no feasible method for testing or measuring it, so it must remain in the realm of speculation.

Another concern about lotteries as a source of revenue does lend itself to empirical test. In some states there have been instances of revenues exhibiting large year-to-year swings. Citing competition from other states and illegal gambling in addition to consumer fickleness, the economists John Mikesell and C. Kurt Zorn warn, "Clearly, a state cannot rely on net revenue from its lottery to be a stable, reliable source of revenue."[7] Our study of revenue data indicates, however, that while lottery revenues have indeed shown more volatility than conventional sources of state revenue, it is relatively rare for revenue in lottery sales actually to decline.

In order to judge the stability of lottery revenues, we compared lotteries to seven kinds of conventional state taxes. These were the sales tax, the individual income tax, death and gift taxes, and the excise taxes on motor fuels, tobacco products, insurance, and parimutuel betting. As sources of revenue these taxes range from the general sales tax (which nationwide generated $75 billion in forty-five states in 1986) to the excise tax on parimutuel betting ($.6 billion in thirty-one states). Lotteries, by comparison, raised $4.8 billion in twenty-three states in 1986. Our sample consisted of five large states that have operated a lottery since the 1970s.[8] Revenues for each source were converted into constant dollars and were tracked over the period 1973 to 1986 in order to examine the volatility and growth of each source.[9] One measure of volatility is the standard deviation (based on year-to-year variation from the state's average) in real annual revenues as a percentage of the average revenue from that tax over the fourteen-year period studied. By this measure lottery revenues are more variable than revenues from the other sources. But part of this apparent volatility is due to the lotteries' rapid growth. To account for the secular trend in revenues, a simple regression was estimated for each revenue source in each state, with time as the sole explanatory variable. While some tax revenues declined in real terms over the period, lottery revenues exhibited rapid growth. When these trends are taken into account, the lottery's relative volatility is far lower, although it remains the highest in the group.

By another measure, however, the lottery appears superior to the other revenue sources; in the states we studied lottery revenues were the most dependable in the sense of showing the lowest frequency of declines in revenue (adjusted for inflation) from one year to the next. The state budget process could count on receiving as least as much real revenue from the lottery each year as it had the preceding year. Even though lottery revenues are subject to an unusual degree of volatility, therefore, much of this has consisted of breathtaking growth. Surely this is a kind of volatility to which few state legislatures would object.

One final concern about the lottery as a revenue source deserves consideration. Some have charged that lotteries are a particularly inefficient way to raise money for government operations, since their ratio of administrative costs to revenue, which is "logically comparable to tax collective cost ratios,"[10] is so high, averaging over 25 percent in 1986. In fact such a comparison is not justified. Lottery agencies are not tax collectors in any normal sense but rather are state enterprises producing and selling a product to the public. This point becomes clear if we imagine a different institutional arrangement. If the lottery were provided by private suppliers at a cost of twelve cents per dollar of sales and the state took its same share of thirty-eight cents, the only relevant administrative cost of collection would be the presumably low one of monitoring the firm's tax payments. Thus the lottery's operating expenses represent the cost of providing a commodity, not a cost of revenue collection comparable to the administrative costs of state taxes.

Viewed as a state enterprise striving to make money, state lotteries appear remarkably successful. Product innovations and aggressive promotions have generated extraordinary growth, and their legal monopoly position has made possible a high rate of profit on sales. Sales have been quite volatile, but because of the high average growth rate states could count on lottery revenues to hold their own even in relatively slow years. Despite this growth, lottery net revenues still amount to only a small portion of the state budget. Furthermore, a proper accounting of the lottery's contribution must take into account the interaction with other sources of revenue and, more speculatively, the long-term effects on productive economic behavior.

The Lottery as a New Consumer Product

It is not sufficient to evaluate lotteries simply as revenue producers, even if that is the primary objective of those who run them. By legalizing and providing lottery tickets, a state in effect creates a new consumer product, and this action makes well-informed buyers better off than they were before. When the state places an implicit tax on this product by keeping a portion of the proceeds, it reduces but does not eliminate the consumer's gain in welfare. The lottery player is not unlike the moviegoer who buys popcorn at inflated prices: he is better off having the opportunity to buy the product than not having it, but would be better off still if the price (or the implicit tax) were not so high. If one makes a comparison with a situation in which lotteries are outlawed, any lottery—even a highly taxed one—could be viewed as a "painless" way to raise revenue.[11] The public has certainly welcomed the lottery in its current version, high tax rate and all. Yet there is little doubt that players would be even more enthusiastic about a lottery with a lower implicit tax rate and correspondingly more generous prize structure.

This argument can be made more precise by placing it in the economist's normative framework for evaluating the welfare effects of an excise tax. Figure 11.1 shows an individual's demand curve for lottery tickets as a function of the takeout rate, the proportion of lottery sales not returned in the form of prizes.[12] Each point on the curve shows how much the person would spend on lottery tickets at each takeout rate. State lotteries typically pay out only half of gross sales as prizes, which corresponds to a takeout rate of 50 percent. At this takeout rate the individual is assumed to spend E_1 on lottery products. Of the E_1 dollars this individual spends on tickets, 40 percent goes into the state treasury. This amount is the implicit tax, or area b in the figure. Altogether, the individual pays $1 for a chance to win prizes which have an expected value of just fifty cents. Yet this is less than the amount he would be willing to pay. The difference between what he would be willing to pay and the amount that he does in fact have to pay, the area a, is what economists refer to as the consumer surplus. This amount is a measure of the individual's net subjective benefit from the lottery.

This conventional economic framework yields two implications. First the legalization and provision of lottery products create consumer surplus. A

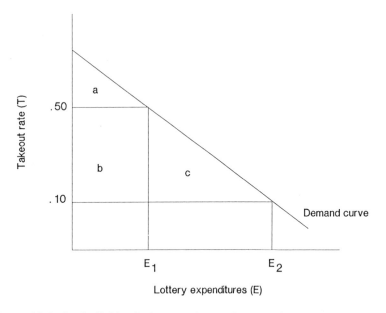

Figure 11.1. An individual's lottery demand curve. (Area a represents consumer surplus, area b the revenue raised, and area c the deadweight loss.)

second implication of the analysis, however, is that this increase in well-being owing to the lottery's introduction would be greater if the takeout rate were lower. If the lottery were to sell tickets with a takeout rate of only 10 percent, for example, the consumer surplus would equal the larger triangular area made up by the sum of areas *a, b,* and *c.*

As is evident from the intense controversy that has surrounded lotteries, not everyone accepts these conclusions. The heart of the matter is whether individual choices with respect to gambling deserve the respect embodied in the principle of consumer sovereignty. Some critics simply dismiss gambling as immoral, thus making a judgment about the worthiness of a taste for this activity. Others do not denounce a taste for gambling, but rather question whether players are sufficiently well informed to make an accurate judgment about whether lottery participation is truly in their best interests.

It is a familiar caveat in welfare economics that consumer demand curves lose their usual normative significance in the case of children and others whose reasoning powers might be subject to question, or when consumers are seriously misinformed about the good being consumed. The prohibition against selling lottery tickets to minors is an implicit demonstration of this condition, as is the concern in many states about the effect of lotteries on problem gamblers. These concerns call into question the appropriateness of using observed demand to measure the benefit of consuming lottery products, especially given the use of advertising to stimulate play. For now, we will not confront these arguments but rather proceed on the assumption that consumer choices with respect to lottery participation accurately reflect worthy preferences.

Recognizing that the lottery entails both the creation and taxation of a commodity allows us to apply conventional concepts of equity and efficiency to the lottery's implicit tax. Relevant to both of these concepts is the fact that lowering the implicit tax on the lottery would increase the utility of players. With regard to equity, we are concerned about the distribution of such benefits (or, conversely, of the costs of raising the implicit tax). Efficiency is concerned with the proper tax rate on lotteries relative to that on other commodities.

Is the Implicit Lottery Tax Inequitable?

Among the traditional criteria for judging taxes, distributional equity has undoubtedly been the issue that has stirred the most vigorous public debate with regard to lotteries. Long lines at lottery outlets in low-income neighborhoods have been a focal point for those concerned about excessive play among the poor.[13] In California jackpots won by illegal aliens and welfare recipients prompted a bill forbidding welfare recipients from using public funds to bet, as well as a suit from a Marin County couple against a welfare recipient who won the lottery.[14] And an advertisement for the Illinois lottery displayed in a poor Chicago neighborhood in 1986 provoked a local church to organize a boycott of the lottery.[15]

Lottery agencies and proponents have shown special sensitivity to this issue. Some of the most outspoken defenders on this score are suppliers of lottery products. In material submitted to a Senate committee investigating lotteries in 1984, for example, an official of Scientific Games, Inc., responded to the charge that lotteries are supported largely by the poor: "Definitely not! Extensive studies of state-run lotteries indicate that an overwhelming majority of ticket purchasers are in the $12,000 to $28,000 salary range. Whereas citizens in the low income range buy lottery tickets, they buy fewer tickets proportionately than their percentage of the population."[16]

Defining Regressivity

A necessary first step in judging the distributional impact of the lottery as a fiscal device is to be clear about definitions, and in particular the meaning of *regressivity*. What criterion should determine whether the implicit lottery tax falls disproportionately on the poor? Since this implicit tax is a constant percentage of expenditures on lotteries, the question can conveniently be answered by using data on expenditures. At least four measures have been used in the debate over the distributional impact, or incidence, of lottery finance. The first focuses on the "typical" player, as in the testimony of the Scientific Games official. Such descriptions are not very enlightening, however, because they fail to make the necessary comparison between players and nonplayers. A second approach does just that. For example, the Washington State lottery, which is required to publish periodically a demographic study of lottery players, compares data on the population with data on lottery players (defined as anyone who had purchased at least six tickets in a year). In 1986 the lottery reported that 30 percent of lottery players had incomes under $20,000, compared to 34 percent for the population at large.[17] While this approach is more informative than focusing on a "typical" player, looking only at players and not at how much they spend ignores the possible large impact of differences in average spending.

A third yardstick for judging whether lottery revenues come disproportionately from those at lower-income levels compares per capita expenditures over the income scale. If the average poor household spends more than the average middle-class household, then the poor are contributing more than their share. An influential study using this approach is John Koza's empirical examination of several lottery states in the late 1970s, which concluded that " 'the poor' participate in the state lottery games at levels disproportionately less than their percentage of the population."[18] This conclusion would be consistent with the expenditure patterns for some of the games discussed in Chapter 6, in which average spending rises with income at lower-income levels. But most of the data presented in Chapter 6 are consistent with the general conclusion that, since absolute expenditures bear no consistent relationship with income, no income group bears a disproportionate share of the lottery burden. However straightforward this yardstick may be, though, it is not the one commonly used in economic studies of tax incidence.

The standard of comparison used in virtually all such studies is income. A tax is called regressive if, as a percentage of income, it falls as income increases, and a progressive tax is one that increases as a percentage of income as one moves up the income scale. The implicit benchmark is a strictly proportional tax. To see how incidence measured by conventional notions of progressivity and regressivity would differ from criteria based on absolute amounts, let us suppose that all households spend exactly $250 on the lottery each year. The expenditure (and the implicit tax) of poor households is then proportionate to their numbers. This distribution is highly regressive, however, in that a household with income of $10,000 would be spending 2.5 percent of its annual income on the lottery, while a household earning $60,000 would only be spending 0.4 percent on the lottery.

Evidence on Regressivity

There have been a number of economic studies of the incidence of lottery revenues, most of them conducted in the 1970s. In addition to reviewing this work, it is important to examine more recent data on the distributional patterns of play because of the dramatic changes that have occurred in the product line in the 1980s. Table 11.1 presents a summary of the various studies of lottery incidence. The measure of incidence used in the table is an index of tax concentration. The index takes on negative values for regressive taxes and positive values for progressive taxes. A perfectly proportional tax would have an index value of zero.[19] For each study that did not report one, a tax concentration index value was calculated. Without exception, the evidence shows that the implicit tax on lotteries is regressive, as shown by the consistently negative index values. Not only are the older games based on drawings regressive, but the instant, daily, and lotto games that now constitute the bulk of sales also have regressive patterns. This conclusion should not be surprising, given the generally flat expenditure patterns for all the games shown in Chapter 6.[20] The implication of regressivity even applies to

Table 11.1.   Studies of the incidence of implicit lottery taxation

Study	State studied	Game	Year	Income of bettors making highest average expenditure ($1,000s)	Tax concentration index[a]
Spiro (1974)	Pennsylvania	Drawings	1971	4–5	−.20
Brinner and Clotfelter (1975)	Connecticut	Drawings	1973	10–15	−.41
	Massachusetts	Drawings	1973	10–15	−.46
	Pennsylvania	Drawings	1973	10–15	−.45
Suits (1977)	U.S. lottery states	Mostly drawings	1974	5–10	−.31
Koza (1982)[b]	Michigan	Instant	1971–76	23–56	−.37
	New Jersey	50-cent drawings	1971–76	23–34	−.38
	Illinois	50-cent drawings	1971–76	23–56	−.37
	Illinois	$1 drawing	1971–76	23–34	−.38
	New York	Lotto	1971–76	23–34	−.39
Livernois (1987)	Western Canada	Draw and lotto	1983	60 +[c]	−.10
Vaillancourt and Grignon (1988)	Canada	All games	1982	40–50[c]	−.18

Chapter 6 of this book	California	Instant	1986	−.32
	Maryland	3-digit nos.	1984	−.42
	Maryland	4-digit nos.	1984	−.48
	Maryland	Lotto	1984	−.36

Sources: Michael H. Spiro, "On the Incidence of the Pennsylvania Lottery," *National Tax Journal 27* (March 1974), 57–61; Roger E. Brinner and Charles T. Clotfelter, "An Economic Appraisal of State Lotteries," *National Tax Journal 23* (December 1975), 395–404; Daniel B. Suits, "Gambling Taxes: Regressivity and Revenue Potential," *National Tax Journal 30* (March 1977), 19–35; John R. Koza, "The Myth of the Poor Buying Lottery Tickets," *Public Gaming 10* (January 1982), 31–40; John Livernois, "The Redistributional Effects of Lotteries: Evidence from Canada," *Public Finance Quarterly 15* (July 1987), 339–351; François Vaillancourt and Julie Grignon, "Canadian Lotteries as Taxes: Revenues and Incidence," *Canadian Tax Journal 36* (March-April 1988), 369–388.

a. For an explanation of how the index is calculated, see text. Midpoints of income are used for closed intervals. Estimated average income for top brackets is based on U.S. Internal Revenue Service, *Statistics of Income, Individual Income Tax Returns* (Washington, D.C.: Government Printing Office), various years. Estimated average income for the $58,000-and-above class in 1980 is $103,000.

b. The Koza study is based on data for winners of 140 different games in five states over the period 1971–1976. For each type of game shown, the state with the most games in the sample is shown for illustration. Income is based on zip code data and is stated in 1980 dollars.

c. In thousands of Canadian dollars. For Vaillancourt and Grignon, income class is based on tabulation for 1984.

Koza's findings, which he used to argue the not inconsistent (but different) point that the poor do not play disproportionally in relation to their numbers in the population. Of all the studies of lottery expenditures, the two indicating the least regressive patterns are based on expenditures in Canada. Exactly what is responsible for this apparently lower degree of regressivity is unclear, but it may reflect the greater use of lotto in Canada than in the United States, and it may also reflect differences in demography and income distribution.

Are some games more regressive than others? Because the studies summarized in the table employ slightly different income classes and methods, the index values cannot be taken as precise measures of relative incidence, but only as rough indicators of incidence relative to a proportional income tax. The only survey that allows such a comparison is for Maryland, which examined expenditures for different games. In that case lotto is the least regressive of the three games covered and four-digit numbers the most. Another study compared the distribution of the daily numbers game and the weekly draw game in Maryland, concluding that the implicit tax in the numbers game is significantly more regressive.[21]

Since the alternative to lottery revenue is usually revenue from conventional tax sources, it may not be sufficient for tax planners to know that lotteries levy a regressive implicit tax. Many popular state taxes are also known to be regressive. So it would be useful to compare lotteries to those other revenue sources. Table 11.2 presents calculated tax concentration indices for several tax bases for the purpose of comparison. For reference, the first two lines give indices for federal taxes, the most progressive element of the U.S. tax structure. The calculated indices confirm that these federal taxes are in fact progressive in incidence. Among state taxes, the income tax is one of the most progressive, as indicated by the positive index value for state and local income taxes in the third line. General taxes on consumption, such as sales taxes, are regressive, but markedly less regressive than most of the indices calculated for lottery games. The Survey of Consumer Expenditures was used to calculate indices for several tax bases used by state governments. For these data, a proportional sales tax on all expenditures would have an index of −.17 and one exempting housing and most services would yield a value of −.16. Both show considerably less regressivity than the implicit lottery tax in the United States. Similarly, excise taxes on alcohol and gasoline are less regressive. Of these excise tax bases, only tobacco approaches the degree of regressivity of implicit lottery taxation. In sum, it is quite clear that the implicit lottery tax is considerably more regressive than other widely used sources of revenue.

Without an explicit statement of what the income distribution "should" be, it is impossible to determine whether the implicit lottery tax is vertically

Table 11.2. Incidence of selected taxes

Selected tax bases[a]	Tax concentration index
Federal income tax	+ .14
All federal taxes[b]	+ .10 to + .15
State and local income tax	+ .09
All consumer expenditures	− .17
Expenditures other than housing and most services	− .16
Alcohol	− .21
Tobacco	− .38
Gasoline	− .23

a. Calculations were performed using U.S. Department of Labor, Bureau of Labor Statistics, *Consumer Expenditure Survey: Interview Survey, 1984* (Washington, D.C.: Government Printing Office, August 1986), tables 1 and 3, pp. 10, 18–21. The index of − .16 was calculated for the following base: all expenditures less shelter, domestic services, maintenance and repair, public transportation, health care, fees and admissions, and education.

b. If the corporate income tax is allocated to capital income, the index is + .15; if it is allocated to labor income, it is + .10. U.S. Congress, Congressional Budget Office, *The Changing Distribution of Federal Taxes: 1975–1990* (Washington, D.C.: Congressional Budget Office, October 1987), p. 77.

equitable. Short of that, however, the evidence is quite clear that the implicit lottery tax is decidedly regressive. That is to say, an increase in the revenue from lotteries has exactly the same distributional impact as the imposition of or increase in the rate of a similarly regressive tax. If dollars spent by those at lower income are given more weight than dollars spent by those with higher incomes, an increase in the rate of implicit tax on lotteries is less desirable than an increase in the rate of tax of most other state taxes on distributional grounds alone.[22]

Earmarking

Up to this point the discussion of incidence has been based entirely on the distribution of the net revenue burden. Is the basic conclusion affected when account is taken of how the lottery revenues are spent? As one lottery proponent has stated, "To the extent profits are used to fund programs which aid the poor, lotteries are arguably progressive."[23] In fact, however, it is unlikely that lottery revenues have much effect on the pattern of expenditures. Suppose, for example, a state earns $100 million from its lottery. If the state law does not earmark that money for a particular purpose, it will go into the general fund and presumably be allocated the same way as additional funds from any other source. Even if state law does earmark lottery income to a particular purpose, there is reason to believe that the budget process nullifies the intended effect. Despite efforts to segregate lottery revenues, it is impossible to prevent the legislature from taking that source of revenue into account when voting on appropriations for an agency receiving earmarked funds. The chairman of the Senate Education Committee in the New York State legislature made it clear that lottery funds are considered a substitute for general revenue funds: "We determine what our whole expenditures are going to be for aid to education and we have 'X' millions set aside toward that purpose from the lottery. So we take that much less out of local-assistance revenue."[24] Earmarking is most likely to have an effect where earmarked revenues are large in relation to a program's total budget. Such may be the case with Pennsylvania's use of lottery funds for senior citizens. In virtually all other instances, however, earmarking appears to have little impact on the pattern of expenditures, so the conclusion of regressivity that emerges from analyzing the implicit tax is unaffected.

Variations within Income Classes

Measures of incidence based on average expenditures obscure a significant element in lottery incidence: participation is heavily concentrated within a small subgroup of the population. As we saw in Chapter 6, only about half of all adults play lottery games at all. Of those who do play, a relatively small group of heavy players accounts for a large proportion of all expenditures. One survey in California showed, for example, that a third of all purchases in California's early instant games were made by about 5 percent of the players, or less than 3 percent of the adult population.[25] Because of this extreme concentration of lottery play, measures of incidence based on mean values alone are likely to miss important distributional aspects of lottery finance. While low-income households on the average spend a larger percentage of their income on lotteries than middle-class households, for example, many people with low incomes contribute nothing at all to the lottery. A complete account of incidence must recognize the variation in implicit tax burden within income classes—variation that derives from differences in people's betting habits.

As a way of bringing evidence on dispersion into the more traditional portrayal of incidence, data from the Maryland survey were used to compare the average expenditures by all adults in each income class with the average for the 20 percent in each class who spent the most on the lottery. This information is given in the first two columns of Table 11.3. In every case the top 20 percent spent over three times the average for the entire class. Especially striking is the very heavy play among the most active players in the lowest-income classes. For the most active 20 percent in the under-$10,000 class, average weekly spending on the lottery was an astounding $32. At a minimum these findings show that the variation in lottery play within income classes is much greater than the variation in mean values among income classes. There are, of course, variations within income classes in all individual taxes, but they tend to be more pronounced the narrower or more idiosyncratic the tax base. This was illustrated in a study by the Congressional Budget Office on expenditures subject to federal excise taxation. Among households with incomes between $20,000 and $30,000, for example, the 20 percent of households that spent the most on various items accounted for 38 percent of the income class's total spending for gasoline, 41 percent for telephone services, 60 percent for tobacco, beer, and wine, 68 percent for liquor, and 99 percent for airfares.[26] A comparable figure for lotteries, based on the $15,000-to-$25,000 income group, was 81 percent.[27] Among these commodities only airfares are more concentrated than expenditures on lotteries.

The variations in lottery play within income groups exhibit predictable patterns. As we saw in Chapter 6, lottery expenditures are associated with such factors as race, education, sex, age, and religion. By definition the incidence of the implicit tax follows the same patterns, and these have been

Table 11.3. Differences in lottery play within income classes, Maryland, 1984

Income	Average weekly expenditure		Percentage of adults betting $10 or more per week		
	All adults	Top 20% of adults	All adults	Whites	Blacks
Under $10,000	$7.30	$32.56	15%	8%	41%
$10,000 to $15,000	5.37	21.85	16	8	27
$15,000 to $25,000	2.99	12.15	10	7	21
$25,000 to $50,000	3.21	14.70	8	7	21
$50,000 and more	2.57	12.48	8	5	32

Source: Calculated from unpublished data from the Gallup Organization, Inc., Gallup Study GO 84190, November 1984; persons giving no information on income are omitted, leaving a sample size of 1,072.

the subject of considerable critical commentary. For example, the fact that participation declines with education appears to support critics' charges that with their relatively high takeout rates, lotteries take advantage of the ignorance of bettors. The pattern of play across racial groups is also a frequent target for lottery critics. That race is a significant factor in lottery play is suggested in Table 11.3 by a comparison of the proportion of people betting more than $10 per week. Heavy lottery play in Maryland was much more prevalent among blacks than whites, and this difference is most striking in the lowest-income class.

Is the Implicit Tax Rate Too High?

According to Adam Smith, a tax should interfere as little as possible with economic choices.[28] Modern tax theory accepts this view and deals with efficiency by examining taxes that will minimize the loss in welfare from tax-induced distortions.[29] The economist's normative framework for evaluating taxes offers at least two possible justifications for taxing a commodity at a high rate. First, a relatively high tax rate is called for if the commodity's production or consumption creates "negative externalities," or harmful effects on others. Second, a higher tax is warranted if it would have relatively little effect on the quantity consumed, owing to insensitivity to price on the part of buyers.

While it is possible to identify possible negative externalities from lottery play, they appear small compared to those associated with, say, alcohol.[30] For example, it may be that the lure of the lottery will cause some players to run up debts that will force them into bankruptcy. An increase in bankruptcies may increase the cost of consumer credit, which would harm those who need to borrow money. But this effect is not large, given that lottery expenditures are small compared to a typical year's increase in total consumer indebtedness. More important, perhaps, are the harmful effects that are not external but are rather suffered by the players themselves and their dependents. But if we assume that consumers are capable of making informed decisions, then concerns about compulsive gambling and neglect of other financial responsibilities are inappropriate.

With respect to elasticity of demand, it is not possible to say precisely how the lottery stacks up against other consumer items. Some evidence, reviewed in Chapter 6, does suggest, however, that lottery expenditures increase when the payout rate is increased, a result that implies demand is elastic. Certainly there is no reason to believe that lotteries have a less elastic demand than, say, alcohol or tobacco products, both of which are taxed at lower rates than lotteries. Thus the elasticity of lottery demand provides little basis for a high tax rate; nor does the lack of large negative externalities.[31]

One ancient and still-important perspective on gambling does offer a principled basis for advocating a high implicit tax. In this view gambling is a vice that should be discouraged, if not by outright prohibition then by restrictions on availability. Consumer preferences, as revealed by the decision to gamble, are not accorded much respect. There are two overlapping arguments here. First, people who play the lottery are often poorly informed about the prize structure, have no intuition about the relevant probabilities, or underestimate the dangers of getting caught up in a gambling habit. It is in their interest (although they may not realize it) if the lottery is designed to be unenticing. Second, a taste for gambling, like a taste for other vices, should be discouraged as a matter of community interest in promoting a wholesome society.[32] So-called sumptuary taxes on activities such as drinking and smoking have long been justified as a way of discouraging consumption when outright prohibition is deemed unenforceable or too costly; the same argument can be readily applied to gambling. A high tax can thus be justified as a protection against imprudent behavior or against sin.

Given this argument, it is interesting to compare the implicit tax rate in the lottery with tax rates on other commodities associated with vice such as drinking and smoking. Table 11.4 presents calculations of the average percentage tax rate on tobacco and alcohol products along with the average rate

Table 11.4. Tax rates on lotteries, alcohol, and tobacco products in the United States, 1985[a]

	Federal	State and local	Total
Lotteries	5%	41%	46%
Liquor	16	14	30
Wine	4	9	13
Beer	4	7	12
Tobacco products	13	20	33

Sources: Distilled Spirits Council of the United States, Inc., *1984/1985 Public Revenues from Alcohol Beverages* (Washington, D.C., 1985), and *Annual Statistical Review 1984/ 85: Distilled Spirits Industry* (Washington, D.C., 1985); unpublished estimates from Frank Sammartino, dated March 27, 1987, used in Frank Sammartino, "The Distributional Effects of an Increase in Selected Federal Excise Taxes," U.S. Congressional Budget Office Staff Working Paper, January 1987; Eric J. Toder, "Issues in the Taxation of Cigarettes," in *The Cigarette Excise Tax* (Cambridge, Mass.: Institute for the Study of Smoking Behavior and Policy, April 17, 1985).

a. For details on the calculation of these rates, see Charles T. Clotfelter and Philip J. Cook, "Implicit Taxation in Lottery Finance," *National Tax Journal* 40, 4 (December 1987), table 11. Components may not sum to total because of rounding.

of implicit taxation in state lotteries. The tax rates are expressed here as a percentage of the gross price paid by the consumer, the price including the tax.[33] In the case of lotteries an estimate of the average federal income tax by type of game is added, but state income taxes are not included. In 1985 the average dollar spent on lottery products contained an implicit tax of forty-one cents and led to an additional federal income tax liability of roughly 5 percent, for a total tax of forty-six cents per dollar. The state component had fallen to thirty-eight cents by 1987, as shown in Table 2.3, but was still relatively high compared with tax markups of about 30 percent on liquor, 13 percent on wine, 12 percent on beer, and 33 percent on tobacco products. Expressed as a percentage of the *net* price, the implicit lottery tax for 1985 was a remarkable 85 percent, compared to 43 percent for liquor and 49 percent for tobacco products. The implicit lottery tax was also higher than the tax on parimutuel wagering, although it is impossible to say by exactly how much because of differences in the forms of betting.[34] As these comparisons show, the implicit tax on lottery products in the United States is quite high, even relative to commodities that have traditionally been subject to high tax rates. It is interesting that in Canada tax rates on alcoholic beverages are higher than the implicit tax rate on its lotteries.[35]

Thus the implicit lottery tax is high even relative to consumer items that have traditionally been the object of a sumptuary argument. The reason for this high implicit tax, of course, is not at all to discourage consumption. After all, the lotteries are doing everything they can in other respects to increase play. Rather, the reason for the high implicit tax is to generate as much revenue for the state as possible. If the objective of enhancing consumer welfare ever replaced the revenue objective, then a lower tax rate would be appropriate.

Appendix   A Lottery's Net Contribution to State Revenue

To consider the net impact of a lottery on a state's revenue, it is useful to apply a simplified model of state income, expenditures, and taxes. Consider a state with an income tax at rate s and a sales or consumption tax at rate t. Income is also subject to the federal income tax at rate f. Factor income Y is fixed, so $dY = 0$. (Cross-state lottery purchases are not taken into account.)

A lottery may add to taxable income over and above factor income if its prizes are taxable but losses are not deductible against ordinary income. Consumers devote their income to expenditures on the lottery, other expenditures, and tax payments.

Y = gross factor income (assumed to be constant)
E = expenditures on nonlottery items
N = lottery net revenue to the state
A = administrative expenses of the lottery

The combined household budget is given by the following:

$$Y = (f + s)Y + (1 + t)E + N + A$$

This expression ignores the deductibility of state income taxes for itemizers in calculating federal tax liability, but this feature has virtually no effect in this case. For convenience, assume that administrative costs are some constant fraction, a, of net revenues, $A = aN$.
Thus

$$Y = (f + s)Y + (1 + t)E + (1 + a)N$$

State government revenue (excluding the lottery's administrative costs) is given by the equation

$$R = sY + tE + N$$

Combining the previous two equations yields

$$R = sY + t[Y - (f + s)Y - (1 + a)N]/(1 + t) + N$$

The net impact of the lottery on state revenue is given by

$$dR/dN = 1 - [t/(1 + t)](1 + a)$$

If t (the average of sales and excise tax rates for all consumption) is .04 and administrative costs are about a quarter as large as net revenues ($a = .25$), then dR/dN is about .95. This result ignores the lottery's effect on state and federal income tax receipts.

To see the effect of considering state and federal income taxation, define

k as W/N, where W is additional taxable income from lottery winnings over and above factor income Y. If $k > 0$, the lottery has the effect of increasing taxable income despite the assumed constancy of factor income. This increases federal tax liabilities and decreases after-tax income, thus decreasing state consumption tax receipts. But this decrease will result in an increase in state income tax receipts if lottery winnings are not exempted from the state income tax. Where $x = 1$ if lottery winnings are subject to state income taxation and $x = 0$ if they are exempt, the two basic equations become:

$$Y = f(Y + kN) + s(Y + xkN) + (1 + t)E + (1 + a)N$$
$$R = s(Y + xkN) + tE + N$$

Thus

$$R = s(Y + xkN) + t[Y - f(Y + kN) - s(Y + xkN)$$
$$- (1 + a)N]/(1 + t) + N$$

The net effect of the lottery on state revenue is now

$$dR/dN = 1 + sxk - [t/(1 + t)] (fk + sxk + 1 + a),$$

or

$$1 - [t/(1 + t)] (fk + 1 + a)$$

if winnings are exempted from the state income tax and

$$1 + sk - [t/(1 + t)] (fk + sk + 1 + a)$$

if they are not exempted.

To illustrate the possible magnitude of these effects, assume k is .50 (taxable winnings equal to half of net lottery revenues), the state income tax rate is .05, and the federal rate is .15. In this case the actual contribution of lottery net revenue to overall state revenue is ninety-five cents per dollar ($dR/dN =$ .95) if winnings are exempt from state income taxation and ninety-seven cents per dollar if winnings are not exempt.

These magnitudes are rough approximations, but they do suggest that the lottery's net contribution to state revenues will be less than the stated net revenue, especially if winnings are not subject to income tax. The model does not account for the possibility that expenditures will "leak out" of the state owing to the lottery, thereby leading to further revenue losses, or that the lottery might have some effect on savings, investment, and economic growth.

12.

Choices

Hope is a good breakfast, but it is a bad supper.

—Francis Bacon, 1624

Linus in the comic strip "Peanuts" once observed, "Life is full of choices, but you never get any." This is a good description of the predicament faced time after time by legislators, governors, and voters who have considered proposals for instituting lotteries in their states. In virtually every case the same model has been debated: a state-run enterprise as the sole supplier of legal lottery games, paying out roughly half of its revenues in the form of prizes, and authorized to use conventional techniques of marketing to broaden the demand for its products. The debate has been posed strictly in terms of whether or not a state should adopt a lottery, not what kind of lottery it should adopt. But there is in fact no reason why a state-sanctioned lottery must conform to this established model. A state could, if it wished, set up a lottery different in any of several key respects. The aim of this concluding chapter is to lay out the policy choices open to any state with a lottery or any state considering a lottery. As a preface to that discussion, the chapter begins with a summary of our observations about the modern lottery in America.

The Lottery Today

A remarkable aspect of the states' enthusiastic promotion of lottery sales is that for the first six decades of this century every state prohibited lotteries. The leap from prohibition to provision and promotion was taken first by New Hampshire in 1964, followed by New York in 1967 and New Jersey in 1970. These pioneer states demonstrated that it was possible for a lottery to be operated honestly, free of the corruption that had been the legacy of nineteenth-century lotteries. By 1976 all the other northeastern states had joined the bandwagon. By 1988 most of the other states outside the South had adopted, and with Florida and Virginia in the lottery business, it seemed likely that other southern states would capitulate as well. The prohibition had been effectively repealed, and the chances that the trend would be reversed seemed no greater than those of a return to the prohibition of liquor.

The modern reemergence of lotteries has been viewed in historical context as one aspect of the third wave of legalized gambling in America. The first wave (from colonial times to the early nineteenth century) and the second (the three decades following the Civil War) both featured lotteries as a popular form of gambling. By 1963, on the eve of New Hampshire's introduction of a lottery, the third wave was well under way: twenty-six of the fifty states had legalized parimutuel betting on horse racing, legal bingo was offered in over half the states, and Nevada's casinos had been in business for three decades. By 1988 few states were still untouched by this third wave, with only a handful maintaining a prohibition on bingo and parimutuel betting. In our era, then, commercial gambling has become pervasive and widely accepted.

As of 1988 only one state in the twentieth century had ever voted down a state-run lottery in a public referendum; once on the ballot adoption proposals have typically passed by healthy margins. But in the politics of state lottery adoption this widespread acceptance has been only part of the story. In virtually every state it was the lottery's opponents, not its supporters, who were most outspoken in debate or who counted major political leaders as allies. With remarkable regularity state governors and legislators have opposed lotteries, only to yield in the end to majority opinion. This opposition has been motivated by ethical concerns that the lottery amounts to a highly regressive tax or that the government should not encourage gambling. These concerns were countered by proponents touting the new revenues that would be generated by the lottery, an argument made more vivid in many states by the proposal to earmark these revenues for education or some other specific use. Commercial interests played a leading role as a source of finance and grass-roots organization for the adoption campaigns of the 1980s. In a number of states the lottery suppliers and convenience store chains worked to galvanize the public majority who supported adoption into an effective political force. Opponents, meanwhile, sometimes received contributions from commercial gambling interests who feared the competition.

The lotteries have proven to be a booming success with the public. National opinion polls have recorded a steady growth in the approval rating for state lotteries from 48 percent in 1964 to 72 percent in 1982. Familiarity has obviously not bred contempt. And participation has grown rapidly: per capita sales rose from $10 in 1975 to $101 in 1988, representing after inflation a remarkable 13 percent annual growth rate over the period. This increase is so large as to suggest that the lotteries have become a qualitatively different phenomenon since the mid-1970s.

Much of the growth in lottery sales has been fueled by the development and introduction of new products. As late as 1973 the only significant lottery game was a passive drawing conducted in much the same fashion as in colonial times. Faced with consumer apathy and flat sales, state lottery agencies introduced two major innovations in the early 1970s, pumping new life into consumer demand for lotteries. The first was the instant game ticket. Although they held out the promise of a quick outcome, these tickets offered only a modicum of the inherent game-playing excitement of other forms of gambling. The second innovation was an on-line computer system that made possible the introduction of a legal numbers game, a high-tech carbon copy of the illegal version long popular in many cities. In addition to offering daily drawings, the state numbers game for the first time allowed players to select their own numbers, thus providing an opportunity to play personal lucky numbers or those suggested by dreams, news events, or betting "systems."

A third major innovation in the early 1980s, lotto, the game of long odds and huge jackpots, quickly came to dominate the popular image of the lottery. By the mid-1980s the original passive game had all but disappeared, leaving the instant games, numbers, and lotto as the mainstays of the product line. But the lottery agencies' quest for new and still more enticing products has continued. Multistate consortiums are being formed for the purpose of creating a larger lotto jackpot than any one state could offer separately, for in lotto bigger has proven better for sales. Several states have recently introduced games based on the casino game of keno, a variant of lotto designed for a sophisticated segment of the gambling market. Still being tested in 1988 were games based on player-activated lottery machines bearing an uncanny resemblance to slot machines. Consideration was also being given to sports betting, a form of gambling widely played abroad. In short, voters who agreed to a lottery a few years back may be surprised by what it has come to encompass and the rapidity with which it is evolving.

The growth in sales has now made state lotteries the leading form of commercial gambling. In 1988 total sales of lottery products in the United States amounted to $14.9 billion, or over $200 per household in lottery states. Half of this amount was returned to players as prizes, leaving $1.8 billion for operating costs and $5.6 billion as net revenue. The amount retained by the states represented over a third of total revenues for all forms of legal commercial gambling nationwide, a larger share than that provided by casinos or parimutuel betting. Furthermore, the states' take from lotteries exceeded the estimated revenues from all forms of illegal wagering combined. Yet there is little evidence that the lottery is undercutting the market for other forms of commercial gambling, and it is not even clear that the illegal numbers game has been hurt. The lottery boom is simply contributing to the general rise in commercial gambling.

Unlike all but one other form of commercial gambling (off-track betting) the lottery is provided directly by the state. Indeed it ranks second among products sold directly by the state to the public, right behind higher education. Lottery gross revenues exceed those of state liquor stores (in states that monopolize liquor distribution) and state-run hospitals. Among all services provided by the state government, whether sold directly to consumers or distributed by some other means, the lottery is uniquely prominent in the eyes of the public, owing to the heavy advertising and intrinsic interest it generates. Thus the states have entered a new business, one that has much more in common with the activities of corporate America than with other government services.

The evidence is abundant that lotteries are structured and managed with the primary goal of maximizing net revenue. Some states express this goal explicitly in their enabling legislation, and whether or not it is stated in law, the objective of increasing revenues underlies the organization and behavior of the lottery agencies. Most of these agencies are set up as separate bureaus under a weak commission, free from the close scrutiny and some of the hiring restrictions placed on other government agencies. This autonomy allows the lottery agency to behave in most respects as a business, responding to the constant pressure to bring in more revenue for the state. A lottery is unlikely to attract attention in the legislature unless it fails to bring in the projected revenues, the lottery directors strive to avoid this sort of attention.

As a business the lottery has the great advantage of being a legal monopoly. Although a number of lottery states allow nonprofit organizations to sell charity game tickets, every state that has established a lottery has granted itself the sole right to provide actual lottery games within its borders. The state monopoly is at the wholesale level, while the private sector handles production and retailing. Most state agencies buy off-the-shelf games and computer systems from private firms specializing in lotteries and then license stores within the state to serve as retail outlets.

The lottery's monopoly position allows it to build in a prodigious profit margin. For every dollar spent on tickets, lottery agencies pay out an average of only fifty cents in prizes, a percentage that differs very little from one state to another. Of the remainder, operating expenses and commissions to retailers consume about twelve cents, leaving profit of thirty-eight cents per dollar that can go into the state's treasury. The 50 percent that lotteries pay out in prizes ranks far below the comparable return offered by other forms of commercial gambling. For example, prizes average 81 percent of the total amount wagered in horse racing, 89 percent in slot machines, and 97 percent in casino table games.

Ironically, although state revenues from lottery operations have grown rapidly since the early 1970s, they are not yet the fiscal bonanza that the public perceives them to be. In 1986 they amounted to 3.3 percent of state own-source revenues in lottery states. Even in the states with the highest per capita sales lottery revenues are not much more than what could be generated by a one-penny increase in the sales tax. The public's perception, influenced by the lottery's wide visibility, is that the lottery makes a much larger difference in state finance. And even this relatively small amount is unlikely to augment spending on the activity for which it is legally earmarked, given the fungibility inherent in the state budget process.

Thus the state lotteries define their success in terms of the bottom line, the amount transferred to the state treasury. Their raison d'être is not the accommodation of widespread interest in this sort of gambling but the stimulation of this interest to generate as much "painless tax" revenue as possible. Whether or not the lottery has been oversold in the political arena, there is no question that lottery directors are dedicated to selling it to consumers. The lottery states have not simply become providers; they have become advocates, trying to persuade more of the public to spend more money more often.

The difference between a lottery agency and any other agency of state government begins with a basic fact: the lottery actively markets a consumer product. Like private firms—but decidedly unlike other units of government—lottery agencies want to increase the sales of their product. To accomplish this they have adopted the methods of modern marketing. Before the first ad is shown, lottery suppliers devote painstaking attention to crucial details of product design and marketing position. In accordance with the modern concept of target marketing, suppliers attempt to distinguish market segments and to identify the product characteristics that will appeal to each segment.

The products themselves are carefully crafted to attract potential players. The lottery agencies turned to numbers games and lotto only after learning in focus groups that consumers wanted big prizes and that they enjoyed the feeling of participation they got from picking their own numbers. In the case of instant games, where player participation is limited to rubbing the coverings off a card, creating play value has been a special challenge. The prize distribution is another variable that can be adjusted by product designers. While the big prizes attract attention and generate sales, lottery marketers believe that for a significant segment of the market small prizes serve as reinforcement to play again. In fact market research has shown that the $2 and $5 prizes are usually "reinvested" immediately, thus feeding the action. Like the corporations they emulate, the lotteries have come to offer a differentiated product line, offering games with high prizes to one market segment and games with higher chances of winning to another.

When it comes to promoting these lottery games the state agencies certainly mean business. Lotteries devote about 2 percent of their total expenditures (including prizes) to paid advertising. This ratio is lower than the comparable ratio for corporations that provide amusement and recreation services but higher than those for all corporations in general and for corporations in the retail industry, and markedly higher than those for public utilities and other state-operated enterprises. Lottery ads constitute the bulk of all ads sponsored by state governments. But comparisons based on paid advertising understate the typical lottery's total promotional effort. Most lotteries pay little if anything to air their drawings on local television stations, which are happy to trade the air time for a boost in audience share. And every lottery agency employs a publicity staff for the purpose of promoting large jackpots and seeking free publicity for other events. Indeed the mass media have been willing collaborators in spreading the word about the prizes, and especially the winners. As a result, lottery promotion has become state government's most prominent message to the public.

Lottery advertising and promotion tend to convey inaccurate impressions about facts such as the true size of the jackpot and the likelihood of winning it. Only a few states require that odds be posted or advertised. More important, perhaps, is that consumers are inundated with images of big winners, both fictional (in commercial television spots) and real (in televised drawings and news accounts). These images lend tangibility to the notion of winning. People typically have little knowledge or intuition about the odds of winning one of the big prizes. Indeed, many players do not approach the lottery as a simple game of luck but rather as one involving a substantial element of skill, challenging them to develop a system or learn to recognize portents that will suggest the winning number. The lottery agencies do nothing to discourage this perception but rather encourage people to play their "lucky" numbers. Superstition is just another angle for selling tickets.

Even in the absence of such promotion the lottery would appeal to an extraordinarily broad audience. A low-priced chance to win a large prize catches almost everyone's attention, and the data indicate that half or more of the adult public in lottery states play at least once a year. One third play regularly. These participation rates are far higher than for other forms of commercial gambling, and for many people, including a significant number of teenagers, buying a lottery ticket is their initiation into gambling. But experienced gamblers also play the lottery when given a chance.

This appeal is not uniform across socioeconomic groups. Lottery play declines with education and is more prevalent among blacks in the East and Hispanics in the West than among non-Hispanic whites. Catholics play more than Protestants, and the middle-aged play more than the young or the old. Of all such characteristics income is the one singled out for the most commentary by critics, and on that score there is a remarkable result: over the broad middle-income range, which includes most households, there is no consistent pattern of lottery play. (Reliable information on the richest and poorest households is hard to obtain.) The evidence suggests that income is not systematically correlated with participation or expenditure. That conclusion further implies that the relatively poor spend a much larger fraction of their income on lottery tickets than the relatively affluent.

Finally, within any broad socioeconomic category, however defined, lottery play is highly concentrated. Most players bet small amounts, but the relatively few who average several dollars a day or more account for the bulk of the lottery handle. Overall, the top 20 percent of players account for 65 percent of the total bet, and 10 percent of players account for about half. Within that upper tail of the distribution are the problem gamblers, those who habitually play more than they can afford. The dream of winning big can lead to harmful consequences if it is carried too far, and increasingly the gambling clinics and hotlines are hearing from people whose primary or only gambling involvement is with the lottery.

These patterns of lottery play have frequently been cited as cause for concern. The lottery, it is said, exploits people's yearnings for a better life, offering them a sucker bet wrapped in promotional hype. Quite a different view is that the lottery does not exploit anyone but rather offers an enjoyable form of entertainment that happens to be more attractive to minorities, people of relatively low education, and people who have a strong taste for gambling. Whatever one's view of this matter, it is useful to consider that there are less aggressive alternatives to the form state lotteries take today, driven as they are by the imperative of supplying ever-greater revenues to the state treasury. We now turn to a discussion of them.

Policy Alternatives

State lotteries today are remarkably alike. Each is a government-operated monopoly. Each pays out roughly fifty cents on the dollar in prizes. Each one is organized as a business enterprise on the wholesale level between a private industry that supplies lottery products and a network of private retailers who sell the products. Each one employs the techniques of modern marketing to design and promote these products. In all that they do, lotteries share a fundamental objective: to generate as much revenue as possible for the state. This revenue-oriented lottery, or Revenue Lottery, is the common model. Yet it is by no means the only functional model imaginable. Few of the characteristics of today's state lotteries are essential to the running of a lottery. Most are nothing more nor less than policy choices that a state has made, often by default. These choices reflect a basic judgment about what the lottery's objective should be. If raising revenue is the primary goal in setting up a lottery, the Revenue Lottery may be appropriate, although there is some question about its net contribution once the effects of lottery promotion on economic growth are taken into account. In any case, if objectives other than revenue are deemed important, then a different model may be preferable.

It is useful to review the four aspects of state lotteries that we have identified: legalization, provision, marketing, and taxation. Each aspect offers an implicit policy choice, but legalization is the only necessary choice among the four. Each of the others presents a range of possibilities, and these constitute the policy alternatives subject to the control of state legislatures.

To clarify the policy choices facing the states—those with lotteries as well as those considering them—we have identified three distinct models. We refer to them as the Revenue Lottery, the Consumer Lottery, and the Sumptuary Lottery (see Table 12.1). The three differ fundamentally, for each of them has a different objective, a different concept of how a lottery serves the public interest. As we have seen, the Revenue Lottery as embodied in current lotteries has as its primary goal the maximization of revenue for the

Table 12.1. Three lottery models

Model	Objective	Promotion	Product variety	Payout rate
Revenue Lottery	Maximize government revenues	Few restrictions	Unlimited	Low
Consumer Lottery	Maximize consumer (player) welfare	Truth-in-advertising restriction	Unlimited	High
Sumptuary Lottery	Accommodate existing demand while discouraging excessive involvement	Informational messages and warnings	Limited	Low

state treasury. The Consumer Lottery takes as its primary objective to serve the interests of its customers. It provides at low cost a product that consumers want to buy and in doing so implicitly accepts the basic implication of consumer sovereignty—that the consumer knows best. In contrast to this nonjudgmental model is the Sumptuary Lottery, which is based squarely on paternalism, emphasizing the hazards of gambling. If the state disapproves of gambling but chooses to legalize it anyway, perhaps in order to take it out of the hands of illegal operators, it could establish a tightly controlled lottery designed to keep consumption to a minimum.

How would these alternative models operate in practice? Let us consider what policy choices the three models would imply for the remaining three aspects of lotteries: provision, marketing, and implicit taxation. Regarding provision, several alternatives to government monopoly exist, ranging from licensing and regulating a single supplier to opening the market to competing suppliers. We believe that the choice of the mode of provision is largely independent of the choice about the lottery's basic objective, and we defer discussion of provision until the end of this section. As for marketing and implicit taxation, there are three specific issues to be addressed: the intensity of promotion, the range of products offered, and the payout rate. Table 12.1 suggests how they would be handled under each lottery model.

Promotion: Information or Enticement?

The most controversial aspect of the Revenue Lottery, as exemplified by the current state lotteries, is their use of Madison Avenue techniques to promote sales. The sales pitch in the lottery ads stresses the possibility of winning big, with the clear intention of giving players an exaggerated impression of both the probability of winning and the size of the jackpot. Hyperbole such as this is a familiar aspect of consumer advertising by private companies, although most ads, including those for promotional sweepstakes, must conform to certain truth-in-advertising requirements. One question about lottery advertising, therefore, is whether a government agency should be held to at least the same standard of candor as private advertisers.

There is more to selling lottery tickets than persuading the public that playing is a good investment. At a more basic level the sales job may be viewed as an education in values, teaching that gambling is a benign or even virtuous activity that offers an escape from the dreariness of work and limited means. Not only does lottery advertising in the Revenue Lottery endorse gambling per se, but it also endorses the dream of easy wealth that motivates gambling. The ads are unabashedly materialistic, and their message is a slightly subversive one—that success is just a matter of picking the right number.

The gospel of wealth based on sweat and a little bit of luck is replaced by one based on luck alone. Needless to say, waiting for fortune to smile is not the formula for success that is usually taught. Indeed, one straightforward test of the acceptability of the message of lottery promotion might be to imagine using lottery ads in the public school curriculum. It would be difficult, for example, to justify teaching children lessons such as "Play your hunch. You could win a bunch."

This perverse education currently being promulgated by lottery agencies may also have the ironic effect of reducing government revenues over the long run by reducing economic growth. If lottery promotion erodes the propensity to work, save, and invest in one's education and training, then the consequence will be attenuated growth in productivity. A full accounting of the effects of the lottery on state revenue must consider these plausible, if unintended, consequences. And if lotteries do erode the values that foster economic growth, the harm is by no means limited to the state treasury.

The Sumptuary Lottery, given its objective of accommodating demand while discouraging players from spending more than they can afford, would eliminate most advertising. Communication about the lottery would be limited to basic information (how the games operate, the prizes, and the chances of winning) and any warnings the state might deem appropriate concerning the hazards of gambling. This approach to advertising is close to the long-established British gambling policy of supplying only "unstimulated demand." In a few states, legislators have shown their concern about the stimulus of vigorous promotion by writing restrictions on the use of advertising by the lottery agency. A singular experiment in restraining the marketing instinct was Missouri's original law, which required ads to be strictly informational and to run the disclaimer that the ad was "not intended to induce any person to participate in the lottery or purchase a lottery ticket." But after two years of disappointing sales the state dispensed with its restrictions on marketing. Virginia and Wisconsin permit their more recent lotteries to provide only informational advertising. This includes information about rules, the probability distribution of prizes, and the location of ticket outlets. Whether those restrictions prove effective in the face of the inevitable revenue pressures remains to be seen.

How would the Consumer Lottery deal with advertising? The basic objective in this model is to serve the customer, and presumably that goal dictates keeping consumers well informed. Thus lottery ads would be subject to the same kind of truth-in-advertising requirements as many other products, including commercial sweepstakes. Statements of the odds of winning and explanations of how prize money is paid out would be routinely included. Furthermore, the Consumer Lottery would discourage ad campaigns that give a distorted view of the prizes or chances of winning, for example by focusing on grand prize winners without giving information on odds and other prizes. Lottery advertising might also be constrained in other ways, such as limiting television ads to adult viewing hours. The Consumer Lottery would not rule out advertisements just because they make playing the lottery look attractive, however. Given the model's underlying assumption that, with sufficient information, consumers can decide for themselves what is in their own best interest, there would be little justification for banning ads that emphasize the fun of playing and the benefits to the state. Ultimately there is no bright line dividing acceptable from unacceptable advertising under this approach. Some might argue that, to a certain extent, advertising that fuels fantasies of wealth and celebrity status is acceptable to the extent that the ads themselves enhance the consumer's enjoyment of the product. While we acknowledge the force of this view, it is hard to argue that it is truly in the consumer's interest to act under an inaccurate impression of the qualities of a product, whether that product be lottery tickets or skin cream. In our conception, then, promotion under the Consumer Lottery would be more informative and less misleadingly evocative than most current lottery advertising.

Product Line

The product line of the state lotteries has evolved from the original passive-drawing game to a showy array of offerings, including instant games, the daily numbers game, and lotto. And lottery marketers are seriously considering ways of increasing the size of the lotto jackpot and initiating sports betting and the use of machines that closely resemble slot machines. The introduction of new games has been a central ingredient in the tremendous growth of lottery sales. The new products offer bigger prizes and more player involvement. Since these new games boost sales and state revenues, they are essential to the Revenue Lottery. The Consumer Lottery presumably would also welcome new games that had a ready market among players, since the demand for them would indicate that they enhance consumer welfare. Advocates of the Sumptuary Lottery, however, might judge these new games to have greater addictive potential than the old and would not allow their introduction. In this regard, most states follow the Revenue Lottery's enthusiasm for new lottery games, and a few of the largest agencies have been active in pursuing product innovations. But in a few states the expansion of the product line has been slowed by continuing debate in the legislatures concerning lottery expansion. Neither Colorado nor Arizona, for example, permits its state lottery to offer daily numbers games.

Payout Rate

In 1988 state lottery agencies paid an average of fifty cents in prizes for each dollar taken in, leaving the remaining fifty cents for administrative costs and net revenues. On the average these administrative costs amounted to about twelve cents, leaving thirty-eight cents as the implicit tax. In small states, where costs constitute a larger share of sales, the implicit tax rate is lower; in the largest states it is somewhat higher. This average rate of implicit tax makes lotteries a much more heavily taxed commodity than, say, alcohol or cigarettes.

Why is the payout rate for lotteries so uniformly low? Presumably lottery directors and legislators believe that the state's profit would fall if the payout rate were raised. Whether or not that belief is correct, and there is no definitive evidence on the subject, the low rate is surely a consequence of the revenue imperative. A Consumer Lottery, by contrast, would raise the payout rate significantly, taking out only enough to pay operating expenses and an excise tax in line with tax rates on similar commodities. One reasonable standard for this lottery tax is the rate imposed on parimutuel betting at the racetrack, which averages roughly 4 percent at the state level.

The low tax rate of the Consumer Lottery could be challenged on the grounds that lottery play has some addictive potential, that it may place a financial burden on the dependents of some participants, and that it may impose costs on society beyond those borne by the players. A higher tax rate would make the lottery less attractive and perhaps discourage some lottery play. This is the traditional justification for sumptuary taxation, and it is also the argument for imposing a special tax on the lottery, which results in the low payout rate of the Sumptuary Lottery. Note that the Revenue Lottery also has a high implicit tax and low payout rate, but for quite a different reason.

Apart from these normative considerations, it is interesting to speculate about what path state payout rates are likely to follow. As we have seen, payout rates have gradually been drifting upward since the 1970s, apparently owing to the belief that offering players more favorable wagers will boost revenue. Another source of upward pressure on payout is interstate competition, especially where urban areas lie near the border of competing lottery states. But this competition would become much more intense if federal restrictions on interstate sales were eased. In that case individual states could lose much of the monopoly status that makes possible the prevailing low payout rates.

In sum, if the focus of state lotteries were redirected from the treasury to the consumer, the major change would be the end of the misleading and even subversive advertising that is the most visible feature of the lottery today. This would probably reduce sales, but it would also reduce the social costs engendered by the sales and the sales pitch. Of course any mechanism for raising public revenues has some social cost; the costs of stimulating lottery sales, however, may be unacceptably high.

Public versus Private Provision

The lottery's objective, then, has rather clear implications for policy choices about marketing and implicit taxation. Does the objective also dictate how the lotteries should be organized and managed? Until 1989 every state lottery was run by an agency of the state government, and in each case this agency was the sole authorized provider of lottery products in the state. Yet other options certainly exist. One variant, used in the Canadian provincial lotteries, is to set the agency up as a public corporation. Although effectively an arm of the provincial government, this structure serves to put some distance, however small, between the government and the lottery agency. In the United States an agency could be structured along the lines of a public utility. A state's governor, along with the legislature, could retain appointive power over a regulatory commission rather than a director or lottery commission. One further step away from government provision would be to allow private firms to bid on the right to operate the state's lottery, a system currently used to award cable television franchises. The franchise could be granted on the basis of an agreement that would stipulate the amount to be paid to the state, the games that would be offered, and the conditions under which the lottery would be operated. Indeed it may be feasible to franchise more than one private firm as a lottery provider and create some competition, especially for games (such as the instant game) in which scale economies are not pronounced.

Although no state has yet considered privatizing the lottery, it is useful to discuss the strengths and drawbacks of private provision relative to provision by a state agency. These forms have certain inherent advantages which take on different weight depending on the objective. Whatever that objective, the state agency form offers at least two advantages over the private alternative. First, provision by a state agency gives the state government substantial control over all aspects of the lottery's operation. If the legislature wishes to limit the introduction of new lottery games or control advertising, for example, it can do so most readily if a state agency operates the lottery or if it closely regulates the lottery. A second advantage of a state agency is its greater potential for avoiding the taint of corruption. One persistent problem in forms of commercial gambling that rely on private providers, especially casinos, is preventing the involvement of organized crime. And while a state agency is not immune to corruption, the notorious Louisiana lottery in the late nineteenth century continues to serve as an object lesson in the special dangers of private provision. In contrast, the state agency model that has been the rule for modern lotteries has been quite successful in avoiding even the appearance of corruption or influence by organized crime.

The Sumptuary Lottery, with its need for tight control on product development, promotion, and pricing, would appear to do best under a state-run or tightly regulated monopoly. But the other models could probably survive under different degrees of privatization. As current practice makes abundantly clear, a Revenue Lottery can be operated under a state agency. But one could argue that lottery provision by a private firm might be a preferable vehicle for a Revenue Lottery, especially if the public understood that the firm was not an arm of the government. To the extent that the lottery's marketing messages conflict with other aims of state government, the current close association between government and the lottery is a disadvantage. Indeed, if a sufficiently high tax rate were levied, a Revenue Lottery could conceivably be operated under some form of open competition with little constraint on the promotional activity of firms. Alternatively, with lower rates and a truth-in-advertising law such as that applying to commercial sweepstakes, competition among private providers could be made to serve a Consumer Lottery. Yet the same aims could be served with a state agency structure as well; all that would be required is a state government willing to accept a lower rate of profit and some limitations on its promotion.

Taking Lotteries Seriously

With the fanfare of a July Fourth parade lotteries reemerged on the American scene following seven decades of prohibition. Dangling the hope of fabulous wealth and fairy-tale transformations, the lottery caught the imagination of the American consumer. Growing at double-digit rates, it soon became the country's most popular form of commercial gambling and a major source of recreation. Revenues from the lotteries grew just as rapidly, producing "painless" income for state governments. The lotteries created hundreds of new millionaires each year, offering hope to the masses of other players just like them. Buoyed by gigantic jackpots and the widespread willingness to take a chance, lotteries have assumed a place in the common culture.

Despite the fun and the hoopla, lotteries have a serious side as well. They have become a new line of business for state governments, and a major one at that. But because of the nature of the product, the manner in which the states are promoting it, and the rate at which they are taxing it, this new activity is worthy of special scrutiny. Lotteries are introducing millions to commercial gambling, and for some unknown fraction of them gambling will become a destructive compulsion. The lottery business places the state in the position of using advertising that endorses suspect values and offers deceptive impressions instead of information. The revenue imperative motivates a search for new products that will attract new players and entice old players to spend more—for some of them more than their families can afford. Because they raise issues related to the very purpose of government, these matters deserve to be taken seriously.

There are substantial policy choices beyond the initial decision to begin a lottery. For both states that already have lotteries and states still considering adoption, the basic question is, what is the purpose of a lottery? Should it be evaluated primarily on the basis of revenue performance, as virtually all conventional lotteries have been, or should other considerations be given weight? For this business the bottom line is not necessarily synonymous with the public interest. It will become increasingly imperative to consider the alternatives as the lottery continues to evolve and grow.

Appendix
Notes
References
Index

Appendix
Supplementary Tables

Table A.1. Prize structure in five lottery games

Lottery	Number of tickets	Amount of prize	Total prize money
Faneuil Hall,	1	$1,000	$1,000
Boston, 1762	1	500	500
	2	200	400
	12	100	1,200
	20	50	1,000
	20	20	400
	30	10	300
	200	6	1,200
	1,200	4	4,800
Total winning	1,486		$10,800
Losing	4,514	0	0
Total tickets[a]	6,000		
Maryland state,	1	$40,000	$40,000
1825	1	20,000	20,000
	1	10,000	10,000
	2	5,000	10,000
	30	1,000	30,000
	20	500	10,000
	50	100	5,000
	100	50	5,000
	5,000	10	50,000
Total winning	5,205		$180,000
Losing	14,795	0	0
Total tickets[b]	20,000		

Table A.1. (continued)

Lottery	Number of tickets	Amount of prize	Total prize money
Maryland Instant	16	$25,000	$400,000
Baseball, 1986	468	1,000	468,000
	8,658	50	432,900
	46,800	25	1,170,000
	173,160	10	1,731,600
	542,880	5	2,714,400
	2,152,800	2	4,305,600
Total winning	2,924,782		$11,222,500
Losing	20,475,218	0	0
Total tickets^c	23,400,000		
Ohio Holiday	4,000	$1,000	$4,000,000
Cash, 1986	41,200	100	4,120,000
	41,200	50	2,060,000
	35,600	25	890,000
	228,000	5	1,140,000
	1,394,800	2	2,789,600
Total winning	1,744,800		$14,999,600
Losing	18,255,200	0	0
Total tickets^c	20,000,000		
Connecticut	1	$1,000,000	$1,000,000
Joker's Wild,	109	10,000	1,090,000
1986	261	1,000	261,000
	15,138	50	756,900
	143,550	10	1,435,500
	475,020	5	2,375,100
	4,410,900	2	8,821,800
Total winning	4,614,979		$15,740,300
Losing	21,485,021	0	0
Total tickets^c	26,100,000		

Sources: John Samuel Ezell, *Fortune's Merry Wheel: The Lottery in America* (Cambridge, Mass.: Harvard University Press, 1960), p. 32; W. Ray Luce, "The Cohen Brothers of Baltimore: From Lottery to Banking," *Maryland Historical Magazine* 68 (Fall 1973), 298; brochure, Maryland State Lottery; unpublished data provided by Ronald L. Nabakowski, September 11, 1986 (for Ohio), expressed per 20 million tickets; *Gaming and Wagering Business* 7 (October 1986), 14.

a. Tickets were $2 each.

b. Tickets were $12 each, and fractions of tickets were sold. Probabilities of winning are based on whole tickets.

c. Tickets were $1 each.

Table A.2.   Effect of date on daily numbers betting, Maryland, October 1 to
9, 1986

| | Straight bets | | |
Number	Placed on matching date (a)	Average of other eight days (b)	"Date effect" (a)/(b)
101	$2,711	$1,871	1.45
102	980	573	1.71
103	1,663	701	2.37
104	2,175	1,009	2.15
105	Sunday (no drawing)		
106	1,076	547	1.97
107	1,496	740	2.02
108	1,961	1,150	1.71
109	1,377	704	1.96

Source: Calculated from unpublished data provided by the Maryland state lottery agency.

ble A.3.   Weekly lottery expenditures for three lottery games, by income, Maryland, 1984

| | | Average weekly expenditures | | | |
come	Sample size	3-digit numbers	4-digit numbers	Lotto	Total
der $10,000	85	$3.65	$1.58	$1.88	$7.30
),000 to $15,000	104	2.99	0.98	1.23	5.37
5,000 to $25,000	226	1.26	0.49	1.22	2.99
5,000 to $50,000	451	1.61	0.40	1.26	3.21
0,000 and over	206	1.19	0.37	0.99	2.57
n't know, refused to say	175	1.44	0.50	0.86	2.79
Total	1,247	$1.86	$0.55	$1.19	$3.46

Source: Calculated from unpublished data from survey conducted by the Gallup Organization, Inc., llup Study GO 84190, November 1984. Components do not add to totals because respondents who not know were excluded, and sample sizes varied.

Table A.4. FY 1986 per capita sales regressions: log linear specification

Independent variable	Numbers sales	Lotto sales
Intercept	−4.50	−18.06
	(.2)	(2.9)
Population[a]	−0.11	0.52**
	(.5)	(6.8)
Income[b]	1.06	1.94*
	(.4)	(2.8)
Black[c]	0.72*	−.14
	(2.7)	(2.0)
Urban[c]	−0.28	1.04*
	(.2)	(2.6)
Payout rate[d]	3.05	2.55*
	(.7)	(2.3)
N	15	16
R^2	0.75	0.89
Root MSE	0.79	0.23
Mean sales	$3.22[e]	$3.44[e]

*p < .05.
**p < .01.

a. Estimates of 1985 population from U.S. Bureau of the Census, *Current Population Reports,* ser. P-25, no. 998 (Washington, D.C.: Government Printing Office, December 1986), p. 15.

b. Per capita income for 1985 from U.S. Bureau of the Census, *State Government Finances in 1986* (Washington, D.C.: Government Printing Office, 1987).

c. Percent black and percent urban for 1980 from U.S. Bureau of the Census, *Statistical Abstract of the United States,* 1986 (Washington, D.C.: Government Printing Office, 1987).

d. Payout rates obtained by telephone from state lottery commissions.

e. Per capita sales computed using FY1986 data from *Gaming and Wagering Business* 8 (May 1987), and provisional population estimates (note a).

Note: All variables are in natural log form. Numbers in parentheses are *t*-statistics.

Table A.5. Regression explaining logarithm of per capita daily lotto sales in eight states, 1986 and 1987

Variable	Coefficient	*t*-statistic
Logarithm of—		
Probability	−0.01	0.3
Jackpot	0.40	40.3
Proportion of prize pool in lower prizes	0.38	4.6
Payout	1.35	1.6
Drawings per week	0.20	3.8
Time trend	−0.00093	3.9
State dummy variable (Ohio omitted)		
Arizona	0.13	2.3
Delaware	−0.14	1.5
District of Columbia	−0.08	0.5
Maryland	0.15	2.3
Missouri	−1.01	8.3
New York	−0.12	1.3
West Virginia	−0.96	6.8
Intercept	−6.8	6.4

Source: Calculated from unpublished data provided by state lottery agencies of Arizona, Delaware, District of Columbia, Maryland, Missouri, Ohio, New York, and West Virginia.

Note: Regression weighted by the square root of state population. $R^2 = 0.92$; N = 1,029.

Table A.6. Multivariate analysis of commercial gambling in complete national sample, 1974 (excludes lottery play)

Bettor characteristics (excluded categories in parentheses)	Fraction of sample	Probit analysis of participation		Log of wager (players only)	
		Probit coeff.	t-stat.	OLS coeff.	t-s
Sex: (female)					
male	0.66	0.116	1.6	0.769	
Race: (white)					
black	0.14	0.112	1.0	1.191	
other	0.10	−0.121	−1.0	0.636	
Religion: (Evangelical Protestant and Southern Baptist)					
Catholic	0.32	0.623	4.0	−0.376	−
Jewish	0.04	0.647	2.8	−0.582	−
Other Protestant	0.49	0.385	2.6	−0.730	−
None or other	0.07	0.183	1.0	−0.708	−
Household income: (< $5,000)					
Missing	0.06	0.180	1.0	0.536	
$5,000–10,000	0.18	0.152	1.1	−0.135	−
10,000–15,000	0.23	0.146	1.1	0.063	
15,000–20,000	0.18	0.207	1.4	0.496	
20,000–25,000	0.10	0.319	2.0	0.205	
$25,000 + more	0.13	0.213	1.4	0.489	
Age: (18–25)					
26–35	0.25	0.072	0.7	0.078	
36–45	0.16	0.109	1.0	0.305	
46–65	0.30	−0.164	−1.6	0.281	
65 and older	0.12	−0.497	−3.3	−0.502	−
Age missing	0.00	−2.127	−0.5	0.000	−
City size: (Over 500,000)					
Size missing	0.01	0.165	0.5	−1.946	−
100,000–500,000	0.10	0.201	1.7	−1.044	−
Suburb	0.07	0.048	0.4	−0.658	−
5,000–100,000	0.28	−0.049	−0.6	−0.416	−
Rural	0.13	0.018	0.1	−0.748	−
Church attendance: (weekly) (>1 per week)					
2–4 per month	0.31	0.231	1.9	0.670	
≤1 per month	0.32	0.414	3.4	0.825	
Never	0.24	0.212	1.7	0.910	

ble A.6.   (continued)

ttor characteristics :cluded categories in ~entheses)	Fraction of sample	Probit analysis of participation		Log of wager (players only)	
		Probit coeff.	*t*-stat.	OLS coeff.	*t*-stat.
ucation: (No H.S.)					
Missing	0.00	0.069	0.1	−0.818	−0.4
Attended H.S.	0.16	0.154	1.2	0.312	0.8
H.S. graduate	0.30	0.262	2.2	0.432	1.2
Attended college	0.21	0.096	0.7	0.121	0.3
College graduate	0.11	0.277	1.9	−0.054	−0.1
Advanced degree	0.06	−0.233	−1.2	−0.387	−0.6
ttery state	0.52	−0.009	−0.1	0.066	0.3
rimutuel state	0.77	0.202	2.2	0.687	2.4
nfederate state	0.13	−0.348	−2.9	0.553	1.4
nstant	—	−1.714	−6.8	2.164	2.6

N = 1,735
Overall participation = 29%

N = 510
R^2 = 0.17

Source: Calculated from unpublished data from a national survey by the University of Michigan ~vey Research Center, "Gambling in the United States," 1975.

Table A.7.   Selected public votes on gambling questions other than adoption of state lotteries

State	Type of gambling	Year	Percenta in favo
Lottery states			
New York	Bingo	1957	61%
	Charitable gambling	1975	50
	Charitable gambling	1984	56
New Jersey	Casino-type amusement games	1959	59
	Bingo	1972	85
	Casinos	1974	40
	Casinos	1976	57
Rhode Island	Dog racing	1972	47
Ohio	Bingo	1973	54
District of Columbia	Jai alai and dog racing	1980	40
Washington	Dog racing	1972	37
Colorado	Bingo	1958	51
	Sweepstakes races	1972	49
	Privately operated lottery[a]	1972	20
	Casinos	1984	33
California	Privately operated lottery[a]	1964	31
	Dog racing	1976	25
	Bingo	1976	70
West Virginia	Bingo	1980	64
Missouri	Horse racing	1971	46
	Horse racing	1984	60
	Easing restrictions on state lottery[b]	1988	58
Kansas	Bingo	1974	70
Montana	Slot machines	1950	28
	Card rooms	1972	61
	Expanded gambling[c]	1982	38
South Dakota	Charitable gambling	1970	59
Florida	Casinos	1978	29
	Casinos	1986	32
Virginia	Gambling[d]	1970	63
	Horse racing	1978	48
	Parimutuel betting	1988	56
Indiana	Horse racing	1968	47
Minnesota	Horse racing	1982	58

ble A.7.   (continued)

ate	Type of gambling	Year	Percentage in favor
lected other states			
Arkansas	Horse racing	1956	53
	Casinos	1964	34
Nevada	Privately operated lottery	1968	24
North Dakota	Charitable bingo and raffles	1982	37
Oklahoma	Horse racing	1974	46
	Horse racing	1982	58
South Carolina	Bingo	1974	63
Tennessee	Parimutuel betting in Davis County	1988	49
Texas	Horse racing	1974	45

Sources: Kathleen M. Joyce, "Public Opinion and the Politics of Gambling," Journal of Social Issues (1979), 144–165; William N. Thompson, "Patterns of Public Response to Lottery, Horserace, and sino Gambling Issues," Nevada Review of Business and Economics 9 (Spring 1985), 12–22; lifornia, Office of Secretary of State, Statement of Vote, general elections, November 6, 1984, plement; South Dakota, Office of Secretary of State, General Election Returns and Registration ures, 1983, pp. 12–13; West Virginia, Office of Secretary of State, General Election Returns, 1980, cember 12, 1980; Colorado Department of State, State of Colorado Abstract of Votes Cast, 1980 81), pp. 144–145. (Question specified that revenues would go to "the conservation trust fund of the te for distribution to municipalities and counties for park, recreation, and open space purposes"); hmond News Leader, November 4, 1987; "Casinos Rejected, but Four States Approve Lotteries," Louis Post-Dispatch, November 8, 1984; State of Missouri, Office of Secretary of State, Roster of te, District, and County Officials, 1985–86 general election returns, biennial, 1985; "Report of the ficial Canvas by County of Votes Cast at the General Election Held in the State of Montana, vember 2, 1982"; State of Nevada, Legislative Counsel Bureau, Additional Constitutional iendment to Be Voted upon in State of Nevada at the General Election, November 5, 1968; ishington Post, May 7, 1980, and November 6, 1980; New York Times, June 16, 1988. Also, phone calls and correspondence to Montana and South Dakota secretaries of state, May 12, 1988; tho, Colorado, and Kansas secretaries of state, May 17, 1988; Florida Board of Elections, May 17, 88; Vermont secretary of state, June 22, 1988; North Dakota attorney general, July 1, 1988. . Both states would have authorized the American Sweepstakes Corporation to operate a lottery for years. The California proposal would have paid the operator 13 percent of sales and paid out 22 cent in prizes, leaving the state with 65 percent of gross sales. Joe and Barbara Saltzman, "Long ds and Sure Things on the California Ballot," Reporter, November 5, 1964, pp. 28–30. The lorado proposal would have allocated 30 percent to the operator, 40 percent for prizes, and 30 cent to the state. Colorado Secretary of State, telephone conversation, May 17, 1988. . Increased allowable prize payout, removed restrictions on operating expenses and advertisements. . Montana's initiative would have expanded the forms of legalized gambling by allowing blackjack ard rooms, punchboards, mechanical gambling devices simulating card games, bingo or keno, and h payoffs for bingo and keno games. Montana Secretary of State, 1982 Voter Information Pamphlet, te General Election, November 2, 1982. . For a description of this question, see Chapter 8.

Table A.8.   Volatility and growth for real lottery revenues and seven selected taxes: averages for five states (percentages)

Revenue source	Variation from the mean[a]	Growth[b]	Variation from the trend[c]	Year-to-year declines[d]
General sales and gross receipts	7.8	−0.4	7.9	46
Individual income taxes	17.0	3.7	8.5	38
Death and gift taxes	22.6	−0.9	24.1	54
Selective excise taxes				
Motor fuels	18.2	−4.9	10.3	77
Tobacco products	26.7	−6.4	6.6	92
Insurance	12.4	0.5	13.2	46
Parimutuel	34.1	−8.3	11.2	85
Lottery net revenues	78.1	15.8	39.0	31
Rank of lottery as revenue source	First	First	First	Last

Sources: U.S. Bureau of the Census, *State Tax Collections,* 1973–1986 (Washington, D.C.: Government Printing Office); annual reports of state lotteries. States are Illinois, Michigan, New York, Ohio, and Pennsylvania.
a. Standard deviation as percentage of mean.
b. Regression coefficient as percentage of mean.
c. Standard error of the regression estimates as percentage of mean.
d. Number of declines as percentage of all year-to-year changes.

Notes

1. A New Role for the States

1. Unless otherwise noted, information on the Illinois lottery is taken from the *Chicago Tribune*. Articles referred to include those for the following dates:

1972: January 24; April 27; June 2, 15, 24, 29
1973: February 11; May 24; June 21, 26; September 19, 27; October 13, 16; November 30; December 2, 15
1974: July 30, 31; August 16; November 14
1975: January 19; April 16; August 8; December 23
1976: January 1; March 14, 19; October 3, 10; December 5
1977: May 30
1978: April 11; December 28
1979: February 18; July 16, 19; September 12, 25, 28, 29
1980: February 19; May 4
1981: March 2; September 20; October 30
1982: March 26; June 22; July 30, 31; November 15
1983: May 30; June 14, 27; July 24
1984: April 11, 27; May 19; July 31; August 4, 23, 28, 31; September 1, 2, 4, 9; October 18
1985: April 9
1986: March 10; April 13; May 25; July 24
1987: March 27; August 12

2. National Association of State Racing Commissioners, *Statistical Reports on Horse Racing in the United States for the Year 1963* (Lexington, Ky., February 1964).

3. Illinois House of Representatives, Policy Numbers Game Study Committee, "Report and Recommendations to the Legislature," June 1975, pp. 137, 211. For descriptions of policy, see Chapter 3 of this book.

4. *Chicago Tribune,* November 30, 1973.

5. See, for example, editorials on June 15, 1972; February 11, 1973; and June 21, 1973.

6. Illinois House of Representatives, "Report and Recommendations," p. 123.

7. *Chicago Tribune,* March 2, 1981.

8. During the month of October 1986 the lottery ran from three to thirteen thirty-second ads per day. Some ten-second ads were used as well. In that month the lottery ran an average of 3.7 minutes of advertising per day on five stations in the Chicago market, or the equivalent of 7.5 thirty-second ads. A day on which approximately this amount of advertising appeared was October 20. On that day seven thirty-second ads were seen at times of the day and during programs as follows: on WBBN, 7:12 A.M., "CBS News"; 6:25 P.M., program break; on WFLD, 6:58 P.M., program break; on WGN, 9:53 P.M., "Independent Network News"; on WLS, 4:47 P.M., "Eyewitness News"; 12:23 A.M., "Nightline"; on WMAQ, 1:19 A.M., "News." Based on October 1986 local advertising schedule for the Chicago market, "Brand Schedules by Parent Company," unpublished tabulations provided by Broadcast Advertisers Reports, Inc.

9. Illinois State Lottery, *1986 Annual Report.*

10. *Chicago Tribune,* August 12, 1987.

11. Illinois Economic and Fiscal Commission, *The Illinois State Lottery: A Special Report,* December 1986, p. 41.

12. Ibid.; *Chicago Tribune,* March 10, 1986. Also, Dean Congbalay, "Priest Assails Lottery for 'Preying on Poor,' " *Chicago Tribune,* March 10, 1986, and Bonita Brodt, "Lottery's Down Side," *Chicago Tribune,* May 25, 1986.

13. Anne Keegan, "Ironworker with Ailing Child Wins $300,000," *Chicago Tribune,* August 16, 1974.

14. Joan Beck, "Our Lottery at Age 1 Is a Winning Kid,"*Chicago Tribune,* August 8, 1975.

15. "Together on Cloud Nine," *New York Times,* August 24, 1985.

16. Russell Baker, "Big Rot Candy Lesson," *New York Times,* September 8, 1984.

17. Tom Witosky, "Babbitt Warns Iowans against State Lotteries," *Des Moines Register,* August 3, 1984.

18. See, for example, Edith Stokey and Richard Zeckhauser, *A Primer for Policy Analysis* (New York: Norton, 1978), pp. 263–264.

19. Dick Netzer, "Legal Gambling, Now That We Have Lots of It," *New York Affairs* 8 (1984), 66.

20. Andy Rooney, "The Lowest Form of Taxation," *Chicago Tribune,* September 20, 1981.

2. Magnitudes

1. Commission on the Review of the National Policy toward Gambling, *Gambling in America* (Washington, D.C.: Government Printing Office, 1976), p. 1.

2. Common law cites three necessary ingredients of a lottery: chance, consideration, and prizes. In some cases chance must be the dominant factor in determining winners. See, for example, the Wisconsin Criminal Code, 945.01(5): "A lottery is an enterprise wherein for a consideration the participants are given an opportunity to

win a prize, the award of which is determined by chance, even though accompanied by some skill." See also Vicki Abt, James F. Smith, and Eugene Martin Christiansen, *The Business of Risk: Commercial Gambling in Mainstream America* (Lawrence: University Press of Kansas, 1985), p. 55.

3. Council of State Governments, *Legalized Gambling* (Lexington, Ky., 1978), p. 6.

4. Two key characteristics of the parimutuel betting system make cheating by an operator less likely: the payoff and odds are a function of betting frequency rather than being predetermined, and the income of operators is a fixed proportion of bets, not a function of the odds.

5. "U.S. and Canadian Gaming-at-a-Glance," *Gaming and Wagering Business* 7 (July 1986), 12–13. Several states, including Maryland, have legalized slot machines for use by charitable groups. See *Gaming and Wagering Business* 8 (November 1987), 7.

6. Terri LaFleur, "Charities Cry 'Foul' as Lotteries Tap into Their Traditional Moneymaking Turf," *Gaming and Wagering Business* 9 (April 1988), 24–25.

7. Fund for the City of New York, *Legal Gambling in New York* (New York, November 1972).

8. Commission on Gambling, *Gambling in America*, pp. 58–60.

9. Ibid., table 4.7, p. 64.

10. *Gaming and Wagering Business* 7 (August 1986), 20–21; "Asian Lottery Sales Could Triple in Next Five Years," *Gaming and Wagering Business* 9 (May 1988), 25. "Spaniards Pick Winners in Lottery Worth $406 Million," *New York Times*, December 23, 1985; James O. Jackson, "Russians Are Hooked on Lottery," *Chicago Tribune*, February 27, 1975.

11. Occasional raids on cockfights in western North Carolina reveal a sustained interest in this form of gambling. For example, in a raid in Madison County in 1987, authorities arrested more than a hundred people, confiscated $5,000 in cash, and found 250 roosters. "Over 100 Are Arrested at Cockfight," *Durham Morning Herald*, July 6, 1987.

12. *Gaming and Wagering Business* 7 (August 1986), 20–21. The countries, in order of the size of their economy, are: the United States, the Soviet Union, Japan, West Germany, France, Great Britain, China, Italy, Canada, and Poland. U.S. Bureau of the Census, *Statistical Abstract of the United States, 1988* (Washington, D.C.: Government Printing Office, 1987), p. 805.

13. Ronald Holloway, "More Gambling, Less Tax?" *Lloyd's Bank Review* 110 (1973), 34.

14. See "Proposes Lottery for Defense Fund," *New York Times*, December 27, 1941.

15. Layn Phillips, "The Premium Savings Bond: Respectable Revenue through Legalized Gambling," *Tulsa Law Journal* 11 (1975), 241–257.

16. Elizabeth H. Hastings and Philip K. Hastings, eds., *Index to International Public Opinion, 1980–81* (Westport, Conn.: Greenwood Press, 1982), pp. 483–497.

17. When New Hampshire legalized lotteries in 1963, twenty-nine states already permitted some kind of legalized gambling.

18. The average household expenditure for lotteries is based on a per capita figure

of $98 in 1988, an assumption of 5 percent of sales accounted for by residents of nonlottery states and an average of 2.6 persons per household. For data on urban consumer units, see U.S. Bureau of Labor Statistics, *Consumer Expenditure Survey: Interview Survey, 1984* (Washington, D.C.: Government Printing Office, August 1986), pp. 18–20.

19. The measure of lottery expenditures used here is comparable to gross wager, or handle, and does not take prize winnings into account. Since winning is decidedly atypical, the use of gross wager is most representative of expenditures. That is, the average family stakes, or is willing to part with, $200 per year, in 1984 dollars. Since winnings (before taxes) amount to about $100, the average net wager is roughly $100.

20. For a description of lotto and other lottery games, see Chapter 4.

21. Estimates based on correspondence with lottery agencies. One country without any lotto game was Japan, with per capita lottery sales of $26 in 1986. Estimate based on sales of $3.1 billion in 1986, given in *Gaming and Wagering Business* 9 (May 1988), 25.

22. The table is based on eighteen states that had lotteries during the entire fiscal year of 1986.

23. The other major form of state-owned enterprise, utilities, is a money-losing operation. U.S. Bureau of the Census, *State Government Finances in 1986* (Washington, D.C.: Government Printing Office, 1987), tables 19 and 21.

24. Calculations based on U.S. Bureau of the Census, *State Government Finances in 1986,* and Council of State Governments, *The Book of States* (Lexington, Ky., 1986), pp. 251–252; sales tax rates are for fiscal 1987.

25. It is possible that lotteries may have the effect of reducing the revenues from other state taxes at the same time that they contribute net revenues to the state. In this case figures for lottery net revenues overstate the total revenue contribution from the lottery. For a discussion of this point, see the appendix to Chapter 11.

3. The Fall and Rise of Lotteries

1. See, for example, C. L'Estrange Ewen, *Lotteries and Sweepstakes* (London: Heath Cranton, 1932), pp. 19–21, 24.

2. Mabel Walker, "Lotteries for Public Revenues—A Medieval Throwback," *American City* 49 (October 1934), 57.

3. John Drzazga, *Wheels of Fortune* (Springfield, Ill.: Charles C. Thomas, 1963), p. 252.

4. John Samuel Ezell, *Fortune's Merry Wheel: The Lottery in America* (Cambridge, Mass.: Harvard University Press, 1960), p. 4, and National Institute of Law Enforcement and Criminal Justice, *The Development of the Law of Gambling: 1776–1976* (Washington, D.C., November 1977), pp. 24–25.

5. Ezell, *Fortune's Merry Wheel,* p. 4. Lotteries remained a fixture in British public finance through the eighteenth century; R.D. Richards, "The Lottery in the History of English Government Finance," *Economic History* 3 (January 1934), 57–76.

6. See Ezell, *Fortune's Merry Wheel,* pp. 55–59, 64, 65–72.

7. National Institute of Law Enforcement, *Development of the Law of Gambling,* p. 74.

8. R. Clay Sprowls, "A Historical Analysis of Lottery Terms," *Canadian Journal of Economics and Political Science* 20 (August 1954), 354.

9. Ezell, *Fortune's Merry Wheel,* p. 54. And see pp. 13, 102, 120, and 272 for a discussion of the problems of debt and tax finance in the eighteenth and nineteenth centuries.

10. A. R. Spofford, "Lotteries in American History," *Annual Report of the American Historical Association, 1892* (Washington, D.C.: Government Printing Office, 1893), pp. 174–175.

11. Ezell, *Fortune's Merry Wheel,* pp. 101–160, 140, 64, 102–108.

12. U.S. Bureau of the Census, *Abstract of the Returns of the Fifth Census* (Washington, D.C., 1832). In 1830 the population was 188,797.

13. Spofford, "Lotteries," pp. 177, 190.

14. Measures of income for this period are difficult to come by and are no doubt unreliable, owing to the absence of a centralized system of money and banking. An estimate for value-added income for four major sectors of the economy is available for 1839, however, and for the period 1897–1901 this value-added figure is about 70 percent of the estimated value of national income. The 1839 estimated value-added income is $1.04 billion. U.S. Bureau of the Census, *Historical Statistics of the United States, Colonial Times to 1957* (Washington, D.C.: Government Printing Office, 1960), p. 139. If, using the ratio from the later period, national income was $1.46 billion in 1839, lottery sales of $53.1 million in 1832 would represent about 3.6 percent of national income.

15. See W. Ray Luce, "The Cohen Brothers of Baltimore: From Lottery to Banking," *Maryland Historical Magazine* 68 (Fall 1973), 302, for a description of the Baltimore firm Cohen's Lottery and Exchange. See also p. 300.

16. Spofford, "Lotteries," p. 177.

17. Ezell, *Fortune's Merry Wheel,* pp. 87, 82–87.

18. Ibid., pp. 105–106.

19. See, for example, Alice Felt Tyler, *Freedom's Ferment: Phases of American Social History from the Colonial Period to the Outbreak of the Civil War* (New York: Harper and Row, 1962), and John B. McMaster, *A History of the People of the United States: From the Revolution to the Civil War* (New York: D. Appleton and Co., 1926), pp. 152–153.

20. Ezell, *Fortune's Merry Wheel,* pp. 221–222, 193, 191.

21. National Institute of Law Enforcement, *Development of the Law of Gambling,* pp. 338–340.

22. Ezell, *Fortune's Merry Wheel,* pp. 212–229.

23. The case of Georgia is illustrative of state policy toward lotteries in many of the southern states. The state outlawed unauthorized lotteries in 1821. National Institute of Law Enforcement, *Development of the Law of Gambling,* p. 271. After the Civil War, however, they were revived briefly beginning in 1867 (Ezell, *Fortune's Merry Wheel,* p. 233), then prohibited in the Reconstructionist Constitution of 1868. Unauthorized lotteries were held in 1871, however, one to build a Confederate monument and another to aid Jefferson Davis. These objectives suggest that the lottery

may have operated as an instrument for the public financing of projects for the deposed Democrats during Radical Reconstruction. In 1876 the state legislature apparently ended lotteries once and for all. Paul Bolster, "Georgia Plays the Numbers: A History of Lotteries in Georgia," *Atlanta Historical Journal* 29 (Winter 1985–86), 101.

24. Ezell, *Fortune's Merry Wheel*, pp. 237–271.

25. John L. Hess, "Scandals and Corruption Ended Last of State Lotteries in 1894," *New York Times*, May 1, 1963.

26. L. N. Robbins, "A Lottery Craze Sweeps across the Land," *New York Times*, September 25, 1932.

27. American Institute of Public Opinion, reported in Edward C. Devereux, Jr., *Gambling and the Social Structure* (New York: Arno Press, 1980), pp. 1045–47. (Originally published as Ph. D. diss., Harvard University, 1949.)

28. Ezell, *Fortune's Merry Wheel*, pp. 95, 250.

29. *France v. United States*, 164 U.S. 676 (1897) and *Francis v. United States*, 188 U.S. 375 (1903); National Institute of Law Enforcement, *Development of the Law of Gambling*, p. 526.

30. Mark H. Haller, "The Changing Structure of American Gambling in the Twentieth Century," *Journal of Social Issues* 35, 3 (1979), 96.

31. The probability of winning such a bet is .0029, or 1 in 345, so the expected value of the prize was 5.8 cents, for a payout rate of slightly under 60 percent. The probability is calculated as $C(75, 9)/C(78, 12)$, where $C(n, m)$ is the number of combinations of n numbers taken m at a time.

32. St. Clair Drake and Horace Cayton, "Policy: Poor Man's Roulette," in Robert D. Herman, ed., *Gambling* (New York: Harper and Row, 1967), pp. 2–5.

33. Haller, "Changing Structure," p. 93.

34. Oliver Quayle and Co., Appendix, in Fund for the City of New York, *Legal Gambling in New York* (New York, 1972), pp. 20–21.

35. St. Clair Drake and Horace R. Cayton, *Black Metropolis: A Study of Negro Life in a Northern City* (New York: Harcourt, Brace and World, 1970), p. 7, and Peter Reuter and Jonathan Rubinstein, *Illegal Gambling in New York: A Case Study in the Operation, Structure, and Regulation of an Illegal Market* (Washington, D.C.: Department of Justice, National Institute of Justice, April 1982), p. 209.

36. Ezell, *Fortune's Merry Wheel*, p. 95.

37. Fund for the City of New York, *Legal Gambling in New York*, pp. 20, 24.

38. National Institute of Law Enforcement, *Development of the Law of Gambling*, p. 199.

39. Commission on the Review of the National Policy toward Gambling, *Gambling in America* (Washington, D.C.: Government Printing Office, 1976), p. 64. Estimate uses a population of 230 million. U.S. Bureau of the Census, *Statistical Abstract of the United States, 1983* (Washington, D.C.: Government Printing Office, 1982); *Economic Report of the President* (Washington, D.C.: Government Printing Office, 1985).

40. *Gaming and Wagering Business* 7 (July 1986), 28.

41. New York State Commission of Investigation, *An Investigation of Bingo Operations in New York State* (New York: New York State Commission of Investigation, December 1961), p. 12.

42. Commission on Gambling, *Gambling in America,* p. 161, and individual state laws.

43. See, for example, Francis Emmett Williams, *Flexible-Participation Lotteries* (St. Louis: Thomas Law Book Co., 1938); "Criminal Law—Lotteries—Necessity of Consideration," *Vanderbilt Law Review* 9 (December 1955), 98–101; Robert P. Gaines, "Criminal Law: Florida's Legal Lotteries," *University of Florida Law Review* 9 (Spring 1956), 93–95; Gerald F. Kaminski, "Promotional Games and the Ohio Lottery Laws," *University of Cincinnati Law Review* 39 (Winter 1970), 163–175; Barry M. Katz, "Lotteries—The Consideration Requirement," *Missouri Law Review* 37 (Winter 1972), 143–149.

44. Henry Chafetz, *Play the Devil* (New York: Clarkson N. Potter, 1960), p. 383; David Weinstein and Lillian Deitch, *The Impact of Legalized Gambling: The Socioeconomic Consequences of Lotteries and Off-Track Betting* (New York: Praeger, 1974), pp. 13–14; William N. Thompson, "Patterns of Public Response to Lottery, Horserace, and Casino Gambling Issues," *Nevada Review of Business and Economics* 9 (Spring 1985), 13.

45. I. Nelson Rose, "The Legalization and Control of Casino Gambling," *Fordham Urban Law Journal* 8 (1980), p. 245.

46. National Association of State Racing Commissioners, *Statistical Reports on Horse Racing in the United States for the Year 1963* (Lexington, Ky., February 1964).

47. Commission on Gambling, *Gambling in America,* p. 161; Council of State Governments, *Legalized Gambling* (Lexington, Ky., 1978), p. 6; "U.S. and Canadian Gaming at-a-Glance," *Gaming and Wagering Business* 7 (July 1986), 12–13.

48. Joel I. Seidman, "Lotteries for Public Revenue," *Editorial Research Reports,* vol. 1 (Washington, D.C., 1934), pp. 306–307.

49. *Congressional Record,* House, January 30, 1934, vol. 78, pt. 2, p. 1638.

50. "Legal Lotteries Urged in 48 States," *New York Times,* September 19, 1935.

51. "State Referendum on Lotteries Sought," *New York Times,* February 10, 1938.

52. See "Proposes Lottery for Defense Fund," *New York Times,* December 27, 1941; "Asks Lottery to Help War Costs," *New York Times,* March 28, 1942; "Senate Gets Bill for Government Lotteries; Pay \$500,000 in Bonds to Winners," *New York Times,* December 2, 1943.

53. Warren Weaver, "Fino Still Bets on a U.S. Lottery," *New York Times,* May 6, 1962.

54. The legislator, Larry Pickett, introduced lottery bills from 1953 to 1963. In 1963 he first suggested earmarking lottery income for education. *Public Gaming* 14 (May 1986), 10.

55. "Women Propose Hospital Lottery," *New York Times,* November 10, 1962.

56. Kathleen M. Joyce, "Public Opinion and the Politics of Gambling," *Journal of Social Issues* 35, 3 (1979), 157.

57. A national survey in 1986 showed that 18 percent of those responding believed that buying a lottery ticket was morally wrong.

58. Daniel Bell, "The Cultural Contradictions of Capitalism," *Public Interest* 21 (Fall 1970), 37.

59. Tom W. Smith, "Atop a Liberal Plateau? A Summary of Trends since World

War II," in Terry Nichols Clark, ed., *Research in Urban Policy: Coping with Urban Austerity,* vol. 1 (Greenwich, Conn.: JAI Press, 1985).

60. *Giving USA* (New York: American Association of Fund-Raising Counsel, 1986), p. 49.

61. Gallup Report, May 1985, p. 22.

62. Deirdre Carmody, "Freshmen Found Stressing Wealth," *New York Times,* January 14, 1988.

63. Bell, "Cultural Contradictions," p. 43.

64. Carmody, "Freshmen Found Stressing Wealth."

65. *Incentive Marketing* (May 1986), 50.

66. "Lotto Beer: Betting on Two Vices," *Business Week,* June 17, 1985, 72.

67. "Prize competitions are currently enjoying a revival as a leading form of incentive marketing." Ronald Holloway, "More Gambling, Less Tax?" *Lloyd's Bank Review* 110 (1973), 34. Also see "Sweepstakes Fever," *Forbes,* October 3, 1988, 164–166.

68. Correspondence from New York Department of State, July 22, 1987. The number of registered games of chance increased from 16 in 1970, to 105 in 1972, to 1,086 in 1985, and to 2,295 in 1986.

69. It is possible to compare different games according to the percentage of total prizes devoted to the top prize. An example of care devoted to lower-tier prizes is a contest for children sponsored by Tinkerbell party products, in which first prize is a trip for four to Disney World. Ronald Smiley, a marketing consultant, states, "But we also paid careful attention to the structure of the lower-tiered prizes. This is especially important in children's promotions since you want to elicit widespread enthusiasm and (figuratively) encourage kids to kick mom and dad in the ankle and make them aware of the contest." *Incentive Marketing* (May 1986), 60.

70. *Code of Federal Regulations,* sec. 16, pt. 419, rev. January 1, 1986 (Washington, D.C.: Government Printing Office, 1986), pp. 233–234.

71. Ezell, *Fortune's Merry Wheel,* pp. 17–18, 259.

72. George W. Cornell, "Methodists Stress Evangelism, Stay Cautious on Social Issues," *Washington Post,* May 14, 1976; "Mormon Leader Opposes Gambling," *Boston Globe,* January 17, 1986; Raymond C. Bell, "Moral Views on Gambling Promulgated by Major American Religious Bodies," in Commission on Gambling, *Gambling in America,* I, 161–239.

73. Kenneth S. Kantzer, "Gambling: Everyone's a Loser," *Christianity Today,* November 25, 1983, 12; Lycurgus Starkey, "Christians and the Gambling Mania," in Herman, *Gambling,* pp. 226–227; James Wall, "Why Isn't the Church Fighting Lotteries?" *Christian Century* 91 (1974), 1163–64.

74. *The Catholic Encyclopedia,* ed. Robert Broderick (Nashville: T. Nelson, 1987), p. 211.

75. Bell, "Moral Views," p. 217.

76. Tabulations based on *Los Angeles Times* Poll, 1986 (see Chapter 6, note 5), show the following illustrative rates of disapproval: Catholics, 8 percent; Jews, 5 percent; non-Southern Baptists, 26 percent; and other Protestants, 24 percent. A 1958 survey in Detroit also revealed that Protestants were much more likely to oppose gambling than Catholics or Jews. The percentage of respondents who thought that

gambling is always or usually wrong was consistently higher among Protestants than among Catholics. Furthermore, the opposition to gambling among Protestants was greatest among active church members, with 80 percent of that group believing that gambling is wrong. But even that opposition lagged behind that of the Protestant clergy, of whom 95 percent thought that gambling is wrong on moral grounds. Similar evidence on attitudes toward gambling is found in Gerhard Lenski, *The Religious Factor* (1961; rpt., New York: Doubleday Anchor Books, 1963), pp. 194, 310–311.

77. Ezell, *Fortune's Merry Wheel,* p.18.

78. *Congressional Record,* Senate, February 24, 1942, vol. 88, pt. 2, pp. 1536–37.

79. See also Larry Braidfoot, "Moral Arguments against State-Operated Lotteries," in U.S. Congress, Senate Committee on Governmental Affairs, "State Lotteries: An Overview," 98th Cong., 2d sess., October 3, 1984, and Braidfoot, *Gambling: A Deadly Game* (Nashville: Broadman Press, 1985); Bell, "Moral Views," pp. 209–210.

4. The Games People Play

1. Vicki Abt, "State Lotteries and Public Policy," paper delivered before the Association for Public Policy Analysis and Management, November 1987, Bethesda, Maryland, p. 8.

2. Descriptions of early games used here are from *Business Week,* March 13, 1971, 45; G. Robert Blakey, "State Conducted Lotteries: History, Problems, and Promises," *Journal of Social Issues* 35, 3 (1979), 78; J. Richard Aronson, Andrew Weintraub, and Cornelius Walsh, "Revenue Potential of State and Local Public Lotteries," *Growth and Change* 3 (April 1972), 6. Data for payout rates in New Hampshire and New Jersey are taken from annual reports of lottery agencies.

3. *Sixth Annual Report of the New Hampshire Pari-Mutuel Commission* (Concord, N.H.: 1987), p. 4.

4. Aronson, Weintraub, and Walsh, "Revenue Potential," p. 6.

5. *Gaming and Wagering Business* 8 (February 1987), 32.

6. West Virginia Lottery, brochure for Lotto 6/36, Easy 8's, 1988.

7. See, for example, Donald Janson, "Legal Gambling Now $10 Billion Tristate Industry," *New York Times,* October 18, 1980.

8. Tom Stevenson, "Mastermind of the Instant Lottery," *New York Times,* January 2, 1977.

9. "Instant Games: Another Successful Experiment for Massachusetts," *Public Gaming* 13 (October 1985), 38.

10. Stevenson, "Mastermind," p. 9.

11. Mark H. Haller, "The Changing Structure of American Gambling in the Twentieth Century," *Journal of Social Issues* 35, 3 (1979), 93.

12. Picking 123 in a box bet, for example, covers the combinations 123, 132, 213, 231, 321, and 312. See Table 4.1.

13. Fund for the City of New York, *Legal Gambling in New York* (New York, 1972), pp. 20–21.

14. Illinois House of Representatives, Policy Numbers Game Study Committee, "Report and Recommendations to the Legislature," June 1975, p. 22.

15. Peter Reuter and Jonathan Rubinstein, *Illegal Gambling in New York: A Case*

Study in the Operation, Structure, and Regulation of an Illegal Market (Washington, D.C.: National Institute of Justice, 1982), pp. xx, 84, and 93; see also Fund for the City of New York, *Legal Gambling in New York*, pp. 21–22.

16. *Gaming and Wagering Business* 9 (February 1988), 21.

17. See Fund for the City of New York, *Legal Gambling in New York*, pp. 18, 64, and testimony by Ralph Batch, Illinois Study Committee, "Report and Recommendations," p. 127, who suggested a payout rate of 75 percent.

18. "Massachusetts Plays the Numbers Right," *Public Gambling* 13 (October 1985), 67.

19. The Maryland lottery, for example, stops play on any number for which bets reach a predetermined level. In October 1986 betting on the number 333 reached this level each day of the month. The only other number that reached this level was 777, on which betting was halted on eleven of the twenty-seven betting days that month. Unpublished tabulations, "Pick-3 Game Sellouts," provided by the Maryland State Lottery Agency, February 5, 1986.

20. The prize (X) in a parimutuel payout system for a bet of A is calculated as $X = AP/W$, where P is the prize pool and W is the total amount bet on the winning combination.

21. In a report on the legalization of numbers in New York, Fund for the City of New York, *Legal Gambling in New York*, p. 18, recommended the fixed-payout approach.

22. The interest rate implied by these figures is roughly 10 percent. At a 10 percent discount rate the present value of twenty annual payments, with the first payment made immediately, is about 9.4 times the annual payment, or about 47 percent of the twenty-year total. Agencies could presumably self-finance these payments by investing the prize money and paying winners each year, but the universal practice has instead been to buy annuities, thus immediately dispensing with the state's liability.

23. The probability of winning a P/D/F game is $C(F - P, D - P)/C(F, D)$, where $C(n, m)$ represents the number of combinations of n numbers taken m at a time.

24. In the New York game based on keno, hitting on all the numbers picked varies in probability from 1 in 72 for three numbers to 1 in 8.9 million for ten. The game even offers a booby prize of $4 if a player picking ten numbers fails to match any of the numbers drawn, making the choice of ten numbers the most likely to yield some prize. For descriptions of keno-type lotto games, see brochures from Pennsylvania and New York and "Keno as Lottery: A Rose by any Other Name," *Gaming and Wagering Business* 7 (July 1986), 37, and "CDC Unveils 7–11–80 Numbers Game in Pennsylvania," *Gaming and Wagering Business* 7 (September 1986), 54.

25. Annual reports of the state lotteries and *Gaming and Wagering Business* 9 (September 1988), 20.

26. Interview with Frances McDonnell, Massachusetts State Lottery Commission, April 3, 1986.

27. *Gaming and Wagering Business* 9 (July 1988), 33.

28. Illinois experimented with such machines briefly in 1985 and 1986 but found sales to be disappointing. *Gaming and Wagering Business* 7 (July 1986), 13; Daniel W. Bower, testimony of October 3, 1984, U.S. Congress, Senate, State Government Affairs Committee, Subcommittee on Intergovernmental Relations, pp. 52–60.

29. "World Lotto Proposed by Canadian Firm," *Gaming and Wagering Business* 9 (November 1988), 1.

30. For further discussion of Delaware's experiment in sports betting and the proposal in New York, see Chapter 9 and William R. Green, "Illegal Sports Betting Called Growing and Intractable Problem in New York," *New York Times,* January 22, 1984.

31. *Gaming and Wagering Business* 9 (July 1988) 1, 40. Each entry involves picking the leading team after each quarter, picking the final score, and matching the random number printed on the ticket with the time of the last score. For a description of other sports games being used in Europe, see *Gaming and Wagering Business* 8 (December 1987), 10.

32. Bob Grotevant, "State Lotteries Weigh Betting on Pro Sports," *Raleigh News and Observer,* December 28, 1981.

33. For an assessment of legalized sports betting, see Fund for the City of New York, *Legal Gambling in New York,* pp. 49–54.

34. The league also argued that the use of team names constituted an infringement of their trademarks. "NFL Sues to Halt Del. Betting," *Washington Post,* August 21, 1976. One official explained the league's opposition to sports-related lottery games: "We are not naive. We are not unaware of the fact that there is a great deal of gambling going on, but we don't think that the state or any governmental authority rightfully should come in and impose a gambling situation on our game . . . Rumors are as destructive to us as actual attempts at fixing." Eliot Marshall, "State Lootery," *New Republic,* June 24, 1978, 20–21.

35. John S. Ezell, *Fortune's Merry Wheel: The Lottery in America* (Cambridge, Mass.: Harvard University Press, 1960), p. 165.

36. Stevenson, "Mastermind," p. 9.

37. Pennsylvania General Assembly, Legislative Budget and Finance Committee, "Report on a Performance Audit of The Pennsylvania State Lottery," September 1987, pp. 77–78.

38. *Public Gaming* 13 (October 1985), 57.

39. The complete prize distribution for these games is given in Table A.1.

40. For references to low-tier and high-tier prize structures of contemporary instant games, see *Gaming and Wagering Business* 7 (November 1986), 9, 30. One way of describing prize distribution is to use a measure of inequality, such as the Gini coefficient, which measures the deviation of any distribution from complete equality. This measure has a minimum value of 0 (indicating that all prizes are the same) and approaches 1 as a maximum (indicating that all prize money is concentrated into one prize). For the games shown in Table 4.4 the degree of inequality in prizes also differs, and it does so in ways seemingly unrelated to the grand prize amounts. A comparison of the 1762 and 1825 lotteries shows that the game that put most of its prize fund into the top prize—the Maryland 1825 game—was more concentrated. This increase in concentration is typical of American and English lotteries during the period. In a study of lottery prize concentration, R. Clay Sprowls found that the average Gini coefficient for a sample of American lotteries held before 1792 was .38 and that for a sample of lotteries held from 1792 to 1835 it was .47. Comparable samples of English lotteries increased from .39 before 1805 to .67 afterward. Sprowls, "A Historical

Analysis of Lottery Terms," *Canadian Journal of Economics and Political Science* 20 (August 1954), 352.

41. Ibid., p. 355.

42. David Stipp, "Picking Birth Dates for Lottery Numbers May Be Why Folks Don't Hit the Jackpot," *Wall Street Journal,* April 28, 1986.

43. John Koza, letter to the editor, *Wall Street Journal,* May 19, 1987.

44. If a player places enough bets on the first round to ensure that he will have winnings to reinvest for fourteen rounds of betting, and if the payout rate for any play is 95 percent, the expected payout for fourteen successive rounds, with winnings reinvested, is .95 raised to the fourteenth power, or .49.

5. Why (And How) They Play

1. See Vicki Abt, James F. Smith, and Eugene Martin Christiansen, *The Business of Risk: Commercial Gambling in Mainstream America* (Lawrence: University Press of Kansas, 1985), chap. 2, for a general discussion of the characteristics of gambling opportunities.

2. *Los Angeles Times* Poll 104, March 1986; Arizona Survey Laboratory, Arizona State University, Fall 1985–Winter 1986, question 60; Hill, Holliday, Connors, Cosmopulos, Inc., "Quantitative Research Findings: The Massachusetts State Lottery Game, Wave II," report prepared for the Massachusetts State Lottery, March 1986.

3. For an analysis of gambling behavior within the economic model of investor behavior, see Richard N. Rosett, "Gambling and Rationality," *Journal of Political Economy* 73 (December 1965), 595–607.

4. The expected value of an uncertain investment is equal to the average return if the investment were to be made many times. In the case of a lottery ticket with a payout of 50 percent, the expected value of a dollar bet is a negative fifty cents, ignoring taxes: that is, the dollar minus the expected value of the prize, which is fifty cents.

5. A jackpot worth $1.5 million before taxes will be worth, in present value, approximately $500,000 after federal and state taxes have been paid. With a probability of winning of 1 in 500,000, the expected value of a dollar bet is therefore about a dollar.

6. For an analysis of which numbers are the best bets in lotto, see William T. Ziemba et al., *Dr. Z's 6/49 Lotto Guidebook* (Vancouver: Dr. Z. Investments, 1986).

7. Herman Chernoff, "How to Beat the Massachusetts Numbers Game: An Application of Some Basic Ideas in Probability and Statistics," *Mathematical Intelligencer* 3, 4 (1981), 166–172.

8. Most state numbers games have fixed payoffs, offering the same prize regardless of how many people have bet the winning number. See Chapter 4 for a description of the two systems for calculating prize payouts.

9. Srully Blotnick, "The Lure of the Lottery," *Forbes,* January 13, 1986, 302.

10. Telephone conversation with Daniel Nagin, former deputy secretary of revenue for Pennsylvania, July 5, 1988. He noted that this use of the legal game by illegal numbers operators was "common knowledge" among state officials involved with the lottery.

11. Bonita Brodt, "Lottery's Down Side," *Chicago Tribune,* May 25, 1986.

12. Daniel Kahneman and Amos Tversky, "Prospect Theory: An Analysis of Decision Under Risk," *Econometrica* 47 (March 1979), 277.

13. Milton Friedman and L. J. Savage, "The Utility Analysis of Choices Involving Risk," *Journal of Political Economy* 56 (August 1948), 299.

14. In terms of microeconomics, the Friedman-Savage explanation for individuals who simultaneously buy insurance and also gamble is that their utility function for money or wealth displays alternating regions of convexity and concavity. For smaller changes the individual could be a risk averter (on a section concave from below, signifying that the utility of the expected value of a lottery is greater than the expected utility of the lottery) yet be a risk taker for larger changes. For a standard treatment of this question, see James M. Henderson and Richard E. Quandt, *Microeconomic Theory* (New York: McGraw-Hill, 1980), pp. 55–60.

For an analysis that links gambling more broadly to economic mobility, see Gabrielle and Reuven Brenner, "A Profile of Gamblers," unpublished manuscript, University of Montreal (March 1987). This study is also a source of data on lottery play in Canada.

15. See Chapter 6, and Charles T. Clotfelter and Philip J. Cook, "Implicit Taxation in Lottery Finance," *National Tax Journal* 40 (December 1987), 533–546.

16. Arizona State University survey, and *Los Angeles Times* Poll survey (see n. 2). In the latter, fewer than 5 percent of blacks and Latinos correctly stated the payout rate.

17. The probability of winning on one bet in a 6/49 game is 1 in 14 million. Playing ten times in each of one hundred drawings a year for fifty-two years yields a probability of winning of .0037, or about 1 in 270.

18. Amos Tversky and Daniel Kahneman, "Judgment under Uncertainty: Heuristics and Biases," *Science* 185 (1974), 1124–31, describe three heuristics that are employed by people in assessing the likelihood of an event, including what they call "availability": "There are situations in which people assess . . . the probability of an event by the ease with which instances or occurrences can be brought to mind."

19. See Chapter 10 for a discussion of the content of lottery advertising.

20. Daniel Kahneman and Amos Tversky, "Choices, Values, and Frames," *American Psychologist* 39 (April 1984), 345.

21. See Ellen J. Langer, "The Psychology of Chance," *Journal for the Theory of Social Behavior* 7, 2 (1978), 185–207, and Langer, "The Illusion of Control," *Journal of Personality and Social Psychology* 32, 2 (1975), 311–328.

22. According to one poll, 40 percent of Americans say some numbers are especially lucky for some people. *Harpers* 273 (October 1986), 11, 76.

23. *Prince Ali Lucky Five Star Dream Book* (New York: Wholesale Book Corp., 1980).

24. Harry B. Weiss, "Oneirocritica Americana," *Bulletin of the New York Public Library* 48 (June 1944), 531.

25. George J. McCall, "Symbiosis: The Case of Hoodoo and the Numbers Racket," *Social Problems* 10 (Spring 1963), 366.

26. Peter Reuter and Jonathan Rubinstein, *Illegal Gambling in New York: A Case*

Study in the Operation, Structure, and Regulation of an Illegal Market (Washington, D.C.: Department of Justice, April 1982), p. 190.

27. St. Clair Drake and Horace R. Cayton, *Black Metropolis: A Study of Negro Life in a Northern City* (New York: Harcourt, Brace and World, 1970), p. 475.

28. Illinois House of Representatives, Policy Numbers Game Study Committee, "Report and Recommendations to the Legislature," June 1975, p. 10.

29. *3 Wise Men* (Philadelphia: Dale Book Co., 1986) gives two numbers for each item. Note that two of the numbers, 148 and 418, are variations of each other.

30. The *National Enquirer's* weekly circulation is about 4.5 million (*Gale Directory of Publications*, 1987), the *Globe's* is 2 million (*Magazine Industry Marketplace*), and the *National Examiner's* is over a million and the *Sun's* is nearly 500,000 (Audit Bureau of Circulations).

31. *Globe,* June 16, 1987; June 23, 1987; and August 4, 1987.

32. *Lottery Player's Magazine* (May 1988), 5.

33. *Newsweek,* September 2, 1985, 16; *New York Times,* August 23, 1985.

34. McCall, "Symbiosis," p. 370.

35. *Los Angeles Times* Poll, March 1986.

36. Blotnick, "Lure of the Lottery," p. 302.

37. "Lottery Cuts Off 'Dream' Bet," *Baltimore Sun,* December 2, 1976.

38. Reuter and Rubinstein, *Illegal Gambling,* p. 105; McCall, "Symbiosis"; *New York Times,* June 9, 1963, p. 9; *Chicago Tribune,* October 2, 1982.

39. Based on unpublished tabulations provided by the Maryland State Lottery Agency. The most popular three-digit number during this period, 123, is not among the top ten numbers shown in Table 5.1. The probable explanation is the gambler's fallacy, discussed later in the chapter. The number was drawn on August 12, 1986, and did not return to the top ten numbers until early 1987. Correspondence from Frank Hemberger, Maryland State Lottery Agency, July 8, 1988.

40. See Table A.2.

41. Straight bets accounted for roughly half the dollar value of bets. The distribution of numbers differed very little on the three different days. More generally, the distribution of bets by number was very stable when analyzed over a one-month period in 1986. As an illustration, of the numbers that ranked in the top twenty on each of the twenty-seven betting days of the month, sixteen of them ranked there every day.

42. In 1986 the lottery agency's rule was to stop taking bets when total liability reached $7 million.

43. Studies of illegal betting by David L. Rados, "The Numbers Game: An Economic and Comparative Analysis," *Quarterly Review of Economics and Business* 16 (Summer 1976) 22, and Reuter and Rubinstein, *Illegal Gambling,* p. 107, show similar distributions of betting frequencies. To indicate how close the distributions are, the percentages of betting on numbers between 100 and 399 were 39 in the Maryland study, 44 in Rados, and 43 in Reuter and Rubinstein. The percentages for numbers between 800 and 999 were 15, 11, and 13, respectively.

Likewise, another study of payoffs in the Massachusetts numbers game was consistent with heavy play on numbers beginning with 1, 2, and 3 and light play on numbers beginning with 0, 8, and 9. Donald J. Smith, "Risk-Efficient Lottery Bets?!" Boston University, July 1986, p. 10. Since payoffs in that state's numbers game are determined on a parimutuel basis, higher-than-average popularity results in lower-than-average payoffs. Although these comparisons are made at a high level of aggregation, they span enough differences in geography, time, and legal status to make the similarity in patterns very striking indeed. See also Kathleen M. Joyce, "Betting Preferences in the Numbers Game," in Reuter and Rubinstein, *Illegal Gambling,* p. 195, who notes that the high frequency of numbers beginning with 1, 2, and 3 corresponds to the more frequent appearance of numbers in this range in dream books. Whatever the reasons why players pick certain numbers, there appears to be a consistency over time and across states in which numbers are chosen most often.

44. Correspondence from Frank Hemberger, Maryland State Lottery Agency, July 20, 1988.

45. According to a "Bet Frequency Report" for lotto provided by the Maryland State Lottery, the frequency of combinations played on August 9, 1986, was:

Number of times selected	Number of combinations	Percentage of total combinations	Number of bets	Percentage of total bets
0	1,191,674	31.0%	0	0%
1	1,334,605	34.8	1,334,605	26.9
2 to 4	1,242,526	32.4	3,054,643	61.5
5 or more	69,575	1.8	576,182	11.6
Total	3,838,380	100%	4,965,430	100%

By comparison, the percentage of straight bets for Maryland's three-digit numbers game was 4.9 percent for the least popular 310 numbers, 26.2 percent for the next 348, 50.3 percent for the next 324, and 18.6 percent for the most popular 18 numbers. Thus, while the numbers game is more concentrated at the very top, lotto is more concentrated in the top third, even though it has parimutuel payoffs.

46. The difference between the distributions for Maryland and New Jersey is discussed later in this chapter.

47. For combinations that won more than once, the implied proportion of bets was averaged, although the differences in proportions, like the observed frequencies for the Maryland data, demonstrated considerable stability in betting patterns over time. Where B represents the number of bets on the winning number and TB represents total bets, and where 50 percent of the bets are paid out in prizes, the payoff (PO) on a one-dollar bet is $PO = .5\,(TB/B)$. The proportion of bets placed on the winning number is $B/TB = .5/PO$. Since New Jersey's payoff reflects betting on boxes and other betting options in addition to straight bets, the total liability of payoffs for all bet variations is used to determine the distribution of betting for Maryland.

48. For discussions of the gambler's fallacy, see, for example, Robert M. Hogarth, *Judgement and Choice* (Chichester: John Wiley and Sons, 1980), pp. 13, 165, and Tversky and Kahneman, "Judgment under Uncertainty." This notion has also been referred to as the principle of the "maturity of chances." Apparently believing it, one historian of gambling in 1909 stated the principle as follows: "In games of chance, the

oftener the same combination has occurred in succession, the nearer we are to certainty that it will not occur at the next coup. It would almost appear, in fact, as if there existed an instant, prescribed by some law, at which the chances become mature and after which they begin to tend again towards equalization." Ralph Nevill, quoted in Edward C. Devereux, Jr., *Gambling and the Social Structure* (New York: Arno, 1980), p. 690n.

49. *New York Times,* August 24, 1985.

50. *The Leader* (Randolph, Mass.: Grove Publishing Co., 1986); the *Globe,* for example January 19, 1988, p. 27, carries lists of numbers that are "due."

51. *3 Wise Men Dream Book,* p. 18.

52. The following equations were estimated:

$$\text{PROBET1} = 0.76 \text{ PBETAVG } (R^2 = .96) \quad \text{and}$$
$$(0.03)$$
$$\text{PROBET2} = 0.46 \text{ PBETAVG } (R^2 = .94)$$
$$(0.02)$$

standard errors in parentheses, where PROBET1 is the proportion of all straight bets placed on a number that won the previous drawing, PROBET2 applies to the second day after the number was drawn, and PBETAVG is the average proportion bet in the two previous drawings.

53. Based on unpublished data on winning three-digit numbers in Maryland during March and April 1988, provided by the Maryland State Lottery.

54. It has also been noted that agencies are reluctant to provide other information that could be useful to bettors. Some states do not report the odds of winning in any readily available source. John G. Cross, *A Theory of Adaptive Economic Behavior* (Cambridge: Cambridge University Free Press, 1983). And it is certainly true that the public—players and nonplayers alike—is ill informed about the probability distribution of prizes. For instance, a survey of lottery players in Massachusetts found that only about one-quarter could correctly state the size of the main prize in the numbers game. Hill, Holliday, Connors, Cosmopoulos, "Quantitative Research Findings." But the question exists whether a better-informed public could make productive use of the information, particularly concerning the odds of winning.

55. Iowa Lottery Annual Report, 1987.

56. West Virginia Lottery, brochure for "Lotto 6/36" and "Easy 8's" brochures.

57. Connecticut State Lottery, "The Daily Numbers Prize Payout Table," brochure.

58. "They add up to $10.7 million," California State Lottery newspaper ad, 1986. Fortunately for the winning player, he got Bob Cousy's number wrong. *Sports Illustrated,* November 24, 1986, 20.

59. Leonard A. Paster, "Quick Pick Design Considerations," *Public Gaming International* 15 (October 1987), 22–23.

60. See Joyce, "Betting Preferences."

61. This skill orientation is suggested by a statement in Marcel Blackerby, *Lucky Number Lottery Guide* (New York: House of Collectibles, 1983), p. 1: "Good judgement and a cool attitude is necessary for the success of any project. Combine this with the lucky number methods in this book, and you could experience greater success and winnings."

6. The Demand for Lottery Products

1. This is also referred to as Pareto's law or the "80/20 rule." See *Handbook of Modern Marketing*, ed. Victor P. Buell, 2d ed. (New York: McGraw-Hill), 1986, pp. 8–10, and *Macmillan Dictionary of Marketing and Advertising*, ed. Michael S. Baker (New York: Nichols Publishing Co., 1984), p. 150.

2. Calculations based on Oliver Quayle and Co., Appendix, in Fund for the City of New York, *Legal Gambling in New York* (New York, 1972), p. 19, indicate that the top 10.5 percent of players in the illegal game made 47.8 percent of the bets, consistent with the 48 percent of bets made by the top 10 percent of players in Maryland. The top 20 percent bet about 67 percent in the illegal game, compared to about 63 percent in Maryland.

3. National Institute of Alcohol Abuse and Alcoholism, *Sixth Special Report to the U.S. Congress on Alcohol and Health* (Washington, D.C., January 1987), p. 3.

4. John Koza, "Who is Playing What: A Demographic Study," pt. 2, *Public Gaming* 12 (March 1984), 72. Likewise, Maryland's advertising agency cites evidence that the great bulk of lottery purchases are made by "regular, loyal, repeat customers," and concludes that it would be incorrect to base a marketing strategy on stimulating impulse sales. Trahan, Burden, and Charles, Inc., *Advertising and Marketing the Maryland State Lottery*, Senate Governmental Affairs Committee, Subcommittee on Intergovernmental Relations, September 1984.

5. The data sets referred to in this section are American Institute of Public Opinion, national survey of gambling, conducted in 1944, summarized in Edward C. Devereux, Jr., *Gambling and the Social Structure* (New York: Arno, 1980), appendix D; University of Michigan Survey Research Center, "Gambling in the United States (ICPSR 7495)," unpublished data from national survey, conducted summer 1975; Gallup Organization, Inc., Gallup Study GO 84190," unpublished data from survey conducted November 1984; Arizona State University, Survey Research Lab, Arizona Survey P1922, unpublished data from survey conducted fall 1985–winter 1986; Field Institute, California Poll 8504, unpublished data from survey conducted November-December 1985; *Los Angeles Times* Poll 103, unpublished data from survey conducted March 1986; Field Institute, California Poll 8602, unpublished data from survey conducted May 1986.

6. Calculations are based on Gallup Study GO 84190.

7. For descriptions of the role of numbers and policy, see, for example, St. Clair Drake and Horace R. Cayton, *Black Metropolis: A Study of Negro Life in a Northern City* (New York: Harcourt, Brace and World, 1970); Illinois House of Representatives, Policy Numbers Game Study Committee, "Report and Recommendations to the Legislature," June 1975; and Fund for the City of New York, *Legal Gambling in New York*. Witnesses testifying on the possible legalization of policy in Chicago agreed about its prevalence in black neighborhoods, some expressing the hope that a legalized and locally administered game would continue to provide employment for blacks. One witness stated: "Policy is an evil in the Black community which we might compare with mosquitoes and flies. None of us like them particularly, but we know they are there to stay and we must live with them." Illinois Study Committee, p. 31. Another

gave the positive side: "Policy offers a positive expectation that one could be lifted out of the most sordid entrapments of life in the ghetto" (p. 17).

8. Calculations are based on Arizona State University, Survey Research Lab, unpublished data from survey conducted fall 1985–winter 1986.

9. Data from household surveys were requested from the Massachusetts and Illinois lottery agencies, but neither consented to their being used for this study.

10. Calculations are based on Gallup survey, 1984 (see note 5), and are corrected for the 9 percent of the population (all nonplayers) who were excluded from the survey.

11. Koza, "Who Is Playing What." For each game regular players were defined so as to account for 80 to 90 percent of all expenditures. Indices of participation were then calculated as the ratio of regular players in a group as a percentage of all regular players to adults in the group as a percentage of all adults. Data were taken from a household survey in New Jersey. Index values for blacks and Hispanics were 199 for four-digit numbers, 197 for three-digit numbers, 131 for lotto, and 105 for instant games.

12. Oliver Quayle and Co., Appendix, p. 9, reports that 20 percent of whites and 40 percent of blacks and Puerto Ricans played the numbers.

13. For example, Roger E. Brinner and Charles T. Clotfelter, "An Economic Appraisal of State Lotteries," National Tax Journal 28 (December 1975), 400, presents data on expenditures by income based on surveys of three states. For none of the states is there a pattern of absolute expenditures with income. Likewise, Daniel Suits, "Gambling Taxes: Regressivity and Revenue Potential," National Tax Journal 30 (1977), 23, tabulates average lottery expenditures by income, based on the national study of gambling in 1974. The average bet rises from $7.48 in the under-$5,000 income class to almost $17 between $5,000 and $14,999, and then falls again to $8.72 in the $30,000-and-above class.

14. Hill, Holliday, Connors, Cosmopulos, Inc. "Quantitative Research Findings: The Massachusetts State Lottery Game, Wave II," report prepared for the Massachusetts State Lottery, March 1986.

15. Koza, "Who Is Playing What."

16. For example, in fiscal 1986 most of the interstate differences in per capita numbers sales could be explained by the percentage of blacks in the population. The correlation between the logarithms of these two variables (per capita sales and percent black) is .87 for the sixteen numbers games operating that year.

17. The states are Arizona, Connecticut, Delaware, Illinois, Maine, Maryland, Massachusetts, Michigan, New Hampshire, New Jersey, Ohio, Pennsylvania, and Vermont.

18. The data are for the period from July 18, 1984, to March 8, 1986. Each of the 170 observations consists of the sum of three days' numbers sales, in thousands of dollars (NUM), corresponding in each case to the three-day period between lotto drawings. The regression equation included a time trend (T), a dummy variable for the second half of the week (SAT), and a variable giving the amount of rollover included in the lotto jackpot (JR), equal to zero if there was a winner in the previous drawing, otherwise the amount advertised as the official jackpot for the preceding drawing, measured in thousands of dollars. The estimated equation (with standard

errors in parentheses) was NUM = 2797 (21) − 0.0018 (.0038) JR + 332 (18) SAT + 4.34 (0.19) T, R^2 = 0.84, mean of dependent variable \$3,331 (thousand). The coefficient on the rollover variable was equal to just one-quarter of its standard error. If taken literally, the point estimate implies that a \$1,000 increase in rollover reduces numbers sales by less than a penny.

19. Calculations are based on *Los Angeles Times* Poll, 1986 (see note 5).

20. It is not plausible that the reinvestment pattern would *by itself* increase net revenue. Even if *all* the additional prize money were reinvested following an increase in the payout rate, the states' net revenue would fall somewhat because a percentage of the additional sales would go to retailers as commissions. Of course, where there are other mechanisms by which the payout rate influences sales, then sales may increase enough to increase net revenue.

21. A series of cross-section regressions of numbers sales was run to estimate the effect of payout rate. Using fiscal 1986 data for the fifteen states that were offering a numbers game at that time, we found that the coefficient estimate on the payout rate in no case exceeded its standard error. A total of seven (log linear) specifications were tried, using various combinations of the following set of variables: percent black, population, per capita income, and percent urban. The only variable that was statistically different from zero by normal standards was percent black. Its coefficient implied an elasticity of about .7. This result is given in Table A.4.

22. See Table A.4.

23. There have been a number of attempts to estimate the payout elasticity of demand using regression analysis of state sales data for all games combined. Unsurprisingly they reach contradictory conclusions on this issue and others. For example, Larry DeBoer, "Lottery Taxes May Be Too High," *Journal of Policy Analysis and Management* 5 (Spring 1986), 594–596, reports a strong positive effect from the payout rate, while Jon David Vasche, "Are Taxes on Lotteries Too High?" *Journal of Policy Analysis and Management* 4 (Winter 1985), 269–271, reports a negative effect. These and other authors chose different sets of control variables, and there is no a priori method of determining which are most appropriate. See John L. Mikesell, "The Effect of Maturity and Competition in State Lottery Markets," *Journal of Policy Analysis and Management* 6 (Winter 1987); Jerome F. Heavey, October 1978, "The Incidence of State Lottery Taxes," *Public Finance Quarterly* 6 (October 1978), 415–426; and Roger E. Brinner and Charles T. Clotfelter, "An Economic Appraisal of State Lotteries," *National Tax Journal* 28 (December 1975), for additional regression analyses of interstate sales patterns.

If the different types of lottery games have independent markets, as we have argued, then the preferred econometric strategy is to estimate separate regressions for sales of each game rather than a single equation on total sales. This is what we have done for numbers and lotto in Table A.4. This disaggregated approach provides the basis for estimating the distinct patterns associated with each game, rather than averaging them together. Most important, separate equations avoid the problem that an overall payout rate is a sort of price average with different weights in each state and is hence endogenous to the pattern of sales.

24. At a payout rate of 50 percent and a marginal cost of administration of 6 percent, the elasticity of sales with respect to the payout rate would need to be 1.14. To

see this algebraically, let net revenue be $N = S(p) - pS - C(S)$, where S is sales, p is the payout rate, and C is the cost of administration (including commissions). The effect of the payout rate on sales is given by $N'(S) = S'(p) - S - pS'(p) - C'(S)$ $S'(p)$, where primes denote partial derivatives. This will be positive if the elasticity of sales with respect to the payout rate, $S'(p)$ (p/S), is greater than $p/[1 - p - C'(S)]$. If the payout rate is 50 percent (.5) and the marginal cost is 6 percent, the elasticity must exceed 1.14.

25. For example, consider a lottery with sales of $100, fixed costs of $5, a payout rate of 50 percent, and commissions and additional administrative costs amounting to six cents per dollar. After subtracting prizes of $50 and operating costs of $11, net revenue would be $39. Could the lottery increase its revenues by increasing its payout rate to 60 percent? It could if sales rose at least 30 percent, to $130. Then deducting prizes of $78 (60 percent of $130), the fixed cost of $5, and other costs of $7.80, net revenues would be $39.20.

26. See Z. Adar and N. M. Edelson, "Gambling Behavior and Lottery Prize Structures," Discussion Paper 72, Fels Center of Government, University of Pennsylvania, May 1975. See also Chapter 4.

27. This account of the history of Holiday Cash was provided by Anne Bloomberg, public information manager for the Ohio state lottery, in a September 1987 telephone call. The lottery also provided weekly sales data for Holiday Cash and other games played just before and after Holiday Cash.

28. A number of regressions (log linear form) were run on fiscal 1986 lotto sales data for the sixteen states that operated lotto games at that time. The specifications included different subsets of the following variables: income per capita, percent black, percent urban, and payout rate. The state population was included in every specification, and was highly statistically significant in each case. The point estimate implies that a 10 percent increase in population causes a 5 percent increase in sales per capita. The results for one specification are given in Table A.4.

29. A pooled sample of sales by drawing period was compiled by eight states' lotto games for calendar years 1986 and 1987. An equation was estimated explaining the logarithm of average daily per capita sales. Independent variables included state dummies, a time trend, and the logarithms of the probability of any ticket's winning the grand prize, the advertised jackpot, the proportion of the prize pool devoted to prizes below the grand prize, and the payout rate. The estimated elasticities of these last variables (with t-statistics in parentheses) were -0.01 (0.3), 0.40 (40.3), 0.38 (4.6), and 1.35 (1.6), respectively. Table A.5 gives the full regression.

30. For example, Elder Witt, "States Place Their Bets on a Game of Diminishing Returns," *Governing* 1 (November 1987), 52: "Bettors want new games or they quit."

31. Chris Wood, "Odds Makers: The Very Profitable Gamble of Canada's Four Public Lottery Corporations," *Canadian Business* 57 (April 1984), 25.

32. One impediment to this sort of competition is the federal prohibition on using the mail to ship lottery materials. As of 1988 that restriction was being circumvented through the use of other shippers, telephone orders, and illegal couriers. But these methods are somewhat costly and inconvenient to players. If federal restrictions were eliminated, a true national market in lottery tickets would emerge, with profound effects on game design and sales patterns.

7. Winners and Losers

1. There is some evidence that the recreational aspects of gambling often have healthy effects on the gambler's personality and interpersonal relations. Igor Kusyszyn, "The Psychology of Gambling," *Annals of the American Academy of Political and Social Science* 473 (July 1984), 142–143.

2. Edward C. Devereux, Jr., *Gambling and the Social Structure* (New York: Arno Press, 1980), pp. 781–782. This hope of wealth may explain both the popularity of lotteries and the widespread dislike for inheritance taxes. Interestingly, for example, 64 percent of California voters in 1982 voted to abolish the state's inheritance tax. *Los Angeles Times,* June 10, 1982.

3. Robert Wagman, *Instant Millionaires: Cashing In on America's Lotteries* (Kensington, Md.: Woodbine House, 1986), p. 2.

4. To estimate the number of such winners we solicited from the larger lottery agencies data on their big winners in 1987. According to the agencies, there were five such winners in Arizona, thirty-five in California, six in Connecticut, forty-three in Illinois, nine in Massachusetts, twenty-four in Michigan, three in Missouri, nineteen in New Jersey, forty in New York, forty-one in Ohio, and fifteen in Pennsylvania.

5. H. Roy Kaplan, *Lottery Winners: How They Won and How Winning Changed Their Lives* (New York: Harper and Row, 1978). These "million-dollar" winners actually received a twenty-year annuity with annual payments of $50,000. Kaplan also interviewed a number of winners of smaller prizes.

6. H. Roy Kaplan, "Gambling Among Lottery Winners: Before and After the Big Score," *Journal of Gambling Behavior* 4 (Fall 1988), 171–182.

7. Wagman, *Instant Millionaires,* p. 6.

8. Kaplan, *Lottery Winners,* p. 45.

9. "One New Yorker's Cure for Hypertension: Win a Million-Dollar Lottery," *New York Times,* June 14, 1987.

10. Wagman, *Instant Millionaires,* pp. 111–112.

11. Kaplan, "Gambling among Lottery Winners," p. 178. Results are based on responses from half of all million-dollar winners.

12. Kaplan, *Lottery Winners,* p. 173.

13. *Raleigh News and Observer,* June 23, 1988.

14. "Gambling Fever: The Survivors Relive Horror Stories," *Chicago Tribune,* October 30, 1981.

15. "Lottery's Down Side," *Chicago Tribune,* May 25, 1986.

16. George B. Merry, "Pinched States Try Lotteries; Hidden Costs May Cancel Gains," *Christian Science Monitor,* January 7, 1983.

17. This brief history is taken from John Rosecrance, *Gambling without Guilt: The Legitimization of an American Pastime* (Pacific Grove, Calif.: Brooks/Cole Publishing, 1988).

18. American Psychiatric Association, *Diagnostic and Statistical Manual,* 3d ed. rev. (Washington, D.C.: American Psychiatric Press, 1980), p. 324.

19. Henry R. Lesieur, *Report on Pathological Gambling in New Jersey* (Jamaica, N.Y.: St. John's University Press, 1988), p. 4.

20. Rosecrance, *Gambling without Guilt,* p. 109.

21. Maureen Kallick et al., *A Survey of American Gambling Attitudes and Behavior*, appendix 2, in Commission on the Review of the National Policy toward Gambling, *Gambling in America* (Washington, D.C.: Government Printing Office, 1976), pp. 74, 93–95.

22. Lesieur, *Pathological Gambling in New Jersey*, p. 1.

23. Robert Colleton, "The Prevalence Rates of Pathological Gambling: A Look at Methods," Rutgers University, Livingston Campus, Urban and Regional Planning, 1987. Colleton is particularly critical of the methods used by the National Study of Gambling, as is Jim Orford, *Excessive Appetites: A Psychological View of Addictions* (New York: John Wiley and Sons, 1985), p. 41.

24. Lesieur, *Pathological Gambling in New Jersey*, p. 27.

25. Rosecrance, *Gambling without Guilt*, p. 117.

26. Derek Cornish, *Gambling: A Review of the Literature and Its Implications for Policy and Research*, Home Office research study 42 (London: Her Majesty's Stationery Office, 1978), p. 6.

27. Lesieur, *Pathological Gambling in New Jersey*, pp. 2, 3.

28. Cornish, *Gambling*, p. 168; Vicki Abt, James F. Smith, and Eugene Martin Christiansen, *The Business of Risk: Commercial Gambling in Mainstream America* (Lawrence: University Press of Kansas, 1985), p. 126.

29. Lesieur, *Pathological Gambling in New Jersey*, pp. 18–19.

30. We should note an interesting attempt to measure the effect of introducing a lottery on rates of larceny, burglary, and robbery; see John Mikesell and Maureen Pirog-Good, "Lotteries and Crime," Indiana University, Bloomington, 1987. They find that lotteries do exacerbate the crime problem by several percentage points. The statistical work, however, is not very persuasive.

31. See generally Jim Orford, *Excessive Appetites: A Psychological View of Addictions* (New York: John Wiley and Sons, 1985), for a complete development of this contextual emphasis in the analysis of appetitive behavior regarding gambling, alcohol, and sex.

32. Legislative Budget and Finance Committee, Pennsylvania General Assembly, "Report on a Performance Audit of the Pennsylvania State Lottery," September 1987, p. 75.

33. In 1987 the average lottery outlet earned $9,000 in commissions. See Chapter 9.

34. Terry Cashin, operations manager, British Columbia Division of Southland Canada, Inc., speech to lottery representatives, Vancouver, B.C., September 1987.

35. The former effect is statistically significantly different from zero only at the 10 percent level ($t = 1.98$), while the latter is significant at the 5 percent level. The dependent variable was the change in per capita convenience store sales in 1985 dollars. The independent variables included eight regional dummy variables, the change in per capita income, and the change in per capita lottery expenditures. Data were taken from *Progressive Grocer*, 55th Annual Report, April 1988, pp. 19, 49–50, and U.S. Bureau of the Census, *Statistical Abstract of the United States*, for various years.

36. *New York Times*, January 15, 1988.

37. William R. Eadington, "Possible Effects of the California Lottery on Nevada's Casino Industry: The Early Evidence," *Nevada Public Affairs Review* 2 (1986), 7–8.

38. The results are reported in Table A.6. The discussion in the text focuses on the coefficient estimates for variable 9, an indicator for lottery state.

39. National Association of Fundraising Ticket Manufacturers, "Effects of Charity Game Ticket Sales on Lottery Sales," Bismarck, N.D., September 1987.

40. One study was Susan A. Simmons and Robert Sharp, "State Lotteries' Effects on Thoroughbred Horse Racing," *Journal of Policy Analysis and Management* 6 (Spring 1987), 446–448. The authors used data on betting at one hundred meets in 1982. They regressed the average daily handle on a number of variables, including whether or not the meet was held in a lottery state. The estimated effect of this variable was substantial and negative. The problem with this approach is the difficulty of knowing which other characteristics of the meets, the local population, and the state significantly influenced the handle. The Simmons and Sharp results are probably very sensitive to the way in which the equation is specified and must be viewed as unreliable.

A second study by Diana Gurley of the Kentucky Thoroughbred Association, "A Preliminary Study of the Effect of Lotteries on Thoroughbred Parimutuel Handle," August 1987, adopted a more promising approach. Average daily handle was plotted for each of a number of meets from two years before the introdution of the lottery to two years after. Gurley found that the handle declined following adoption. She used no control group, however, and it is possible that the decline was simply the result of the general slump in parimutuel betting during this period.

41. Data were provided in a telephone conversation with Chuck Anderson of the Nevada State Gaming Control Board, August 16, 1988. Growth rates in taxable gaming revenues were as follows: 1983, 8.3 percent; 1984, 8 percent; 1985, 7.8 percent; 1986, 5.1 percent; 1987, 12.7 percent.

42. Peter Reuter and Jonathan Rubinstein, "Illegal Gambling and Organized Crime," *Society* 20 (July–August 1983), 52.

43. Floyd J. Fowler, Jr., Thomas W. Mangione, and Frederick E. Pratter, "Gambling Law Enforcement in Major American Cities: Executive Summary" (Washington, D.C.: National Institute of Law Enforcement and the Administration of Justice, Law Enforcement Assistance Administration, U.S. Department of Justice, September 1978), pp. 25, 36.

44. Peter Reuter and Jonathan Rubinstein, *Illegal Gambling in New York; A Case Study in the Operation, Structure, and Regulation of an Illegal Market* (Washington, D.C.: Department of Justice, National Institute of Justice, April 1982).

45. U.S. Department of the Treasury, Internal Revenue Service, Office of the Assistant Commissioner (Planning, Finance and Research), Research Division, *Income Tax Compliance Research: Estimates for 1973–1981* (Washington, D.C., July 1983).

46. Reuter and Rubinstein, "Illegal Gambling and Organized Crime," pp. 53, 55.

47. The earlier report was *Estimate of Income Unreported on Individual Income Tax Returns,* Publication 1104(9–79) (Washington, D.C.: Internal Revenue Service, 1979). It is cited in Abt, Smith, and Christiansen, *The Business of Risk,* pp. 245–246.

48. Abt, Smith, and Christiansen, *The Business of Risk,* p. 67.

49. Fowler, Mangione, and Pratter, "Gambling Law Enforcement," p. 57.

50. Rosecrance, *Gambling without Guilt,* p. 89; H. Roy Kaplan, "The Social and Economic Impact of State Lotteries," *Annals of the American Academy of Political*

and Social Science 474 (July 1984), 101; "Maryland Gets a Winning Number," *Washington Post,* July 29, 1977; telephone conversation with Dennis Last, Washington, D.C., Metropolitan Police Vice Squad, July 2, 1987.

51. Reuter and Rubinstein, "Illegal Gambling and Organized Crime." Abt, Smith, and Christiansen, *The Business of Risk,* p. 224, estimate that the illegal game has an average takeout rate of 51 percent.

52. Conversation with Dennis Last (see note 50); "State Lottery Losing Millions to Illegal Rackets, Police Say," *Chicago Tribune,* May 30, 1983; "Numbers Racket: The City's Underground Lottery," *Syracuse Post-Standard,* March 10, 1988.

53. The estimates are prepared by Eugene Martin Christiansen. His method for arriving at his original estimate is explained in Abt, Smith, and Christiansen, *The Business of Risk,* p. 247.

54. U.S. Department of the Treasury, *Income Tax Compliance Research,* table G-17. In subsequent updates, Eugene Martin Christiansen has assumed that the illegal numbers game is growing at the same rate as the legal three-digit game. See *Gaming and Wagering Business* 7 (July 1986).

55. "Despite State Lotteries and Raids, Numbers Racket Thrives," *New York Times,* November 20, 1987; "Three- and four-digit lottery games have significantly cut into the appeal of numbers betting in many areas." The *Syracuse Post-Standard* (see note 52) quotes one operator in Syracuse who says that the state game has cut deeply into the street game ("better than three-quarters"). Sergeant Vince Stehlin, supervisor of the Gambling Section of the St. Louis Police Department, observed in a telephone conversation, August 24, 1987, that a lucrative policy game had existed in black neighborhoods prior to the early 1970s but that it had begun to lose popularity and was eventually wiped out by the advent of the Illinois lottery and later the Missouri lottery. The sociologists William Blount and H. Roy Kaplan studied records seized by police from a gang operating in the Miami area; its gross from the numbers racket dropped after the legal numbers game was initiated but recovered after the gang started taking bets on the legal number; Blount and Kaplan, "The Impact of the Daily Lottery on the Numbers Game," paper presented at the 1989 Annual Meeting of the American Criminal Justice Society.

56. John Dombrink, "The Touchables: Vice and Police Corruption in the 1980s," *Law and Contemporary Problems* 51 (Winter 1988).

57. *Chicago Tribune,* May 30, 1983. Judith H. Hybels, "The Impact of Legalization on Illegal Gambling Participation," *Journal of Social Issues* 35, 3 (1979), 27–35, notes that Nevada has been very successful in eliminating illegal gambling and attributes this success to the fact that gambling enforcement is not in the hands of the police but rather rests with a separate regulatory body.

58. Significantly, more blacks than whites (28 percent compared with 19 percent) agreed. It is notable that these percentages are smaller than for other Western countries: 29 percent in Switzerland, 30 percent in West Germany, and 32 percent in Canada; Scholarly Resources, Inc., *The Gallup Poll* (Wilmington, Del.: 1984), pp. 27–28.

59. Paul Jacobs, "State Lottery Creates 'Culture of Gambling,' Arizona Governor Says," *Los Angeles Times,* October 31, 1984.

60. Delaware Council on Gambling Problems, "The Impact of State Sponsored Gambling on the Community," mimeographed report, 1979.

61. Henry R. Lesieur and Robert Klein, "Pathological Gambling among High School Students," *Addictive Behaviors* 12 (1987), and Robert Ladouceur and Chantal Mireault, "Gambling Behavior among High School Students in the Quebec Area," *Journal of Gambling Behavior* 4 (Spring 1988).

62. In correspondence and telephone conversations Duran F. Jacobs has described his research, some of which was based on a paper in progress, D. F. Jacobs et al., "Prevalence of Gambling Activity among High School Students in California," 1988. When asked whether they had gambled for money, 22 percent of the students surveyed in 1984 said that they had. In the 1987 survey the percentage had increased to 45 percent who had gambled for money in the preceding twelve months.

63. Edward C. Devereux, Jr., "Gambling," in David L. Sills, ed., *International Encyclopedia of the Social Sciences,* vol. 6 (New York: Macmillan and Free Press, 1968), 53–62.

8. State Politics and the Lottery Bandwagon

1. James Madison, *Federalist Papers,* no. 20.

2. *Miami Herald,* February 21, 1985.

3. Estimate of industry income calculated as 2.2 percent of $12 billion, where 2.2 percent is the estimated portion of sales paid to vendors (based on Maryland's ratio) and $12 billion was total lottery sales in 1986.

4. David Weinstein and Lillian Deitch, *The Impact of Legalized Gambling: The Socioeconomic Consequences of Lotteries and Off-Track Betting* (New York: Praeger, 1974), pp. 14–15; *New York Times,* April 19, 1963.

5. Weinstein and Deitch, *The Impact of Legalized Gambling,* p. 15.

6. Foreign-born white stock as a percentage of the population was 7.2 percent in New Hampshire, compared to a national average of 5.2 percent. U.S. Bureau of the Census, *Statistical Abstract of the United States 1970,* (Washington, D.C.: Government Printing Office, 1969), pp. 14, 30. In 1973, 36 percent of the state's population was Catholic, compared to a national average of 22 percent. Douglas W. Johnson, Paul R. Picard, and Bernard Quinn, *Churches and Church Membership in the United States 1971* (Washington, D.C.: Glenmary Research Center, 1974), pp. 1, 3.

7. *New York Times,* May 1, 1963; April 19, 1963; April 20, 1963; May 1, 1963. John Gould, "The Lottery, The Puritan, and the Devil," *New York Times Magazine,* May 19, 1963.

8. Commission on the Review of the National Policy toward Gambling, *Gambling in America* (Washington, D.C.: Government Printing Office, 1976), pp. 17–18.

9. *New York Times,* March 7, 1964; May 3, 1964; I. Nelson Rose, "the Legalization and Control of Casino Gambling," *Fordham Urban Law Journal* 8 (1980), 256n.

10. *New York Times,* January 30, 1966.

11. Ibid., November 9, 1966; September 14, 1966; August 27, 1966; January 27, 1966.

12. Table A.7 presents the voting results for selected state referenda on gambling issues other than lottery adoption since the 1950s.

13. Commission on Gambling, *Gambling in America*, p. 70.

14. Jack L. Walker, "The Diffusion of Innovations among the American States," *American Political Science Review* 3 (September 1969), 897.

15. *Wall Street Journal*, February 7, 1986.

16. Walker, "Diffusion of Innovations," p. 890.

17. It is worth noting one rather elaborate model used to explain the pattern of adoption of state lotteries. John D. Jackson, David S. Saurman, and William F. Shughart, in "Instant Winners: Legal Change in Transition and the Diffusion of State Lotteries," November 1987, an unpublished paper presented at the Southern Economic Association meetings, analyze the number of years since a state has adopted a lottery, with zero for nonlottery states, using Tobit estimation. Explanatory variables include the number of bordering lottery states as a percentage of all lottery states at the time of adoption, the size of the state house of representatives relative to the senate, the number of voters per representative, the highest marginal tax rate in the state's tax structure, a dummy variable indicating a greater-than-average percentage of Baptists in the state, per capita income, and a dummy variable indicating that a state's lottery revenues are earmarked for education. Because several of the explanatory variables are relevant to the year before adoption or are relevant only if a state has adopted a lottery, there is clearly a problem of endogeneity in the estimation. For example, the positive sign on the earmarking variable is not surprising since that dummy variable is other than zero only for lottery states, many of which do earmark their revenues. The variable for proximity to lottery states has a positive coefficient, which is consistent with the contagious nature of lottery adoption, discussed in this chapter, but this variable also suffers from endogeneity. The tax-rate variable, which is taken as a measure of revenue pressure, is insignificant. The Baptist variable has the expected negative effect.

18. Opponents maintained that, after the additional administrative expenses were deducted from the 22 percent lottery fund, only 2 percent would be left for prizes.

19. Joe and Barbara Saltzman, "Long Odds and Sure Things on the California Ballot," *Reporter*, November 5, 1964, 28–30.

20. *Los Angeles Times*, June 14, 1978; January 13, 1982; May 28, 1983; September 14, 1983.

21. A company spokesman said that "from a marketing standpoint" it was useful to earmark lottery funds for education: "they're always screaming they don't have enough bucks for education." Paul Jacobs, "Ticket Supplier Underwriting State Lottery Drive," *Los Angeles Times*, October 8, 1984.

22. Ibid. The Arizona lottery director said: "My one question is the timing of it. Can California start a lottery in the best interest of the state in 135 days? I'm sure it was put in there to give [Scientific Games] an advantage."

23. *Los Angeles Times*, September 11, 1984.

24. Ibid., October 28, 1984; October 23, 1984; May 23, 1984; October 31, 1984.

25. A statistical analysis of the referendum results by Eva M. Herbst, "The State Lottery: Who Is Supporting Its Adoption?" Duke University, Fall 1985, showed that approval rates were higher in counties with larger percentages of the population who were unemployed, older, born outside the country, high school graduates, or male.

Approval rates were lower in counties with higher proportions of blacks and low-income households.

26. Robert Mote, quoted in the *Los Angeles Times,* October 8, 1984.

27. Speech quoted in John Dombrink and William N. Thompson, "The Last Resort: Success and Failure in Campaigns for Casinos," University of California, Irvine, December 1986, p. 57.

28. *St. Petersburg Times,* August 24, 1986.

29. *Miami Herald,* March 29, 1985.

30. *St. Petersburg Times,* March 1, 1985.

31. Ibid., September 25, 1986; March 17, 1986.

32. Ibid., August 24, 1986.

33. In 1986 the state education budget was $5.3 billion. U.S. Bureau of the Census, *State Government Finances in 1986* (Washington, D.C.: Government Printing Office, 1987), p. 20.

34. *Miami Herald,* November 5, 1986.

35. Ibid., November 5, 1986.

36. *Richmond Times-Dispatch,* March 21, 1969; January 27, 1970; November 2, 1978; January 4, 1970.

37. Ibid., January 27, 1970; January 18, 1978; November 5, 1978; November 8, 1978.

38. *Washington Post,* December 22, 1986.

39. *Richmond Times-Dispatch,* January 12, 1985; January 28, 1984; January 24, 1985; March 23, 1987; February 2, 1982; February 7, 1983.

40. Ibid., March 1, 1987; February 28, 1987; January 25, 1987. See also Chapter 1 for a discussion of this controversy.

41. *Washington Post,* February 9, 1987.

42. *Richmond Times-Dispatch,* February 28, 1987; March 28, 1987.

43. Ibid., April 18, 1987. The Virginia Chamber of Commerce was also opposed; ibid., July 18, 1987.

44. *Virginia Pilot,* October 28, 1987. *Richmond Times-Dispatch,* October 31, 1987.

45. *Richmond Times-Dispatch,* July 17, 1987; November 4, 1987.

46. A regression weighted by the square root of the number of voters was estimated for Virginia's counties and independent cities. Where Y is percent voting yes, CATH is the percentage of the population who are Catholic, BAP is the percentage who are Baptists, BLK the percentage black, OV65 the percentage over 65, URB the percentage living in urban areas, and MED is median income, the estimated equation (t-statistics in parentheses) is as follows:

$$Y = 0.50 \text{ CATH} - 0.08 \text{ BAP} + 0.33 \text{ BLK} - 1.14 \text{ OV65} + .005 \text{ URB}$$
$$(3.4) \quad\quad (1.0) \quad\quad (7.5) \quad\quad (5.7) \quad\quad (0.3)$$
$$+ 0.000039 \text{ MED}, R^2 = .55.$$
$$(0.2)$$

9. The Suppliers

1. Washington State, Legislative Budget Committee, "Performance Audit of the Washington State Legislature," November 21, 1986.

2. "In practice the organization form seems unimportant." See David Weinstein

and Lillian Deitch, *The Impact of Legalized Gambling: The Socioeconomic Consequences of Lotteries and Off-Track Betting* (New York: Praeger, 1974), p. 22.

3. Survey of state lotteries, 1988. See appendix to this chapter.

4. For a description of the Kentucky Lottery Corporation, see *Gaming and Wagering Business* 10 (January 1989), 10; for the Georgia House of Representatives Bill 1164, 1986, see *Public Gaming Magazine* 14 (June 1986), 66. A bill introduced in Minnesota would have established a lottery board to oversee the lottery's operations and a franchise tax equal to 20 percent of gross sales. *Gaming and Wagering Business* 9 (April 1988), 6.

5. The Illinois law is typical. Prohibited from receiving retail licenses are convicted felons, professional gamblers or gambling promoters, bookmakers or others involved in illegal gambling, those convicted of fraud or misrepresentation, and anyone "who is not of good character and reputation in the community." *Illinois Annotated Statutes,* Cumulative Supplement (St. Paul: West Publishing, 1985), sec. 120(1160.1), p. 137.

6. *Illinois Annotated Statutes,* Cumulative Supplement (St. Paul: West Publishing, 1985), sec. 120(1157.4), p. 134.

7. *California: West's Annotated Codes,* Cumulative Supplement (St. Paul: West Publishing, 1986), sec. 12.5(8880.57), pp. 62–63.

8. For comparison, see Table 2.3 for a tabulation of the actual percentages devoted to prizes, administrative costs, and net revenues in 1987.

9. See Ben A. Franklin, "Maryland Judge Casts Doubt on Plan for 2 New Stadiums," *New York Times,* July 8, 1987.

10. *California: West's Annotated Codes,* sec. 12.5:8880.5, pp. 51, 53.

11. Edward Powers, "Do You Want to Start a State Lottery?" *Public Gaming* 11 (January 1983), 28.

12. Pat Wood, press secretary for the Pennsylvania Department of Revenue, quoted in Jane Carroll, "The Lure of the Lottery," *State Legislatures* (April 1986), 1.

13. California's lottery director argued that Ohio's switch from placing revenue in the general fund to earmarking it for education increased public interest in playing. Roxanne Arnold, "Lottery Improves Its Odds by Dipping into Grab Bag of Marketing Ideas," *Los Angeles Times,* June 22, 1986.

14. A second set of federal laws applies specifically to lotteries and their activities that cross state lines. Although state-run lotteries were exempted from many of the restrictions that arose in response to corruption in the nineteenth century, lotteries are still prohibited from mailing lottery tickets across state lines. Congressional Research Service, "Overview of State Lottery Operations," Committee Print for Subcommittee on Intergovernmental Affairs, Committee on Government Affairs, September 25, 1984, p. 29. Yet this prohibition is apparently ignored by at least one state. Alfred N. King, "Public Gaming and Public Trust," *Connecticut Law Review* 12 (Summer 1980), 752.

15. In addition two states, Iowa and Pennsylvania, officially tax lottery winnings but provide for the tax to be paid out of lottery proceeds rather than a winner's earnings.

16. Designers of Washington's lotto game set the share of the prize pool for matching five out of six numbers at $550. In Massachusetts' 6/36 game second prize was a flat $400.

17. *Gaming and Wagering Business* 7 (December 1986), 10; Congressional Research Service, "Overview of State Lottery Operations," p. 35. The Commission on Review of the National Policy toward Gambling, *Gambling in America* (Washington, D.C.: Government Printing Office, 1976), recommended exempting lottery winnings from taxation.

18. *California: West's Annotated Codes*, sec. 12.5(8880.5), p. 51.

19. *Delaware Code, Annotated, Revised*, Cumulative Supplement, 1984 (Charlottesville, Va.: Michie, 1983), sec. 29(4815), p. 29.

20. *Michigan Compiled Laws, Annotated*, Cumulative Supplement, 1985 (St. Paul: West Publishing, 1978), sec. 432.9, p. 174.

21. *Arizona Revised Statutes, Annotated*, Cumulative Supplement (St. Paul: West Publishing, 1985), sec. 5(504.B), p. 296.

22. *Vermont Statutes, Annotated*, Cumulative Supplement (Orford, N.H.: Equity Publishing, 1985), sec. 31(14.658C), pp. 286 and 19; *West Revised Code of Washington, Annotated* (St. Paul: West Publishing, 1985), chap. 67.70.040(1).

23. *West Virginia Code, Annotated*, Cumulative Supplement (Charlottesville, Va.: Michie, 1985), sec. 29(22.9).

24. See Terri LaFleur, "Bans on Lottery Advertising Becoming More Common," *Gaming and Wagering Business* 8 (October 1987), 14.

25. *Missouri Annotated Statutes*, Cumulative Supplement (St. Paul: West Publishing, 1986), sec. 313(320.2).

26. Weinstein and Deitch, *Impact of Legalized Gambling*, pp. 32–33.

27. "Who's Running North America's Lotteries," *Public Gaming International* 15 (December 1987), 27–34.

28. Missouri Department of Revenue, State Lottery Commission 1988, "Program Decision Item, Form 5," unpublished budget document.

29. Pennsylvania, Legislative Budget and Finance Committee, "Report on a Performance Audit of the Pennsylvania State Lottery," September 1987; 1988 survey of lotteries, described in the appendix to this chapter.

30. "Public Opinion Held to Be Sacred," *Gaming and Wagering Business* 7 (November 1986), 26.

31. Irwin Ross, "Corporate Winners in the Lottery Boom," *Fortune*, September 3, 1984.

32. "2 Charged in Rigging of Lottery," *New York Times*, May 4, 1988.

33. See, for example, Ray Gibson, "10 Charged in Bids to Defraud Lottery," *Chicago Tribune*, June 14, 1983.

34. Joseph Egelhof, "N.Y. Sends Its 'Ripoff' Lottery off to Boot Hill," *Chicago Tribune*, December 2, 1975.

35. Ronald Koziol, "State Lottery Hits String of Bad Luck," *Chicago Tribune*, July 24, 1983.

36. See, for example, Michael Weisskopf, "Alleged Maryland Lottery Bribes Probed," *Washington Post*, October 19, 1977. U.S. Congress, House of Representatives Appropriations Committee, *Hearings on District of Columbia Appropriations for 1988*, 100th Cong., 1st sess., p. 2631.

37. Lottery agencies prefer mechanical devices for picking numbers over computer algorithms because people appear to trust the former more than the latter. See James

Gleick, "The Quest for True Randomness Finally Appears Successful," *New York Times,* April 19, 1988.

38. See the 1983–84 annual report for the Arizona Lottery (*Arizona Lottery 1983–84,* n.d.) and the 1986–87 Iowa annual report.

39. See Terri LaFleur, "On-Line Problems: Software Burglary Poses a Major Threat to Lottery On-Line Systems," *Gaming and Wagering Business* 7 (November 1986), 26.

40. "Director on the Watch for Ticket Scams," *Gaming and Wagering Business* 7 (November 1986), 27, and K. F. Suzuki, "Dual Security: The Most Effective Safeguard for the Instant Game," *Public Gaming* 14 (June 1986), 54–55.

41. Marvin R. Brams, "The Failure of the Delaware Lottery," *Proceedings of the 68th Annual Conference on Taxation,* National Tax Association–Tax Institute of America, November 2–5, 1975 (1976), pp. 271–275. In light of the current success of lotto and numbers games, it is ironic that one reason given for the failure of this game was the requirement that players pick their own numbers; see pp. 274–275.

42. "Delaware Halts Lottery Game, To Repay $95,929," *Chicago Tribune,* December 13, 1976; King, "Pubic Gaming and Public Trust," pp. 756–757.

43. "Program Decision Item," unpublished document obtained with 1988 survey; see appendix to this chapter. The lottery was requesting changes in the "current restrictions . . . so that Missouri's lottery could operate as a normal lottery and compete more effectively with bordering lottery states." The lottery recommended: (1) removing revenue restrictions on size of prizes, (2) removing the 10 percent restriction on operating costs "so the lottery could continue to support products with appropriate levels of advertising," (3) earmarking revenues "so Missourians could see the tangible benefits of their participation," and (4) removing restrictions on advertising. The legislature failed to adopt these in 1987 and took $40 million out of $57 million in reserve funds. In June 1987 the lottery commission ordered cuts in spending and reduced advertising expenditures from $12.8 million to $3 million. Estimates indicated that the reserve fund would be depleted at the end of fiscal 1989.

44. For the full statement, see Chapter 10.

45. Powers, "Do You Want to Start a State Lottery?" p. 28. Vicki Abt, James F. Smith, and Eugene Martin Christiansen, *The Business of Risk: Commercial Gambling in Mainstream America* (Lawrence: University Press of Kansas, 1985), use the term "revenue imperative" to describe the urge on the part of commerical gambling to increase takeout rates. See, for example, p. 99.

46. For detailed reports on the management of several lotteries, see Citizens' Task Force to Review the Michigan Lottery, "Final Report," submitted to Governor James J. Blanchard, January 8, 1988; Pennsylvania General Assembly, Legislative Budget and Finance Committee, "Report on a Performance Audit of the Pennsylvania State Lottery," September 1987; Washington State Legislative Budget Committee, "Performance Audit of the Washington State Lottery," November 21, 1986.

47. Commission on the Review of the National Policy toward Gambling, *Gambling in America* (Washington, D.C.: Government Printing Office, 1976), p. 150.

48. Michigan Citizens' Task Force, "Final Report," p. 32.

49. *Gaming and Wagering Business* 9 (April 1988), 9.

50. Holiday Cash, begun November 19, 1986.

51. "Instant Games: Another Successful Experiment for Massachusetts," *Public Gaming* 13 (October 1985), 19ff., and Michigan Citizens' Task Force, "Final Report," pp. 28–32.

52. Sales for the state's ninth instant game were 67.6 percent higher than those for the eighth game in the grocery chain, 59.2 percent higher in the convenience store chain, and 48.1 percent higher for the state as a whole. Cynthia Cameron Combs, "Take 5 Test Market Research Report," Iowa Lottery, June 1987.

53. See *Gaming and Wagering Business* 7 (July 1986), 38 and 39, and 8 (December 1987), 73.

54. Pennsylvania General Assembly, "Performance Audit," p. 64.

55. New Jersey introduced a random draw in its four-digit game to spur interest in the game. *Gaming and Wagering Business* 7 (July 1986), 40.

56. If the coverage rate (c) is a constant, the probability of having no winner on two successive drawings is $(1 - c)^2$. This probability was .37 for Connecticut and .10 for Maryland.

57. "Hughes Announces Lottery Cutback," *Washington Post*, September 25, 1981.

58. Maryland, Department of Budget and Fiscal Planning, *Maryland State Lottery Agency: Analysis of Organizational Structure, Procurement Practices, and Marketing Operation*, January 1987, p. 135. Also see Chapter 10.

59. Pennsylvania General Assembly, "Performance Audit." See also Illinois Economic and Fiscal Commission, "The Illinois State Lottery," special report, December 1986.

60. Chon Gutierrez, in California State Lottery, *Annual Report 1987*, n.d., p. 2.

61. Weinstein and Deitch, *Impact of Legalized Gambling*, p. 20, suggests the latter franchising relationship.

62. Martech Associates, Inc., "Oregon State Lottery Communications Study," report for the Oregon State Lottery Commission, October 1986, p. 8.

63. New Jersey State Lottery, "Advertised Bid Proposal, on Line Numbers Selection Games," bid proposal, 1983.

64. Unpublished table, form M-127, provided by the Maryland State Lottery Agency, April 1, 1988. See also Maryland Department of Budget and Fiscal Planning, "Maryland State Lottery Agency: Analysis of Organizational Structure, Procurement Practices, and Marketing Operation," January 1987, pp. 110–115, for 1986 figures.

65. Oregon paid its contractors $6.96 million out of sales of $127.8 million, based on fiscal 1987 figures.

66. Unpublished data provided in response to survey.

67. See *Gaming and Wagering Business* 7 (June 1986), 50; 7 (August 1986), 11; and 8 (November 1987), 6, for descriptions of instant game contracts, and Irwin Ross, "Corporate Winners in the Lottery Boom," *Fortune*, September 3, 1984, 21.

68. *Gaming and Wagering Business* 8 (October 1987), 3.

69. "Lottery Agents Continue to Cash In on Commissions," *Gaming and Wagering Business* 8 (June 1987), 26. Calculations based on 1988 survey of lotteries and data, ibid. The averages were highest in Maryland ($21,900), Pennsylvania ($20,800), Michigan ($16,900), New York ($16,400), and Ohio ($15,700).

70. Eric Freedman, "Lottery System Creates a Controversy," *Government Computer News*, November 20, 1987, 109.

71. Larry DeBoer, "The Administrative Costs of State Lotteries," *National Tax Journal* 38 (December 1985), 479–487.

72. There are several well-known models of the behavior of government agencies based on the maximization of budget size. See, for example, William Niskanen, *Bureaucracy and Representative Government* (Chicago: Aldine Press, 1971), and Geoffrey Brennan and James M. Buchanan, "Tax Instruments as Constraints on the Disposition of Public Revenues," *Journal of Public Economics* 9 (1978), 301–318.

73. A survey conducted by the Washington State legislature found that 79 percent of respondents agreed that the state should continue to have a lottery. See Washington State Legislative Budget Committee, "Performance Audit of the Washington State Lottery," November 21, 1986. In New Jersey a 1988 survey showed a 77 percent approval rate for the state's lottery. *Newark Star-Ledger*/Eagleton Poll, "New Jerseyans Support State Lottery Though Many See Negative Social Costs," news release, February 28, 1988.

74. In Michigan the contractor was Syntech International, which employed one hundred people in the state and depended on the Michigan lottery for half of its business. *Government Computer News,* November 20, 1987, 109. In Illinois it was Bally Manufacturing, which had its headquarters in the state. See, for example, "Battle Royal over Lottery," *Chicago Sun-Times,* June 12, 1988, and *Gaming and Wagering Business* 9 (November 1988), 3.

75. Arizona State Lottery, "Statewide Distribution of Lottery Funds," n.d., for fiscal 1986–87.

76. Iowa Lottery, "Where the Money Goes: Lottery Benefits for Iowa," pamphlet, June 1987.

77. Data collected in 1988 survey of state lotteries (see appendix to this chapter). Of the fifty-nine bills mentioned, nineteen related to the distribution of revenues, five to the games that could be offered, including video lotteries and multistate lotto, three to the payout or odds of existing games, three to the use of unclaimed prize money, and twenty-eight to other details of operation. One bill would require odds to be publicized. In Missouri a package of bills was introduced which would change the ceiling for operating expenses and revenue restrictions on advertisements.

78. Ross, "Corporate Winners," p. 25.

79. For an analysis of the role of the weapons industry in national defense, see Richard A. Stubbing, *The Defense Game* (New York: Harper and Row, 1986).

10. The Sales Pitch

1. "New Jersey Lottery Plans Changes in Sales Marketing," *Public Gaming* 13 (October 1985), 12–13.

2. Mary Faulk, "An Introduction to the Washington State Lottery," *Public Gaming* 14 (June 1986), 10.

3. John Hurst, "Lottery Ads: Soft Sell on a Big Budget," *Los Angeles Times,* April 17, 1985.

4. Philip Kotler, *Marketing Management,* 5th ed. (Englewood Cliffs, N.J.: Prentice-Hall, 1984), p. 386.

5. "New Jersey Lottery Plans Changes in Sales Marketing," *Public Gaming* 13 (October 1985), 13.

6. Excerpted pages from 1986–87 marketing plan for the Iowa Lottery, provided by Creswell, Munsell, Fultz, and Zirbel, Inc., Des Moines.

7. Maryland Department of Budget and Fiscal Planning, "Maryland State Lottery Agency: Analysis of Organizational Structure, Procurement Practices, and Marketing Operation," report, January 1987, p. 147.

8. "Lottery: How to Sell Tickets without Promoting Gambling," *Los Angeles Times,* April 17, 1985.

9. Illinois Economic and Fiscal Commission, "The Illinois State Lottery," special report, December 1986, pp. 78–79.

10. Trahan, Burden, and Charles, Inc., "The Maryland State Lottery," report for the Maryland State Lottery, Baltimore, 1984. For a similar statement from the Ohio lottery's media plan, see Marcus Advertising, "Ohio Lottery: 'SuperLotto' Introduction, Media Recommendation," report for the Ohio Lottery, September 18, 1985, p. 2.

11. Kotler, *Marketing Management,* pp. 134–135, 250–252, and 258–262.

12. Ibid., p. 345.

13. See, for example, "Focus Groups Give Answers about Lottery Vending Machines," *Public Gaming* 13 (October 1985), 43.

14. Glenn Shippee, Donna Schwartzman, and Kim Reynolds, "Using Demographics to Increase Lottery Sales," *Public Gaming* 11 (August 1983), 14, 17.

15. For a description of the ACORN residential segmentation and its application to lottery marketing, see John R. Koza, "Who Is Playing What," pt. 4, *Public Gaming* 12 (June 1984), 52, 64.

16. See, for example, "California Awards Ethnic Advertising Contract," *Public Gaming* 15 (May 1987), 4.

17. *Chicago Tribune,* March 14, 1986.

18. Illinois Economic and Fiscal Commission, "The Illinois State Lottery," pp. 6, 58, 63.

19. See Arnold Mitchell, *The Nine American Lifestyles* (New York: Macmillan, 1983), and Kotler, *Marketing Management,* pp. 134–135, for discussions of this system.

20. William Meyers, *The Image-Makers* (New York: Times Books, 1984), p. 15; John Koza, "Who Is Playing What: A Demographic Study," pt. 3, *Public Gaming* 12 (March 1984), 19.

21. Mitchell, *Nine American Lifestyles,* pp. 9–22.

22. Koza, "Who Is Playing What," pt. 3, pp. 60–61.

23. Ibid., p. 61.

24. Tabulations based on unpublished reports prepared by Rumrill-Hoyt, Inc., "Salespersons Time Schedule," for New York Lottery radio ads for the period January 5–18, 1987, and Broadcast Publications, *Broadcasting/Cablecasting Yearbook* (Washington, D.C., 1987 and 1988), showed that the average number of one-minute advertisements per station in selected format groups was fourteen for "easy listening," thirteen for country-and-western, twelve for black music, one for diversified format, two for foreign language, four for "oldies" and middle-of-the-road music, and zero for educational and classical music stations.

25. Kotler, *Marketing Management,* pp. 68–70.

26. "Instant Games," *Public Gaming* 13 (October 1985), 57.

27. Pat Stimpson, "Lotto: A Change for the Better," *Public Gaming* 14 (June 1986), 20, 22.

28. Earl Sedlick and Rolf Rautenberg, "Instant Stub Games 'Reinvent the Deal' and Increase Sales," *Public Gaming* 14 (June 1986), 16.

29. Tom Stevenson, "Mastermind of the Instant Lottery," *New York Times,* January 2, 1977.

30. Terri LaFleur, "Ticket Shops Prove a Boon for Western Canada Sales," *Gaming and Wagering Business* 7 (August 1986), 6.

31. For further discussion of the price of lottery products, see Chapters 6 and 11.

32. Letter from Mary Faulk, director, Washington State lottery, June 12, 1986.

33. G. Robert Blakey, "State Conducted Lotteries: History, Problems, and Promises," *Journal of Social Issues* 35, 3 (1979), 78–79.

34. "Instant Games," p. 38.

35. For a discussion of the selection of the face-value ticket price in the Massachusetts instant game, see ibid.

36. See *Gaming and Wagering Business* 8 (February 1987), 38, and 7 (August 1986), 6.

37. Survey of state lotteries described in the appendix to Chapter 9; U.S. Bureau of the Census, *Statistical Abstract of the United States 1987* (Washington, D.C.: Government Printing Office, 1986).

38. "Instant Games," p. 58.

39. For games that require tickets to be transported, some lottery agencies use field representatives to deliver tickets rather than using banks as distribution centers, as had been the practice. "New Jersey Lottery Plans Changes in Sales Marketing," *Public Gaming* 13 (October 1985), 13, 58.

40. H. Roy Kaplan, "The Social and Economic Impact of State Lotteries," *Annals of the American Economy* 474 (July 1984), 104, notes the importance of convenience, availability, and proximity as factors contributing to compulsive gambling.

41. Letter from Tom Seaver, July 24, 1987. Officials in Massachusetts attribute part of their success in instant games to the use of bright and attractive graphics, designed to appeal to impulse buyers. See "Instant Games," p. 38.

42. The success of the instant game dispenser in three New England states is cited admiringly in the report of the Citizens' Task Force to Review the Michigan Lottery, "Final Report," submitted to Governor James J. Blanchard, January 8, 1988, p. 32.

43. Kotler, *Marketing Managment,* p. 603.

44. *Public Gaming* 14 (May 1986), 6.

45. Terri La Fleur, "New York Debuts Win-10," *Gaming and Wagering Business* 8 (March 1987), 43.

46. "Instant Games," p. 39.

47. Kotler, *Marketing Management,* p. 663. In 1979 over 81 billion coupons were distributed, or 1,200 per household, of which only 4 percent were redeemed.

48. "Instant Games," p. 39.

49. *Gaming and Wagering Business* 9 (January 1988), 12. Terri LaFleur, "Michigan

Uses Parody Promos to Boost Daily 4," *Gaming and Wagering Business* 7 (July 1986), 39.

50. Pennsylvania General Assembly, Legislative Budget and Finance Committee, "Report on a Performance Audit of the Pennsylvania State Lottery," September 1987, pp. 41–42.

51. "California State Lottery Start-Up Smooth and Successful," *Lottery Journal* 2, 1 (1985), 4, 32–33.

52. "Lottery Public Relations: Expense or Investment," *Gaming and Wagering Business* 8 (February 1987), 18.

53. *Gaming and Wagering Business,* 9 (September 1988), 38.

54. Arizona State survey, 1985–86. See Chapter 6, note 5.

55. For a description of one lottery's arrangement with a local television station, see Maryland Department of Budget and Fiscal Planning, "Maryland State Lottery Agency: Analysis of Organizational Structure, Procurement Practices, and Marketing Operation," January 1987, pp. 110–111.

56. Calculated from Broadcast Advertisers Reports/Leading National Advertisers Multi-Media Service, *Class/Brand YTD $,* January-December 1984 (New York: Publishers Information Bureau, 1985), and U.S. Bureau of the Census, *Statistical Abstract of the United States 1988* (Washington, D.C.: Government Printing Office, 1987), p. 18. By comparison, estimated total advertising for the top ten lottery states in 1987 was $128 million. *Gaming and Wagering Business* 8 (June 1987), 14.

57. Unpublished information provided by Arbitron, Inc., based on its May 1988 survey.

58. Calculated from Broadcast Advertisers Reports, *Class/Brand YTD $,* and U.S. Bureau of the Census, *Statistical Abstract 1988,* p. 18.

59. Calculations based on sales and advertising figures for fiscal 1988 in *Gaming and Wagering Business* 9 (September 1988), 34.

60. "Instant Games," p. 39. Missouri's strategy was the same, at least before budget cuts reduced its advertising effort. Letter from Tom Seaver, July 24, 1987.

61. Sedlik, *Nine American Lifestyles,* p. 16.

62. Marcus Advertising, "Ohio Lottery," pp. 8–9.

63. In requesting samples of ads, we offered to pay for the cost of reproducing television tapes. The lotteries for which ads were received (and the number of ads collected) were Arizona 10, California 27, Iowa 16, Maryland 6, Michigan 31, Missouri 9, New Jersey 4, New York 16, Ohio 65, Oregon 33, Pennsylvania 17, Washington 25, and the District of Columbia 23. Unsuccessful requests were made to Colorado, Connecticut, Illinois, Rhode Island, and Massachusetts.

64. Terri La Fleur, "Lottery Ad Budgets Remain Flat in Fiscal 87," *Gaming and Wagering Business* 8 (June 1987), 15.

65. Maryland Legislative Budget, Review Analyst, "Analysis of the Maryland Executive Budget 1988," report excerpt, sec. 24.04.00, p. 370.

66. "Ad Restrictions in State's Lottery Proposal Criticized," *Richmond Times Dispatch,* June 3, 1987.

67. See Terri La Fleur, "Lotteries Push Benefits, Tug Heartstrings to Sell Tickets," *Gaming and Wagering Business* 7 (November 1986), 1, 21.

68. "Scientific Games Lures Lifestyles," *American Demographics* 8, (October 1986), 26–27.

69. *New York Times,* July 22, 1984.

70. Meyers, *The Image-Makers,* p. 58.

71. "Becoming a Successful Lottery Is an Evolutionary Process," *Public Gaming* 12 (October 1985), 16.

72. Trahan, Burden, and Charles, "Advertising and Marketing the Maryland State Lottery," report prepared for U.S. Congress, Senate Committee on Governmental Affairs, Subcommittee on Intergovernmental Affairs, *State Lotteries: An Overview,* 98th Cong., 2d sess., October 3, 1984 (Washington, D.C.: Government Printing Office, 1985), p. 63.

73. In a Washington series not part of our sample, Lady Luck complains that no one needs her anymore because the lottery has made it so easy to win by setting 1 in 5 odds in instant games: "Unaided random recall of Lady Luck skyrocketed to the equivalent of 'Meow Mix' during our successful campaign." Sedlik and Rautenberg, "Instant Stub Games," p. 16.

74. Vance Packard, *The Hidden Persuaders* (New York: Pocket Books, 1957), p. 40.

75. See, for example, Illinois Economic and Fiscal Commission, "The Illinois State Lottery," p. 77, and John Mikesell and C. Kurt Zorn, "Another Look at the Structure and Performance of State Lotteries," Indiana University, August 1987, pp. 36–37.

76. John G. Cross, *A Theory of Adaptive Economic Behavior* (Cambridge: Cambridge University Press), 1983, p.87.

77. Illinois Economic and Fiscal Commission, "The Illinois State Lottery," p. 79.

78. Ibid., p. 75.

79. *U.S. Code of Federal Regulations,* rev. (Washington, D.C.: Government Printing Office, January 1, 1986), sec. 16, pt. 419.

80. For a discussion of the fairness of rules governing Canadian lotteries, see D. R. Bellhouse, "Fair is Fair: New Rules for Canadian Lotteries," *Canadian Public Policy* 8, 3, (1982), 311–320, which argues for federally enforced rules for stating odds and describing prize distributions.

81. *Gaming and Wagering Business* 8 (November 1987), 20. Reprinted by permission of the Oregon State Lottery.

82. Amos Tversky and Daniel Kahneman, "Judgment under Uncertainty: Heuristics and Biases," *Science* 185 (1974). For a comparison of government statements about lotteries and other unlikely events, see Jeryl Mumpower, "Lottery Games and Risky Technologies: Low-Probability/High-Consequence Events," *Risk Analysis* 8, 2 (1988).

83. National Association of Broadcasters, *Radio Code* and *Television Code* (Washington, D.C., 1971).

84. National Association of Broadcasters, "Lottery Advertising Guidelines," *Guidelines and Interpretations,* rev. (Washington, D.C., 1975).

85. Michael Schudson, *Advertising: The Uneasy Persuasion* (New York: Basic Books, 1984), p. 10.

86. Elder Witt, "States Place Their Bets on a Game of Diminishing Returns," *Governing* 1 (November 1987), 52–57, for example, writes: "Aggressive advertising

is as essential for a successful lottery as it is for any business, lottery officials agree." Mikesell and Zorn, "Another Look at State Lotteries," p. 29, state: "The lottery must be aggressively marketed and promoted; without these sizable costs, total and net proceeds will be disappointing." Also see Fund for the City of New York, *Legal Gambling in New York* (New York, 1972), p. 7.

11. A "Painless Tax"?

1. This statement has been attributed to Jefferson: "A lottery is a wonderful thing; it lays taxation only on the willing." See, for example, a letter from Landon Taylor, *Washington Post,* October 4, 1987. The closest thing yielded by a search of Jefferson's writings, however, were these statements, made in his declining years, when he was desperate for money and hoped to persuade the Virginia legislature to approve a lottery to help him pay his bills for Monticello: "Money is wanting for a useful undertaking, as a school, etc., for which a direct tax would be disapproved. It is raised therefore by a lottery, wherein the tax is laid on the willing only, that is to say, on those who can risk the price of a ticket without sensible injury for the possibility of a higher prize." He argued that a lottery was an appropriate vehicle for disposing of a large property in order to repay debts: "The lottery is here a salutary instrument for disposing of it, where many run small risks for the chance of obtaining a high prize." Thomas Jefferson, "Thoughts on Lotteries," February 1826, in A. Lipscomb, ed., *The Writings of Thomas Jefferson,* vol. 12 (Washington, D.C.: Thomas Jefferson Memorial Association, 1904), p. 450. In his earlier years he was no supporter of lotteries. In a letter of 1810 he wrote, "Having myself made it a rule never to engage in a lottery or any other adventure of mere chance, I can, with less candor or effect, urge it on others, however laudable or desirable its object may be." Thomas Jefferson, *Writings* (New York: Library of America, 1984), p. 1222. See also John Samuel Ezell, *Fortune's Merry Wheel: The Lottery in America* (Cambridge, Mass.: Harvard University Press, 1960), pp. 168–169.

2. Ronald Alsop, "State Lottery Craze Is Spreading, but Some Fear It Hurts the Poor," *Wall Street Journal,* February 24, 1983.

3. Adam Smith, *The Wealth of Nations* (New York: Modern Library, 1937), pp. 777–779.

4. John C. Mikesell and C. Kurt Zorn, "Another Look at the Structure and Performance of State Lotteries," Indiana University, August 1987, p. 20.

5. Whether current nonlottery states would, if they adopted lotteries, match the per capita revenue levels of the urbanized states is also uncertain. To make revenue projections for nonlottery states based on averages for current lottery states, as lottery proponents have done, engenders excessive optimism. Even projections based on regression analysis may be biased if lottery states differ systematically from nonlottery states in ways not reflected by included variables. See, for example, an advertisement by Scientific Games, Inc., "What it Costs Your State by *Not* Joining the Lottery Majority," in *Public Gaming* 14 (December 1986). Estimates of net revenues for nonlottery states are based on performance in lottery states. For a projection of lottery revenues based on regression analysis, see Mark E. Stover, "Revenue Potential of State Lotteries," *Public Finance Quarterly* 15 (October 1987), 428–440.

6. See Brian McGrath, "Economic Effects of a Lottery in Idaho," Boise State University, September 1986.

7. Mikesell and Zorn, "Structure and Performance of State Lotteries," p. 21.

8. Of the eight most populous states in 1983, those that had lotteries in 1975 were chosen for the analysis: Illinois, Michigan, New York, Ohio, and Pennsylvania. U.S. Bureau of the Census, *State Tax Collections in 1986,* GF 86, no. 1, (Washington, D.C.: Government Printing Office, March 1987).

9. The medians for the five states are shown in Table A.8.

10. Mikesell and Zorn, "Structure and Performance of State Lotteries," p. 27.

11. An alternative argument for why the lottery tax is "painless" is that it is entirely voluntary. But of course the same thing could be said about a tax on any other item that is not a necessity of life. See Daniel Suits, "Economic Background for Gambling Policy," *Journal of Social Issues* 35 (Summer 1979), p. 51.

12. The demand curve is a compensated one. See Charles T. Clotfelter and Philip J. Cook, "Implicit Taxation in Lottery Finance," *National Tax Journal* 40 (December 1987), for a further discussion of these points.

13. See, for example, Alsop, "State Lottery Craze Is Spreading," p. 31.

14. "Playing Lottery on Welfare," *New York Times,* September 21, 1986.

15. *Chicago Tribune,* March 14, 1986.

16. Robert Mote, "Questions and Answers about a State Lottery," in U.S. Congress, Senate Committee on Governmental Affairs, Subcommittee on Intergovernmental Affairs, *State Lotteries: An Overview,* 98th Cong., 2d sess., October 3, 1984, p. 346.

17. Washington State Lottery, *1986 Annual Report,* n.d.

18. John Koza, "The Myth of the Poor Buying Lottery Tickets," *Public Gaming* 10 (January 1982), 40.

19. The index, suggested by Daniel B. Suits, "Gambling Taxes: Regressivity and Revenue Potential," *National Tax Journal* 30 (March 1977), is based on a diagram in which the cumulative percentage of household income is measured on the horizontal axis and the cumulative percentage of taxes—or, in the case of lotteries, expenditures—is shown on the vertical axis. A tax that is exactly proportional to income would result in a curve along the diagonal line because each income class would pay in taxes the same share as its share in total income. A regressive tax would collect a higher percentage of income from lower-income households than their share of total income and thus would result in a curve above the diagonal. By the same token a progressive tax would show up as a curve below the diagonal. It is possible to summarize the incidence of any tax with an index of tax concentration based on the deviation of these curves from the diagonal line. Where A is the area under the tax concentration curve and T is the area under the diagonal line, the index is defined as $(T - A)/T$.

If the tax concentration curves corresponding to these indices do not cross, the calculated index yields an unambiguous ranking of regressivity. If the curves cross, however, it is uncertain whether one is justified in comparing index values. See Thomas W. Calmus, "Measuring the Regressivity of Gambling Taxes," *National Tax Journal* 34 (June 1981), 267–270, and John P. Formby, W. James Smith, and Paul D. Thistle, "On the Measurement of Global Tax Progressivity," University of Alabama, September 23, 1987, for a discussion of the theoretical issues involved. In the cases of the indices calculated for Maryland lotto and the four-digit numbers game, the curves do not cross, so there is no ambiguity in making this comparison.

20. To illustrate the effect of a perfectly flat expenditure pattern, the tax concentration was calculated using data on the income distribution from the Consumer Expenditure Survey for a hypothesized flat expenditure. The calculated index was − .43.

21. Charles T. Clotfelter, "On the Regressivity of State-Operated 'Numbers' Games," *National Tax Journal* 32 (December 1979).

22. See Shlomo Yitzhaki and Joel Slemrod, "Welfare Dominance: An Application to Commodity Taxation," National Bureau of Economic Research Working Paper no. 2451, December 1987, for a discussion of "welfare dominance" in the context of commodity taxation.

23. Robert Mote, "Lotteries and 'The Poor': The Verdict Is In," U.S. Congress, Senate Committee on Governmental Affairs, Subcommittee on Intergovernmental Affairs, *State Lotteries: An Overview,* 98th Cong., 2d sess., October 3, 1984, p. 469.

24. Gene I. Maeroff, "Some Call Big Lotto Revenue No Boon to Schools," *New York Times,* August 23, 1985. Governor George Deukmejian of California expressed reservations about a lottery based on the inability of an earmarking provision to control for the appropriations of future legislatures. See John Balzar, "Governor Raps Lottery as Way to Help Schools," *Los Angeles Times,* May 23, 1984. For a more general analysis with the same conclusion, see Steven Gold, "The Pros and Cons of Earmarking," *State Legislatures* (July 1987), 28–31.

Empirical studies have found similar effects in categorical grants from one level of government to a lower level. See Edward M. Gramlich, "Intergovernmental Grants: A Review of the Empirical Literature," in Wallace Oates, *The Political Economy of Fiscal Federalism* (Lexington, Mass.: Lexington Books, 1977), pp. 219–239. In Gramlich's terms, these funds "will probably get lost in the shuffle" (p. 233). Other studies addressing the effect of earmarked lottery revenues have found that earmarking for education has no measurable effect on total state spending for education; but these findings are far from conclusive, since they are based on simple comparisons of expenditures before and after the lottery's introduction, with no account taken of the amount of lottery revenue or other determinants of educational spending. See Mikesell and Zorn, "Structure and Performance of State Lotteries," pp. 23, 26, and Mary O. Borg and Paul M. Mason, "Earmarked Lottery Revenues: Positive Windfalls or Concealed Redistribution Mechanisms?" University of North Florida, October 1987.

25. See Table A.3.

26. Frank Sammartino, unpublished data used in U.S. Congressional Budget Office, "The Distributional Effects of an Increase in Selected Federal Excise Taxes," Staff Working Paper, January 1987.

27. The $12.15 spent by the top 20 percent of players alone was $2.43 per adult, or 81 percent of the class average of $2.99. The ratio for the next highest class was 92 percent.

28. Smith, *Wealth of Nations,* p. 778.

29. For a discussion of this literature, see Harvey Rosen, *Public Finance,* 2d ed. (Homewood, Ill.: Irwin Publications in Economics, 1988).

30. Carl Shoup, *Public Finance* (Chicago: Aldine, 1969), p. 423, for example, argues for taxes on betting "since the negative externalities here are so great."

31. Economists have developed models that combine considerations of efficiency (minimizing the deadweight loss owing to misallocation of resources) and equity (weighting the gains and losses to individuals according to society's evaluation of the importance of dollars to people at different income levels). Where there are no externalities and production is subject to constant costs, for example, Martin S. Feldstein, "Distributional Equity and the Optimal Structure of Public Prices," *American Economic Review* 62 (March 1972), has developed a tax rule combining efficiency and distributional considerations. One special case he obtains is a modification of the familiar Ramsey pricing rule for the special case in which cross-elasticities of demand are zero. Any externalities in production or consumption are ignored. Where the p's are gross prices including taxes, and the m's are marginal costs, E_{11} and E_{22} are the own-price elasticities of demand for goods 1 and 2, and D_{12} corresponds to the "distributional characteristic" of the two goods, the ratio of optimal tax-inclusive proportional tax rates on the goods is given by:

$$t_1/t_2 = D_{12} (E_{22}/E_{11})$$

The distributional factor D_{12} given here is a function of the pattern of consumption of both goods over the income distribution and the marginal social utilities assigned to income at different incomes. As the percentage of good 1 bought by the poor rises, D_{12} falls. If both goods are purchased at the same relative magnitudes over the income distribution, $D_{12} = 1$ and the rule reduces to the simple inverse elasticity condition. As the relative concentration of purchases of good 1 among lower-income purchasers rises, however, the optimal markup for that good falls, reflecting distributional considerations.

32. Richard A. Musgrave and Peggy B. Musgrave, *Public Finance in Theory and Practice* (New York: McGraw-Hill, 1980), p. 448, offer the notion of a "demerit good," one whose consumption is subject to social disapproval.

33. This "tax-inclusive" basis differs from the manner in which sales and excise taxes are usually expressed, which is as a percentage of the net of tax price, or on a tax-exclusive basis, and results in lower-percentage tax rates. For example, a 40 percent rate on a tax-inclusive basis would be equivalent to a 67 percent rate (40/60) on a tax-exclusive basis.

34. As we noted in Chapter 2, comparing the handle for different forms of gambling can be problematic because of the more rapid turnover of winnings in some games. As a percentage of gross parimutuel wagering ($15.607 billion in 1985), state parimutuel excise taxes ($646.6 million in fiscal year 1986) were 4 percent. As a percentage of gross revenue to the supplier ($3.046 billion), however, the average tax rate was 21 percent. Of course both rates are far below the 41 percent for lotteries. U.S. Bureau of the Census, *State Government Finances in 1986* (Washington, D.C.: Government Printing Office, 1987), table 6.

35. Frank T. Denton and Byron G. Spencer, "Indexation of Commodity Taxes: A Case Study of Alcoholic Beverages in Canada," QSEP Research Report no. 118,

McMaster University, Ontario, Canada, November 1984, p. 24, report the following tax rates as a percentage of gross price for Canada in 1983: 42 percent for beer, 84 percent for liquor, and 67 percent for wine.

References

Books, Journals, and Reports

Abt, Vicki. "State Lotteries and Public Policy." Paper prepared for the Association for Public Policy Analysis and Management, Bethesda, Maryland, October 1987.

Abt, Vicki, James F. Smith, and Eugene Martin Christiansen. *The Business of Risk: Commercial Gambling in Mainstream America.* Lawrence: University Press of Kansas, 1985.

Adar, Z., and N. M. Edelson. "Gambling Behavior and Lottery Prize Structures." Discussion Paper 72, Fels Center of Government, University of Pennsylvania, May 1975. Photocopy.

Aranson, Peter H., and Roger LeRoy Miller. "Economic Aspects of Public Gaming." *Connecticut Law Review* 12 (Summer 1980): 822–853.

Aronson, J. Richard, Andrew Weintraub, and Cornelius Walsh. "Revenue Potential of State and Local Public Lotteries." *Growth and Change* 3 (April 1972): 3–8.

Bailey, Thomas A. *The American Pageant.* Boston: D. C. Heath, 1961.

Bell, Daniel. "The Cultural Contradictions of Capitalism." *Public Interest* 21 (Fall 1970).

Bellhouse, D. R. "Fair Is Fair: New Rules for Canadian Lotteries." *Canadian Public Policy* 8 (September 1982): 311–320.

Blakey, G. Robert. "State Conducted Lotteries: History, Problems, and Promises." *Journal of Social Issues* 35, 3 (1979): 62–86.

Blotnick, Srully. "The Lure of the Lottery." *Forbes,* January 13, 1986, 302.

Bolster, Paul. "Georgia Plays the Numbers: A History of Lotteries in Georgia." *Atlanta Historical Journal* 29 (Winter 1985–86): 95–104.

Borg, Mary O., and Paul M. Mason. "Earmarked Lottery Revenues: Positive Windfalls or Concealed Redistribution Mechanisms?" University of North Florida, October 1987. Photocopy.

———. "The Budgetary Incidence of a Lottery to Support Education." *National Tax Journal* 41 (March 1988): 75–86.

Braidfoot, Larry. *Gambling: A Deadly Game.* Nashville: Broadman Press, 1985.

Brams, Marvin R. "The Failure of the Delaware Lottery." In *Proceedings of the 68th Annual Conference on Taxation,* National Tax Association–Tax Institute of America, November 2–5, 1975.

Brennan, Geoffrey, and James M. Buchanan. "Tax Instruments as Constraints on the Disposition of Public Revenues." *Journal of Public Economics* 9 (1978): 301–318.

Brenner, Gabrielle A., and Reuven Brenner. "A Profile of Gamblers." Unpublished manuscript, University of Montreal, March 1987.

Brinner, Roger E., and Charles T. Clotfelter. "An Economic Appraisal of State Lotteries." *National Tax Journal* 28 (December 1975): 395–404.

Broadcast Advertisers Reports/Leading National Advertisers Multi-Media Service. *Class/Brand YTD $,* January-December, 1984. New York: Publishers Information Bureau, 1985.

California Office of the Legislative Analyst. *Tax Expenditure Budget.* Sacramento: Legislative Analyst, January 1987.

Calmus, Thomas W. "Measuring the Regressivity of Gambling Taxes." *National Tax Journal* 34 (June 1981): 267–270.

Campbell, Felicia. "Gambling: A Positive View." In *Gambling and Society,* edited by William R. Eadington. Springfield, Ill.: Charles C. Thomas, 1976.

Carroll, Jane. "The Lure of the Lottery." *State Legislatures* (April 1986).

Chafetz, Henry. *Play the Devil.* New York: Clarkson N. Potter, 1960.

Chernoff, Herman. "How to Beat the Massachusetts Numbers Game: An Application of Some Basic Ideas in Probability and Statistics." *Mathematical Intelligencer* 3, 4 (1981): 166–172.

Citizens' Task Force to Review the Michigan Lottery. "Final Report." Report submitted to Governor James J. Blanchard, January 8, 1988. Photocopy.

Clotfelter, Charles T. "On The Regressivity of State-Operated 'Numbers' Games." *National Tax Journal* 32 (December 1979): 543–548.

Clotfelter, Charles T., and Philip J. Cook. "Implicit Taxation in Lottery Finance." *National Tax Journal* 40 (December 1987): 533–546.

Code of Federal Regulations. Sec. 16, pt. 419, rev. January 1, 1986. Washington, D.C.: Government Printing Office, 1986.

Commission on the Review of the National Policy toward Gambling. *Gambling in America.* Washington, D.C.: Government Printing Office, 1976.

Congressional Research Service. "Overview of State Lottery Operations." Committee on Government Affairs, Subcommittee on Intergovernmental Affairs, September 25, 1984. Photocopy.

Council of State Governments. *Gambling: A Source of State Revenue*. Lexington, Ky.: Council of State Governments, 1973.

———. *Legalized Gambling*. Lexington, Ky.: Council of State Governments, 1978.

———. *The Book of States*. Lexington, Ky.: Council of State Governments, 1986.

"Criminal Law—Lotteries—Necessity of Consideration." *Vanderbilt Law Review* 9 (December 1955): 98–101.

Cross, John G. *A Theory of Adaptive Economic Behavior*. Cambridge: Cambridge University Press, 1983.

DeBoer, Larry. "The Administrative Costs of State Lotteries." *National Tax Journal* 38 (December 1985): 479–487.

———. "Are Taxes on Lotteries Too High?" *Journal of Policy Analysis and Management* 4 (Spring 1986): 594–596.

Delaware Council on Gambling Problems. "The Impact of State Sponsored Gambling on the Community." Study conducted April–September 1979. Photocopy.

Denton, Frank T., and Byron G. Spencer. "Indexation of Commodity Taxes: A Case Study of Alcoholic Beverages in Canada." QSEP Research Report no. 118, McMaster University, Ontario, November 1984. Photocopy.

Devereux, Edward C., Jr. "Gambling." In *International Encyclopedia of the Social Sciences,* edited by Donald L. Sills, vol. 6. New York: Macmillan and Free Press, 1968.

———. *Gambling and the Social Structure*. New York: Arno Press, 1980.

Dombrink, John, and William N. Thompson. "The Last Resort: Success and Failure in Campaigns for Casinos." Unpublished manuscript, December 1986.

Drake, St. Clair, and Horace R. Cayton. *Black Metropolis: A Study of Negro Life in a Northern City*. New York: Harcourt, Brace and World, 1970.

Drzazga, John. *Wheels of Fortune*. Springfield, Ill.: Charles C. Thomas, 1963.

Due, John F., and Ann F. Friedlaender. *Government Finance*. Homewood, Ill.: Richard D. Irwin, 1977.

Edmondson, Brad. "Scientific Games Lures Lifestyles." *American Demographics* (October 1986): 26–27.

Ewen, C. L'Estrange. *Lotteries and Sweepstakes*. London: Heath Cranton, 1932.

Ezell, John Samuel. *Fortune's Merry Wheel: The Lottery in America*. Cambridge, Mass.: Harvard University Press, 1960.

Feldstein, Martin S. "Distributional Equity and the Optimal Structure of Public Prices." *American Economic Review* 62 (March 1972): 32–36.

Formby, John P., W. James Smith, and Paul D. Thistle. "On the Measurement of Global Tax Progressivity." University of Alabama, September 23, 1987. Photocopy.

Freedman, Eric. "Lottery System Creates a Controversy." *Government Computer News,* November 20, 1987, 109.

Friedman, M., and L. J. Savage. "The Utility Analysis of Choices Involving Risk." *Journal of Political Economy* 56 (August 1948): 279–304.

Fund for the City of New York. *Legal Gambling in New York.* New York: Fund for the City of New York, 1972.

Gaines, Robert P. "Criminal Law: Florida's Legal Lotteries." *University of Florida Law Review* 9 (Spring 1956): 93–95.

Gold, Steven. "The Pros and Cons of Earmarking." *State Legislatures* (July 1987): 28–31.

Hacker, George A. "Taxing Booze for Health and Wealth." *Journal of Policy Analysis and Management* 6 (Summer 1987): 701–708.

Haller, Mark H. "The Changing Structure of American Gambling in the Twentieth Century." *Journal of Social Issues* 35, 3 (1979): 87–114.

Hastings, Elizabeth H., and Philip K. Hastings, eds. *Index to International Public Opinion, 1980-81.* Westport, Conn.: Greenwood Press, 1982.

Heavey, Jerome F. "The Incidence of State Lottery Taxes." *Public Finance Quarterly* 6, 4 (October 1978): 415–426.

Henderson, James M., and Richard E. Quandt. *Microeconomic Theory.* New York: McGraw-Hill, 1980.

Herman, Robert D., ed. *Gambling.* New York: Harper and Row, 1967.

Hill, Holliday, Connors, Cosmopulos, Inc. "Quantitative Research Findings: The Massachusetts State Lottery Game, Wave II." Report prepared for the Massachusetts State Lottery. Boston, Mass.: March 1986. Photocopy.

Hogarth, Robert M. *Judgement and Choice.* Chichester: John Wiley and Sons, 1980.

Holloway, Ronald. "More Gambling, Less Tax?" *Lloyd's Bank Review* 110 (1973): 34.

Illinois Economic and Fiscal Commission. "The Illinois State Lottery: A Special Report," December 1986. Photocopy.

Illinois House of Representatives. Policy Numbers Game Study Committee. "Report and Recommendations to the Legislature." Springfield, Ill.: June 1975. Photocopy.

Jackson, John D., David S. Saurman, and William F. Shughart. "Instant Winners: Legal Change in Transition and the Diffusion of State Lotteries." Paper presented at the Southern Economic Association meetings, Washington, D.C., November 1987. Photocopy.

Jefferson, Thomas. *Writings.* New York: Library of America, 1984.

Johnson, Douglas W., Paul R. Picard, and Bernard Quinn. *Churches and Church*

Membership in the United States, 1971. Washington, D.C.: Glenmary Research Center, 1974.

Joyce, Kathleen M. "Public Opinion and the Politics of Gambling." *Journal of Social Issues* 35, 3 (1979): 144–165.

———. "Betting Preferences in the Numbers Game." In Peter Reuter and Jonathan Rubinstein, *Illegal Gambling in New York.* Washington, D.C.: U.S. Department of Justice, April 1982.

Kahneman, Daniel, and Amos Tversky. "Prospect Theory: An Analysis of Decision under Risk." *Econometrica* 47 (March 1979): 263–291.

———. "Choices, Values, and Frames." *American Psychologist* 39 (April 1984): 341–350.

Kallick, Maureen, et al. *Survey of American Gambling Attitudes and Behavior.* Appendix 2 of Commission on the Review of the National Policy toward Gambling, *Gambling in America.* Washington, D.C.: Government Printing Office, 1976.

Kaminski, Gerald F. "Promotional Games and the Ohio Lottery Laws." *University of Cincinnati Law Review* 39 (Winter 1970): 163–175.

Kantzer, Kenneth S. "Gambling: Everyone's a Loser." *Christianity Today* 27, November 25, 1983, 12.

Kaplan, H. Roy. "The Social and Economic Impact of State Lotteries." *Annals of the American Academy of Political and Social Science* 474 (July 1984): 91–106.

———. "State Lotteries: Should Government Be a Player?" Unpublished paper, May 1988.

———. "Gambling among Lottery Winners: Before and After the Big Score." *Journal of Gambling Behavior* 4, 3 (Fall 1988): 171–182.

Katz, Barry M. "Lotteries—The Consideration Requirement." *Missouri Law Review* 37 (Winter 1972): 143–149.

King, Alfred N. "Public Gaming and Public Trust." *Connecticut Law Review* 12 (Summer 1980): 740–761.

Kotler, Philip. *Marketing Management.* 5th ed. Englewood Cliffs, N.J.: Prentice-Hall, 1984.

Koza, John R. "The Myth of the Poor Buying Lottery Tickets." *Public Gaming* (January 1982): 31–40.

———. "Who Is Playing What: A Demographic Study." *Public Gaming* 12 (March–June 1984).

Kusyszyn, Igor. "The Psychology of Gambling." *Annals of the American Academy of Political and Social Science* 473 (July 1984): 133–145.

Ladouceur, Robert, and Chantal Mireault. "Gambling Behaviors among High School Students in the Quebec Area." *Journal of Gambling Behavior* 4 (Spring 1988): 3–12.

Langer, Ellen J. "The Illusion of Control." *Journal of Personality and Social Psychology* 32, 2 (1975): 311–328.

————. "The Psychology of Chance." *Journal for the Theory of Social Behavior* 7, 2 (1978): 185–207.

Lenski, Gerhard. *The Religious Factor*. Garden City, N.Y.: Doubleday, Anchor Books, 1961.

Lesieur, Henry R. *Report on Pathological Gambling in New Jersey*. Jamaica, N.Y.: St. John's University Press, 1988.

Lesieur, Henry R., and Robert Klein. "Pathological Gambling among High School Students." *Addictive Behaviors* 12 (1987): 129–135.

Lipscomb, Andrew K., ed. *The Writings of Thomas Jefferson*. Washington, D.C.: Thomas Jefferson Memorial Association, 1904.

Lipset, Seymour Martin, and William Schneider. *The Confidence Gap*. New York: Free Press, 1983.

Livernois, John. "The Redistributive Effects of Lotteries: Evidence from Canada." *Public Finance Quarterly* 15 (July 1987): 339–351.

Luce, W. Ray. "The Cohen Brothers of Baltimore: From Lottery to Banking." *Maryland Historical Magazine* 68 (Fall 1973): 288–308.

Marcus Advertising. "Ohio Lottery: 'SuperLotto' Introduction, Media Recommendation." Report for the Ohio Lottery, Cleveland, September 18, 1985.

Marshall, Eliot. "State Lootery." *New Republic,* June 24, 1978, 20–21.

Martech Associates, Inc. "Oregon State Lottery Communications Study." Report for the Oregon State Lottery Commission, October 1986.

Maryland Department of Budget and Fiscal Planning. "Maryland State Lottery Agency: Analysis of Organizational Structure, Procurement Practices, and Marketing Operation." Report, January 1987.

McCall, George J. "Symbiosis: The Case of Hoodoo and the Numbers Racket." *Social Problems* 10 (Spring 1963): 361–371.

McGrath, Brian. "Economic Effects of a Lottery in Idaho." Boise State University, Idaho, September 1986. Photocopy.

McMaster, John B. *A History of the People of the United States: From the Revolution to the Civil War*. New York: D. Appleton, 1926.

Meyers, William. *The Image-Makers*. New York: Times Books, 1984.

Mikesell, John L. "The Effect of Maturity and Competition on State Lottery Markets." *Journal of Policy Analysis and Management* 6 (Winter 1987): 251–253.

Mikesell, John L., and Maureen A. Pirog-Good. "Lotteries and Crime." Unpublished paper, Indiana University, 1987.

Mikesell, John L., and C. Kurt Zorn. "Another Look at the Structure and Performance of State Lotteries." Indiana University, August 1987. Photocopy.

Mitchell, Arnold. *The Nine American Lifestyles*. New York: Macmillan, 1983.

Mumpower, Jeryl. "Lottery Games and Risky Technologies: Communications

About Low-Probability/High-Consequence Events." *Risk Analysis* 8, 2 (1988): 231–235.

Musgrave, Richard A., and Peggy B. Musgrave. *Public Finance in Theory and Practice*. New York: McGraw-Hill, 1980.

National Association of State Racing Commissioners. *Statistical Reports on Horse Racing in the United States for the Year 1963*. Lexington, Ky.: National Association of State Racing Commissioners, February 1964.

National Institute of Alcohol Abuse and Alcoholism. *Sixth Special Report to the U.S. Congress on Alcohol and Health*. Rockville, Md., January 1987.

National Institute of Law Enforcement and Criminal Justice. *The Development of the Law of Gambling: 1776-1976*. Washington, D.C., November 1977.

Netzer, Dick. "Legal Gambling, Now That We Have Lots of It." *New York Affairs* 8 (1984): 59–66.

New York State Commission of Investigation. *An Investigation of Bingo Operations in New York State*. New York, December 1961.

Niskanen, William. *Bureaucracy and Representative Government*. Chicago: Aldine, 1971.

Oates, Wallace. *The Political Economy of Fiscal Federalism*. Lexington, Mass.: Lexington Books, 1977.

O'Donnell, William T. "A Chief Executive's Views on the Necessity for Comprehensive State Control and Regulation in the United States Gaming Industry." *Connecticut Law Review* 12 (Summer 1980): 727–739.

Oliver Quayle and Co. Appendix. In Fund for the City of New York, *Legal Gambling in New York*. New York: Fund for the City of New York, 1972.

Orford, Jim. *Excessive Appetites: A Psychological View of Addictions*. New York: John Wiley and Sons, 1985.

Packard, Vance. *The Hidden Persuaders*. New York: Pocket Books, 1957.

Pennsylvania General Assembly, Legislative Budget and Finance Committee. "Report on a Performance Audit of the Pennsylvania State Lottery," September 1987. Photocopy.

Peterson, Virgil W. "A Look at Legalized Gambling." *Christian Century,* May 26, 1965, 675–679.

Phillips, Layn. "The Premium Savings Bond: Respectable Revenue through Legalized Gambling." *Tulsa Law Journal* 11 (1975): 241–257.

Quinn, Bernard, et al. *Churches and Church Membership in the United States, 1980*. Atlanta: Glenmary Research Center, 1982.

Rados, David L. "The Numbers Game: An Economic and Comparative Analysis." *Quarterly Reveiw of Economics and Business* 16 (Summer 1976): 19–36.

Reuter, Peter. "Easy Sport: Research and Relevance." *Journal of Social Issues* 35, 3 (1979): 166–182.

Reuter, Peter, and Jonathan Rubinstein. *Illegal Gambling in New York: A Case*

Study in the Operation, Structure, and Regulation of an Illegal Market. Washington, D.C.: Department of Justice, National Institute of Justice, April 1982.

Richards, R.D. "The Lottery in the History of English Government Finance." *Economic History* 3 (January 1934): 57–76.

Rose I. Nelson. "The Legalization and Control of Casino Gambling." *Fordham Urban Law Journal* 8 (1980): 245–300.

Rosen, Harvey S. *Public Finance.* 2d ed. Homewood, Ill.: Irwin Publications in Economics, 1988.

Rosett, Richard N. "Gambling and Rationality." *Journal of Political Economy* 73, 6 (December 1965): 595–607.

Ross, Irwin. "Corporate Winners in the Lottery Boom." *Fortune,* September 3, 1984, 21.

Saltzman, Joe, and Barbara Saltzman. "Long Odds and Sure Things on the California Ballot." *Reporter,* November 5, 1964, 28–30.

Sammartino, Frank. "The Distributional Effects of an Increase in Selected Federal Excise Taxes." U.S. Congressional Budget Office Staff Working Paper, January 1987. Photocopy.

Schudson, Michael. *Advertising: The Uneasy Persuasion.* New York: Basic Books, 1984.

Sedlick, Earl, and Rolf Rautenberg. "Instant Stub Games 'Reinvent the Deal' and Increase Sales." *Public Gaming,* June 1986.

Seidman, Joel I. "Lotteries for Public Revenue." *Editorial Research Reports.* Vol. 1. Washington, D.C.: Editorial Research Reports, 1934.

Shoup, Carl. *Public Finance.* Chicago: Aldine, 1969.

Simmons, Susan A., and Robert Sharp. "State Lotteries' Effects on Thoroughbred Horse Racing." *Journal of Policy Analysis and Management* 6 (Spring 1987): 446–448.

Smith, Adam. *The Wealth of Nations.* New York: Modern Library, 1937.

Smith, Donald J. "Risk-Efficient Lottery Bets?!" Boston University, July 1986. Photocopy.

Smith, Tom W. "Atop a Liberal Plateau? A Summary of Trends since World War II." In *Research in Urban Policy: Coping with Urban Austerity,* edited by Terry Nichols Clark. Vol. 1. Greenwich, Conn.: JAI Press, 1985.

Snyder, Lester B. "Regulation of Legalized Gambling: An Inside View." *Connecticut Law Review* 12 (Summer 1980): 665–726.

Spiro, Michael H. "On the Incidence of the Pennsylvania Lottery." *National Tax Journal* 27 (March 1974): 57–61.

Spofford, A. R. "Lotteries in American History." *Annual Report of the American Historical Association, 1892.* Washington, D.C.: Government Printing Office, 1893.

Sprowls, R. Clay. "A Historical Analysis of Lottery Terms." *Canadian Journal of Economics and Political Science* 20 (August 1954): 347–560.

Stokey, Edith, and Richard Zeckhauser. *A Primer for Policy Analysis*. New York: Norton, 1978.

Stover, Mark E. "Revenue Potential of State Lotteries." *Public Finance Quarterly* 15 (October 1987): 428–440.

Stubbing, Richard A. *The Defense Game*. New York: Harper and Row, 1986.

Suits, Daniel B. "Gambling Taxes: Regressivity and Revenue Potential." *National Tax Journal* 30 (March 1977): 19–35.

———. "Economic Background for Gambling Policy." *Journal of Social Issues* 35 (Summer 1979): 43–61.

Thomas, W. I. "The Gaming Instinct." *American Journal of Sociology* 6 (July 1900–May 1901): 750–763.

Thompson, William N. "Patterns of Public Response to Lottery, Horserace, and Casino Gambling Issues." *Nevada Review of Business and Economics* 9 (Spring 1985): 12–22.

Thurow, Lester C. "Cash versus In-Kind Transfers." *American Economic Review* 64 (May 1974): 190–195.

Trahan, Burden, and Charles, Inc. "The Maryland State Lottery Fiscal 1987 Advertising Plan." Report for the Maryland State Lottery, Baltimore, n.d.

Tversky, Amos, and Daniel Kahneman. "Judgment under Uncertainty: Heuristics and Biases." *Science* 185 (1974): 1124–31.

Tyler, Alice Felt. *Freedom's Ferment: Phases of American Social History from the Colonial Period to the Outbreak of the Civil War*. New York: Harper and Row, 1962.

U.S. Bureau of the Census. *Abstract of the Returns of the Fifth Census*. Washington, D.C.: Government Printing Office, 1832.

———. *Historical Statistics of the United States, Colonial Times to 1957*. Washington, D.C.: Government Printing Office, 1960.

———. *State Government Finances in 1986*. Washington D.C.: Government Printing Office, 1987.

———. *Statistical Abstract of the United States*. Washington, D.C.: Government Printing Office, various years.

U.S. Congress. Congressional Budget Office. *The Changing Distribution of Federal Taxes: 1975–1990*. Washington, D.C.: Congressional Budget Office, October 1987.

U.S. Congress. House of Representatives. Appropriations Committee. Hearings on District of Columbia Appropriations for 1988. 100th Cong., 1st sess. Washington, D.C.: Government Printing Office, 1988.

U.S. Congress. Senate Committee on Governmental Affairs, Subcommittee on Intergovernmental Affairs. *State Lotteries: An Overview*. 98th Cong., 2d sess., October 3, 1984. Washington, D.C.: Government Printing Office, 1985.

Vaillancourt, François, and Julie Grignon. "Canadian Lotteries as Taxes: Revenues and Incidence." *Canadian Tax Journal* 36 (March-April 1988):369–388.

Vasche, Jon David. "Are Taxes on Lotteries Too High?" *Journal of Policy Analysis and Management* 4 (Winter 1985): 269–271.

Viti de Marco, Antonio de. *First Principles of Public Finance*. New York: Harcourt Brace, 1934.

Walker, Jack L. "The Diffusion of Innovations among the American States." *American Political Science Review* 3 (September 1969): 880–899.

Walker, Mabel. "Lotteries for Public Revenues—A Medieval Throwback." *American City* 49 (October 1934): 57–58.

Washington State. Legislative Budget Committee. "Performance Audit of the Washington State Lottery," November 21, 1986. Photocopy.

Weinstein, David, and Lillian Deitch. *The Impact of Legalized Gambling: The Socioeconomic Consequences of Lotteries and Off-Track Betting*. New York: Praeger, 1974.

Weiss, Harry B. "Oneirocritica Americana." *Bulletin of The New York Public Library* 48 (June 1944): 531.

"Why Isn't the Church Fighting Lotteries?" *Christian Century,* December 11, 1974, 1163–64.

Williams, Francis Emmett. *Flexible-Participation Lotteries*. St. Louis: Thomas Law Book Company, 1938.

Witt, Elder. "States Place Their Bets on a Game of Diminishing Returns." *Governing* 1 (November 1987): 52–57.

Wood, Chris. "Odds Makers: The Very Profitable Gamble of Canada's Four Public Lottery Corporations." *Canadian Business* 57 (April 1984).

Yitzhaki, Shlomo, and Joel Slemrod. "Welfare Dominance: An Application to Commodity Taxation." National Bureau of Economic Research. Working Paper no. 2451, December 1987. Photocopy.

Zola, Irving K. "Observations on Gambling in a Lower-Class Setting." *Social Problems* 10 (Spring 1963): 353–360.

State Laws

Arizona Revised Statutes Annotated. Cumulative Supplement. Vol. 2, sec. 5(501–525). St. Paul: West Publishing, 1985.

California: West's Annotated Codes. Cumulative Supplement. Vol. 32B, sec. 12.5(8880.1) and seq. St. Paul: West Publishing, 1986.

Colorado Revised Statutes. Cumulative Supplement 1985. Vol. 10, sec. 24(35:201–218). Denver: Bradford Publishing, 1982.

Connecticut General Statutes Annotated. Cumulative Supplement 1986. Vol. 6A, sec. 12(565–570). St. Paul: West Publishing, 1983.

Connecticut State Agencies, Regulations of. Sec. 12(568–569). St. Paul: West Publishing, 1985.

Delaware Code Annotated, Revised. Cumulative Supplement 1984. Vol. 14, sec. 29(48). Charlottesville, Va.: Michie, 1983.

District of Columbia Code Annotated. Cumulative Supplement 1985. Vol. 3, sec. 2(2501–2537). Charlottesville, Va.: Michie, 1981.

Florida Statutes Annotated. Cumulative Annual Pocket Supplement. Vol. 1, sec. 24(309–326). St. Paul: West Publishing, 1988.

Illinois Annotated Statutes. Cumulative Supplement. Sec. 120(1151–1176). St. Paul: West Publishing, 1985.

Iowa Code Annotated. Cumulative Supplement. Vol. 6, sec. 99.E. St. Paul: West Publishing, 1986.

Kansas Statutes Annotated. Cumulative Supplement 1987. Vol. 5A, Article 87, 74–8701 and seq. Topeka: Division of Printing, Department of Administration, 1985.

Maine Revised Statutes Annotated. Cumulative Supplement 1985. Vol. 3, sec. 8 (14:351–367). St. Paul: West Publishing, 1980.

Maryland: Annotated Code. Sec. 9(100–125), Article 88D(1) and seq. Charlottesville, Va.: Michie, 1984.

Massachusetts, Annotated Laws of. Cumulative Supplement 1986. Sec. 10(22–38). Rochester: Lawyers Cooperative Publishing, 1980.

Michigan Compiled Laws Annotated. Cumulative Supplement 1985. Vol. 20A, sec. 432.1 and seq. St. Paul: West Publishing, 1978.

Missouri Annotated Statutes. Cumulative Supplement. Vol. 16A, sec. 313(200–335). St. Paul: West Publishing, 1986.

Montana Code Annotated. Vol. 4, Title 23, chap. 5–1001 and seq. Helena: Montana Legislative Council, 1987.

New Hampshire: Revised Statutes Annotated. Cumulative Supplement 1985. Vol. 2.D., chap. 284(21) and seq. Orford, N.H.: Equity Publishing, 1977.

New Jersey Statutes Annotated. Cumulative Supplement 1986. Sec. 5:9.1 and seq. St. Paul: West Publishing, 1973.

New York Codes and Regulations. Vol. 21.C, chap. 44, pt. 2800 and seq. Albany, N.Y.: Department of the State, 1985.

Ohio Revised Code Annotated. Cumulative Supplement 1985. Sec. 3440.01 and seq. Cincinnati, Ohio: Anderson Publishing, 1980.

Oregon Revised Statutes. Legislative Council Committee, 1985. Vol. 3A, sec. 461.

Pennsylvania Code. Sec. 61(5:801) and seq. Mechanicsburg, Pa.: Frey Communications, 1984.

Rhode Island, General Laws of. Cumulative Supplement 1985. Vol. 6C, sec. 42(61:1) and seq. Charlottesville, Va.: Michie, 1984.

South Dakota Codified Laws Annotated. 1987 pocket supplement. Vol. 12B, sec. 42–7A(39–52). Charlottesville, Va.: Michie, 1985.

Vermont Statutes Annotated. Cumulative Supplement. Vol. 8, sec. 31(14). Orford, N.H.: Equity Publishing, 1985.

Virginia, Code of. Cumulative Supplement 1987. Vol. 8A, sec. 58.1–4000 and seq. Charlottesville, Va.: Michie, 1984.

Washington, West Revised Code of, Annotated. Chap. 67(70). St. Paul: West Publishing, 1985.

West Virginia Code Annotated. Cumulative Supplement. Vol. 9, sec. 29(22). Charlottesville, Va.: Michie, 1985.

Index

Relation of the Directors to the
Work and Publications of the
National Bureau of Economic Research

1. The object of the National Bureau of Economic Research is to ascertain and to present to the public important economic facts and their interpretation in a scientific and impartial manner. The Board of Directors is charged with the responsibility of ensuring that the work of the National Bureau is carried on in strict conformity with this object.

2. The President of the National Bureau shall submit to the Board of Directors, or to its Executive Committee, for their formal adoption all specific proposals for research to be instituted.

3. No research report shall be published by the National Bureau until the President has sent each member of the Board a notice that a manuscript is recommended for publication and that in the President's opinion it is suitable for publication in accordance with the principles of the National Bureau. Such notification will include an abstract or summary of the manuscript's content and a response form for use by those Directors who desire a copy of the manuscript for review. Each manuscript shall contain a summary drawing attention to the nature and treatment of the problem studied, the character of the data and their utilization in the report, and the main conclusions reached.

4. For each manuscript so submitted, a special committee of the Directors (including Directors Emeriti) shall be appointed by majority agreement of the President and Vice Presidents (or by the Executive Committee in case of inability to decide on the part of the President and Vice Presidents), consisting of three Directors selected as nearly as may be one from each general division of the Board. The names of the special manuscript committee shall be stated to each Director when notice of the proposed publication is submitted to him. It shall be the duty of each member of the special manuscript committee to read the manuscript. If each member of the manuscript committee signifies his approval within thirty days of the transmittal of the manuscript, the report may be published. If at the end of that period any member of the manuscript committee withholds his approval, the President shall then notify each member of the Board, requesting approval or disapproval of publication, and thirty days additional shall be granted for this purpose. The manuscript shall then not be published unless at least a majority of the entire Board who shall have voted on the proposal within the time fixed for the receipt of votes shall have approved.

5. No manuscript may be published, though approved by each member of the special manuscript committee, until forty-five days have elapsed from the transmittal of the report in manuscript form. The interval is allowed for the receipt of any memorandum of dissent or reservation, together with a brief statement of his reasons, that any member may wish to express; and such memorandum of dissent or reservation shall be published with the manuscript if he so desires. Publication does not, however, imply that each member of the Board has read the manuscript, or that either members of the Board in general or the special committee have passed on its validity in every detail.

6. Publications of the National Bureau issued for informational purposes concerning the work of the Bureau and its staff, or issued to inform the public of activities of Bureau staff, and volumes issued as a result of various conferences involving the National Bureau shall contain a specific disclaimer noting that such publication has not passed through the normal review procedures required in this resolution. The Executive Committee of the Board is charged with review of all such publications from time to time to ensure that they do not take on the character of formal research reports of the National Bureau, requiring formal Board approval.

7. Unless otherwise determined by the Board or exempted by the terms of paragraph 6, a copy of this resolution shall be printed in each National Bureau publication.

(Resolution adopted October 25, 1926, as revised through September 30, 1974)